Dissimulation and the Culture of Secrecy in Early Modern Europe

The publisher gratefully acknowledges the generous support of the Ahmanson Foundation Humanities Endowment Fund of the University of California Press Foundation.

Dissimulation and the Culture of Secrecy in Early Modern Europe

Jon R. Snyder

UNIVERSITY OF CALIFORNIA PRESS

Berkeley / Los Angeles / London

University of California Press, one of the most distinguished university presses in the United States, enriches lives around the world by advancing scholarship in the humanities, social sciences, and natural sciences. Its activities are supported by the UC Press Foundation and by philanthropic contributions from individuals and institutions. For more information, visit www.ucpress.edu.

University of California Press
Berkeley and Los Angeles, California

University of California Press, Ltd.
London, England

First paperback printing 2012

Library of Congress Cataloging-in-Publication Data

Snyder, Jon R., 1954–.
    Dissimulation and the culture of secrecy in early modern Europe / Jon R. Snyder.
        p.   cm.
    Includes bibliographical references and index.
    ISBN 978-0-520-27463-1 (pbk. : alk. paper)

    1. Italy—Social life and customs—16th century.   2. Italy—Social life and customs—17th century.   3. Italy—Social life and customs—Sources.   4. Secrecy—Social aspects—Italy—History.   5. Truthfulness and falsehood—Social aspects—Italy—History.   6. Interpersonal communication—Italy—History.   7. Europe—Social life and customs.   8. Secrecy—Social aspects—Europe—History.   9. Truthfulness and falsehood—Social aspects—Europe—History.   10. Interpersonal communication—Europe—History.   I. Title.

DG445.S64   2009
302.22094'0903—dc22   2008050735

Manufactured in the United States of America

20   19   18   17   16   15   14   13   12
10   9   8   7   6   5   4   3   2   1

This book is printed on Cascades Enviro 100, a 100% post consumer waste, recycled, de-inked fiber. FSC recycled certified and processed chlorine free. It is acid free, Ecologo certified, and manufactured by BioGas energy.

*In memory of my father, Asa Edward Snyder,
and my mother, Jean Mosher Snyder*

*Qual ritratto della vita umana più al naturale si può trovar
che l'ombra?*
What more natural portrait of human life may be found
than shadow?

Salvator Rosa, *Il teatro della politica*

Contents

Illustrations

Lost Horizons

Early in the seventeenth century the young René Descartes (1596–1650) wrote, "Like an actor wearing a mask, I come forward, masked, on the stage of the world."[1] With these famous words—*larvatus prodeo*—Descartes at once recognized the political, social, and cultural difficulties of the task that lay ahead of him as a philosopher, and proposed a means by which to overcome them: dissimulation.[2] He was, of course, hardly original in choosing to take this route. Many other members of early modern society had done the same before him, and many more would follow in due course. In fact, on Descartes' family coat of arms was inscribed the motto "he lives well who is well hidden."[3] Descartes may not, however, have understood the art of dissimulation as well as he claimed. A masked actor openly acknowledges the artifice of the stage, whereas the dissimulator does the opposite, announcing nothing and allowing no one to know even if a mask is or is not in use. For many inhabitants of early modern Europe, dissimulation was a compelling—and often disturbing—feature of their lives, precisely because there was no way to detect with certainty its presence or absence in the world around them: it was at once everywhere and nowhere, and the dissimulator was like an evanescent *homo bulla* who would vanish into thin air without a trace, if one were to come too close. Cutting across many nations, cultures, languages, and institutions, this book examines early modern attitudes toward the shadowy art of dissimulation in the sixteenth and seventeenth centuries.

Dissimulation provoked conflicting and often powerful emotions in those who suspected it, as well as in those who wrote about it. As Louis

D'Orléans complained in a 1594 diatribe against Henry IV, King of France, "being a secret and hidden animal, man withdraws within himself like the oyster, and only opens up when and to whom it pleases him to do so. His thoughts cannot be made transparent by the brightest light or the sun's most blazing rays, and this is why it is as difficult to judge them as it is difficult to judge a false or genuine diamond in the darkness of night, or a beautiful or ugly painting amidst dark shadows."[4] In these few lines D'Orléans expressed a view of personhood that was widely held between the sixteenth and seventeenth centuries. The mind was—or ought to be—"secret," "hidden," "withdrawn," well-defended and shut tight "like the oyster." Thoughts were inscrutable and masked in impenetrable shadows; they could be read by others only if one chose to "open [oneself] up" and reveal the inner workings of the heart and mind to them.[5] Knowing when, where, and with whom it was appropriate to disclose one's thoughts was just as important as knowing when, where, and with whom to disguise them. Humanity was, in short, well versed in the art of dissimulation. Because it could render one's thoughts and feelings completely inaccessible to others, this art effectively denied anyone the chance to know the true identity of the dissimulator: all were left, D'Orléans lamented, as if "in the darkness of night."[6] Although there were those who for this very reason celebrated dissimulation's defensive powers, many others—such as D'Orléans—were deeply troubled by its capacity to establish an inviolable security zone around persons, making dissimulation one of the most controversial and contested of all the early modern virtues.

A book on early modern attitudes toward the art of dissimulation might be suspected of having something to hide. This preface, however, attempts to throw light on the methodological choices that were made in writing the present work. The title, *Dissimulation and the Culture of Secrecy in Early Modern Europe,* is perhaps the most logical place to start. Intellectual and cultural historians of Europe have long identified the period with which I am concerned, namely the years 1500–1700, as formative for the establishment of the modern state. In the pages that follow I do not, however, offer the reader a historical account of the development of the state security apparatus, from espionage and secret police services to technologies of surveillance and encryption. Nor do I consider the dissidents and underground religious groups who were targeted by repressive regimes during these same years. What I mean by "the culture of secrecy" is something quite different. The present book is concerned specifically with the emergence of a discourse on dissimulation among the dominant social groups of the Old Regime, especially (but far from exclusively) in Italy. I argue in chapter 1 that these elites cultivated and disseminated the early modern discourse on dissimulation in order to legitimate or, in some cases, to critique their own highly disciplined practices of self-management and self-representation. If a secret involves not saying something that is or was, then dissimulation is a species of secrecy; and if it was one of the cornerstones of the Old Regime, as this book attempts to show, then the latter may be defined as a culture of secrecy.

The single most extensive body of scholarship on early modern dissimulation belongs to the French historian Jean-Pierre Cavaillé. His prolific output of essays and editions concerning the early modern period led to the publication of *Dis/simulations* in 2002.[7] In this study of the writings of five seventeenth-century heterodox figures—Giulio Cesare Vanini, François La Mothe Le Vayer, Gabriel Naudé, Louis Machon, and Torquato Accetto—Cavaillé sets out to expose what he calls "a reflexive practice of dis/simulation" which can be found, with a nod to the philosopher Leo Strauss, in "a writing of persecution and censorship" that embodies "a poetics and . . . a practice of the secret at once subjective and subjectivizing."[8] By this the historian means that what has been intentionally hidden in the texts of these Old Regime writers is at least as significant as what is immediately visible in them. Although they belong to different strands of early modern libertinism—and experienced the pressures of contemporary censorship in vastly different ways—these five writers nonetheless share a common concern for secrecy. In their works is not deliberately hidden a mystical or metaphysical secret, that is, a recondite meaning that can be recovered thanks to the proper interpretive key. Rather, Cavaillé finds in them the tactical use of secrecy as a constitutive component of self-expression and self-representation, in which a unique portrait of the writer emerges even as he withdraws from us. In the implementation of this strategy, in which evasions and elisions are generated in ways not always foreseen or controlled by the writer, we witness these early moderns' ongoing negotiations with their particular political circumstances, as well as with the era's dominant protocols of socialization. The result is a vision of the singularity of each individual "practice of the secret," set in a specific context, rather than a general theory of its workings.[9]

Cavaillé sees the turn to dis/simulation between the sixteenth and seventeenth centuries as marking a shift toward secularization ("from transcendence to immanence") in European culture.[10] The practice of dis/simulation can best be traced, he contends, in the history of Inquisitorial and judicial investigations, persecutions and interrogations, as well as in Nicodemite religious writings.[11] The major early modern theories of this practice may serve as a guide in reading persecuted texts, but these theories cannot be abstracted from their sociopolitical context. What motivates the turn to dis/simulation for so many individuals in the sixteenth and seventeenth centuries, Cavaillé contends, is the pressing need to master appearances, while hiding from sight "the inner space of conscience," whether in the realm of politics or faith.[12] The neologism "dis/simulation" expresses Cavaillé's belief that dissimulation is often inseparable from simulation, although the two are nonetheless dissociated because "it is one thing to keep a secret and another thing to lie."[13] His book shuttles back and forth between the analysis of libertine texts and those setting out a general theory of dis/simulation, from Vanini's subversive theology to the Machiavellianism of Machon (whose treatise on the subject "lifts at least a little the veil of dissimulation, insofar as he is himself unable to dissimulate") or Accetto's politics of resistance.[14] In Cavaillé's view, the seventeenth century in particular is full of individuals in inner revolt against the absolutist system, and thus "we must listen for the wounded cry in the text that keeps silent."[15]

Over and beyond the singularity of each work, *Dis/simulations* identifies other, broader issues raised by the early modern theory and practice of dis/simulation. First, there is a radical tension between "the concern to publish the truth and that of protecting it by the development of justifiable procedures of dis/simulation," which in Cavaillé's view is no more and no less than "a fundamental element of Western culture."[16] The elites who monopolized the public space of discourse in early modern Europe did not see themselves in a reciprocal relationship with the rest of society, and spoke to one another through the use of complex linguistic and cultural codes that belonged to them alone. In other words, there were exoteric and esoteric modes of reading the early modern text, and this double register served to preserve the social status quo by restricting knowledge of its full (if hidden) significance to the exclusive few. This same social logic of a privileged inside and an unreadable outside extends to dis/simulation itself, which could be subversive, in seeking to elude censorship or persecution, but also encouraged accommodation with the Old Regime by splitting off the inner life of the person from outward appearances. The libertine might freely think heterodox thoughts but regularly attend religious services, for instance, in order to maintain his appointed place in society. This was not due to hypocrisy, a desire for accommodation, or an instrumentalist orientation toward social existence, as we would naturally think of anyone acting in this way today, but rather was a function of the double register of interior conscience and public conformity. Second, Cavaillé ironically sees the Catholic church through its renewed post-Tridentine emphasis on the doctrine of the confession (or penance), in which secrets are revealed and concealed beyond the reach of law and social discipline, as greatly increasing the domain of dis/simulation in early modernity. Although the penitent must confess his most secret sins, the priest can never betray them to others; indeed, according to canon law, the confessor must guard these secrets with his very life, and dissimulate them in the face of any threat against him. Conscience is formed in a secret space, in other words, where the transparency of the individual confession is kept completely separate from the realm of social relations.[17] If the church allows for the existence of legitimate secrets of the heart and mind—and by definition the sacrament of confession deals in these—then libertine culture draws from this the lessons needed for its conquest of a private, interior, autonomous secular conscience, withdrawn from institutional spiritual oversight.

Cavaillé's insights are invaluable for anyone working in the field of early modern studies, but the present book takes a fundamentally different direction. In his historical investigations of simulation and dissimulation, Cavaillé starts from the premise that these two terms cannot be viewed in isolation from one another. Philosophically speaking, any coherent distinction between them cannot be sustained for long: hence the need to invent a term ("dis/simulation") that can capture the essence of both at once. I have instead chosen to take very seriously the fact that, from the perspective of many early modern European writers, there was indeed a significant difference between simulation and dissimulation, which defined a conflict between distinct moral economies. Rarely were the two terms accorded the same treatment, or condemned in the same way: they were not Siamese but fraternal twins. Perhaps there was no logical foundation to this belief, as Cavaillé contends, but it nevertheless informed the world of the Old Regime, in which distinction(s) mattered a great deal. Evidently faced with what seemed at the time like the unstoppable spread of the culture of secrecy, many contemporary writers intervened by trying to define its subtle ground rules and to influence future attempts to deploy, detect, or deter dissimulation. Although some were outspoken in their criticism of its practice, no matter what the intent behind the act may be, there were many who recognized that dissimulation might, under certain well-defined conditions, possess a specific moral valence distinguishing it from simulation, and at times even justifying its use. The early modern discourse on dissimulation was largely organized, for better or for worse, around the assumption that one could separate it from its evil twin, and I have adopted this stance as the basis for my own investigation.

In the pages that follow, I examine mainly treatises and manuals, or fragments of treatises and manuals, on dissimulation. Whether published or unpublished, I take these—like Peter Burke's exemplary study of early modern conversation, another elusive object of intellectual history—as indicative of a practice that has otherwise proved difficult to locate through the lens of history. They are not, however, documents of the performance of dissimulation itself, only of attitudes toward the art of dissimulation, just as there are no records of (let us say) actual early modern dreams, only the dream-narratives that recount them. As Burke notes,

> the value of the treatises on conversation to a cultural historian is that they make explicit norms which were usually implicit. Actually the last statement, obvious as it may seem, needs to be qualified. The authors of the treatises cannot be assumed to be articulating a social consensus. Different social groups within the same society may follow different rules for communication, while some authors may be subverting the rules current in their own culture. . . . To coax information about practice from treatises . . . means reading the texts against the grain, with all the dangers implied by that procedure.[18]

Burke may have said the obvious, but it bears repeating. These texts make visible to us the conceptual norms of "different social groups within the same society," which, in the case of the discourse on dissimulation, were those of the dominant groups under absolutism.[19] My book explores the discursive paths taken by these elites in an attempt to get to grips with, articulate, legitimize, or contest the norms of dissimulatory practice.

This should not be confused, however, with the practice purportedly subject to these norms, which remains beyond the scope of the present work. As Burke warns, the dangers of trying "to coax information about practice from treatises" are legion, and likely to lead into blind alleys. Even a report in which an ambassador claims to have dissimulated some important state secret while in conversation with a foreign potentate may, of course, be nothing other than a dissimulation in its own right: even with an archive at hand, we would be on dangerous ground in thinking that we could fully know the truth about his claim. On the other hand, the majority of these treatises may appropriately be read as instances of another sort of practice, namely the development of a normative disciplinary discourse serving as a horizon within or against which individuals and groups oriented themselves with the intent to perform, legitimize, interpret, or contest dissimulatory acts. Although they do not allow us to reconstruct all the ruses of the early modern dissimulator, these texts define the contours of a mode of comportment or *virtù* within which practitioners of this art were likely constrained to remain, or against which they felt compelled to work. Even the early modern writers most vehemently critical of dissimulation confirm the widespread awareness of such a code of behavior within the dominant groups involved in both the production and reception of this discourse (although, once again, behavior itself—the putting-into-work of dissimulation—certainly may have been at variance with this code). In short, I will examine the ways in which a discourse on dissimulation was born, lived, and died without claiming to be able to know, after the passage of many hundreds of years, who was actually dissimulating and who was not. What we can instead recover at this point in time—however partially or provisionally—are those lost horizons of dissimulation that informed the subjectivity and practices of early modern men and women.

The interdisciplinary and international Europa delle Corti group of scholars has persuasively argued since the 1970s that the culture of absolutism (*la cultura classicista*) cannot be confined to traditional schemes of historical periodization or national literatures, because it functioned as a highly diffuse and enduring paradigm of cultural homologation in Europe.[20] The present study, taking its cue from this approach, follows an itinerary traversing a number of exemplary moments in the discourse on dissimulation over a long period of time and a large geographical area, without pretending to treat exhaustively any one text, author, national literature, or historical period. Any attempt to write a book about this elusive subject must inevitably result in a work in which a great deal is missing: I can only try to cast a net around the question of early modern attitudes toward dissimulation, although some, perhaps much, will slip through. If Italy is the focus of much of the book, however, it is because so many of the *maîtres penseurs* of dissimulation—such as Baldassar Castiglione, Niccolò Machiavelli, and Torquato Accetto (to name only three)—were Italians and wrote in the vernacular of the peninsula. I do not provide detailed biographical information for the many writers, either famous or obscure, whose works are discussed in the following pages. Without denying the relevance of such data, and without trying to suggest that discourses can be disembodied, I confess that my interests lie elsewhere.

I have provided both the original text and an English-language translation (if needed), preferably a published one, for every citation in the main body of the book. In some cases this has meant using contemporary early modern translations, a few of which are still adequate for the purpose, while in other cases more recent translations have been employed. If not otherwise indicated in the notes, however, all translations are my own. I have generally preferred not to modernize or correct the orthography and punctuation of the early modern texts that I cite, although in those instances in which critical editions are available, I make full use of them.

A final caveat. The kinds of dissimulation examined in this book have been generally discredited in the West for more than two centuries now. The Romantic revolution, in privileging the rhetoric of sincerity and transparency, signaled the end of the long reign of the Old Regime, as well as its social and cultural protocols. Dissimulation has not vanished from our world, but it no longer constitutes an art with its own recognized set of rules: its value is merely operational. Today the media-saturated society of the West, built around the principle of publicity, cannot tolerate even the slightest suspicion of dissimulation in those persons who are chosen to be put (profitably) on display. Never have seeming and being been more perfectly merged than they are now, or so most would want—and be expected—to think. Perhaps, however, it is time to think again.

Acknowledgments

Although this is a book about dissimulation, I profess the utmost sincerity in saying that there are many to whom I am most grateful for their assistance. My thanks go to the librarians of the University of California library system, the Huntington Library, the Biblioteca Nazionale Marciana, the Berenson Library of the Villa I Tatti, the Biblioteca Nazionale Centrale di Firenze, the Biblioteca Marucelliana, the Biblioteca Nazionale Universitaria di Torino, the Biblioteca Angelica and the Biblioteca Casanatense in Rome, the Biblioteca Nazionale di Napoli, the Biblioteca Comunale dell'Archiginnasio in Bologna, and the Bibliothèque Nationale de France. Although their contributions are often anonymous, I wish to acknowledge all those who have developed and maintained online scholarly databases, text repositories, digital archives and Web search engines over the past decade, which have transformed research in the field of early modern European studies. I am particularly grateful to those colleagues who invited me to speak in public about my research as it evolved: Albert Ascoli, the late Jean-Pierre Barricelli, Franca Bizzoni, Lina Bolzoni, JoAnn Cavallo, Massimo Ciavolella, Jean-Jacques Courtine, Nadeije Dagen, Francesco Erspamer, Marcello Fantoni, Maurizio Ferraris, Werner Gundersheimer, Manfred Hinz, Colin Jones, Mariapia Lamberti, Giuseppina Muzzarelli, Amedeo Quondam, and Carlo Vecce. The insight and encouragement that I received on these occasions were invaluable. Among those who provided me with research assistance or materials along the way, I wish to acknowledge the contributions of Monica Fintoni, Paul Kottman, Simona

Foà, Roberto Mancini, Christine Maisto, and Tanja Christensen. Albert Ascoli and David Quint read an earlier version of the manuscript and freely shared with me their vast knowledge of early modern European literature and culture. The Ufficio di Cultura of the city of Cherasco, in Piedmont, was consistently helpful to me: *mille grazie*. At the University of California Press, Laura Pasquale and Stanley Holwitz displayed patience in the face of project delays, and provided guidance and support when it was needed the most. My thanks are due, moreover, to the entire production team at the Press, especially Caroline Knapp. A special thank-you goes to Kathleen MacDougall for her work as copyeditor of the manuscript. To my friends Cesare Mozzarelli and Sergio Mamino, who gave generously of their time and expertise, but did not live to see the end result, I owe more than I can say.

My intellectual debts are numerous, and readers will recognize many of them without difficulty. One, however, runs deep beneath the surface of this work: as an undergraduate, I had the great good fortune to study with the historian Carl Schorske, whose limitless passion for—and knowledge of—the cultures of Europe did so much to inspire me to become a scholar. Later on, as a graduate student in comparative literature, I began to consider the issue of dissimulation while researching a chapter, on the Baroque philosopher-poet Tommaso Campanella, of my doctoral dissertation. Campanella's terrible trials in the dungeons of Spanish Naples, and the ruses that he used to survive them, made a lasting impression on me. Although my studies subsequently led me in other directions, I always knew that I would one day return to write this book. By a twist of fate, Campanella is not in it, but much that I learned from him is to be found here. Finally, I had already completed the first draft when I came across the publications of Jean-Pierre Cavaillé: his perspective on early modern dissimulation, although very different than mine, helped me to revise and refine my arguments. The responsibility for any and all shortcomings of the present book is, however, entirely my own.

Initial support for this project came from a Huntington Library summer research fellowship, followed by a year as a fellow at Villa I Tatti (Harvard University's Center for Italian Renaissance Studies). The Academic Senate of the University of California, Santa Barbara, subsequently provided research funding, and the Division of the Humanities the release time to complete the manuscript. The Cassamarca Foundation graciously hosted me in Treviso for several weeks while I worked in Venetian libraries and archives. The most significant support of all, however, has come from my family. Lucia and Isabella have meant so very much for me over the long years of writing and rewriting this book. I could never dissimulate my debt to them: as Torquato Accetto remarks with a Baroque flourish at the beginning of chapter 14 of *Della dissimulazione onesta,* "amor, che non vede, si fa troppo vedere."

A portion of chapter 2 was first published as "Truth and Wonder in Naples circa 1640," *Culture and Authority in the Baroque,* eds. Massimo Ciavolella and Patrick Coleman (Toronto: University of Toronto Press, 2005): 85–105. It appears here in modified form with the kind permission of the University of Toronto Press.

CHAPTER I

Not Empty Silence

The Age of Dissimulation

La dissimulation est des plus notables qualitez de ce siècle.
Dissimulation is among the most notable qualities of this century.

Michel de Montaigne, "Du dementir"

Il non fidarsi del vivere è necessario per fidarsi del vivere, cioè per vivere alla moderna.
Not to trust life is necessary in order to trust life, that is to say, to live in the modern way.

Pio Rossi, "Ingannare"

"A Profession to Which One Cannot Profess"

It was an evening in early January 1612, and the city of Turin was in the frigid grip of the Po Valley winter. Vespers were long past and the streets were dark and silent, but not everyone was asleep. Alessandro Anguissola, Count of San Giorgio and Lord of Cimmafava, was in his chambers, where he was often to be found when not engaged in his official duties. Anguissola, who had served since 1601 as Serenissimi Ducis Sabaudiae Consiliarius (Counselor to His Most Serene Highness the Duke of Savoy) at the court of Charles Emmanuel I, the Duke of Turin and Prince of Piedmont, devoted these hours by himself to writing down his thoughts on the early modern prince. His manuscript had slowly grown to more than two hundred pages, but he had shown only a few of these to the duke. This evening, however, Anguissola decided to make His Most Serene Highness the gift, in a few days' time, of a fair

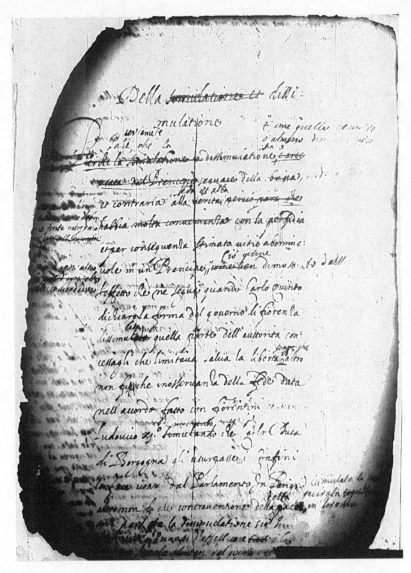

FIGURE 1. Alessandro Anguissola, "Della dissimulatione," manuscript page with emendations. Biblioteca Nazionale di Torino, MS M.III.6. Reproduced by permission of the Biblioteca Nazionale di Torino.

copy of one of the chapters of his work, entitled *Del buon governo del principe* (On good government by the prince). He drew out a copy of the manuscript and shuffled through the papers until he came to the chapter that he had already selected in his mind, "Della simulatione et dissimulatione" (On simulation and dissimulation). Then he took up his quill—and cancelled systematically the words *simulatione et* in the manuscript. When he presented the fair copy to the duke, along with a letter dated 20 January 1612, the title of the chapter read simply "Della dissimulatione." Charles Emmanuel I was apparently pleased with the gift, which survived in the Royal Library in Turin until lost in the catastrophic 1904 fire.[1]

Why did Anguissola—an able courtier and man of the world— suppress any mention of "simulation" in his gift? What led him to consider "dissimulation" alone as a topic worthy of the duke's attention and advantageous to associate with his own name? After all, in drafting the original version of his never-to-be-published work on the fashionable theory of "reason of state," as the extant manuscript shows, Anguissola treated both simulation and dissimulation as essential techniques for the early modern elites. However, as the crossing out in Figure 1 shows, he chose to present his sovereign with a concise manual on dissimulation alone. Why was the one so much more legitimate than the other? Did not both of them involve some degree of deception, if not falsehood? We likely will never know if some event at court near the beginning of 1612 made up Anguissola's mind to revise his original text, or if his gift had long been contemplated in this form. In revising this chapter of his manuscript for the eyes of his sovereign, however, Anguissola clearly must have thought that dissimulation was an attractive subject, as well as an important one, for his gift. Turin was not the cultural or political capital of the peninsula, but there was no shortage of sophistication or intrigue at the Savoy court, where both the poet G. B. Marino and the composer Sigismondo d'India were also in residence in 1612. The author of "Della dissimulatione" was surely acquainted with the latest trends in early modern culture; his choice of topic here could not have been random or casual, and the duke's acceptance of the gift would seem to confirm this.

Perhaps Anguissola found it imprudent openly to discuss simulation as a component of statecraft—at least not in the company of princes, most of whom were not pleased to be considered masters of this art, or to take instruction in its fine points.[2] If so, by 1612 he was certainly not alone in seeing simulation as a contested category of contemporary political culture, for the same gesture of erasure had been performed by others before him writing elsewhere in the Italian states.[3] Neither was the decision to compose a work about dissimulation an isolated act. On the contrary, "Della dissimulatione" was inscribed in many networks of discourse that traversed early modern Europe. If he thought his own little work to be beyond controversy, however, Anguissola must not have spent much time at the booksellers in Turin. Dissimulation was debated, and likely practiced, from the courts of Old Regime Italy to the bustling cities of the Low Countries, from the outposts of the Spanish empire to the great English country houses, from austere Geneva to the glittering palaces of the Roman popes. Catholics and Protestants, courtiers and princes, great aristocrats and their secretaries, diplomats and soldiers, saints and heretics: all praised dissimulation or denounced it vehemently.

What stirred the hearts and minds of these Europeans was the role that dissimulation played in the establishment of the early modern culture of secrecy. As states and societies grew in size and complexity, the production, circulation, and reception of information came to be seen as involving a number of new and vexing problems for rulers and subjects alike. The Spanish Jesuit moralist Baltasar Gracián y Morales (1601–1658), one of the keenest observers of the culture of secrecy, warned that "much of our lives is spent gathering information. We see very few things for ourselves, and live by trusting others. The ears are the back door of truth and the front door of deceit. Truth is more often seen than heard. Seldom does it reach us unalloyed, even less so when it comes from afar. It always bears something mixed in by the minds through which it has passed."[4] In this context of ever-increasing circulation, contamination, transformation, and appropriation, how could information best be managed securely and secrets kept by individuals or by governments? Was the truth always to be told? Who was to have the right to keep something hidden, and under what conditions? And how could the practice of secrecy itself be kept secret from others? There was no simple answer to these questions, and few clear-cut cases to which to refer. If some—like Anguissola—were inclined to divulge the workings of dissimulation, few were willing publicly to acknowledge its use. Except in the form of this discourse on its performative norms and protocols, dissimulation has persistently escaped the gaze of history, striving to remain covert, incognito, and unspoken. As Torquato Accetto, the greatest of all early modern theorists of the topic, reminded his readers in 1641, "dissimulation is a profession to which one cannot profess."[5]

THE SOCIAL TECHNOLOGY OF SECRECY

The sixteenth and seventeenth centuries have been called "the age of dissimulation" in Europe. Even today these years still summon up not only remarkable cultural achievements ranging from the Italian Baroque to the French *grand siècle* and the Spanish *siglo de oro,* but also what later came to be known to many Italians as *la leggenda nera* (the dark legend): hackneyed images of Don Juan, Volpone, Tartuffe, Iago, poison rings, secret passageways, ciphers scrawled in invisible ink, duplicitous Jesuits, paranoid Inquisitors, exquisite tortures, spectacular betrayals, hasty midnight executions, and all the rest of the Old Regime mythology. Dissimulation most certainly played a key role in the processes by which authority and subjectivity were constructed within the early modern period, but it has no place in such an archaic mythology. Rather, we may consider it a central component of the early modern social and cultural technology of secrecy, which was of paramount importance to those who lived in that period. For example, when offered the chance in 1584 to surrender to the overwhelmingly superior Spanish army led by Alessandro Farnese, Duke of Parma, during the most violent religious conflict that early modern Europe had yet known, the outmanned Dutch rebel forces defending Antwerp hesitated, doubtless recalling the atrocious fate of other towns that had fallen to Parma's ferocious predecessor, the Duke of Alba. To convince them to lay down their arms, the commander of the Dutch garrison assured his men that Parma was "void of all dissimulation" and would therefore keep to the terms of the surrender.[6]

For these desperate Dutch fighters, as for countless other early modern men and women, it was completely legitimate—and quite routine—to suspect dissimulation in the words of others, whether overt enemies or not. There was nothing unusual either in the rebel commander's assessment of Parma's words and motives, or in his decision to communicate to his troops the absence of dissimulation in the Spanish general. In extreme cases such as military conflicts, to grasp the techniques of dissimulation—in order to know who was sincere and who was not—could make the difference between life and death. But knowledge of these techniques was also needed in the everyday negotiations of the individual, who was, like Antwerp itself, besieged, in this case by the sweeping social, political, religious, and economic changes in the new Europe. Dissimulation was the most radically subversive and most feared of all dialogue games involving the early moderns caught up in these many changes, for it was often difficult, if not impossible, for those taking part in the dialogue to tell who was playing and who was not.

Early modern dissimulation involved first and foremost the exercise of strict self-control over the expression of thoughts, emotions, or passions. As a practice of self-censorship, dissimulation assisted those who sought not to reveal or disclose anything of their own interiority, but were at the same time intent upon not uttering any untruth to others. Gracián urged his readers: "Without lying, do not tell all truths. Nothing requires more skill than the truth, which is like a letting of blood from the heart. It takes skill both to speak it and to withhold it."[7] Dissimulation offered a range of techniques for safeguarding one's secrets by rendering them unreadable or invisible to others. Through the disciplined use of reticence, taciturnity, diffidence, negligence, omission, ambiguity, irony, and tolerance (that is, pretending not to have seen or heard something), dissimulators aimed to frustrate any outside attempts to connect their words and gestures to their true inner state. Dissimulating language was therefore nonmimetic, as artificial as a highly stylized work of art. A common metaphor for dissimulation in early modern culture was the mask. On the anonymous cover of a lost portrait from the early sixteenth century, sometimes attributed to Ridolfo del Ghirlandaio, appears a haunting image of a mask with the inscription *sua cuique persona* (to each his own mask). Two points are made by the creator of this unusual object. First, its motto asserts that each of us has a mask (or *persona*) that can be worn whenever needed, in order to hide or disguise some truth about us. Second, as the inscription warns anyone about to gaze at the portrait within, no one can know with certainty whether the face is itself already a mask and its owner no different than an actor in a comedy: in the culture of secrecy, the natural was always already artificial, and mimesis was fundamentally unreliable. Thus, as Valentin Groebner suggests, to think about dissimulation means to consider the limits of human perception and of the capacity to make distinctions.[8]

The aim of the dissimulator was to arrive at a "zero degree" of communication, without leaving the conversation or lapsing into either muteness or falsehood.[9] In other words, dissimulating language always clung as closely as possible to silence, like a shadow to a body, approximating but not being taken for the latter: as any number of early modern writers pointed out, if one were to remain truly mute in conversation, the effort at dissimulation would be evident to all and therefore doomed to failure. It was meant to be a rhetorical act that was "hard to follow": balancing precariously on an intersubjective tightrope, the dissimulator attempted to detach from the conversation without disappearing from it entirely. As Accetto noted archly, "some men of excellent virtue are sometimes almost buried alive."[10] Dissimulation was a finely woven cultural covering that allowed its user to avoid appearing to others either as a statue, like those stone-faced Stoics mocked by Erasmus, or as a blatant hypocrite, while little more than marginally engaged in the present exchange of words and emotions. The true master of this art of secrecy was to pass—Accetto observed memorably— "without leaving a trace, like smoke in the air."[11]

In 1578 the Flemish humanist Justus Lipsius (1547–1606), in his famous *Epistola de fructu peregrinandi et praesertim in Italia* (Letter on the benefit of traveling, especially in Italy) addressed to an ex-disciple from the Lowlands inquiring about travel to Rome, admonished his reader to follow three basic rules while in Italy, and especially in the corrupt city of the Popes: *frons tibi aperta, lingua parca, mens clausa.*[12] Dissimulation required much more, however, than simply keeping one's eyes open and one's mouth (and mind) shut. The foundation of successful self-effacement was thorough self-analysis on the part of the dissimulator, who was to subject every word, gesture, and gaze to rigorous inner examination. Prior to representing any part of one's heart or mind to others in conversation or writing, one had to consider how to minimize the possibility of revealing what was better kept hidden or secret. To withhold the truths of the heart or mind from others, however, it was first necessary to find out what those truths were. In order to dissimulate successfully with others, one therefore could not dissimulate with oneself.

The master dissimulator relied on probing psychological self-critique, to be sure, but sought to scrutinize with equal rigor the motives and abilities of all those participating in the conversation as well. Only in this way could one understand what might be safely or profitably revealed to them. Norbert Elias, in his classic studies of the court, understood this to mean that there was established under early modern absolutism "a correspondence between self-observation and the observation of others" that led in the seventeenth century to the birth of the discipline of psychology.[13] This did not indicate, as has already been suggested, that either such intensive labor of self-analysis and analysis, or the fruits of its discoveries, could be openly discussed in the exchange between speakers. Dissimulation had to stay as secret as those secrets it intended to preserve, and could only succeed if the dissimulator managed to remain unnoticed: one's words or actions had to be taken by others as signs of mere diffidence, indifference, or nonchalance. This was no mean feat in the age of absolutism, which greatly valued the visual and gave priority to the eyes over all the other senses.[14] Dissimulation had to exist unseen, paradoxically, in a social context that placed a premium on display and on observation. Some expert practitioners of this shadowy art, many early moderns assumed, nonetheless managed to do just this. "We have no news," warned Accetto, "of those excellent dissimulators who have been, nor of those who are."[15]

PRUDENCE

Although dissimulation was a watchword for the European elites of the sixteenth and seventeenth centuries, there was no general agreement on its significance as a practice pertaining to these groups.[16] Until the early modern era, prudence, or *phronesis,* occupied the most prominent position in philosophical and moral reflection on how to evaluate and adapt to changing circumstances and the shifting winds of fortune. There was relatively broad consensus that prudence was a matter of practical conduct and practical reason, as Aristotle had argued in book 6 of the *Nicomachean Ethics* (1140A–1145A). It was neither a kind of wisdom nor mere clever opportunism, for it dealt with universal principles and particular cases.[17] In the wake of Aristotle, Cicero too had closely identified prudence with practical knowledge in his *De Inventione* (On invention, II.53), setting it over and against theoretical or philosophical knowledge of universal truths. Prudence was the exercise of *versatilitas,* involving foresight, preparation, judgment, patience, quickness, perspicacity, maturity, and caution.[18] Concerned as it was with the ever-changing affairs of the individual, prudence required, above all else, relativism and flexibility in the application of moral and ethical principles to any given situation in which there was a choice to be made.

It has been observed that "prudence, from providence, means foresight. Such anticipatory inner vision requires experience, and prudence may be said to be the use of the past in the present for the sake of the future." Titian's famous *Allegory of Prudence* (ca. 1565) offered its viewers a striking image of three human heads and three emblematic animal heads linked together by the inscription: "from the past, the present acts prudently lest it spoil future action."[19] The prudent person drew on the fruit of lived experience in order to discover the right course of action for the present ("for its end," Aristotle observed, "is what should or should not be done").[20] This, however, did not mean, at least in early modern eyes, that the "right course of action" might go against this same individual's most vital interests. If prudence was a virtue concerned with proper choices and the circumstances in which they must be made, it was not, in practical terms, conceivable to interpret moral and ethical principles in such a way as to harm or endanger oneself: self-preservation was a fitting end for the prudent or "honest" early modern man or woman. As a response to contingency and uncertainty that was at once practical and principled, prudence required careful rational reflection based on experience and on knowledge, but without losing sight of the Aristotelian goals of happiness and success in future life. Between the sixteenth and seventeenth centuries, however, we may in fact detect an important shift in European thinking about prudence: writers on the topic increasingly abandon the motive of self-preservation and turn toward a more instrumental notion of self-interest.[21]

In the transformation of European culture that occurred in these years, the emergence of the discourse on dissimulation accompanies the collapse of the longstanding consensus concerning prudence.[22] Accetto remarked, in the most extreme reformulation of an ancient adage, that *qui nescit fingere nescit vivere* (whoever does not know how to dissemble does not know how to live).[23] He meant, of course, to say that "whoever does not know how to dissimulate does not know how to belong to polite society, which is the only sort of life worth living." However, his motto eloquently captures the life-and-death nature of this undertaking for many of those living in the age of dissimulation. More than a few early modern treatise-writers, for instance, held that the prince or courtier wishing to subject prudence to ethics would literally not survive the risky intrigues of contemporary courts or politics. Not unless, that is to say, the operations of prudence also allowed for recourse to the social and cultural technology of secrecy. Thus in 1589 Lipsius put forward a theory of *prudentia mixta,* or mixed prudence, in order to absorb dissimulation into the more traditional category of prudence. This tactical reorientation subsequently became so widely accepted that a half-century later a Frenchman complained that "when one wishes to make a virtue of dissimulation, one calls it prudence."[24]

But the boundaries of this particular virtue were blurry to most Europeans, some of whom invested considerable energy in trying to define its rules, norms, and procedures. Over and over again the question was posed: What exactly was dissimulation, when and how was it to be

practiced appropriately, and by whom? Without an answer, there could
be no consensus as to what it meant—in a social order obsessed with the
rules of conduct—to practice "honest" rather than "dishonest," or "prudent" rather than "imprudent," dissimulation. The interplay between
this normative discourse and the practices evoked by it certainly was not
without tension. Individual members of early modern society may have
tried to shape their conduct in such a way as to manipulate, evade, or
defy the rules and norms, as well as to confirm and reproduce them, according to their particular purposes. Whatever practical strategy these
persons chose to pursue, however, had inevitably to refer to a normative
disciplinary discourse. Thus the foundations of the culture of secrecy
had to be brought to light and into discourse: since there were only a
few widely scattered classical or medieval authorities to which to refer,
this discourse had to be largely invented *ex nihil,* something that early
modern culture was always hesitant to do—but was, as we shall see, extremely good at doing.

HARPOCRATES' FINGER

The cults of the classical age bequeathed to posterity numerous potent
symbols of taciturnity and silence. Images of the Sphinx, the Egyptian
god of secrecy and enigma, circulated widely in the ancient and early
modern worlds. Harpocrates, the Egyptian god of silence also known
to the Greeks and Romans as Sigalion, was usually represented as
pressing the forefinger of his right hand to his lips, as if enjoining initiates to keep the sacred mysteries shrouded in secrecy. The Egyptians
placed his statue at the entrance to the temples of Isis and Serapis. The
cult of Harpocrates was adopted by the ancient Romans, who set his
statues at the entrance to their temples and used his name in an id-
iomatic expression meaning "to reduce someone to silence."[25] Many
centuries later, Harpocrates' importance was not lost on those humanists intent on recuperating the classical past.[26] Vincenzo Cartari, in his
fundamental iconographical work entitled *Le imagini de i dei de gli antichi* (The images of the ancient gods; first ed., 1556), noted that "the
peach tree was dedicated to Harpocrates because its leaves resemble
the human tongue, and its fruit resembles the human heart; just as the
tongue may display what is in the heart, but should not do so without
careful reflection."[27] Another, later, iconographic tradition represented
Harpocrates as being covered with eyes and ears, but without a mouth.
In this tradition he wore the pelt of a wolf, and his hat—symbol of

FIGURE 2. Engraving of two versions of Harpocrates (*lower left and right*) and Angerona (*on pedestal*). Vincenzo Cartari, *Le imagini de i dei de gli antichi*, 1571 ed., private collection.

freedom—meant that no one could speak freely, but all could freely keep silent.[28] Angerona, the Roman goddess of silence, was usually represented with her mouth bound and gagged, and her festival fell on the winter solstice, the briefest day of the year.[29] Another Roman goddess of silence, Tacita, was said to have been greatly venerated by Numa himself.[30] And the very word *mysterium* (referring to religious mysteries or secrets) had as its Greek root the concept of closing the lips or eyes.

The silence linked to dissimulation was controversial among both the ancient Greeks and Romans because it was always understood to disguise some kind of content, as opposed to indicating a philosophical position preferring silence to speech in general, or a prophetic and mystical stance. Such dissimulating silence was never empty. Another mythic deity, Momus, the god of pleasantry, ridiculed Vulcan because, in the human form which the blacksmith of the gods had made of clay, the latter had not placed a window in the breast, by which whatever was done or thought there might easily be brought to light without relying on the treacherous medium of language.[31] The mythical figure Bellerophon bore a letter to the king of Lycia with a request that the bearer of the letter be put to death, thus giving the name *littera Bellerophontae* to any letter that harms the person bearing it; like dissimulation itself, its cover or envelope cloaks a secret and potentially dangerous message.[32] The ancient epic poets Homer and Virgil, fountainheads of the Western poetic tradition, offered conflicting accounts of dissimulation. The protean Odysseus disguised not only his body but his emotions upon his return to Ithaca after twenty years' absence, and willfully made his eyes as hard as "horn or iron" to hide what was in his heart (*Odyssey* XIX.204–212).[33] Moreover, he warned Telemachus to observe strict silence about the plan to kill Penelope's suitors (XIX.40ff.). On the other hand, in book 4 of the *Aeneid* the spurned Dido raged at the departing Aeneas, "False one! Did you also hope to dissimulate so foul a crime, and to pass from my land in silence?"[34] If the doomed queen of Carthage thought no lover should practice dissimulation, in the *De arte amandi* (The art of love) the worldly Ovid nevertheless assured his readers that it could indeed prove useful in love. In this same work he promoted, moreover, the strategic use of "affability" in social interaction, later to become a fundamental component of early modern conduct books and treatises on *honnêteté* or politeness. Given that these poets took such divergent approaches to the same theme, however, sixteenth- and seventeenth-century readers of classical poetry were left to draw their own conclusions about the meaning of dissimulation for ancient art, culture, and myth.

Nor did the ancient philosophers share a common position on the topic. Despite his notorious expulsion of the poets from the *Republic*, Plato acknowledged the strategic value of untruth in more than one place in the dialogues, many of which were later to be read by the humanists as allegories whose true meaning lay hidden beneath the surface of the text.[35] Most famously, Plato's portrayal of Socrates suggested that *docta ignorantia*, or learned ignorance, was the tool of the true philosopher. Socratic irony was often considered a species of dissimulation, inasmuch as Socrates seemed not to know what he asked of his interlocutors.[36] Alcibiades remarked in the *Symposium* (215A–B) that "What [Socrates] reminds me of more than anything is one of those little sileni that you see on the statuaries' stalls; you know the ones I mean—they're modeled with pipes or flutes in their hands, and when you open them down the middle there are little figures of the gods inside."[37] Silenus, a demigod and a companion of Bacchus, was generally represented in classical statuary as a cheerful old drunk riding on an ass, but he was also considered by many to be a great philosopher. Despite his grotesque appearance, Alcibiades suggested, Socrates—like Silenus or the statues of him—contained within himself sublime philosophical truths, but his dissimulating words needed to be cracked open in order to gain access to the god-like knowledge hidden within them.

Plato's most famous pupil, Aristotle, argued instead for transparent truth-telling and against too great a reliance on the use of Socratic irony. In the *Nicomachean Ethics* (1124A), he exalted the magnanimous or high-minded individual (*megalopsychos*) for outspokenness "concerning his hatreds and friendships, for secrecy is a mark of fear; and he will care for truth more than for reputation; and he will speak and act openly, because he has contempt for fear and secrecy and falsity. And hence he will be truthful, except when he is ironical, and if ironical, it will be only towards the many."[38] Aristotle defined the ironizing Socratic dissimulator as "denying the qualities that he possesses, or minimizing them," and as speaking through attenuation in order "to avoid exaggeration . . . [and] those qualities that give men fame, just as Socrates did."[39] Such understatement had the virtue of avoiding boasting and pomposity, but was bound to fail if the things dissimulated were too insignificant or self-evident, which paradoxically led others to notice them all the more. Aristotle gave as an example the exaggeratedly sober clothing of the Spartans, which seemed to boast about the Spartans's supposed modesty rather than effectively dissimulate it. This was a warning, in no uncertain terms, about the difficulties of any undertaking to dissimulate honestly.

The skeptic Pyrrhon and his followers aspired to *ataraxia,* or imperturbability, by withholding judgment and stating nothing positive. The followers of the philosopher Pythagoras were said to have observed self-imposed silence (sometimes for years at a time) as an ascetic exercise in mental and spiritual discipline rather than as a means to disguise the truth.[40] Founded by Spartan colonists, the mute city of Amyclae (mentioned in *Aeneid* X.778) was thought by some to have been devoted to the Pythagorean cult of silence. Legend has it that when the city was about to be attacked, the guards on watch held their tongues out of respect for the cult, and Amyclae was taken by the enemy without a sound. But the Pythagoreans were far less influential than the Stoics, who promoted the prudent use of dissimulation at the right time, in the right place, and with the right persons. Seneca, the Stoic who would alternately be adored and despised by his early modern readers, not only urged his followers to exercise self-control but contended that "one must also know how to withdraw into oneself" (*multum et in se recedendum est*).[41]

Plutarch, the Platonic moral philosopher and staunch opponent of the Stoics, praised silence and secrecy in the *Moralia* (On matters relating to customs and mores). In his treatment of loquacity, Plutarch provided an emblematic image of prudence in the use of one's tongue: "therefore the tongue must be fenced in, and reason must ever lie, like a barrier, in the tongue's way, checking its flow and keeping it from slipping, in order that we may not be thought to be less sensible than geese, of whom they relate that when from Cilicia they cross Mt. Taurus, which is full of eagles, they take a great stone in their mouths to serve as a bolt or bridle for their scream, and pass over at night unobserved" (510A–B).[42] In addition to the philosophers, rhetoricians stretching from Isocrates to Cicero (*Oratio pro Milone;* Speech in defense of [Titus Annius] Milo) and Quintilian (*Institutionum Oratorium;* Institutes of oratory, book XII.1) endorsed the use of dissimulation under certain circumstances, or allowed, as did Quintilian, for untruths to be told *utilitatis gratia.*[43] The ancient rhetoricians, particularly Cicero, also displayed a keen interest in picturing, training, and modifying the passions, and this too would find an echo in the early modern discourse on dissimulation. Although these classical sources—as well as others—were well known in the sixteenth and seventeenth centuries, it was generally accepted that the chief authority of the ancient world on the subject of dissimulation was neither a philosopher nor a rhetorician but rather the Roman historian Tacitus.

Tacitus's works began to be rediscovered long before they came into vogue in early modern Europe. Giovanni Boccaccio read some of the manuscripts that had come to light in the fourteenth century, and the *editio princeps* appeared in Venice around 1470. Marc-Antoine Muret and the sixteenth-century anti-Ciceronians used Tacitus as a point of reference in their critique of exaggerated humanist eloquence. However, it was the great 1574 edition by Lipsius that triggered the revival known as "Tacitism" throughout Europe.[44] Tacitus's laconic account of the deeds and misdeeds of Rome's imperial rulers seemed to speak directly to many of those who found themselves living in a new age of absolutism. In Spain, France, and northern Europe, as in Italy, Tacitus's writings attracted a large and diverse readership for whom the *Annals* and *Histories* meant many often contradictory things. Depending upon the Old Regime state to which they were subject, some of Tacitus's interpreters found him to be an opponent of absolutism, while others used his authority to defend the doctrine of reason of state. Sometimes he served as a convenient means of referring in a backhanded manner to Machiavelli, whose writings were on the Index of Forbidden Books, but more often than not his works were of interest in their own right. The almost perverse subtlety of the ancient historian's depiction of the relationship between ruler and courtiers in imperial Rome was particularly fascinating to his early modern readers, and his accounts of life in Rome under Tiberius and Domitian (who was "never to be more greatly feared than when he smiled") became staples of political discussion across Europe.

In particular, Tacitus's remark in the *Annals* (IV.71) concerning Tiberius's love of dissimulation was to be invoked repeatedly to legitimate or critique the practice of dissimulation by both early modern ruler and courtier: "Of all his virtues, as he regarded them, there was none which Tiberius held in such esteem as his power of dissimulation; whence the chagrin with which he received this attempt to reveal what he chose to suppress."[45] The innovative Piedmontese Tacitist, humanist, and diplomat Carlo Pasquale drew the conclusion, in the first full political commentary on Tacitus (published in Paris in 1581), that "not only Tiberius, but many other princes count dissimulation among those special virtues which it is necessary for them to have; and so they care for none of the other virtues as much; and even today they say that it is necessary for a prince."[46] Thus the ancient historian's works held the key to understanding the virtues and vices of Europe's princes as well as the emperors of imperial Rome, all of whom wished to surround themselves with a cloak of secrecy.[47] Indeed, most Tacitists, well acquainted with the arcana of absolutism, would have agreed with the cutting epigram penned by Gracián in the mid-seventeenth century. For this worldly Baroque wit, a reading of the above passage from the *Annals* revealed that Tiberius's fatal shortcoming as a tyrant consisted merely in that "Tiberius affected dissimulation, but did not know how to dissimulate dissimulation."[48] Many early modern rulers, as Gracián knew only too well, would be careful not to make the same mistake.

HEARTS OF GLASS

Christianity, which inherited and transformed classical culture, developed a language for describing the moderation and control of the passions. Tertullian's praise of patience in his *De patientia* (On patience, 200–203 A.D.) supplied an early example of this sort of ascetic Christian self-discipline. Tertullian recommended that silence and humility be employed to express the serenity of the soul, even in moments of extreme distress:

Now then! If you will, let us try to grasp the features and appearance of patience. Its countenance is peaceful and untroubled. Its brow is clear, unruffled by any lines of melancholy or anger. The eyebrows are relaxed, giving an impression of joyousness. The eyes are lowered, in an attitude rather of humility than moroseness. The mouth is closed in becoming silence. Its complexion is that of the serene and blameless.[49]

This silence disguised nothing, and fully expressed the inner peace of the devout. However, early Christian theologians and thinkers held contrasting positions on the matter of dissimulation, as they did on the question of lying. The Bible combined prohibitions against lying or dissembling, on the one hand, with examples of those who had done so for good reasons.[50] Job's lament (Job 3:26) was translated in the Vulgate: "Did I not dissimulate? Did I not keep silent? Did I not keep calm? And yet I was overcome by the wrath of God."[51] Between 387 and 405 A.D., Jerome, the author of the Vulgate text, and Augustine debated the interpretation of Paul's rebuke to Peter for having dissembled his faith in Antioch (Galatians 2:11–14). Jerome contended that the meaning of the passage was that "(dis)simulation may sometimes be accepted as useful."[52] In this he was not alone among the Church fathers, as Origen, Cassian, Clement of Alexandria, Didymus of Alexandria, and St. John Chrysostom all took positions favorable to the withholding of the truth under certain circumstances.[53]

Augustine disagreed, insisting that nothing in the Scriptures could be understood to support anything other than the "necessity of truth."[54] This position, which he used to counter the followers of Priscillian, was developed at length in his *De Mendacio* (On lying, ca. 395) and *Contra Mendacium* (Against lying, ca. 420). In the former, Augustine provided his famous definition of a lie as "a false statement made with the intention to deceive" (enuntiationem falsam cum voluntate fallendi) and condemned all such statements, even when meant as an equivocation rather than a lie. The *Contra Mendacium* also flatly rejected all justifications of deception, including religious dissimulation in the face of persecution.[55] In the *Enchiridion* (The Enchiridion, or on faith, hope and love), moreover, Augustine reaffirmed his belief that, for the Christian, the only choice was to tell the truth: "for who, except in error, denies that it is bad to approve the false as though it were the truth, or to disapprove the truth as though it were falsehood, or to hold what is certain as if it were uncertain, or what is uncertain as if it were certain?"[56] In sharp contrast to Jerome, he thus envisioned the ideal Christian as a *homo fenestratus,* whose face ought to be an open book and whose heart ought to be as transparent as glass. Augustine was still indebted here to the discourse on the classical virtue of *parrhesia,* according to which one must say everything that one thinks. *Parrhesia* — literally pan (all) + *rhema* (that which is said) — is concerned not so much with the formal correctness of discourse as with the right or duty to tell the truth to others, and to put it into frank and sincere words, no matter what the cost may be. This insistence on the continuity between what one thinks and what one says creates a specific relationship between the individual and truth, and thus stands as the polar opposite in antiquity of the discourse on dissimulation.[57]

Augustine's rigorous doctrinal position was to become the reigning orthodoxy for many centuries to come, yet it was not unconditionally endorsed by the medieval Church. According to some medieval legal scholars, *dissimulatio* was to be employed by those ecclesiastical authorities obliged to overlook an irregular act or situation that could not be prevented but who wished to make it clear that they were simply "closing their eyes" rather than approving or tolerating irregularities. The doctrine of *dissimulatio* made its official appearance during the papacy of

Alexander III (1159–1181). The aversion of the ecclesiastical gaze simply recognized that something could not be effectively opposed at that moment; by seeming to ignore it, the Church did not give up its moral standards but merely abstained temporarily from applying them. Thus dissimulation provided a means of defending the Church from a greater evil while marking time in anticipation of the moment at which to rectify a given state of affairs. Such a practice was closely related to "economical silence" (defined as the "unspoken acceptance of the current state of things"), and differed considerably from tolerance, which invoked the "tacit admission" of a right.[58]

Few philosophers have ever had as encyclopedic a range as Aquinas, and—not surprisingly—he dealt with dissimulation in his *Summa Theologiae* (Summary of theology). Although Aquinas viewed lying and deceit just as negatively as Augustine had, "it is nevertheless," he added, "licit to conceal the truth prudently under some dissimulation" (*licit tamen veritatem occultare prudenter sub aliqua dissimulatione*).[59] That is to say, while "deception, which meant a false signification by outward acts, was identical with lying," and was therefore reprehensible, for Aquinas it was equally true that "to pretend (*fingere*) [was] not always to lie, for a pretense sometimes has reference to a further meaning and conveys a truth figuratively," just as keeping silent—or keeping a secret—is not always to lie. Feigning (*fingere*) was at times a morally acceptable response to a situation that demanded it.[60] Thus Aquinas, in recovering the distinctions that Augustine had rejected regarding the legitimacy of feigning and dissembling, anticipated the early modern shift in attitude toward dissimulation. But the medieval notion of the sacred *concordia* or *consonantia* between heart, mind, and voice, making us fundamentally similar to God in this respect, did not encourage much general interest in the topic. The monastic practice of silence, moreover, was intended both as a display of disciplined self-mortification and as an end in itself, and thus was different from the taciturnity described by the ancients and the Church fathers.[61]

Missing Persons: A Typology of Early Modern Dissimulation

Louis Machon, an obscure member of Cardinal Richelieu's circle in Paris in the 1640s, argued, in his manuscript entitled *Apologie pour Machiavelle en faveur des Princes et des Ministres d'Estat* (Apology for

Machiavelli, for the benefit of princes and ministers of state), that dissimulation could be either *civile et morale* or *politique*.[62] Machon's encyclopedic work was left unpublished, but his attempt to sort out the tangled strands of the early modern discourse on dissimulation was not without merit. If reflection on dissimulation was widely dispersed across a number of discursive fields traversing the principal European cultures, these fields often intersected with one another, making their definition difficult to fix. For instance, the boundary lines could and did grow blurry at times between the discourse on the court and the discourse on civility, for the court served as the model for the manners of those social groups who aspired to it. Baldassar Castiglione's *Il Libro del Cortegiano* (The book of the courtier) served as a source for both discursive fields, as did Baltasar Gracián's *Oráculo manual y arte de prudencia* (The oracle: A manual on the art of prudence). Likewise, discussions about the court sometimes crossed over into the territory of reason of state. As Lorenzo Ducci was to show in his *Arte aulica* (The courtier's art), for example, there was a relationship of mutual dependency that bound prince and courtier together, and which could affect the decisions of the former as well as the destiny of the latter.

The chief early modern discursive fields for which the legitimacy of dissimulation was an issue included: (i) civility or good manners, (ii) the court, (iii) the prince and reason-of-state politics, (iv) moral philosophy, and (v) religious dissent. The last of these is excluded from this book for two reasons. First, religious dissimulation (and discussions of it) involved many powerful individuals or well-known intellectuals, to be sure. The majority of those practicing religious dissimulation were, however, ordinary people who often belonged to socially marginal splinter groups and radical sects. Popular and elite cultures intermixed under absolutism, as the new historicists have tried to show with varying degrees of success, but this does not mean that there was a symmetrical relationship between the two. This book is concerned with the production of the discourse on dissimulation in the dominant early modern culture, centered on the courts and state apparatus, which was subsequently absorbed and transformed by other social strata. Religious dissimulation had a long history reaching back into the Middle Ages and beyond (one need only think of Dante's explanation for Statius's Christianity in *Purgatorio* XXII.89–90), but the insistently secular discourse on dissimulation at court, in politics, or in polite society was chiefly a product of the sixteenth and seventeenth centuries.[63] Second, the phenomenon of religious dissimulation, which employed mental reservation, amphibological speech, and outward shows of conformism, has attracted considerable interest from historians in recent years, and interested readers have a number of useful studies to which to turn.[64] Even orthodox religious thinkers such as Martin Berbeeck, confessor of Emperor Ferdinand and author of a well-known manual on the religious controversies of the age, distinguished between Nicodemitism and other sorts of dissimulation: "it is one thing to deny faith, which is not permitted," he noted, "but it is another thing to keep silent, to dissimulate and to hide."[65] Libertinage (which sometimes included the practice of religious dissimulation) also became increasingly important over the course of the period that concerns me here, but the profoundly heterodox positions of free-thinkers such as Giulio Cesare Vanini or Ferrante Pallavicino place them outside of the scope of the present inquiry.[66] Thus, the following pages will concentrate on the first four discursive fields—all deeply embedded in the culture of the early modern elite social groups—and the problems posed by dissimulation for them.

"MORAL AND CIVIL" DISSIMULATION

The cult of civility, with its exceptionally elaborate codes of comportment, recognized that dissimulation was essential for all those who wished—or were compelled—to exist together in polite society. At least three Italians who wrote about civility and manners were practically household names across Europe by the early seventeenth century: Baldassar Castiglione, Giovanni Della Casa, and Stefano Guazzo.[67] But there were many others as well, of course, and as Italy gradually lost its cultural primacy these newer authors tended to be French or Spanish. Castiglione's famous neologism *sprezzatura* became identified throughout Europe with the worldly dissimulation emanating from the Italian courts and from those who sought to emulate the fashions of the latter. Castiglione's ideal courtier, whether in riding, dueling or dancing, knew how to hide from others the considerable effort—and ambition—that lay behind what appeared to be inherently graceful and natural. Della Casa and Guazzo both were careful readers of Castiglione's dialogues, and suggested a number of ways in which dissimulation and secrecy could be applied to matters of everyday "civil conversation" by the gentry and urban bourgeoisie. *Chi non sa tacere non sa parlare*, warned Guazzo, repeating a commonplace of the age derived from Seneca: who does not know how to keep silent does not know how to speak.[68] Throughout the rest of the early modern period, dissimulation continued to be acknowledged as a virtue for persons wishing not only to practice, but also to display, self-control and hence acquire social distinction.

Although approaches to dissimulation from the perspective of personal ethics and morality were few and far between in the first half of the sixteenth century, gradually this too began to change. What Machon called "moral and civil" discourse on the topic began to flourish with the revival of Stoic philosophy in the last part of the century, together with the emergence of the essay form. Giovanni Pontano and others had, in the early Cinquecento, defined dissimulation as a component of prudence itself, which was founded on reason and allowed one to adapt to circumstances through foresight, preparation, caution, judgment, patience, and so on. Such later writers as Michel de Montaigne, Justus Lipsius, and Francis Bacon, among others, went further into the analysis of dissimulation while exploring the infinitely complex nature of human subjectivity. Drawing on currents of Neostoicism, they probed the mechanisms of psychological and emotional self-control needed to endure in an age of great social, religious, and political unrest. This same self-control, which enabled those who practiced it to attain the happiness of the "good life" through moderation of the passions, was also one of the cornerstones of all successful dissimulation. For the critical self-examination that it demanded was a prerequisite for the acquisition of authentic self-knowledge, without which dissimulation was destined to fail.

The intersection of these two discourses was thus perhaps inevitable, and Torquato Accetto's *Della dissimulazione onesta* (On honest dissimulation, 1641) was the single most important work to appear at this crossroads. Accetto's brief treatise—the only one of its kind ever to be published—pushed the discourse on dissimulation to the extreme limits of paradox, in an attempt to define, for the early modern individual caught up in a web of social, cultural, and political coercion, the possibilities of freedom of thought and emotion. When faced with demands for conformity in comportment, Accetto's honest dissimulator was able to withdraw and to become a missing person, through strict observance of the rules of secrecy, silence, and reservation governing the art of dissimulation. Self-expression was generally recognized in early modernity as essential to personal well-being, insofar as the carefully regulated expression of the passions and emotions was a defining trait of subjectivity itself.[69] The very logic of dissimulation suggested that the possibility of hiding one's feelings within the depths of the heart was dependent upon the prior possibility of expressing those feelings. Each person—through the exercise of will and reason—was nonetheless responsible for deciding when and where and how to put emotions and passions into words, or not to do so. Dissimulation came to represent for Accetto the paradox of carefully controlled self-expression *through* the choice of secrecy and silence. How was one to sustain this paradoxical performance over a long period of time, however, and at what cost? The precarious balancing act that constituted the culture of secrecy was perhaps never any more clearly in view than it was here, as were the extraordinary demands made on participants and observers alike. It can therefore hardly be surprising that, not long after Accetto faded into obscurity near the middle of the seventeenth century, a revolt against the rule of dissimulation began to develop, which is discussed in chapter 5.

COURTLY DISSIMULATION

At the epicenter of the patronage networks of the Old Regime societies, the court provoked perhaps the most vexed reflection by its own members, as well as by its enemies, on the issue of dissimulation. Given the overriding importance of appearances at court, it was perhaps no wonder that courtiers were reviled or praised as experts in the art of hiding their true thoughts and feelings behind localized displays of etiquette, conversational skills, and rituals of power.[70] As Jean de La Bruyère remarked, "a man who knows the court is master of his gesture, his eyes and his face; he is deep and impenetrable; he dissimulates bad deeds done to him, smiles at his enemies, controls his temper, disguises his passions, denies his heart, and speaks and acts against his own feelings."[71] Much translated and often republished across Europe, Castiglione's *Il Libro del Cortegiano* once again defined the terms of the debate, but a host of other voices joined in as the courts grew in size, number, and influence, from Florence and Rome to Madrid, Versailles, and London.

From the well known (Antonio de Guevara, Torquato Tasso, Nicolas Faret) to the little known (Lorenzo Ducci, Philibert de Vienne) to the anonymous, writers who dealt with dissimulation at court after Castiglione probed the motives and practices of its members in an effort either to exonerate or criticize their tireless struggle for status and distinction under the controlling gaze of the prince. Was the courtier's *sprezzatura* part of an ethically balanced and respectable project to advance at once secret personal ambitions and the interests of the sovereign, as Castiglione seemed to suggest? Or was the courtier, as Henri

Estienne claimed in his diatribe against the court, *Deux Dialogues du nouveau langage françois italianizé* (Two dialogues on the new Italianized French language, 1578), a paragon of some of the most morally questionable traits of humanity, intent only upon self-aggrandizement and the furthering of self-interest? "Take three pounds of impudence (but of the finest sort, which grows on a rock called 'sheer shamelessness'), two pounds of hypocrisy, one pound of dissimulation, three pounds of the science of flattery, and two pounds of borrowed airs. Cook together in the juice of good grace for a day and a night. . . . Afterwards pass this concoction through a cheesecloth made of lax conscience. . . . And there you have a capital potion for becoming a courtier of absolutely perfect courtiership."[72] The discourse on dissimulation, in general, split along these same fault lines, in some cases lauding and in other cases ridiculing the courtier and the court for relying on such extensive recourse to the art and culture of secrecy in order to guarantee that appearance and reality would never coincide.

POLITICAL DISSIMULATION

The development of the doctrine of reason of state (*raison d'état, ragion di stato*) accompanied the consolidation of European absolutism between the sixteenth and seventeenth centuries. Many saw, in the bloody violence and instability of the religious conflicts of the age—from the civil strife in France to the revolt of the Low Countries to the Thirty Years' War—and the increasingly fierce economic competition between the great European superstates, a clear justification for the use of extreme means to preserve and maintain the state, even if this in turn concentrated great fiscal, bureaucratic, and military power in the hands of the prince.[73] The centralized state, with its growing ability to tax, to exercise a monopoly on the use of coercive violence through the army and the police, and to expand its territories in Europe and overseas through its military and commercial organizations, was founded on a logic of self-interest sustained by force, not on republican or religious principles.[74] While continuing to endorse and embody many traditional Christian values, the prince was increasingly obliged to rule with whatever means—including dissimulation—might assist in providing security to his subjects and stability to his state. In particular, there was keen awareness throughout Europe of the need for governments to control tightly all access to the *arcana imperii,* or secrets of state, upon which the prince's power often depended, and which spies, traitors, and other enemies of the state sought to discover in his words, gestures, or countenance. Indeed, wherever reason-of-state doctrine was debated in this period, it provided one of the principal platforms for debate over the nature and function of dissimulation.

The doctrine of reason of state and of the *arcana imperii* inevitably hinged on the question of whether or not political discourse should or could free itself of the constraints of ethics and religion. Europeans split into rival camps over this issue, which tended to crystallize around the interpretation of the works of Machiavelli and Tacitus. The so-called *politici* or *politiques* (that is, the exponents of the doctrine of reason of state), followed Machiavelli—and later claimed to be following Tacitus—in separating politics from ethics and religion. Some writers such as Giovanni Botero, in his pathbreaking *Della Ragion di Stato* (On reason of state, 1589), took a middle ground, justifying princely dissimulation as a requisite tool for the preservation of the state and the social order while promoting the image of the absolutist ruler who governs virtuously with justice and liberality for all, and without recourse to fraud or tyranny. Anti-Machiavellians, such as Innocent Gentillet and Virgilio Malvezzi, contended instead that Christian virtues and traditional practices of truth-telling should suffice for the prince, who ought never be bound by the demands of statecraft to commit acts of deception. Although each of these positions had passionate advocates and detractors, none could do without reference to the prevailing culture of secrecy and the crisis of traditional ethical and religious values that it invoked. Thus the debate over dissimulation in early modern European statecraft seems, from our vantage point some four hundred years later, to be about the incipient process of secularization itself.

Paper Bodies

It was perhaps inevitable that the first age of mechanical reproduction (that is, with the advent of printing) would have the question of identity at its very core. Print was the first means of mass communication in early modern Europe, but the medium was not a strictly neutral instrument for the transmission of thought. The paper bodies it (re)produced—from the cheapest broadside to the most priceless incunabula—profoundly affected those persons who came into contact with them, opening up a perspective in which the word was perceived in a fundamentally new way: it now belonged as much to material space as to consciousness alone. Mind and text, interior and exterior, seemed poised to mirror each other as never before in the early modern period: print promised to transform one's thoughts, no matter how intimate, into so many objects readily recognizable to anonymous readers or viewers near and far.[75] This development fits part and parcel with the incessant demands for self-disclosure that mark all phases of modernity.[76] At the same time, however, those same objectified thoughts were not only highly mobile but could multiply ad infinitum thanks to the new media, leaving the orbit of the author far behind them and, as Plato had warned, becoming vulnerable to appropriation or abuse by others. Not coincidentally, this was also a period of profound anxiety and intense confrontation about controlling identity, or, in other words, of regulating "relations between the interior and the exterior," as Valentin Groebner has defined the process of identification.[77]

Dissimulation seems designed, among other things, as an antidote for this anxiety about identity, for it produces a dissimilarity (if not a rupture) between inside and outside.[78] In other words, it deliberately sets out to shatter the mirror-model upon which the process of identification was generally thought to depend: in the act of dissimulating— whether in speech or in writing—neither heart nor mind will perforce be represented as they really are. The dissimulator truly is, in the words of the Italian historian Anna Maria Battista, *l'uomo dissociato* (the dissociated individual).[79] One of the points that was debated most heatedly in the controversy over dissimulation is the moral legitimacy of this attitude toward self-expression. But if one's thoughts are not contrary to, but only different than, what is said in a dialogue, do these words constitute a falsehood?[80] Dissimulation permits its practitioners to speak or act *next to or beside* what they think, deflecting or deterring any and all attempts by others to connect definitively thoughts with words, interior with exterior, being with appearance. It thus short-circuits the primary mechanisms for the representation of personal identity, rendering that representation at least partially unintelligible, and leaving others to doubt the evidence of their own eyes and ears. The historian John Martin has argued that the experience of a "divided self," in which convictions, passions, and emotions were disguised in response to legal, administrative, and religious pressures to define one's identity clearly and publicly, was common in early modern societies.[81] This may certainly be the case. It should be added here, however, that in its unquestionable power, across a broad spectrum of social institutions and modes of interaction, to challenge assumptions about visual rationality, and even to destabilize the very notion of an uncontestable visual reality itself, dissimulation occupied a unique role in early modern Europe, anticipating radical developments in the aesthetic field of the Baroque.[82]

For the moment, however, let us turn our backs, like rowers, away from the place toward which we are going, and first look more closely at the intertwined discourses of civility and the art of dissimulation.

CHAPTER 2

Taking One's Distance

Civil and Moral Dissimulation

Civil Conversations

> *La cortesía . . . es un tipo de hechizo.*
> Courtesy . . . is a kind of enchantment.
> Baltasar Gracián, *Oráculo manual*
> *y arte de prudencia*

Early modern civility is inextricably linked to the civilizing process itself. Over the past few decades the reception of Norbert Elias's *Über den Prozess der Zivilisation* (The civilizing process), which first put forward this theorem, has not been without controversy among scholars.[1] The gradual, incremental standardization of self-constraint among elite groups across Europe between the end of the Middle Ages and the end of the Old Regime is by now widely accepted as an indicator of the civilizing process first defined by Elias.[2] It is still an open question, however, if conduct books—as opposed to socially instilled thresholds of shame and delicacy—disseminated new standards regulating and automating the comportment of the members of these groups. To claim, as Elias does, that manuals on good manners were always and only instruments of social disciplining implies that they were read univocally by their early modern readership, and this is unlikely to have ever occurred. Anyone familiar with the contrasting contemporary interpretations of the major treatises on conduct in the sixteenth and seventeenth centuries will recognize that these works offered multiple possible meanings, leading in quite different directions, to their readers.[3] It would be more accurate to say that conduct books operated as the publicity for various behavioral models, rather than as instruments of their direct inscription into the life-world of polite persons.

The function of such texts was not solely to deploy new protocols for conduct and, subsequently, to reinforce them, but to represent and legitimate, or criticize, the conduct in which prominent figures—courtiers, aristocrats, princes—were already actively engaged. Such behavior may be so secret that only a select few would know of its existence without an exposé, or outsiders may want or need to learn more about its codes and nuances, or the author of the work may desire to revise or condemn it. Manuals on conduct intervened in the activities that they described, in any event, by spreading knowledge among readers outside of the court and the aristocracy. This could and did occur in unforeseeable ways, depending upon the reception given to the works by these same readers. Elias fails to account satisfactorily, moreover, for the representation of conduct itself in an increasingly theatricalized and aestheticized culture. One critic has acutely observed that early modern conduct books project "the sense of an unrepresented, perhaps unrepresentable, inner self [that] is the specific product of relatively more powerful regimes and technologies of representation—regimes that both encourage the expression of inwardness and limit the forms it can take."[4] In the discourse on civil dissimulation, in particular, the story told by conduct books presents a troublesome paradox that Elias does not address. For if these texts articulate the ground rules of the culture of secrecy, making them visible to all, do they not at the same time recommend that readers (in order to further their own interests) participate fully in that very same culture? What could be less disciplined than to display a model of self-controlled comportment whose very basis may be undermined by such a display? We will need to look beyond the conceptual limits of Elias's *Civilizing Process* in order to grasp the significance of dissimulation for polite society in early modern Europe.

In composing his study in the 1930s in London, Elias largely overlooked the corpus of sixteenth-century Italian treatises on civility that provided the basis not only for the early modern discourse on politeness but on civil dissimulation as well. This omission is particularly glaring, given the renown that these works enjoyed for so many decades and in so many countries. The Italian philosopher Giordano Bruno remarked that "orators, courtiers and those who in any event know the rules of behavior are more effective at civil conversation when they employ the hidden dissimulation of artifice . . . for not a small part of art is to use it while dissimulating it."[5] Although he was of modest social extraction and was not renowned for his social graces, Bruno must have learned a great deal about the rules of politeness during his years of wandering through Europe, where he often interacted with ambassadors, patricians, and their peers. His observations here, however, seem to have been drawn not from life but from two of the fundamental texts of Renaissance conduct literature, namely Baldassar Castiglione's *Il Libro del Cortegiano* (The book of the courtier, 1528) and Stefano Guazzo's *La civil conversazione* (The civil conversation, 1574). These two works, together with Giovanni Della Casa's *Il Galateo* (Galateo, 1558), virtually defined the discourse on conduct in the second half of the sixteenth century and the early part of the seventeenth century; they were, as Amedeo Quondam has observed, truly pan-European books.[6]

The three Italian treatises glide effortlessly across discursive boundaries. Castiglione's work on the court was widely read for its insights into general etiquette, just as many readers took the subject of Della Casa's brief treatise to be the confluence of civil and courtly manners (in 1663 the *Galateo* was translated into English as *The Refin'd Courtier, or a Correction of Several Indecencies Crept into Civil Conversation*).[7] The civil discourse on conduct drew upon the literature of the court but concerned itself chiefly with specific protocols of socialization for those persons performing acts of politeness in everyday life, outside of the shared institutional etiquette of courts and academies. Dissimulation was recognized by this discourse to be one of the contributing factors in the worldly success of all who mastered the art of "civil conversation." The latter included everything appropriate to courteous behavior in the ensemble of civil relations constituting "good society" at large.[8] Dissimulation enabled those who were adept in this art to operate under cover, as it were, concealing the applied sociocultural technology of good manners behind a screen of apparent naturalness, spontaneous grace, and warm conviviality. As Bruno recognized, paraphrasing Castiglione, in matters of manners dissimulation was something that had to be present everywhere and visible nowhere.

The following four sections of chapter 2 explore the discourse on civil dissimulation that circulated throughout Italy and Europe during the early modern period. To those involved, etiquette appeared as the common sense of ethics or, in other words, as an approximation of the ethical ideal of existence (namely the achievement of happiness, in this case through the rewards for successful social interaction). Etiquette is the universal script and politeness is its particular performance; the two stand in a relationship analogous to that of the maxim and the aphorism.[9] Nevertheless, despite its seemingly sound ethical foundation, the system of courtesy depicted in early modern conduct books was unable to function without recourse to reservation, discretion, and dissimulation.[10] The cult of civility, with its complex codes of comportment and respect for social hierarchy, made it essential for those who wished—or were compelled—to live together in an aristocratic or semi-aristocratic culture to exercise mastery over passions and emotions, most often by masking them through impassivity and polite silence. As Elias argued in *The Court Society*, civility made the establishment of distance an end in itself, in order to preserve and conserve a hierarchical structure of social relations, and the vigilant self-control required for the achievement of this end was the very basis of the civilizing process.[11] Dissimulation was therefore not only a means to establish distance between persons but a condition of possibility of polite coexistence, *il vivere associato*. As Torquato Accetto noted in regard to the relationship between morality, civility, and dissimulation, "Turning now to the usefulness of dissimulation in moral affairs, I will start with the most necessary things, namely the art of good manners, which amounts to nothing other than the skillful practice of dissimulation. In reading what Monsignor Della Casa wrote of this matter, it can be seen that the whole of that most noble doctrine thus teaches us to restrict excessive desires, which are the cause of troublesome actions, like appearing not to see the errors of others, so that the conversation will be in good taste."[12]

DISCRETUM

> What a deale of cold business doth a man mis-spend the better part of life in! in scattering *complements,* tendring *visits,* gathering and venting *newes,* following *Feasts* and *Playes,* making a little winter-love in a darke corner.
> Ben Jonson, *Timber: or, Discoveries; Made Upon Men and Matter* . . . [1641]

Etiquette guarantees not only participation but social integration into the existing hierarchical order, by providing for the distribution of social positions.[13] It is not difficult to see how the art of good manners could function in the relatively close quarters of the court, but what of the wider sphere of urbane good society spreading far beyond the center of political power? Such a refined social milieu, consisting of minor aristocrats, urban patricians who had "aristocratized" themselves, professionals, members of religious orders and others, was experienced by its members as the *discretum* of everyday life.[14] As a series of discrete ritual events occurring in a variety of settings, this stood opposite the *continuum* or total cultural system of court life. In 1604 a posthumously published work by the ecclesiastic Bernardino Pino da Cagli (ca.1530– ca.1601) explained that the everyday was the arena of the gentleman (*il galant'huomo*), who was distinguished from striving courtiers by the use of discretion and prudence in everything that he did.[15] He added: "'Gentleman' means a wise, discreet, and prudent man, who governs himself prudently in all places, at all times, and with all persons, and who is so capable in word and deed that he is always worthy of praise. . . . It is our intention and firm proposal to show how in every human act a man can be called a gentleman."[16] As the fluid domain of interpersonal communication governed by the rules of gracefulness and courtesy, the *discretum* was precisely what Guazzo and Bruno called the "civil conversation."[17]

This conversation arose in the gap between the court and the town, between the *palazzo* and the *piazza,* between the taste-makers at court and those influenced by them, and was to be found in or around such important sites of everyday social interaction as churches, streets, bed- rooms, and dinner-tables. As Montaigne remarked in his essay entitled "Ceremony of Interviews between Kings" (1.13), "not only each country but each city has its particular forms of civility, and so has each occupa- tion. . . . [I]t . . . is a very useful knowledge, this knowledge of social dexterity."[18] Outside of the court, the principle of civil conversation be- came generally recognized by persons of various ranks and roles, pro- moting and establishing an exchange between groups and forms of so- cial life, while respecting existing hierarchical power relations and class divisions.[19] Both Guazzo and Della Casa, for instance, in separating daily life into discrete episodes, attempted to distinguish the norm, for- mulate the precept, and assign the level of linguistic or conversational competence suited to the situation, in order to develop a grammar of the quotidian centered on the concept of the need to communicate without conflict and with social dexterity.[20]

The task of civil conversation—*bon ton, buona creanza,* good manners—was, moreover, to order the most intimate aspects of per- sonal behavior. In fact, the further civil conversation delved into the minimal and the trivial details of everyday existence, the greater its power over the polite individual became.[21] One had to display one's acceptance of this power in order to belong to the social exchange that aspired to civility: all were expected to play by the same complex rules of the "world." These established a dialectic of proximity and distance between the various interlocutors. To participate in the civil conversation meant to be with others in society, and yet to maintain, in adhering to the intricate code of proper comportment, a certain distance from them.[22] This in turn opened up a role for dissimulation, for in the polite exchange the subjective element was always presumed to be radically subordinate to the social element or, to put it another way, to the outwardness of identity. As Jacques Revel has argued, civil dissimulation functioned as a display of the absolute primacy of the forms of social life (gesture, attitude, speech) over the interiority of the individual, which was supposed to be readily intelligible to all involved.[23]

In disguising idiosyncratic passions and emotions through politeness, dissimulation allowed the speaker to affirm the values of the civil conversation, by displaying what appeared to be instead an intimacy ordered and governed by the social imperatives of grace, tact, and good manners. If there was a certain lack of sincerity in such acts of civility, the enhancement of one's own status and prestige through polite conversation, and the contribution of an aesthetic dimension to sociability, were far more important to those engaged in the conversation than was the authentic expression of thoughts or passions. For the former not only created and sustained the "good society" to which they aspired but allowed these individuals to come into social existence by entering into the discrete rituals of the civil linguistic exchange.[24]

The necessary involvement of dissimulation in politeness invokes in turn the concept of the limit as the unspoken law of civility itself. The polite woman or man not only had to possess a sharply critical self-regard but to make it manifest to others through the exercise of restraint in self-expression. Such a practice—with its rational calculus of subject positions and of applications in the public sphere of conversation—was aimed at impulse management, to be sure. One had to know, however, exactly what the rules of the game were at any given moment, and what were the limits of expression, in order to maintain the harmony and to respect the hierarchy of the conversation. And this was perhaps the most difficult thing to do of all, precisely because this knowledge was not rational but social in nature: conversational events were quite unlike ceremonies, which were intended to follow a preordained pattern. Participants in the civil conversation constantly negotiated the limits of *contenance,* that is to say, the harmony of behavior, person, and place. These limits were not hard and fast, and were inherently difficult to trace, in order to exclude from the exchange all but those who shared tacit knowledge of the elusive, indefinable *je ne sais quoi* or *non so che* that was needed to affirm social distinction.[25] Dissimulation permitted those who inhabited the sphere of the *discretum* to search—behind a veil of prudent discretion and reservation—for the boundaries of what could be said or done, reducing the risk of an error that could result in social death. The law of civility, which sentenced the socially maladroit to such a death through public loss of face, was only invoked if the invisible limit of the unspeakable was violated in conversation.

ON TOLERANCE AND INTOLERANCE

> O dissembling courtesy!
> William Shakespeare,
> *Cymbeline* 1.i.84

Throughout the course of daily social interaction, the polite person had to be *costumato* or well-mannered, as Della Casa noted, in order to reduce social friction to a minimum, even if this meant dissembling and disguising one's passions and thoughts.[26] The *Galateo* states:

If someone is prepared to tell something, it is wrong to ruin it for him or to say that you already know about it. Or, if he scatters some lies about while getting on with his story, it is wrong to reproach him for it either with words or with actions, such as shaking one's head or screwing up one's eyes, as many usually do, claiming that they cannot bear the bitterness of lies in any way. But this is not the reason, which is rather the [unripe] citrus and aloe of their rustic and harsh nature, which makes them poisonous and bitter in the company of men, and which makes all refuse [to be with them].[27]

This quality of discretion and *costumanza* described by Della Casa resembles nothing so much as civil dissimulation. One was obliged to tolerate and overlook others' conversational faults for the sake of politeness and the conviviality that it produced. Without dissimulation of this sort there would be only solitude, for all would find themselves deprived of "the company of men" *(il consorzio degli uomini)*. Thus this passage underlines the often problematic nature of the relationship between etiquette and ethics in Della Casa's treatise: self-improvement was not necessarily ethical improvement.[28] But the civil conversation would cease if each interlocutor were to reveal an awareness of the untruths told by others, and Della Casa—so keenly aware of the importance of individual behavior for successful social relations—desired above all else for the exchange to continue to exist.[29]

This was not, however, a license to lie freely. Although Della Casa suggested that lying is something that occurs frequently in the civil conversation, sometimes for good reasons, he castigated many different kinds of liars, including those who lie for the fun of it (*come chi beve non per sete ma per gola di vino* [like he who drinks, not out of thirst, but out of a taste for wine]), those who lie out of vainglory (*per vanagloria di se stessi*), and those who claim to be better or worse off than they actually are. As he warned his readers, "one must keep carefully from falling into such foolishness."[30] Castiglione's ideal courtier was likewise called upon in *Il Libro del Cortegiano* to dissimulate through clever displays of conversational wit rather than to resort to such falsehoods. According to Bernardo Bibbiena, one of the interlocutors in the dialogue, "of the same sort is a certain spicy and sharp dissimulation, when a man (a prudent one, as I have said) pretends not to understand what he does understand."[31] Here *dissimulatio* is a form of tactical irony, in which a speaker or listener wants something not to become known because it would be inappropriate for the situation. It is for this reason that ethics has always had difficulty in dealing with such irony and the forms of courtesy that it has generated.[32] Bibbiena also pointed out to his companions in Urbino that a courtier may, in telling witty tales, freely make use of certain fictions and lies to embellish the truth, as long as they are convincing and delightful. But the courtier was not supposed to become widely known as a liar or hypocrite: "I would also take care not to have our courtier acquire the name of liar."[33] Indecorous falsehoods threatened not only the reputation of those who spoke them but also that of those who could not tolerate such lies entirely, and were compelled to violate the rules of polite conversation—and the decorum of social relations—to denounce them.

Guazzo barely referred to dissimulation in *La civil conversazione* (it is directly mentioned three times all together), preferring the term *simulazione,* and without distinguishing one from the other. Although he made no secret of his admiration for Castiglione's treatise, Guazzo did not consider dissimulation one of the most useful kinds of knowledge but merely a part of the immense repertory of knowledges and practices necessary to the new "man of the world." To read *La civil conversazione* was an act of *askesis* (in the sense of "practice" and "training") for polite persons seeking to construct a general matrix for their own behavior.[34]

In the first book of the dialogue, the two interlocutors—the physician Annibale Magnocavalli and the Cavaliere Guazzo (the author's brother)—undertake a wide-ranging discussion of feigning and dissembling.[35] The physician first reviews the military applications of such stratagems as feinting in swordplay, but soon turns to another, more controversial argument. For there are, he contends, any number of socially accepted forms of feigning commonly practiced even among friends. For instance, the person who pretends to be ill in order to avoid going to the theater, or who wears a disguise in order to go out at night incognito, is deceiving others in an inoffensive and perfectly acceptable way, for such actions harm no one.[36] The physician concludes that deception is a part of the conversational and ethical status quo: by implication, then, dissimulation is at least as legitimate, since it does not promote falsehood. It is not a vice to feign, the physician contends, as long as it is "disinterested and without intent to offend others."[37]

In the first book, the physician Annibale defends lying as a practice of "discreet and praiseworthy astuteness," as long as the lies are directed at "an honest end."[38] Lying is, in other words, a socially valuable skill; the limit to its usefulness is imposed by the moral purpose to which it is put. The Cavaliere gives an example taken from the court to illustrate this. He recounts the tale of a young prince, perhaps twelve years old, who never blew his nose, to the despair of his tutor. One day the boy met by chance an old beggar with a hideously deformed cancerous nose, and his tutor told him that the man's disease was caused by his having never cleaned his nose. Horrified, the young prince began to blow his nose regularly, thus observing the rules of politeness to the benefit of all and amply justifying his tutor's recourse to a falsehood.[39] Furthermore, in the first book the physician explains that if, on the street, one greets an acquaintance for whom one does not care by doffing one's hat, no deception is committed: "if, in an act of good manners, I doff my hat to an acquaintance whom I do not love, I am not to be considered at fault, because I honored him more as a sign of courtesy and civility than as a sign of love."[40] Guazzo's argument here is strongly reminiscent of Della Casa's doctrine of *buon costume:* the naked truth was at times antithetical to the practices of courtesy and civility necessary for the highly formalized and theatricalized relations of early modern polite society. Reflecting on the court, La Rochefoucauld would later reformulate this observation in the following terms: "human beings would not live long together in society if they did not deceive each other."[41] Whether in the provincial palaces of Casale Monferrato or at the French court, those trained in the cult of courtesy found themselves very far from the Augustinian position first established in *De Mendacio*. Proponents of polite conversation or of dissimulation, for which the exercise of deception was one of the basic requirements of civility, preferred a far more pragmatic and nuanced approach to sociability.

HOW TO STAY AFLOAT

> *Sea uno primero señor de sí, lo será después de los otros.*
> If one is first master of oneself, one will then be the master of others.
>
> Baltasar Gracián, *Oráculo manual y arte de prudencia* 166 (aphorism 55)

As Quondam notes in his superb 1993 edition of *La conversazione civile,* Guazzo pays little direct attention to dissimulation per se, giving only slightly more heed to simulation.[42] Nonetheless, the perfect gentleman had to master the art of being silent at the right time and with the right persons, in keeping with a vast body of *exempla,* proverbs, and mottos concerning silence that circulated throughout early modern culture.[43] As the physician Annibale comments, "the principal virtue is to know how to rein in one's tongue."[44] The thematics of silence, self-control, and secrecy, which are (not surprisingly) prominent in the text of Guazzo's dialogue, strongly suggest the influence of Francesco Guicciardini as well, and point to the subterranean presence of a strand of the discourse on dissimulation. If the two interlocutors agreed that silence is golden, in accordance with the fundamental precepts of sixteenth-century classicism, it was because one must be master of oneself in order to participate in the civil conversation.[45] Secrecy is praised by the Cavaliere, for example, on the grounds that "knowing how to keep silent, and rein in one's tongue, is an eminent virtue."[46] This held true whether the secrets to be protected were our own or those entrusted to us by others. A good secretary had to guard the master's secrets with silence, and friends kept secrets out of friendship for each other. But to hide one's own secrets, as was often the wisest course of action, meant to work as one's own private secretary, censoring and filtering information about oneself before it circulated: "certainly whoever dearly wanted to keep his thoughts hidden should not reveal them to others, but be his own secretary."[47] Secrecy of this sort was beyond reproach, however, because in the civil conversation silence was to be taken as a sign of courtesy. It indicated that one was listening to others out of respect for the principle of social exchange, while displaying self-mastery in *facendo resistenza a se stesso,* or resisting oneself.[48] The resulting conversation would be graceful, delightful, and balanced, reflecting core values for Guazzo's theory of civility. The physician not surprisingly reaches the conclusion that "knowing how to keep silent gathers no less admiration than skillful speech, because if the latter displays eloquence and doctrine, the former bears signs of gravity and prudence."[49] Through the *topoi* or commonplaces of prudence and silence, the discourse on civility hints at its own only partially hidden "secret," namely its pragmatic dependence on dissimulation.

Some thirty years after Guazzo, Pino da Cagli echoed the words of *La civil conversazione* in promoting, in his aptly entitled treatise *Del Galant'huomo* (On the gentleman), the prudent use of silence as a defining feature of polite behavior: "the virtue and nature of the gentleman may be found in his speaking and keeping silent at times."[50] Pino da Cagli's concept of the gentleman was more inclusive even than Guazzo's ("in every human act a man can be called a gentleman"), extending the range of the civil conversation to ever-larger segments of early modern society. His text is a compendium of precepts, maxims, and the like drawn from Castiglione, Della Casa, Guazzo, and a host of classical and classicizing sources, but it displays the more open interest in dissimulation that typifies many works of the turn of the century. Discretionary silence displays the gentleman's good judgment because, when employed at the right time, in the right place, and with the right person, it means that he knows something should be left unsaid or gracefully passed over without comment in conversation, either for the benefit of good society, for his own benefit, or for the benefit of both. As was the case for Guazzo, at times this taciturnity—so highly prized in the Old Regime as a cornerstone of civility—resembles nothing other than the essence of dissimulation: "The gentleman or prudent man will adopt silence or taciturnity when he realizes that he cannot defeat such adversaries as he may at times engage, or repel a lie by an envious interlocutor, and reserves speaking until a more suitable moment, and prudently keeps silent until a better occasion [arises] for explaining his own position, so that it may be better understood, and his adversaries more clearly confounded."[51] In many circumstances self-cancellation may be a purely defensive maneuver, but in civil conversation it is also something more. For whoever chooses silence is more alone than whoever chooses to speak and participate in such conversations. The former acquires a certain singularity in this way, however; such silence signals the potential presence of a secret hidden within. By not displaying the hidden content of this silence to others, a certain amount of attention will inevitably be attracted, and any further words—no matter how rare or few—in the conversation are likely to be accorded new scrutiny and perhaps even new weight.[52]

Not only the wise use of silence but even the true gentleman's choice of words, Pino da Cagli added, may produce this same dissimulating reserve:

Two things worthy of consideration are found in this mode of prudence and wisdom: the first is when one keeps silent without speaking, by not answering someone urging or proposing that one speak, as Thaletes did; and the other is when one does not answer the person doing the proposing or urging, but rather someone else instead, in order to create greater confusion or [sense of] neglect in the former. . . . And this second well-considered means is pleasant and even airy when done with the gentleman's [good] judgment, so that one may stay on top, or (as is said) afloat, without offending the person about whom one is speaking, and without being thought to be sharp.[53]

The ultimate goal of the civil conversation, for the individual *galant'-huomo,* is to remain "afloat" rather than to lose face and sink in social prestige. As the above passage makes clear, this can be achieved through the careful display of neglect, indifference, and nonchalance when in conversation with someone asking potentially difficult or damaging questions. If done skillfully, such dissimulation should not cause offense or loss of esteem for the gentleman. In this sense, *Del Galant'huomo* embraces the project of the civil conversation to distribute grace, delight, and social recognition to all of its participants. Yet it also betrays Pino da Cagli's anxiety about the precarious—and possibly temporary—position of the worldly individual in such conversations. Guazzo, for whom the participants in civil conversation are bound together by enduring mutual self-interest, seems far more serene on this point. Behind the cautiously defensive and largely invisible maneuvering of the *galant'-huomo* in his efforts not to see his status submerged, and to avoid being left alone and outside of the conversation, is the practice of patience.[54] A popular *topos* in the early modern discourse on dissimulation (appropriated by Neostoicism from Christian and humanist thought), patience is repeatedly invoked as a means of prudently bearing or tolerating injuries done to oneself by fate or by other, usually more powerful and influential, members of society. The true secret of the *galant'huomo* is, in so many words, his own lack of power in relation to others in the civil conversation, the only remedy for which is patience. Its presence here (as in *La civil conversazione*) indicates yet another point of convergence of the various strands of this discourse, from the civil and moral to the political.

BETWEEN OLD FRIENDS

> *Dal conoscer gli altri nasce quella piena autorità che l'uomo ha*
> *sopra se stesso quando tace a tempo, e riserba pur a tempo.*
> That full authority that man has over himself when, at the
> proper moment, he keeps silent or withholds something,
> comes from knowing others.
>
> Torquato Accetto, *Della dissimulazione onesta* 25

Pietro Andrea Canonieri (15??–1639) published his treatise entitled *Il Perfetto Cortegiano et dell'Ufizio del Prencipe verso 'L Cortegiano* (The perfect courtier and the duty of the prince to the courtier) in 1609. Then at the outset of his career, Canonieri was to prove an erudite and prolific writer of works on modern politics, history, literature, medicine, and philosophy, among other subjects. He was certainly well read in the debate over dissimulation: in the second book of his treatise, for example, he discusses texts by Baldassar Castiglione, Antonio de Guevara, Scipione Ammirato, Lorenzo Ducci, and other authorities on courtly and princely dissimulation.[55] But in this same book, Canonieri provides early modern readers with the most comprehensive look at civil dissimulation to appear in print in Italian prior to 1641. Ostensibly a work on the courts and princes of the present day, *Il Perfetto Cortegiano* recognized that, although especially suited to the courtier, "dissimulation is a necessity for everyone."[56] A component of the civil conversation, it is as necessary in everyday affairs as in courtly life. This does not mean, however, that every sort of dissimulation is equally justifiable. Canonieri acknowledged that "not every dissimulation is good and honest, only that which has a good and honest end, and which, given the proper circumstances, does not deny the truth or go against what is right. Such dissimulation is a part of, and a term for, prudence, and is done for the most part through keeping quiet, and for these reasons."[57] His treatise considered dissimulation legitimate for many of the usual reasons: it has a good end, it is not a lie nor does it exclude sincerity and truth-telling, and it does not cover up anything wrong; it is really a practice of prudent silence and an integral part of sociability itself. None of this was particularly new or original, not even when Canonieri calls such dissimulation "honest," making it morally justifiable because fully inscribed in the Old Regime code of polite conduct.

Canonieri assembles a series of "causes" or reasons for the practice of silence, whether at court or anywhere else in the social world. This list has few rivals as a concise summary of the state of the discourse on civil dissimulation in the early years of the seventeenth century. One should keep silent, he explained,

- in order not to reveal an intention which, if revealed, would not attain its end;
- in order not to show that we see others' thoughts, or the evil thoughts that others have set against us, or against those whom we love, or the good thoughts that others have for those who are our enemies;
- in order not to make public that someone has violated our trust;
- in order not to reveal something that, if known, could cause a scandal;
- in order not to show that we know someone's faults or someone's evil deed, because flawed and guilty men, when they are known as such, hate whoever knows what they are;
- in order not to show that we know of an offense done to us, or that we consider it to be an offense to us, or that we hold it to be one;
- in order not to make it necessary for us to inflict harm or ruin upon ourselves by answering when not required by the thing, person, place or time;
- in order not to harm or shame ourselves, or others, and to bring benefit and honor to ourselves and others.[58]

In all of these cases, a prudent silence may be considered good (*buono*). It might be used even between friends, Canonieri added, in order "that the greatest respect is not lacking, and we do not do worse to ourselves."[59] This sort of dissimulation possesses a defensive quality, such as might be needed at court (for instance, to avert harm to one's self or position by not revealing anything more about oneself than is strictly necessary), but it might also be employed in a conversation in order to maintain civility, avoid scandals, insults, or quarrels, and bring "benefit and honor" to all participants. In its regard for others, this practice differs distinctly (as is shown later in the present chapter) from the honest dissimulation espoused by Accetto, which was to be chiefly for the benefit of the dissimulator alone.

At other times, Canonieri allows, it is necessary to speak and nonetheless dissimulate. This requires more skill than that used in keeping silent, obviously enough: "this dissimulation needs greater artifice, because speaking cannot be avoided [in some cases], and we want to save ourselves both from the danger of telling lies and from the danger of telling the truth." Some might try, as Pino da Cagli suggested, to end the conversation or change the subject quickly, but this might not always work, or not always be enough. Others might say that they did not know the answer to a question, but this is an error, Canonieri objects, because it denies the truth. Instead, he observes, "the response must therefore resemble a retreat, which is done without fleeing, and without fighting saves property and life."[60] One had to respect three precepts at all times in dissimulating through polite speech: "Do not deny the truth. Do not say what you do not have to say. And leave the mind of the person asking the question as it was before."[61] One could implicitly or explicitly refuse to answer a question on the grounds that it is "impertinent," but this has to be done according to "the respect due to persons and the particular circumstances," in order to avoid disrupting the civil conversation.[62] Moreover, dissimulation may legitimately be used in such conversation to "make [others] believe that we see things that we did not see and feel things that we did not feel." Finally, one may dissimulate through appearance and actions, in particular by controlling the expression of the passions and emotions, "when for the aforementioned reasons and ends we abstain from demonstrating happiness, sorrow, hope, fear, or other emotions that may be ours."[63]

Thus dissimulation is extremely valuable, Canonieri concludes, "in the entire life of humanity and in all of its doings." Operating as an "antidote" or "cure" for the poisons and evils that mar our existence, dissimulation has the ability to save humans from "infinite harmful things."[64] At the end of *Il Perfetto Cortegiano* Canonieri adds that he has just seen a few sheets of a new book by Bonifacio Vannozzi, still in the process of being printed.[65] This remark was part of an exchange of civilities between these two writers, both residents of Rome at the time. Vannozzi in turn incorporated extensive passages from *Il Perfetto Cortegiano,* a work—as he notes with a flourish—"del mio dottissimo, e gentilissimo, Sig. Pierandrea Canoniero," in the final volume of his own encyclopedic *Della Supellettile degli Avvertimenti Politici, Morali, et Christiani* (An apparatus of political, moral and christian counsels, 1609–1613) under the heading "Della dissimulatione."[66] Vannozzi was vehemently anti-Machiavellian but found nothing wrong with the notion of civil or honest dissimulation; and certainly—out of civility—would have dissimulated any differences with Canonieri on this subject. In his text Vannozzi borrows much of Canonieri's text virtually verbatim, taking it upon himself to extend the latter's maxims for courtiers to all of polite society:

Everyone should therefore refrain, while holding their tongue, from speaking with head or body movements, laughter or other physical gestures; because these clues are often enough to reveal inner thoughts and the secrets of the mind. What is needed is caution and very great skill to ensure that dissimulation is neither known nor discovered.[67]

Like his friend, Vannozzi freely blends together reflections on dissimulation at court and in the civil conversation or everyday acts of the moral individual, for he sees them all as belonging essentially to the same social and cultural field of polite comportment. Dissimulation does not exclude sincerity and truth but is justified both as a part of the pleasure of *politesse* and as a means of protecting oneself from loss of social status or prestige. And although perhaps, as Elias and others have argued, social discipline was most spectacularly displayed in the ceremonies of courtesy at court, this same disciplining process made "respectful behavior"—the art of pleasing others, or *l'art de plaire*—an act of calculated self-interest for parvenus of lower social extraction, as well as for all those involved in the civil conversation.[68] In these same years, however, another group of European men of letters, drawing on developments in moral philosophy, proposed a new approach to the discourse on dissimulation that would be distinct from these, and claim the name "honest dissimulation" for itself.

The Art of Pleasing Oneself

> *Qui probe dissimulare scit, Dissimilem quasi esse.*
> Who knows how to dissimulate honestly is, so to speak,
> "dissimilar."
>
> Rudolf Gottfried von Knichen,
> *Opus Politicum* 507A

The system of values expressed and embodied in the civil conversation remained relatively stable over most of early modernity; ceremonies and fashions may have changed, sometimes drastically, but among the elites there was only very gradual erosion of the principles of politeness. Throughout Europe, treatises on manners continued to rework Castiglione, Della Casa, and Guazzo well into the seventeenth century, and the texts of these three arbiters continued to be read and pondered until the end of the Old Regime.[69] The discourse on honest dissimulation, as I will call it here, was instead most prominent in the late sixteenth and early seventeenth centuries. During these years interest was extremely keen in the individual management of the ebb and flow of passions and emotions, as well as their expression. Indeed, this activity was taken as a defining trait of subjectivity itself. It was incumbent on each individual member of society to know how to express carefully or to disguise deliberately the passions and emotions, according to the place, the time, and the setting in which they made themselves felt. As François Senault observed in De l'Usage des passions (On the use of the passions, 1656), nature generates but cannot control passions—only human beings can, and must, do so.[70] One of the most brilliant and enigmatic Baroque moralists, Baltasar Gracián, explained to readers of his Oráculo manual y arte de prudencia (1647) that "no mastery is greater than mastering yourself and your own passions."[71] He added, by way of motivation, that "if one is master of oneself, one will then be the master of others."[72] This culture of rational self-control, not surprisingly, was fertile ground for the discourse on honest dissimulation, for which the capacity for "honest" expression of passions and emotions was crucial. In his earlier El Héroe (The hero, 1637), Gracián noted that "this art would be useless if, after prescribing restraint to the limit of its capacity, it did not entrust the impulses of the passions to dissimulation."[73] Expertise in the art of dissimulation, and domination of the drives (los afectos) surging beneath the skin, seemed to demand the same thing of the individual: the discovery of the proper distance to maintain not only from others but from oneself.[74]

Many Europeans sought this self-mastery outside of the confines of polite society and the court, struggling to find a new psychic equilibrium at a moment in which the hegemony of organized religion over conscience had been weakened by schisms in the Church and bloody religious conflict.[75] The culture of self-control offered individuals an emotional and mental compass in a time of spiritual uncertainty and widespread social turmoil. The rise of the discourse on dissimulation seemed to acknowledge that familiar systems of identification no longer functioned under these conditions. If, on the one hand, dissimulation invoked the "extreme mobility" of human relationships through its power to disorient those against whom it was employed, it also provided its adepts with the means to anchor themselves to the bedrock of their own secrets.[76] One of these was the secret of the nearness of distance—namely the distance that the honest dissimulator kept from his own inner life, which John Michael Archer has called "self-spying."[77] Certainly considerations of *savoir-vivre*, sociability, and court fashion were never too far from the minds of the members of the aristocracy and urban bourgeoisie, including the *uomo medio* or average man (as Accetto termed him). They also sought to define for themselves another rationale for dissimulation, however, rooted in a rigorous moral and ethical analysis that would lead from self-scrutiny to self-discipline and the socially acceptable expression of passions and emotions. One had to know how to live not only with others but with oneself, or, in other words, to please oneself as well as others. Thus early modern moral philosophy also took up the issue of dissimulation. Much of the time, of course, there was an implicit social calculus at work in this discourse on the most intimate secrets of subjective experience and the self-distance needed to keep them under control. How could one come to know and understand oneself, and others, well enough to turn the mysteries of the heart to one's own advantage within the social order of the Old Regime?

Such diverse figures as the Italian polymath Girolamo Cardano (1501–1576), medical doctor and scientist; Michel de Montaigne (1533–1592), nobleman and leading late-sixteenth century French exponent of the new humanism; Francis Bacon (1561–1626), high-ranking English statesman and philosopher; and Torquato Accetto (ca. 1590–after 1641), obscure secretary and minor Baroque poet, all addressed the intricate dealings—via honest dissimulation—through which individuals could cope with the pressures brought to bear upon them by the world of absolutism. Accommodation to that world was taken for granted, but some means was needed not to give oneself away to others, who would likely only use this gift against the giver. As Gracián warned, "even in allowing oneself to be understood, one should avoid frankness, just as in one's dealings not everyone should be able to look inside of one."[78] These evasive maneuvers, which allowed passions and thoughts to be displayed only when consistent with one's own interests, exacted a moral and psychological price. In exchange for a gain in personal security, thanks to the ability to control the flow of information about one's inner state, the honest dissimulator had to submit to pitiless self-analysis: the old adage—"think before you speak"—was taken to remarkable new extremes. In a relentless effort to manage the outflow of information about the state of one's own heart and mind, the dissimulator was compelled to censor every word and monitor every gesture. This self-vigilance meant the abandonment of any pretence to spontaneous self-expression, and, together with it, the very possibility of sincerity and frankness in exchanges with others. In such opaque conversations as were to be had in the world, trust was neither to be given nor expected.

CUTTLEFISH INK

> *La buena exterioridad es la mejor recomendación de la perfección interior.*
>
> A fine exterior is the best recommendation of inner perfection.
>
> Baltasar Gracián, *Oráculo manual y arte de prudencia* 186 (aphorism 130)

The emergence of huge and overcrowded cities by the early years of the seventeenth century in Europe helped to create the conditions in which the culture of dissimulation took firm root. Within those teeming and increasingly complex urban societies, in which, as Gracián noted, "you need more resources to deal with a single person these days than an entire nation in times past," the cost of failing to rein in the free expression of passions and thoughts was clear to many.[79] The commonplace Baroque metaphor of the theater of the world did not only imply that everyone was an actor but also that all were spectators: almost invariably social intercourse seemed to involve onlookers as well as interlocutors, and even one word too many might have considerable social consequences beyond the immediate circle of a conversation.[80] There were those people who simply could not act prudently, inevitably revealing their secrets to others, and there were those who could. The latter were labeled "foxes," "lynxes," or the like, while the former, who ignored or defied the rule of dissimulation, were felt to risk loss of face or even—in extreme cases—loss of life. Treatises often retold the story of the flight of the disguised King Seleucus from a defeat on the battlefield, during which he was helped by a peasant who did not seem to recognize him. As the king departed, however, the peasant said, "Farewell, sire." The king ordered the peasant to be killed immediately so that he could not possibly betray him to his pursuers. The anecdote was interpreted to mean that if the peasant had simply kept silent and dissimulated any awareness of the king's true identity, as it was in his own self-interest to do, he would have been safe and perhaps even rewarded.[81] Truth-telling was not necessarily an obligation under all circumstances, and could at times prove extremely risky.

The advantages of the regimentation of displays of inner experience were equally evident, because of the special power that secrecy grants to those who practice it. As Gracián observed, "the passions are the gates of the spirit. The most practical sort of knowledge lies in dissimulation. . . . Oppose lynxes of discourse with inky cuttlefish of interiority. Let no one discover your inclinations, no one foresee them, either to contradict or to flatter them."[82] Greater than the exercise of self-mastery alone, honest dissimulation was integral to a practical moral philosophy—*el más plático saber*—grounded in prudence, discretion, and realism as well as in secrecy. Gracián's memorable conceit of the *jibias de interioridad*—inky cuttlefish of interiority—gave vivid shape to this special function of secrecy which, by forestalling social and emotional subjugation of oneself by others, allowed for the possibility of eventual complete self-mastery.[83] Moreover, along with other related early modern practices of self-control, honest dissimulation helped to reduce the distortions that the expression of the passions could at times provoke in communication between persons. Spontaneous outbursts of rage, fear, or hatred could in this way be kept from interfering with the transactions of everyday social life, thus benefiting the community as a whole. Such dissimulation was seen in a positive light precisely because it withheld intimate—and sometimes unsettling—secrets from the ongoing public exchange of opinions, ideas, and passions.

The moral and ethical implications of this "inky" strategy, however, were troubling to many who nevertheless recognized that, as Accetto so succinctly put it, "there are many foxes among us and they are not always known to us."[84] The term "honest dissimulation," now generally associated with Accetto's 1641 treatise, had long been in circulation in the West.[85] Born from the perceived need to adapt to the social and political circumstances of absolutism without resorting to hypocrisy and lying, honest dissimulation differed fundamentally from the dissimulations practiced by princes and courtiers. To practice honest dissimulation was to acknowledge that, for persons caught up in the *discretum* of daily affairs, there were intolerable risks involved in being fully transparent in most intersubjective exchanges. Honest dissimulation aimed to subtract from the gaze of others—but in a morally acceptable manner—an interiority constructed out of a range of mental and emotional states and events, whose manifestation (unlike the Freudian unconscious) could be fully regulated by the instrumental exercise of reason. As the personal physician of Louis XIV, Marin Cureau de la Chambre (1594–1669), sniffed, "Among Actions, the External may be disguis'd under contrary appearances; and the Internal, which are the Thoughts and the Passions, may be easily dissembled."[86] The theory of honest dissimulation appeared as a new kind of realism in its revaluation of the role of the conversing body as an "image" of the mind.[87]

"THE SECRET HOUSE OF HIS HEART"

> In countenance be as courteous as you can . . . in talk as affable as you shall see cause; but keep your mind secret unto yourself, till you come to those whose hearts are as yours.
>
> John Stradling, *A Direction for Travailers* C4

Contemporary historians as different as Carlo Ginzburg, Perez Zagorin, and Rosario Villari have depicted dissimulation in the sixteenth and seventeenth centuries as a mode of resistance to oppressive social, cultural, and religious norms. Many early modern intellectuals had, however, already suggested as much. Virgilio Malvezzi (1595–1653), one of the greatest of Baroque prose stylists, wrote that "it is not always a good idea to say everything that one has in one's heart, even though what one has in one's heart is good: at times one has to restrain oneself from speaking freely, when the free life is already corrupt."[88] There were other important dimensions to this phenomenon as well. The practice of honest dissimulation was dialectically linked to the Old Regime culture of display and observation: the invisibility or inner nature of "internal" actions—as Cureau de la Chambre called them—permitted passions and thoughts to arise and persist undetected by others. Such experience could be defined as freedom from the pervasive obligation to display or perform. This did not, however, necessarily lead to a complete break with the regime of visibility, for such a rupture would threaten one's social rank, prestige, and place in the social order.

Those pursuing the path to such freedom had to divert the gaze of others through the ruses of reservation and silence, but without disappearing entirely from the civil conversation. Honest dissimulators could discover and explore the components—heart and mind—of individual interior experience or subjectivity, but only through a process of self-analysis of which no one else could be cognizant. Such a practice promised no loss of face, prestige, or power, on the one hand, or violation of one's moral integrity, on the other. This was not a matter merely of avoiding the pressure to conform to the norm, or of making a show of adapting to the norm while retaining one's moral conscience intact. Rather, interiority was taken to be the site of full self-coincidence, split off from the classical notion of "con-science" as a "knowing with others." As Accetto observed in *Della dissimulazione onesta,* "what is ours is what is in us."[89] Thus honest dissimulation allowed mental and emotional representations to emerge, shielded by a chiaroscuro play of shadow and light, within a secret inner space to which all access from the outside had been barred. Here they could be kept and examined by the dissimulator who was unwilling to articulate them openly and unable to repress them completely.[90]

Such an approach could function successfully only through the establishment of a critical relationship to oneself as well as to others. To put it another way, in dissimulating with others one had to be extremely careful not to dissimulate with oneself. There was no place in early modern theories of dissimulation for an unconscious (Id) that might work against the dissimulator's conscious intentions, or for a potentially disruptive impersonal entity such as fortune. Nor could the workings of language, with its slippery, elusive figures of speech, be held responsible for undermining efforts at honest dissimulation. Shining a glaring light into the most remote recesses of the mind and heart (into *quanto è in noi medesimi*, as Accetto put it), dissimulators aimed to arm themselves with knowledge of all that was "in" them. With this knowledge in hand, they were then expected to exercise caution at all times and in all places, and to extinguish spontaneity and sincerity in speech through the proper use of reason and will. The foundational moment of honest dissimulation was, in short, the achievement of full self-consciousness or self-transparency.

The Socratic *nosce te ipsum,* or know thyself, required for such a plenitude of consciousness was warmly endorsed by Gracián in the *Oráculo manual:* "know yourself: your character, intellect, judgment and emotions. You cannot master yourself if you do not understand yourself. There are mirrors for the face, but the only mirror for the spirit is wise self-reflection."[91] Accetto made a similar point to his readers, and added to it a striking image. Dissimulation, he noted, was like so many blinding rays of light exiting from the breast of the dissimulator to trace or spin a web around those listening or looking on. Once caught in this shining net, no interlocutor or onlooker could see the secrets of the dissimulator's heart buried within the breast: "in this way one cannot deceive oneself, presupposing that the mind cannot lie with the knowledge that it is lying to itself, because that would mean seeing and not seeing. . . . The lines of dissimulation are drawn from the center of the breast to the circumference of those who are around us."[92] Cast out like dazzling beams of light, these lines do not envelop the dissimulator's own mind and heart, precisely because one cannot—and must not—deceive oneself. Thus the honest dissimulator defined the relationship to the self first of all in ethical as well as practical terms.

If limited only to this, however, the project of honest dissimulation would be just a footnote to prior attempts in Western philosophy and moral thought to attain full and complete self-knowledge. Accetto noted along these lines that "therefore first of all one ought to try not only to get some news of oneself and one's concerns, but a complete report, and dwell not only on the surface of opinion, which is often mistaken, but in the depth of one's thoughts, and take the measure of one's talent and the true definition of what one is worth."[93] What distinguished honest dissimulation from the Socratic-Platonic and Augustinian philosophies was its transformation of that hard-won "news" about the self into a secret—that is, into something not only dissimilar from others but fundamentally unknowable for others.

The nature of this secret defined the very (limited) possibility of psychic freedom for those living under the Old Regime who were unwilling to submit fully to its rule. As has already been shown, by keeping one's "news" secret from others, the theorists of honest dissimulation thought it possible to maintain one's position in absolutist society and at the same time avoid a complete neutralization of intimate mental and emotional experience. To paraphrase Gracián, to master the art of secrecy meant to have no master other than that art itself. Within the framework of a morally and ethically tolerable inner experience, free of falsehood, the honest dissimulator sought a degree of liberation from the constant pressure of being-with-others. One could in this way move within the secure confines of one's own mental and emotional sphere, although denied the possibility of a sincere exchange with others. Accetto noted with no small amount of irony that "one admires, as the grandeur of men of high rank, their remaining within the walls of the palace, and in the secret rooms therein, encircled with iron and men guarding their persons and interests; nevertheless it is clear that, without such expense, every man can, although exposed to everyone's gaze, hide his affairs in the vast and secret house of his heart."[94] The practice of honest dissimulation, with its defensive and accommodative nature, was neither a mode of revolutionary resistance to power nor a banal instrument of worldly ambition. It played a formative role in the appropriation of an interiority—at once secularized and psychologized—in which to hold the secrets of the early modern individual, who had to know when and whether to express those secrets or, as far as possible, keep them silent.

EARLY SIXTEENTH-CENTURY VOICES

> *Officio della mente è il pensare, della lingua il parlare.*
> *Gl'imprudenti confondono quest'ordine e questi officij:*
> *prima parlano e poi pensano.*
> The task of the mind is to think, and that of the tongue
> is to speak. Imprudent people confuse this order
> and these tasks: they speak first, and then they
> think.
>
> Pio Rossi, *Il convito morale* (1657) 296

There were relatively few endorsements of honest dissimulation anywhere in Europe before the final years of the sixteenth century. Not long after the French invasion of northern Italy in 1494, which signaled the beginning of a long period of upheaval in the social, political, economic, and cultural order of the peninsula, the Neapolitan humanist Giovanni Pontano (1426–1503) named dissimulation as a component of prudence, and therefore as a valuable mode of practical knowledge of the sort later to be lauded by Gracián. In his *De Prudentia* (On prudence), which first appeared posthumously in 1505 but was composed near the turn of the sixteenth century, Pontano contends that prudence is the opposite of fortune, and that dissimulation, as one of the modes of prudence, is therefore also a practice set in opposition to the irrational nature of fortune.[95] Although he acknowledges that both simulation and dissimulation are "modes of behavior that honest people ought to consider unworthy," he notes that "nonetheless at times the power of fortune and the variety and inconstancy of human events are such that, in the right time and place, it is necessary not only to simulate or dissimulate, but also to make use of fictions: and this is considered extremely honest and worthy of highest praise. Even in Virgil, in fact, Aeneas shows hope on his face while smothering great pain in his heart."[96] Pontano finds a justification for dissimulation in the ill winds of adverse fortune and in the shifting tides of human events, both of which are beyond the control of men and women, who nevertheless need to navigate even under such conditions.

Such "honest" (as he terms it) dissimulation was a morally acceptable and "necessary" expedient, in other words, at certain times and in certain places, even if it would be preferable to do without it. Indeed, he goes so far as to call even feigning and simulation—those related terms often used by critics to smear dissimulation—"worthy of highest praise" in the right circumstances. The real technical difficulty lies in the decorum of dissimulation, that is, in knowing when and where it is appropriate to be prudent by remaining silent.[97] In his treatment of the theme, Pontano recalls the medieval scholastic literature on the virtues of holding one's tongue with the aid of, among others, simulation and dissimulation. In this perspective, silence is the foundation of all social virtue, and the keystone of the *secreta cordis* or nontransparency of the soul for all others except God, knower of all human mysteries.[98]

In the early years of the Cinquecento, the Ferrarese humanist, antiquarian, soldier, and diplomat Celio Calcagnini (1479–1541) wrote a brief composition in hexameters entitled "Simulatae virtutis defensio" (A defense of the virtue of simulation), which offered a general defense of dissimulation, without targeting specific social groups or institutions. Franco Bacchelli, who published this text for the first time, points out that for Calcagnini—at this point in his dialogue with the radical Reformation ideals then circulating in Ferrara—"dissimulation was to serve to hide practices contrary to current morals, rather than mask religious dissidence."[99] Calcagnini writes in his poem that "all things follow with easily moving foot, provided that he does with cautious mind whatever he does that should be concealed under night; and so the doctrines of the sanctified Christ teach: 'Either avoid sins or cover them under sleep-bringing night.'"[100] Like many of his contemporaries, such as Machiavelli, in this poem Calcagnini freely mixes references to simulation and dissimulation. Nevertheless he sees in these techniques a means to the end of "living honorably" in an age "so greatly ruined and imbued with rust."[101] Later in life Calcagnini authored a brief *Descriptio silentii* (Description of silence), which contains a florilegium of ancient sayings, mottos, and anecdotes concerning the virtues of silence: "nothing," he concludes, "is dearer and is more pleasing to the gods and humankind than silence."[102] Many of these same passages concerning the virtues of silence for ancient gods, heroes, and philosophers were later to become *topoi* in the discourse on dissimulation.

The Dutch humanist Desiderius Erasmus (1466/69–1536) first assembled his collection of *Adagia* (Adages) in Paris in 1500, subsequently revising and publishing them many times before his death. In his adage

III.iii.1, entitled "Sileni Alcibiadis" (The sileni of Alcibiades), which appeared for the first time in the 1508 Aldine version but was greatly augmented in the 1515 edition, Erasmus draws on an emblematic image that had already been used by Giovanni Pico della Mirandola in a letter of 1485 to Ermolao Barbaro.[103] This particular adage was popular with contemporary readers and saw many separate editions in Latin as well as translations into most of the major European languages. In it Erasmus explores the meaning of the ancient Greek sileni, which were small figures or statuettes made of wood and containing another, radically different figure hidden within them. These objects were named for Silenus, a comic figure who was Bacchus's tutor and the court jester of the gods of poetry, renowned for his ugliness. The outer figure "looked like a caricature of a hideous flute-player" but when opened "suddenly displayed a deity."[104] In the *Symposium,* Alcibiades explicitly compares Socrates to the sileni, "because like them he was very different on close inspection from what he seemed in his outward bearing and appearance."[105] Erasmus draws from the description of Socrates' looks and manners an explicit parallel with Christ, that "marvellous Silenus." He then proceeds to criticize savagely the leaders of the contemporary Church—and the powerful in general—as so many sileni turned "inside out" and thus unlike Christ, whom they nonetheless claimed to emulate.[106]

Although Erasmus does not touch directly on the topic of dissimulation, he formulates for his large readership an indelible image of the reserved Christian individual who possesses, beneath a mask of irony and indifference to the values of the world, a precious inner core that will be revealed only to a few: "such, to be sure, is the nature of things really worth having. Their excellence they bury in their inmost parts, and hide; they wear what is most contemptible at first glance on the surface, concealing their treasure with a kind of worthless outward shell and not showing it to uninitiated eyes."[107] According to the circumstances, the honest dissimulator had, like the sileni, to hide his or her emotions and thoughts behind an opaque and impenetrable screen, or to open up in order to reveal, to those who could be entrusted with such knowledge, the true nature of the treasure within. Not only are the inside (the core of affect and intellect) and the outside (comportment, appearance) of the person often radically and willfully divergent; there is, in Erasmus's eyes, nothing wrong with this state of affairs, as long as an acceptable ethical justification for it can be established.[108]

"HALFE LIGHTS" AND FULL SHADOWS

> *Frons tibi aperta, lingua parca, mens clausa.*
> An open face, few words, an inaccessible mind.
>
> Justus Lipsius, *Epistolarum selectarum* 35,
> letter 22

Neither Pontano, Calcagnini, nor Erasmus thought of dissimulation as involving any particular technical expertise, apart from a grasp of the rules of decorum, and did not target any specific social group or institution. With the strengthening of the Counter-Reformation, however, the discourse began to shift in a different direction. In 1570, near the end of his troubled life, the northern Italian physician and philosopher Girolamo Cardano wrote a work entitled *Proxeneta,* which was to appear in print only some fifty-odd years later under the auspices of the erudite French libertine Gabriel Naudé (1660–1653). A work variously thought by seventeenth-century publishers to be concerned with civil prudence, with human wisdom, or with the secrets of court politics or statecraft (perhaps in order to sell more copies), the *Proxeneta* affirms, in a chapter devoted wholly to dissimulation, that "dissimulation . . . is different from simulation above all for the fact that it consists in something that truly exists and produces nothing."[109] To be employed "against personal enemies and princes," Cardano's brand of dissimulation draws on the techniques of prudence itself, requiring those who practice it to be "grave, modest, and pure" in everything that is said, and adopt "silence" and "calm" as models of demeanor.[110]

It is thus more "charming" than simulation, and its exercise involves a detached attitude as well as an ability to equivocate by "doing and saying" something other than what one wants to do or say.[111] For Cardano, its most important representative was Socrates, who pretended in his dialogues with others not to know what he instead knew well (for "we dissimulate principally that which we know").[112] Because Socrates died for having spoken the truth, dissimulation is instead to be considered a less "dangerous" practice when speaking to the powerful.[113] Thus Cardano, whose manuscript may have been unpublished but not unknown in the late sixteenth century, draws a distinction between dissimulation and simulation—grounded in ancient moral philosophy—that would subsequently prove fundamental to the development of the discourse on honest dissimulation. Although some critics argued that the tactical adoption of silence and outer calm differed not in the least from the simulation or false representation of an inner state of quiet, others answered that the principal purpose of honest dissimulation was to defend oneself against others, not to offend established morality.[114] It was meant to bar access to "something that truly exists" (that is, the interior life of the individual) for those who wished to penetrate and discover those secrets. The true scandal of dissimulation was not that it produced a false representation of "that which we know" but rather that it was a blank page, representing nothing at all.

Among the voices raised against such a practice in the late sixteenth century, perhaps Michel de Montaigne's was the most eloquent. Despite his early affinity for Neostoicism, Montaigne professed disdain in the *Essais* (Essays, 1580, 1588, 1595) for the current vogue of dissimulation. In 1580 he wrote in his essay "On Presumption": "for as for this new-fangled virtue of feigning and dissimulation, which is so greatly in vogue at this moment, I mortally hate it; and, of all vices, I know none that testifies to so much cowardice and baseness of heart."[115] Montaigne resided at his country estate near Bordeaux while writing his essays and was able to observe the French political and religious crisis without the impediment of the pressures of the court. From the relative solitude of his study, he declared himself to be—unlike courtiers and princes—governed as far as possible by the principles of sincerity and openness: "a generous heart should not belie its own thoughts; it wants to reveal itself even to its innermost core. Everything in it is good, or at least everything in it is human. . . . It would be a great piece of simplicity in anyone to allow himself to be beguiled by the countenance or word of a man who prides himself on being always another thing without than he is within, as Tiberius did."[116] The moral failure of the dissimulator who never removes his mask to reveal his heart lies, according to Montaigne, not in the deliberate short circuit between the heart's innermost core and its self-representation but in the choice not to be "true to one's nature or temperament."[117] Such an individual seems to violate one of the principal tenets of Stoic doctrine. Only the *homo fenestratus* can be said to have a genuine moral conscience, because he willingly attempts to make his "generous heart" as fully visible to others as possible. In any person who professes dissimulation, on the other hand, a refusal to show oneself as one is, Montaigne suggests, is a sign of "cowardice" and "baseness," and any avoidance of the responsibility of truth-telling indicates a lack of virtue.[118]

Montaigne also offers an objection to dissimulation on technical grounds. As he explains in the same essay, "now, for my part, I had

rather be troublesome and indiscreet than a flatterer and a dissembler. . . . I have not a wit subtle enough to evade a sudden question and
to escape from it by some shift, nor to invent a truth, nor memory
enough to retain what I have invented, and certainly not enough assurance to maintain it; and so I put on a bold face out of weakness."[119] In
other words, dissimulation is overly difficult to put into practice without "a subtle wit" or "enough memory" to carry it off. These are qualities in which Montaigne considers himself to be—with more than a
touch of self-deprecating Socratic irony—sadly lacking. The only practical option is to speak artlessly and sincerely, trusting in fortune to keep
him from doing harm to himself or others.

Montaigne's declared willingness to entrust himself to artlessness
rather than submit to the rule of dissimulation is, however, not unqualified. This can hardly be surprising in the context of the *Essais,* which often probe several contradictory facets of the same issue, shifting focus
with each successive revision, as its author moves toward a more openly
skeptical stance. In fact, as John Martin has suggested, in the essays both
sincerity and prudence appear as ideals, and Montaigne endlessly nego-
tiates the tensions between them in his writing.[120] Montaigne warns his
readers, for instance, that they should be prepared to defend themselves
against the cunning traps set for them by others. "Duplicitous men are
useful in what they bring; but one must take care that they take away
with them only as little as possible."[121] The great essayist also acknowledges that it would be a serious mistake to underestimate or to deny
the importance of indirection in human affairs. "I do not wish to de-
prive deceit of its place; that would be to misunderstand the world.
I know that it has often proved profitable, and that it maintains and
nourishes the majority of human occupations."[122] Complete frankness
may at times be foolish, moreover, and risk "indiscretion and incivility"
(indiscretion et incivilité), both of which would put an end to polite conversation.[123] To violate the rules of civility through sincerity would be
to "misunderstand" the very nature of social interaction, he notes, for
"innocence itself could neither negotiate among us without dissimulation nor bargain without lying."[124] Thus the only reasonable choice,
Montaigne seems to suggest, lies in a compromise between telling
truths and avoiding them. "A man must not always say everything,
for that were folly; but what a man does say should be what he thinks;
otherwise it is knavery."[125] On this last point, at least, Montaigne's
thought coincides neatly with the growing consensus in Europe that
dissimulation constituted a morally acceptable mix of silence and speech.

It would be left to Montaigne's contemporary readers, however, to establish a more cohesive framework for the discourse on honest dissimulation.[126]

Francis Bacon, Lord Verulam and Viscount St. Albans, was one of these. He belonged to the highest administrative class of Elizabethan and Jacobean England and, despite his checkered political career and spectacular final fall from royal grace, produced some of the most important philosophical works of the age.[127] His *Essayes* first appeared in 1597, and the work saw its greatly enlarged and revised final edition, *The Essayes or Counsels, Civill and Morall,* in 1625. In this latter edition there appeared for the first time the essay entitled "Of Simulation and Dissimulation," which was to be read widely in the seventeenth century.[128] Bacon was not only an enthusiastic reader of Montaigne's essays but also an influential exponent of English Tacitism and an advocate of Machiavelli's political and philosophical realism, as well as of Lipsius's "mixed prudence." His own essay, written in razor-sharp prose and greatly indebted to Lipsius (who is considered in chapter 4), distinguishes between three kinds of "Hiding, and Vailing of a Man's Selfe" in everyday life.[129] It would be best to speak freely at all times, Bacon admits, but only the greatest leaders have the keen intelligence and judgment needed to do so; most must resort to covering their thoughts.

The first and most valuable kind of covering for the self Bacon calls "*Closeness, Reservation,* and *Secrecy;* when a Man leaveth himselfe without Observation, or without Hold to be taken, what he is.*" Secrecy of this sort differs from dissimulation in being not strictly for defensive purposes. Like a vacuum that nature seeks to fill, the person who is well known to be secretive and reserved will receive the "confessions" of others seeking to "discharge their Mindes" and ease their hearts. By hiding their own thoughts, "*Secret* Men come to the Knowledge of Many Things" that others think. Whether they want to or not, silent and secretive individuals will find many ready and willing to "turne their Freedome of Speech, to Freedome of thought," even if they do themselves a disservice. A cloak of secrecy allows one the freedom to explore incognito, and in some safety, the opinions of others, while giving nothing away to them. Bacon returns to a by now familiar theme in adding that this undertaking will never be successful without the exercise of rigorous control over the expression of the passions, especially in the privileged site of the face, "for the Discovery, of a Mans Selfe, by the Tracts of his Countenance, is a great Weaknesse, and Betraying." The face must not "speak" for the mind; it must not be "as a book where men may read strange matters" (*Macbeth* 1.v); it must be blank, silent, illegible. The body, so quick to betray its innermost secrets, is unruly and must be disciplined through conscious force of will, just as the unruly body politic must be forcefully governed by its absolute sovereign. And inasmuch as those who are held to be "Talkers and Futile Persons" are usually "Vaine, and Credulous" as well as dangerously transparent, Bacon adds, "Therfore set it downe, *That an Habit of Secrecy, is both Politick, and Morall.*"[130]

Dissimulation, on the other hand, is but the second degree of secrecy. The latter always has both temporal and ontological priority over the former, which trails behind secrecy like a shadow. For Bacon, dissimulation occurs "when a man lets fall Signes, and Arguments, that he is not, that he is." To act in this way is not a mere caprice or vice, for one dissimulates chiefly "by a necessity" rather than choice, in order to protect an important secret that risks discovery. Such a stratagem is therefore to be defined "in the *Negative*": dissimulation is made possible not only by the fact that the speaker has something to hide, but also by the necessary skills to keep it hidden. In Bacon's eyes, dissimulation always accompanies secrecy in a second moment, serving as its "Skirts or Traine" in an effort to shield us from the "cunning" of others who would pry into the vicissitudes of our minds and hearts. One of the chief flaws of this defensive technique is that it "cannot hold out long"—at least not legitimately—against persistent questioning that aims to uncover a secret and bring it into the open.

Most of the tactics treated in the discourse on honest dissimulation are, the essay acknowledges, inadequate to the task. Withdrawal within a conversation is not a practical choice, for others will not allow one to maintain for long "an indifferent carriage" without expressing an "Inclination, one way." As Bacon warns, "they will so beset a man with Questions, and draw him on, and picke it out of him." Taking refuge in "an absurd Silence" will not work either, for this would simply tip the dissimulator's hand, and others "will gather as much by his Silence, as by his Speech." Neither will rhetorical devices relying on amphibological figures and enigmas, such as "Equivocations, or Oraculous Speeches," persuade others to desist from seeking out one's secrets. There can be no permanent and morally legitimate way to defend one's secrets from discovery, but a "seasonable use" of dissimulation can help to delay the unwelcome event, and must be used judiciously from time to time to this end.

After excoriating simulation as a "Vice" of value only "if there be no [other] Remedy," Bacon explains to his readers that both dissimulation and simulation nonetheless offer some "great *Advantages*." Here, however, he would seem to lapse into contradiction, for all three of these advantages may belong to anyone making general use of "*Closenesse, Reservation, and Secrecy*" rather than the particular defensive techniques of dissimulation that he defined earlier in the essay. The first of the three advantages is found in the element of "Surprize," for both simulation and dissimulation help to lay "asleepe Opposition." If "a Mans Intentions, are published, it is an Alarum, to call up, all that are against them," and thus the element of surprise allows one to strike against or slip past opponents effectively. The second of these advantages is, Bacon notes, the possibility of a "faire Retreat": "for if a man engage himselfe, by a manifest Declaration, he must goe through, or take a Fall." Either through the use of simulation or dissimulation, one may keep oneself from committing openly to a course of action that does not allow for withdrawal at a later time. The third and final advantage consists in discovering "the Minde of another," although this is exactly what others are trying to do to the simulator/dissimulator as well.

In an attempt to follow the model of Montaigne's essays, Bacon then proposes to "set it even" by listing three "*Disadvantages*" that might cancel these out. All three of these disadvantages extend and deepen Bacon's prior critique of simulation and dissimulation by insisting on the social and public cost of practicing such arts. For, first of all, their use displays a "Shew of Fearfulnesse" which risks spoiling "any Business." As much as they conceal about one's secret intentions, the indirections of dissimulation or the simulacra of simulation also reveal the user's underlying anxiety, fear, and doubt about the business at hand: and this can only have a negative effect on negotiations with others. The second disadvantage is to be found in the social isolation of anyone deploying the evasions and fictions of simulation/dissimulation. Unable to speak to the point, such a figure "pusleth and perplexeth the Conceits of many; that perhaps would otherwise co-operate with him," leaving him "to walke, almost alone, to his owne Ends." Because of this express intent to sow confusion in the minds of others, Bacon observes, an inevitable social vacuum forms around the adepts of these arts: they find themselves "almost alone," cut off from the bonds of companionship. Finally, the "third, and greatest" of these disadvantages is the loss of "*Trust* and *Beleefe*" that simulation/dissimulation may cause in those at whom it is directed, especially if they are even in the least aware of its presence. Trust and belief are key lubricants of social interaction, and without them the simulator/dissimulator courts failure in every undertaking that may involve other members of society. While underscoring these particular disadvantages, which threaten to poison the atmosphere necessary to sustain civic life, Bacon suggests in his essay that any regime so dependent on the use of secrecy would ultimately collapse under the weight of its own internal contradictions.[131] He could not have imagined, however, how long it would take for this prophecy to come to pass.

Marking Time: Torquato Accetto

> *Personam coactus fero; licet in Italia nemo sine ea esse possit.*
> I am obliged to wear a mask, because no one in Italy may
> go without one.
>
> Paolo Sarpi, letter to Jacques Gillot, 12 May 1609

As far as anyone now knows, between 1618 and 1641 Torquato Accetto lived chiefly in Naples, and briefly in Rome, where he served as a secretary to the powerful and wrote some moderately successful verse. If today Accetto is considered one of the finest Baroque prose stylists in Italian, however, his contemporaries seem to have been supremely indifferent to his one known prose work. So far no proof positive has been found of any contemporary reaction to the appearance in print of his treatise entitled *Della dissimulazione onesta* (1641), and, after its publication in Naples with a regular *imprimatur,* Accetto himself vanished from the view of history.[132] Rediscovered nearly three hundred years later by Benedetto Croce, this slender text is—like Gracián's *Oráculo manual*—not an expression of a systematic moral philosophy but a warning about the complexity of the "world," before which each of us stands alone. Accetto did not specifically endorse the Christian preference for the spiritual life, the Stoic withdrawal from the world, or the imperturbability of the Skeptics, although these currents freely intermingle in his discourse on the "honest" nature of dissimulation.[133] Salvatore S. Nigro's 1997 edition of the text has convincingly shown Accetto's treatise to be a compendium of the main themes of this particular strand of the early modern discourse on dissimulation.[134] They are: (i) communication with others risks revealing one's inner state; (ii) masterful self-control is required in all social situations; (iii) knowledge of the techniques of dissimulation is essential; (iv) psychologically speaking, its practice exacts a high price; and (v) the theme of time, especially in waiting and in memory, is central to honest dissimulation. This chapter's treatment of civil and moral dissimulation will conclude by examining in turn each of these five master keys to the topic.

COMMUNICATION AND CONSCIOUSNESS

Early in *Della dissimulazione onesta,* Accetto writes: "I recall the damage that an unrestrained love of speaking the truth could have caused me."[135] This is one of the most deliciously ironic understatements to appear in his treatise. As the historian Rosario Villari has argued, the social, economic, and political situation in Naples in the early seventeenth century under the viceroy was extremely volatile, and dissent was dealt with harshly. The municipal authorities employed everything from censorship to spectacular acts of public terror to maintain order.[136] This in turn fostered a climate in which dissimulation may have flourished at more than one level of Neapolitan society.[137] The city was the administrative and economic center of the Kingdom of Naples, a Hapsburg state integrated into the Spanish empire and governed by the viceroy and the Consejo de Italia (Council of Italy), but the decline of Spanish power in the seventeenth century brought economic crisis to Naples, with its enormous population of around 250,000 people (making it one of the largest cities in Europe). Spain's disastrous foreign wars and downward economic spiral led to increasing taxation of its semicolonial territories in Italy, resulting in further impoverishment of the Neapolitan masses; not long after the publication of Accetto's treatise, Masaniello's revolt broke out among the *lazzari* in the streets of the city (1647).[138] The decade from 1640 to 1650, which saw six significant revolutions in Europe and the climax of the debate over dissimulation, may well have marked the true beginning of the modern era.

Unlike most Baroque works of its kind, *Della dissimulazione onesta* bears no dedication to a powerful patron or, for that matter, to anyone else. This does not indicate, however, that politics is absent from the text of the treatise. All of chapter 19 deals with the vital need to control self-expression under tyranny: "it is not permitted to sigh when the tyrant does not allow one to breathe."[139] Accetto's scathing if indirect criticism of the Spanish domination of Naples in this chapter is followed, in chapter 20, by a clear warning of the danger that comes with not having total control of one's words and gestures in every public situation: "some are ready for any sort of vendetta, and because of a gesture that is not to their liking, they wish to penetrate into others' thoughts and complain about them as if they were public offenses."[140] Even the most minimal expression of thought or passion threatens to place the speaker at risk of being publicly "outed" and victimized by others, most likely those of higher social rank, who rightly or wrongly may sense latent hostility to them. Whether verbal or gestural, communication constitutes a potential trap for the careless and the unwary, who may reveal much too much about themselves. In these same years, Baroque science had begun to target the secrets of nature and was attempting to expose them with the use of such wondrous devices as the microscope and telescope (Evangelista Torricelli was to invent the barometer in 1643, just two years after the publication of Accetto's work). The value of dissimulation, Accetto suggests, lies in its power to forestall any possible discovery of one's secrets by investigators probing for ways to get "inside" one's heart and mind in order to ferret them out. Such dissimulation may be accomplished honestly, he argues, through the practice of reservation and the reduction of language to a mere "seeming not to be much" *(parer da poco)*.[141] Probably under the influence of philosophical currents of Skepticism, Accetto accepts self-consciousness as stable and positive, naturally centered in itself and set in opposition to social laws, rules, and conventions. He sees the defensive nature of honest dissimulation as a legitimate means of preserving this entity; to dissimulate in such a way means nothing more or less than *conservatio sui ipsius,* or self-preservation.

SELF-CONTROL

In contrast to Montaigne's claims in his essays, Accetto notes that "in this life one should not always have a transparent heart."[142] In order to achieve the proper degree of opacity, the expression of passions and ideas must be meticulously monitored from within. The arguments used by Accetto to make this point draw heavily from Neostoicism, in particular the work of Lipsius, whose influence (as a writer with works on the Index) is skillfully dissimulated in *Della dissimulazione onesta.*[143] Neostoic moral philosophy turned sharply away from the Aristotelian ideal of temperance and moderation of the passions. These did not emerge in inner experience only to be repressed by reason, for, in the Neostoic perspective, the passions were not irrational but rather corrupted forms of reason itself. They were therefore best controlled by the elimination of beliefs that could cause unsuitable passions to arise in the first place: instead of taming them, in other words, the Neostoics sought to uproot and eliminate those passions that led to a loss of tranquility, security, and happiness. What was needed was the will to direct oneself in this difficult undertaking; as Charron remarked, will is the one thing that is wholly one's own, for everything else can be tampered with from the outside. The true sage—who was the happiest of men—carried out this undertaking in the most coherent and systematic way possible. Therefore the task of the honest dissimulator was not to find an expedient means to a temporary end but to transform permanently his own subjectivity. Accetto remarks that "[one should] put a brake on affect, so that it may be satisfied to accommodate itself to necessity, not as tyrant but rather as subject to reason, and in the role of an obedient citizen."[144]

Dissimulation is not a neutral rhetorical technique, for it would be of scant use to someone whose heart is in turmoil. It is instead one component of a rigorous moral philosophy of self-management that institutes the obedience of the passions to reason by eliminating harmful beliefs and reinforcing beneficial ones. Consistent with the arguments of numerous other thinkers of the age, Accetto holds anger to be the most dangerous of all emotions for the successful practice of dissimulation: "the greatest peril to dissimulation is anger, which is the most manifest type of affect and, more than any other, precipitates words that display what is in one's mind."[145] The loss of self-command manifested in the expression of wrath puts one's secrets at risk by making explicit to others "what is in one's mind." When turbulent passions start to rise upward from the hidden depths of the heart, the honest dissimulator has to find a way to delay their expression by introducing a pause for reflection, giving the turbulence time to subside. But this in itself is a sign that one has not yet perfected the art of self-management; the aim of honest dissimulation is to purge oneself, as far as possible, of beliefs that could cause such undesirable emotions to form in the first place.

Accetto concludes that "it is of greater delight to triumph over oneself, while waiting for the storm of the affects to pass, and in order not to deliberate in the confusion of one's own tempest."[146] To win out over oneself constitutes the "most glorious victory that anyone can achieve" and the very meaning of honest dissimulation.[147] For this triumph in turn ought to lead to the greatest of earthly delights, namely happiness itself, brought about by the disappearance of all traces of conflict within heart and mind. Such a state, for Accetto, can be nothing other than "inner peace, which is a good of incalculable value and belongs to innocence."[148] No amount of worldly wealth, fame or power can provide us with the "incalculable value" offered by inner calm and outer detachment; no social, political, or religious institution can restore to us this *tranquillità del vivere,* or tranquility of living. Genuine harmony between thoughts, passions, and emotions can be achieved only by the solitary *homo secessus* who withdraws into himself in order to practice honest dissimulation.[149]

THE ART OF OBLIVION

By no stretch of the imagination can Accetto's treatise be considered a "how-to" manual for would-be dissimulators. Although he notes that honest dissimulation is "a veil composed of honest shadows and violent deferences," the techniques for fabricating this "veil" are treated by him only vaguely at best.[150] Like his predecessor Lipsius, Accetto warns his readers that the foundation of all successful dissimulation lies in a healthy skepticism, "not believing in every promise, not nourishing every hope."[151] Once this skepticism is thoroughly engrained in one's habit of mind, the life-enhancing goal of creating for oneself *una moderata oblivione,* or moderate oblivion—as opposed to the complete and permanent oblivion of death—may then be pursued as a project for a wise existence.[152] Accetto does not dwell in his treatise on the details of how this is to be accomplished, apart from recommending a mastery of patience, prudence, and tolerance. In particular, in-depth psychological analysis of the human heart sustains the dissimulator's art, for "a shrewd mind will make use of the abysses of the heart, which in spite of its small size is infinitely capacious."[153] Those seeking self-erasure can hope to lose their pursuers in the labyrinth of the heart, scattering them along its innumerable pathways, as long as care is taken not to get lost in the maze themselves: the honest dissimulator must already know the way. As Gracián admonished his readers only a few years later, "a breast without reserve is an open letter. Have depths where you can hide your deepest secrets: great spaces and little coves where important things can sink to the bottom. This comes from having mastered yourself, and winning out over oneself in this is the genuine triumph."[154]

The sole technical note in the treatise, one that was apparently congenial to Accetto's thoroughly Baroque sensibility, is found in chapter 11, entitled "Del dissimular con li simulatori" (On dissimulating with simulators):

But there are many foxes among us and they are not always known to us. When we do discover them, it is nonetheless very difficult to use art against art. In such cases whoever best knows how to seem to be a fool will end up being the wisest one, because by making a show of believing the person who wishes to deceive us, it may be that he will in turn believe what we wish; and it is part of a great intelligence to be able to be seen not to see—precisely when one sees the most—so that the game is thus played with eyes that seem closed but are open within themselves.[155]

Here it might reasonably be objected that these are not techniques of dissimulation at all. By pretending to play the credulous fool, the dissimulator has in fact become a simulator and resorted to using "art against art," just as Accetto elsewhere advises his readers not to do. Whoever feigns to be blind but in fact is watching carefully can also be legitimately considered a simulator. The semicolon signals a turning point in Accetto's argument, however, whose essential meaning emerges only in the final part of the passage. The dissimulator plays the "game" or practices the "art" of dissimulation by appearing not to register the effects of a conversation or a gesture, that is, by not reacting or by remaining oblivious. If others mistakenly persist in believing that someone is blind or foolish—and can thus "be seen not to see"—it is not the duty of the person being observed to disabuse them of this notion. For the honest dissimulator's eyes are not secretly open instead of shut, as would be the case in a false representation. Rather, they remain technically "open within themselves," not watching—or watching out for— anything other than themselves, seemingly closed and indifferent to the outside world, and patiently awaiting with a sense of detachment the moment at which they can once again open wide. What they "see" so clearly is the impossibility of seeing, at least for the time being.[156]

This withdrawal behind a mask of indifference, reminiscent of the Stoic concept of *adiaphoron,* is at once intended to preserve personal moral integrity and to enhance patience: "you [dissimulation] are none other than the art of patience, which teaches both not to deceive and not to be deceived."[157] Such an art raises the threshold higher, in terms of complexity, for those seeking to discover the secrets hidden in others who may be dissimulating either honestly or dishonestly. Certainly this search for others' secrets is one of the most important tasks that Accetto sets for his readers. Well schooled in the art of patience, the dissimulator should know better than to be easily provoked into a display of passion or led into a subtle trap designed to reveal the innermost truths of heart and mind. How could these obstacles be overcome in turn by the kind of honest person that Accetto describes? How is it possible to be a sharp-eyed "lynx," in Gracián's terms, when those being observed are so skilled in the defensive techniques of dissembling? Even the most capable dissimulator must surely be eventually betrayed by some gesture or sign, no matter how small or seemingly trivial: but how is one to know what to look for? If Accetto has the answer, he keeps it to himself in *Della dissimulazione onesta*. Secrets cannot remain eternally hidden, after all, as both Montaigne and Bacon make clear; but it is no simple matter to learn to see them revealed—at the opportune moment—either written on the face or articulated in words and gestures.[158] Every aspect of the honest dissimulator's behavior, then, must be destined to intensive scrutiny by those engaged in the search for those secrets, and, in reciprocal fashion, the former must try to probe the latter's defenses just as carefully. The enhanced security provided to the early moderns by mastery of the art of honest dissimulation was to be countered by a corresponding expansion of the culture of suspicion.

THE HIGH COST OF LIVING HONESTLY

According to Seneca and the Stoics, the limits of dissimulation lay in the suffering that one was willing to undergo for it.[159] As we have seen, Accetto finds considerable rewards in honest dissimulation's ability to control the self, observing that such "dissimulation is honest and useful and, moreover, full of pleasure" *(onesta ed util è la dissimulazione, e di più, ripiena di piacere)*. Indeed, chapter 10 bears as its title "The delight found in dissimulation." Yet there is also, he admits, a bitter truth underlying the practice of this particular art. For whether because of the tyranny or fraud or violence of others, the "honest" person is always compelled to resort to dissimulation when in crisis: this practice is never, in other words, strictly a matter of free choice, but is imposed by external pressures *volens nolens*. It is thus a grating and ever-present reminder of one's authentic lack of freedom of action in the contemporary world. Ever sensitive to the psychological nuances of his theme, Accetto recognizes (as had Lipsius before him) that some psychic pain was inevitable in the practice of honest dissimulation: "not a little pain is felt when we keep silent what we would like to say, or when we do not try to carry out what our desires urge upon us."[160] This does not mean that there could not be a measure of pleasure in such pain, for the "sweet victory" of full self-mastery partially compensates for the lost ability to express spontaneously one's emotional and mental experiences. Solitude and self-denial cost the honest dissimulator dearly, but cannot be done without; it is not in anyone's best interest to risk revealing secrets to others, no matter how friendly the latter might appear to be, and no matter how great a psychic release such a gesture seems to promise.[161]

TIME AND MEMORY

Reflections on the temporality of dissimulation abound in *Della dissimulazione onesta*. Secrets may endure as long as silence is kept; but once discovered they vanish in a flash, and can never return to their former status. Memory too plays a key role in the art of honest dissimulation, as Accetto takes pains to explain. It had long been objected in the discourse on dissimulation that, as the treatise-writer Giovanfrancesco Lottini pointed out in 1574, "it is not possible for someone to be dissimilar from himself for a long period of time."[162] In other words, truth progresses over time—*veritas filia temporis*. If truth, no matter how skillfully masked, must eventually emerge, then dissimulation is weaker than truth, just as appearance is weaker than being.[163] Accetto is quick to agree that dissimulation cannot be carried out continuously over a long period of time: "it seems to me that one cannot successfully always put dissimulation into practice."[164] Although one simulates naturalness some of the time, in certain places and with certain persons, one has to dissimulate artifice all of the time, in every place and with everyone. The sole exception to this exacting regimen is in exchanges with the most intimate and trusted of beings, such as a lover, a best friend, or God, the loci of the "proffered heart" (as the historian John Martin has eloquently called them), where it is possible to be sincere at last.[165]

The decorum of dissimulation is thus fundamentally different from that of simulation. Memory serves the honest dissimulator as a means of keeping the past in view at all times, in order to avoid contradicting previous words or gestures that would betray his true intentions at the present moment. To forget one's own secrets could prove fatal, and thus secrets have to be hidden where memory will not fail to find them, namely not far below the surface layers of mental life. A crowning paradox of the discourse on honest dissimulation is that one's own secrets are always in danger of being lost, and therefore must never be hidden too well.[166] The function of memory in dissimulation is to be found, Accetto observes, "in the consideration of time past, in order not to contradict the present and to be able to evaluate the future."[167] The past is always part of the present, and between these two points there are to be no ruptures or radical breaks. The seamless continuity of temporality is, in a sense, the very being of the honest dissimulator.[168]

Moreover, honest dissimulation, by insisting on the cardinal importance of waiting for the right moment to arrive at which to abandon the mask of silence and negligence, is oriented toward a future that is always yet to come: namely, the moment at which sincerity may return to its rightful role in human affairs. For Accetto, dissimulation is an art of patience for which the Book of Job serves as a paradigm.[169] The act of temporal deferral—together with the renunciation of satisfaction in the present moment—stands at the very core of his project: "from knowing others is born that full authority than one has over oneself when one keeps silent at the right time, and also reserves at the right time, those thoughts which tomorrow will perforce prove good and which today are pernicious."[170] The successful practitioner of the art of honest dissimulation has to know how to mark time patiently in the (perhaps vain) hope of a favorable change in circumstances, all the while *tollerando, tacendo, aspettando*—tolerating, keeping silent, waiting.[171] Hope, however tenuous, is the ultimate motive behind Accetto's enterprise: implicit in the dissimulator's waiting game is the hope of a different and better future that makes the present bearable. Although knowing full well that no one can keep this game up forever, Accetto admits that only at the end of time itself, on the apocalyptic Day of Judgment, is it absolutely certain that the rule of dissimulation will finally come to an end as well: "the necessity of using this veil is so great that it will only disappear on the last day."[172] No dissimulation will be used in addressing God when the trumpet sounds, the universe blazes with light, and time ceases to exist. Only then will there be no more *savoir-vivre*, no more personal security zones, no more secrets, and no more need to recede into the shadows or strain in the murky half-light to see what, if anything, lies behind the masks of others.

CHAPTER 3

Confidence Games

Dissimulation at Court

They dissemble, as some men do that live within compass o' th' verge.

John Webster, The White Devil V.iii.52–53

Questo è un secolo d'apparenza, & si va in maschera tutto l'anno.
Pur che altri appaia d'essere, non si cura d'esser da dovero.
This is a century of appearances, and one wears a mask all year round. As long as one seems to be someone else, no effort is made to be what one should be.

Bonifacio Vannozzi, Della Supellettile degli
Avvertimenti Politici, Morali, et Christiani

The Courts of the Old Regime

The Italian Wars (1494–1559) shattered the system of city-states that had long maintained a balance of power on the peninsula, replacing it by and large with the Old Regime patchwork of absolutist states. Across Italy there arose dynasties dominated by a single figure, the *signore* or prince, who surrounded himself with an entourage of courtiers to whom he accorded honor, distinction, and wealth and from whom he demanded participation in increasingly elaborate court ceremonials and ritual acts that recognized and sanctioned his authority. Although the court was hardly a new phenomenon in Italy or elsewhere, under absolutism its importance grew steadily, and in many places it became the chief institution mediating between the center of state power, namely the prince, and the social order. Many noble families built their fortunes through members who became courtiers, often after service in the bureaucracy, army, or Church: but the goal of these other career paths was always to get to court and to maintain a presence there.[1] As well as fulfilling its key economic function of royal patronage, the court was the focus of the social existence of the elites and supplied the paradigm of legitimation of social relations in general.[2] Its fashions and models of social interaction were transmitted far and wide, through the network of connections that developed between court and periphery. Court society, however, could not entirely absorb the masses of individuals who aspired to gain entrance to it. No matter how large the courts grew in size (at the Medici court in Florence, for instance, the number of court personnel went from seven in 1549 to 792 in 1692), participation in their ceremonies—and access to their opportunities—remained restricted to relatively few privileged figures.[3] The courts of Europe, which grew in power and number during the early modern period with the weakening of feudalism and rise of absolutism, drew extensively on the Italian model at first, only subsequently to surpass it, a process culminating at Versailles under Louis XIV.

Norbert Elias's *The Court Society,* first published in 1969 (but composed nearly forty years earlier), proposed a theoretical model of early modern courts in Europe that helped to stimulate new interest among scholars in issues of ritual, legitimation, and representation during absolutism. However, Elias's model, dependent upon an outmoded vision of class struggle that linked the "civilizing" of the French nobility to the concomitant rise of the bourgeoisie, has been subjected to extensive revision as historical research has progressed in recent decades. For instance, Jeroen Duindam, in his critique of Elias's work on early modern court society, paints a rather different picture of the court. For Duindam, it was not only the place where power networks formed in support of the elites and where royal authority was on display; in its function as a gathering point, the court made visible both the emerging contours of the state and of a privileged social model of comportment. In the dynastic Old Regime states, prince and nobles stood in a relation of symbiosis that confirmed the authority of both parties; their copresence at court was a sign of compromise, not only of obligation. Nor were the elites by any means a single homogeneous entity, although they acted in unison in restricting access to the court for those many individuals of lower social extraction—men of letters or arms, for instance—who gravitated there.

Indeed, the courts (and the prince) often struggled to maintain equilibrium between competing factions and resident interest groups—something of which courtly literature shows a keen awareness. For power was permanently at stake in every relationship, and flowed in sometimes unpredictable and capillary ways through the web of interrelations at court. It was reproduced and augmented in the ceremonials and rituals of the court, in ways that could increase or decrease the authority of courtiers or princes. Thus, despite Elias's contention to the contrary, the growth of the absolutist courts did not necessarily signify the nobility's progressive loss of power to the central authority of the monarch. Rather, if the courts produced a code of comportment and demanded mastery of it from members, this meant that performance was fundamental for obtaining or retaining power: no one—not even the prince—could ignore this rule. Court life involved "both the presentation and legitimation of power. Paradoxically, the noble code of behavior served simultaneously as an impediment and as a vehicle for social mobility: those who could crack it found the way open to higher status."[4] Thus competition was keen among the members of the court, who sought—through performance of its particular code—to acquire prestige and reputation in the eyes of the nobles, and favor in the eyes of the sovereign. In one respect, however, Elias was quite correct: such intense struggle between its members for social, cultural, and political capital led to a new art of observation of human behavior at court. And this, in turn, led to new developments in the discourse on the art of dissimulation.

This is not the place for an essay on the court. I am concerned here with the development of the discourse on dissimulation within the genre of writing about courtiers and court society, which was, as many scholars have noted, perhaps the most successful elite institution of the early modern period.[5] In treating texts ranging from the early sixteenth century to the middle of the seventeenth century, I have concentrated on the ways in which dissimulation was represented as a constituent part of the courtier's art, and thus was transformed from an unwritten but widely enforced disciplinary code into a text. The intersection of numerous powerful and often competing interest groups at court, from patronage networks to the state bureaucratic apparatus, compelled courtiers to exercise caution and astuteness in their dealings with its other members. If the court system founded new practices of knowledge, in particular in the management and conduct of the courtier, dissimulation was certainly included among them. I have focused here chiefly on Italian writers, for if the literature on the court displayed great awareness of the problem posed by dissimulation for courtly rationality, this problem was often—especially in France and England—considered an export product of Italy.[6]

Philibert de Vienne complained in *Le Philosophe de Court* (The court philosopher, 1547): "in his actions, the Italian does not seem at all hasty, but rather coldly and hardly seems to consider all the circumstances, and, as it were, test the waters, which is part of prudence . . . moreover, there is no need to say how [the Italians] hide and repress their emotions, [or to speak of] their patience and dissimulation. In a word, they are born courtiers there."[7] Philibert's target text was Baldassar Castiglione's *Il Libro del Cortegiano* (The book of the courtier), published in 1528, which was the single most influential work on the court published in the sixteenth and seventeenth centuries in Europe, and the fountainhead of all early modern discourse on dissimulation at court.[8] Whether in terms of the history of its publication or reception, Castiglione's book was a huge success both in Italy and elsewhere; around sixty-two editions of the text were published in Italy alone in the sixteenth and seventeenth centuries, while at least sixty-nine were published in various European languages in these same years.[9] The historian Peter Burke has estimated that *Il Libro del Cortegiano* had, remarkably, some 300,000 readers in the early modern period alone.[10] Castiglione introduced, in other words, generations of courtiers and would-be courtiers to the arts of courtiership, including that of courtly dissimulation, and eventually became synonymous—through his many readers, exegetes, and epigones—with the transnational court culture of the Old Regime.

Sprezzatura

The suavely elegant dialogues found in *Il Libro del Cortegiano* embodied the ideals of the court of Duke Guidubaldo di Montefeltro in Urbino, at which Castiglione (1478–1529), Pietro Bembo, Bernardo Bibbiena and many other distinguished figures served in the first years of the Cinquecento. Although in these dialogues the courtiers bandied about many terms that were soon to become the common currency of the discourse on the court, including "grace" (*grazia*), "perfection" (*perfezione*), and "affectation" (*affettazione*), one in particular, *sprezzatura*— a term coined in *Il Libro del Cortegiano* and often translated as "nonchalance" or "negligence"—became the emblem of Castiglione's courtier. Once absorbed within the immense textual machinery of classicism, the language of Castiglione's courtiers was transformed into a set of *topoi,* or commonplaces, to be recycled endlessly in the writings on the court, establishing the bedrock that would support this discourse for well over a century.

It was clear to many sixteenth- and seventeenth-century readers of the dialogues that, in the context of court society, there was not such a great difference between *sprezzatura,* as the very touchstone of the courtier's existence, and the more controversial term "dissimulation." Subsequent works on the court split, not surprisingly, into pro- and anti-Castiglione camps, and an anti-court literature flourished throughout the early modern period alongside the numerous reprints, rewritings, and translations of *Il Libro del Cortegiano.*[11] Ignoring the remarkable publishing history of the book after 1528, too many scholars have portrayed Castiglione's four dialogues as the melancholic and nostalgic expression of a fading High Renaissance culture, a fleeting and final backward glance at the greatness that had been Italy before its decline into absolutism and cultural marginality, rather than as the inauguration of a discourse that fascinated several successive generations of Europeans.[12]

Despite his claim in the preface that "I was moved . . . to write these books of the Courtier: which I did in but a few days," Castiglione probably began work on *Il Libro del Cortegiano* in 1507 or 1508, and continued to revise it, layer upon layer, until its publication in 1528, just a year prior to his death in Spain.[13] The main body of the text seems, in any event, to have been completed by 1524, the date by which pirated copies of the manuscript were already circulating in Italy. Although it belonged to a genre enjoying considerable popularity in the sixteenth century because of the widespread desire to emulate the influential model of the court society, Castiglione's treatise on the courtier was far more than a mere list of rules prescribing proper behavior at court and elsewhere. One of the most sophisticated of all literary works produced in the vernacular in the sixteenth century, its *soavi ragionamenti* (sweet conversations) were modeled on the great dialogues of antiquity. The dialogues formed a kind of *gioco,* or game, as the courtiers in Urbino called it, in which the speakers vied with one another in creating a composite portrait of the perfect court and the perfect courtier.[14] Any number of early modern and modern critics, from Torquato Tasso to Giuseppe Toffanin, have seen the idealization of the court and the courtier as the key to reading this text.

But Castiglione's work was also enmeshed with the deepening political crisis on the peninsula and took its idealistic impetus in part from the fact that, in the troubled principalities of early sixteenth-century northern and central Italy, the term *cortegiano* had already become "a byword for dishonesty and faithlessness."[15] Through his composite portrait of the qualities of an ideal courtier and an ideal court, Castiglione set out to correct the already common image of the courtier as a flatterer, sycophant, and hypocrite, and of the court as "a shop of masks, where only false goods made to serve deceit are for sale," as Traiano Boccalini was later to put it.[16] The work depicted the political wisdom, humanistic learning, military prowess, aesthetic sensibility, ethical rigor, amorous art, and refined manners of the courtiers as the one way of being in the one world (and the one social class) that really mattered, and the courtiers participating in these conversations were portrayed as gifted individuals possessing the highest moral and intellectual qualities. The final version of the manuscript of *Il Libro del Cortegiano* was charged with Neoplatonism, especially in the fourth book: in the visions of Ottaviano Fregoso and Pietro Bembo, the court became the "site of the transparency and synonymity of knowledge and power" and the courtier became "the expression of a supreme human balance, a transhistorical ideal" of perfect harmony, proportion, and sublimity.[17]

Perfection, of course, can be considered a legitimate philosophical concept. But in the context of the court it was also possible to see "perfection" as a sought-after marker of social advancement, for the courtier's claim to perfection was meant to guarantee and validate success in gaining recognition in the eyes of the prince and the other courtiers. *Il Libro del Cortegiano* was, even in its enthusiastic search to define the modalities of courtly perfection, a study of power as well as of the social and aesthetic ideals of the Urbino court. No matter how flawless the performance, the courtier's claim to perfection—and hence to increased status and power at court—was subject to confirmation or challenge by the other courtiers, all of whom were locked into the same structure of competition and mutual interdependence under the watchful eye of the prince. The autocratic power of Duke Guidubaldo, himself conspicuously absent from the dialogue, cast a long shadow across Castiglione's book, and the courtiers were regularly reminded of its presence as they conversed. In a place such as Urbino, the so-called "city in the form of a palace" *(la città in forma di palazzo)*, there were few places where the presence of the ruler and the court society could not be felt. The city thus appeared as a paradigm of the court as *continuum,* or regime of disciplined social interdependency, a closed circuit in which every gesture was codified, homogenized, and inscribed in a ritual scene meant to enhance the prestige of the courtiers in each others' eyes and in the prince's. Perfection, in Urbino, therefore meant to serve perfectly (*perfettamente servire*).[18]

The appearance of the neologism *sprezzatura* in the text of *Il Libro del Cortegiano* indicates a key moment of conceptual tension in Castiglione's treatment of the ideal conduct of the early modern courtier. Keenly aware of its controversial status in moral philosophy and theology, as well as its pejorative meaning for the anti-courtier critics, Castiglione seems to have decided that *dissimulazione* itself had to be dissimulated and transformed into *sprezzatura* in his dialogue. The decision to displace the former term—but not the function that it signified—from the center of the work suggests that he understood well the potentially difficult reception facing his discourse on conduct at court. Although not directly named as the essence of the courtier's art, the term *dissimulazione* appears in *Il Libro del Cortegiano* in a number of places and never figures negatively in the text.[19] On the contrary, it supplies the essential link between *grazia* and *sprezzatura*, between grace and negligence.[20] The semantic couple *sprezzatura/dissimulazione* makes its best-known appearance in the famous passage in book 1 (par. 26) in which Count Ludovico da Canossa observes:

I have found quite a universal rule which in this matter seems to me valid above all others, and in all human affairs whether in word or deed: and that is to avoid affectation in every way possible as though it were some very rough and dangerous reef; and (to pronounce a new word perhaps) to practice in all things a certain *sprezzatura*, so as to conceal all art and make whatever is done or said appear to be without effort and almost without any thought about it. . . . Therefore we may call that art true art which does not seem to be art; nor must one be more careful of anything than of concealing it, because if it is discovered, this robs a man of all credit and causes him to be held in slight esteem. And I remember having read of certain most excellent orators in ancient times who, among the other things they did, tried to make everyone believe that they had no knowledge whatever of letters; and, dissembling their knowledge, they made their orations appear to be composed in the simplest manner and according to the dictates of nature and truth rather than of effort and art; which fact, had it been known, would have inspired in the minds of the people the fear that they could be duped by it.[21]

This passage is so well known, and has been so thoroughly discussed elsewhere, that there is no need to comment on it further here, other than to point out that the Count compares his theory of *sprezzatura* to the dissimulation of the ancient orators or, it may be inferred, Socratic irony itself: the courtier's art of dissimulation acquires legitimacy from its origins in, or proximity to, classical rhetoric and philosophy.[22]

Castiglione's innovative use of the category of dissimulation in order to define the perfect courtier's code of conduct represents, as Jacques Revel suggests, an attempt to discover a new form of social distinction; for only one group—the members of the court—could know exactly what the "universal rule" (*regula universalissima*) of courtly etiquette was.[23] *Il Libro del Cortegiano* reveals that this universal rule was to be "an art that does not seem to be art," that is, the practice of *sprezzatura*. As a means of "not letting things be seen as they are," *sprezzatura* could only figure as a species of dissimulation, for if one simulates that which is not, then one dissimulates that which is.[24] The practice of *sprezzatura* was appropriate to the particular circumstances of the court, in which ruler and courtiers alike tacitly agreed to accept the fiction that something was what it appeared to be, namely a spontaneous act of grace devoid of personal ambition, while knowing full well that at court "nothing is but what is not" and that appearance had to prevail over being. Those who were masters of the practice of *sprezzatura*—and who knew how to dissimulate self-interest in this way—formed the true aristocracy of the court, as opposed to the traditional aristocracy of bloodlines.[25]

To be a courtier meant not only to be an agent within a specific institutional context but an interlocutor in an exchange arising in and through language and serving as the space of disclosure (conversation) sustaining the culture of the court.[26] Dissimulation at court was a supremely self-conscious art of producing an image of oneself for others through language, gesture, and action, among other things, even if such a representation was intended to disclose little or nothing about the courtier's true intentions: *sprezzatura* was expressly designed to uncouple representation from intention. As seen in chapter 2 of the present book, such a doubling possesses a distinct temporal structure: there has first to be self-recognition on the part of the dissimulator before it is possible to act to prevent others from recognizing the inner workings of that same self. This temporal lag in the process of producing dissimulation has, in turn, two consequences for the courtier. On the one hand, as was widely acknowledged in early modernity, dissimulation is wholly dependent on secrecy, and hence the successful dissimulator is obliged, through a conscious process of internalization, to make the interests of heart and mind a private matter. The dissimulating courtier has to impose an absolute limit or threshold to displays of inner life—a vanishing point of subjectivity, beyond which all must remain invisible—and never violate that limit in negotiations with others. A solitary interrogation of one's inner being was no longer the choice of the ascetic, as it had been in antiquity and the Middle Ages, but rather the obligation of the worldly, courtly, or polite individual.

On the other hand, however, the choice of dissimulation also invokes a dialogical and intersubjective dimension. The courtier wishing to carry through successfully with dissimulation has to take others fully into account, and never—at the risk of discovery and loss of face—make the mistake of underestimating the resources at their disposal. To practice the art of dissimulation at court means, in so many words, to respect the otherness of interlocutors in the conversation, as well as one's own intimate truths. It is necessary for the courtier to negotiate with others' intelligence and astuteness in order to produce the proper socially operational self-representation. (Any genealogy of the libertine art of seduction in the neoclassical age and the Enlightenment must consider the early modern theory of dissimulation as one of its legitimate precursors.)[27] If courtly dissimulation is to succeed, then, it has to be convincing for most participants in the conversation at court, who expect it to satisfy such aesthetic criteria as the completeness and perfection of the courtier's performance. Not only are the courtier's intimate mental and emotional experiences to be erased from view of others, but this erasure is itself part of an elaborate and aesthetically pleasing display of competence in courtly etiquette. *Il Libro del Cortegiano* acknowledges, in other words, that the dialogical dimension of dissimulation leads to the aestheticization of the courtier's existence.

Given that dissimulation—as a philosophical concept, as a code of conduct, and as a trope—was not without controversy in the sixteenth century, it seems remarkable that the members of the court of Urbino taking part in the dialogues should have seemed so serenely oblivious to this fact, especially when it is clear that Castiglione's great contemporaries Guicciardini and Machiavelli were not.[28] There seems, however, to be little sense in the text of *Il Libro del Cortegiano* of the problematic moral and ethical status of dissimulation in the Western tradition, apart from the lame protests of Gaspar Pallavicino in book 2.[29] Perhaps this was due to the fact that, for Castiglione's courtiers, "the ethic of social life takes its point of departure in aesthetics—that is to say, the values of the beautiful are the basis of the values of the good," making the treatise therefore a Neoplatonic "*exemplum* of an aesthetic legitimation of the moral."[30] The function of dissimulation in the creation of the aesthetic experience of the court had to be viewed in terms of the moral value of the beautiful *qua* the good, and traditional reservations regarding the morality of dissimulation had to be thrust aside in order to theorize adequately aristocratic courtly culture.

In the early modern court, the exercise of sovereignty inevitably involved public display. The court was an ensemble of glittering surfaces in which all seemed to be visible; the court, and the courtier, were governed by the gaze of the ruler and by a general economy of the eye.[31] Courtly dissimulation was thus the product of a split consciousness— the courtier's—torn between the infinite private labor (*fatica*) required for success and the equally compelling need for its concealment in public.[32] This split or double vision generated, in the context of the courtly *continuum,* a heightened sense of awareness both of the way in which the courtier produced an image of himself—allowing others to view it as a continuous aesthetic performance—and of the "effacement of the traces of [its] production." This is the essence of the "social trope" of dissimulation, or, as Castiglione preferred to call it, *sprezzatura.*[33] The courtier's mind had self-reflexively to scrutinize, discipline, and master itself, in an effort to see exactly what others at court saw of oneself, and account for this in the representations that it produced. By the same token, the actions of others had to be seen "as one presumes to be seen oneself (is he doing that because I am watching him?)."[34] This relationship to oneself *as if another* is the basis of the courtier's aesthetics and the source of the courtier's alienation; the eye, after all, cannot see itself except in the form of a reflection.[35]

The Captain of All Figures

Dissimulation is a trope in *Il Libro del Cortegiano* as well as a program of conduct.[36] Early modern educators explicitly linked the physical training of the body—the management of its gestures—and the acquisition of mastery over language through training in the rhetorical tradition. The exercise of self-control over language and body functioned as formalizations of individual behavior. Although a treatise on courtiership rather than an educational manual, *Il Libro del Cortegiano* extends this same discourse of self-control to the *institutio* of the courtier. Bibbiena reminds his listeners in the second book of the dialogue that "quite a nice sort of pleasantry is that too which consists in a certain dissimulation, when one thing is said and another is tacitly understood."[37] *Dissimulatio*—here defined in terms of elementary rhetorical irony ("when one thing is said and another is tacitly understood")—is a figure in many ancient, medieval, and Renaissance rhetorics.[38] However,

Bibbiena's definition of dissimulation as rhetorical irony, part of his lengthy discussion of ironic wordplay, does not completely convey the way in which it functioned in the discourse of the court. Such ironic statements would normally depend upon a tacit understanding shared by both speaker and listener. In rhetorical dissimulation of this kind, in other words, the figurative or double meaning of the speaker's words is transparent, or ought to have been, for most listeners. This is, however, the opposite of what occurs in the *dissimulatio* at the basis of the courtier's art.

Courtly *dissimulatio* consists, rather, in the concealment of one's own meaning from others.[39] It further consists, as Bibbiena notes, in the concealment of one's understanding of the meaning of the words of others: "of like kind is a certain spicy and keen dissimulation wherein a man (a man of wit, as I have said) pretends not to understand what he does understand."[40] To transfer this to the terms of the court's economy of the visible, the dissimulating courtier would in such cases appear not to have seen or heard something.[41] The trope of *dissimulatio* in this context resembles *reticentia,* while the opposite of such a figure would be *sinceritas* or *confessum,* either one of which was anathema to Castiglione's courtier.[42] In the rhetorical treatises, *dissimulatio* (in the mode of concealment) is considered a figure of tactical irony in which a speaker or listener wants something not to become known because it would be inappropriate for the situation. It is for this reason that ethics has always had great difficulty dealing with such irony and the forms of courtesy that it has generated.[43] It should in any case be clear that the figure of *dissimulatio* constitutes in and of itself a basic program of conduct, just as *sprezzatura* is both a system of persuasion and a rhetorical figure for the courtier ("the chief ringleader and capitaine of all other figures," as Puttenham put it).[44]

Tactical irony, which uses dissimulation as its chief device, rather than rhetorical irony, defines the conduct of the courtier as both speaker and listener in the conversation at court.[45] The courtier's words display a mask of *sprezzatura* in order to hide the prime secret of the heart (that is, the truth of its distance from itself), which would be fatal to reveal in the context of the court. Unlike simulation, this mask does not form a false representation but rather an inscrutable one, whose persuasive power derives from the apparent absence of affectation and visible traces of ambition in the courtier. The essential element in the equilibrium between concealment and display is secrecy, or, more precisely, the "setting apart of the secret from the non-secret."[46] Secrecy has everything to do with the civility and courtesy of the courtier, for the ambition and effort behind the image of one's own perfection had to be kept from others.[47] Moreover, Castiglione's ideal courtier has continually to recall to mind—but only in order not to disclose them—the practical rules for setting apart the truth of the relation that one must have to oneself at court and segregating it from the rest of the self-representation. Memory is therefore one of the keys to secrecy, dissimulation, and etiquette at court, as well as a cornerstone of its social and power relations: to forget to remember this would fatally compromise the courtier in the eyes of the others.

Sprezzatura may be considered the withholding of a secret, or rather, the twin secrets of effort and ambition, as well as the recollection of the cardinal rules of the art of dissimulation. In the context of the court, this practice serves to guard not just the courtier's own particular secrets but access to the underlying experience of secrecy.[48] The display deserving of favor—produced by the highly skilled exercise of *sprezzatura* and the consequent elimination of affectation—figures, in the visual economy of the court, as a gift to the eye of the observer, who may be dazzled by a graceful dance step, a witty remark, fancy swordplay, or an offhand erudite citation. The point of such a charismatic performance, however, is precisely that it is not only a gift. Rather, it is like a one-way mirror behind whose shimmering images lie the courtier's hidden behavioral calculus. In seeking to attract admiration, gain favor, and advance one's interests at court, the ambitious courtier in Urbino has to perform without revealing any suspect underlying mental and emotional states: only this may lead the prince to bestow his favor.

The work of the members of the court, inscribed in an apparently gratuitous economy of the gift (of *grazia*)—namely, what is sought after, admired, expected— therefore has to involve something else as well.[49] According to *Il Libro del Cortegiano,* every courtier is a spectator who knows enough of the code of *sprezzatura* to suspect a secret (ambition) hidden behind the highly polished surface of effortless grace displayed in a given courtly performance. In other words, every courtier has every reason to read between the lines when confronted with acts intended to form an impenetrable screen of dissimulation, revealing only the art that is not an art, while covering over all traces of ambition. Otherwise one risks becoming a dupe, losing face, and falling into disgrace—that is, experiencing social "death." Although these masterful performances may be necessary to the proper functioning of the court, Castiglione's dialogue suggests, its members are compelled to scrutinize them for signs pointing out the secrets hidden beneath them, which could reveal the true state of the performer's heart and mind. In this sense, it is not enough to speak of the courtier's conduct as a mode of showing rather than being, for what is not shown at court—what lies outside of the economy of the eye—is as essential as what can be seen.[50] No matter how self-assured in appearance, the early modern courtier and practitioner of *sprezzatura* was anxiously aware that, behind the aesthetically gratifying screen of nonchalance and effortlessness that was to be constantly on display, there was always something cached in a recess of the others' minds and hearts, just out of sight, namely the will to dissimulation itself.[51] One could be a successful courtier, in other words, only inasmuch as one still had something left to hide.

The Anti-Courtier

Although *Il Libro del Cortegiano* was widely popular in the years following its publication—the emperor Charles V was said to love to read only three books: *Il Libro del Cortegiano,* Machiavelli's *Discorsi* (Discourses), and Polybius's *The Histories*—it had many detractors as well. Several treatises appeared in the first half of the sixteenth century that took exception to Castiglione's program of courtly conduct.[52] Little is known of the life of Philibert de Vienne, who penned a vigorous mid-century satire of courts and courtiers, *Le Philosophe de Court*. A lawyer who served at the Paris parliament, Philibert expresses in his treatise the anti-courtier and anti-Italian sentiments shared by many of his compatriots.[53] Mocking Castiglione's main thesis in *Il Libro del Cortegiano,* he remarks that while no one approves of dissimulation whose intent is to hide one's true being, it is not thought fraudulent at court to accommodate oneself "to everyone's imperfections, when this is not to one's own detriment." Such dissimulation could be innocuous, Philibert notes ironically, if its aim is merely "to please men" *(de complaire aux hommes)*.[54] He explains what this means for the philosophy of the court: "it is thus highly praiseworthy to moderate our emotions, so that they do not appear to others, and thus dissimulate and accommodate ourselves to everyone, for it is an easy means for attracting the benevolence of other men, from which come honor and good reputation."[55] The irony is so sustained in *Le Philosophe de Court* that it is not difficult to see how the work could have been misread by sixteenth-century students at Cambridge (among others) as meaning exactly what it says, and as belonging in a class with Castiglione himself.[56] In the Lucianesque vein of the treatise, however, such a philosophy of the court was meant to be understood as wholly reprehensible.

Indeed, Philibert notes, even those who carry their dissimulation too far, exaggerating their use of *sprezzatura,* cannot stain the spotless reputation of dissimulation at court, where it is wholly necessary to the functioning of courtly conversation: "when the finesse of some dissimulators is subject to reprehension, we should not for that reason blame dissimulation in general, for rogues are poor at all things. . . . One should therefore hardly blame this mental agility which allows man to change and transform himself in accordance with the pleasure of others."[57] Dropping his mockery, he proposes instead a return to the classical Aristotelian and Ciceronian virtues of magnanimity, temperance, prudence, and liberality among courtiers. But these virtues, Philibert admits a touch acidly, have little to do with the customs of the contemporary courts: "here is the way that true courtiers live, reining in their own emotions in order to follow our virtue and to please men. Here is the true source of that good grace which is to be found primarily (as we see) in modesty and temperance. . . . The courteous gentleman is never subject to himself: if one ought to laugh, he laughs; if one should grow sad, he weeps."[58] The courtier is, in short, a Protean figure—but scarcely heroic. Both simulator and dissimulator, the contemporary courtier willingly abandons any pretense to coincidence between being and appearance, devoting every effort instead to the production of a fundamentally false self-image that might be pleasing to others and helpful to one's own advancement at court. In the critical perspective of *Le Philosophe de Court,* the ideal courtier of *Il Libro del Cortegiano* was nothing other than a shameless, two-faced opportunist bent solely on personal gain rather than on service to the sovereign, and willing to employ dissimulation (among many other nefarious devices) to achieve that end.

Shortly after the publication of Philibert's vitriolic attack on Castiglione, there appeared in Italy Lucio Paolo Rosello's *Dialogo della vita de' cortegiani, intitolato 'La patientia'* (Dialogue on the life of the courtiers, entitled "Patience" [1549]), a critique by this Nicodemite religious reformer of the corrupt values of the contemporary Italian courts. Born in Padua, where he studied law at the university, Rosello (?–1552) lived much of his life in Venice, to which he fled after the sack of Padua during the war of the League of Cambrai. The author of various treatises (on topics such as nobility or the court), he was known as a poet and orator as well as an ecclesiastic with marked sympathies for the Reformation.[59] The label "Nicodemite" is today applied to the heterogeneous underground groups of religious dissidents ranging from Catholic evangelicals to various unorthodox Protestant congregations that existed in the early modern period in a number of European countries. These groups were well known for their doctrine of dissimulation in dealing with persecution.[60] In Italy the Counter-Reformation, launched in 1542 with the reconstitution of the Roman Inquisition, forced Italian religious dissidents such as Rosello to choose between exile, a clandestine existence, and silence. Although many dissidents fled abroad, the majority seems to have stayed in Italy and continued religious observances under the cover of dissimulation, usually while continuing to attend Mass and receive the sacraments.[61] Even though no mention is made of this issue in his dialogue on the court, Rosello's approach to the topic of dissimulation is enmeshed with the Nicodemite experience of the 1540s in Italy, as the administrative apparatus of the Church and state began to turn its attention to the ferreting out of heretics and dissidents. In rejecting Castiglione's doctrine of *sprezzatura*, he proposes—not surprisingly—a different doctrine of dissimulation in its place.

One of the two speakers in the dialogue, Marco Montalbano (the other being Rosello himself), condemns the conduct of contemporary Italian courtiers in no uncertain terms: "as for the practices of which you speak, those seem wicked to me that know how to deceive a companion with gestures and words, feign to love him and hate him deeply, have as many faces as the people that one meets, and all of them false, and finally never to be sincere, and to have conspired against truth, a thing which is so very troubling and displeasing to nature."[62] This litany of evils contains most of the standard *topoi* of the anti-court literature of the age.[63] The courtiers traffic in deceit (*ingannare co' gesti e parole*), duplicity (*haver tante faccie . . . tutte finte*), hypocrisy (*non esser mai di sincero animo*), and falsehood (*haver congiurato contra la verità*). The social and political transparency for which Montalbano longs in the dialogue is seemingly the polar opposite of the ceremonial worldliness described by Castiglione. Like Philibert de Vienne, Rosello sees the political realism of the courtiers as undermining traditional Christian values of transparency, solidarity, and truthfulness then being championed by John Calvin and other reformers. However, dissimulation or mental reservation is not included by Montalbano on his list of the courtiers' sins. This glaring exclusion undermines any possibility that the dialogue could belong only to the literature of the *contempto curiae*.

Not only are words spoken at court not a reliable index of the mind of the speaker, Montalbano complains, but the very principle of mimesis is undermined by the predominance of ritual display and ceremony. Life at court—"this external apparatus that displays such gaiety with all its pomp"—is as intolerable as life in Plato's cave, in which everything appearing on the wall is a flickering simulacrum of reality.[64] Thus at court "opening and closing our eyes we see the shadows of things, but we cannot handle things themselves, for they are not there."[65] The speakers in Rosello's dialogue clearly grasp the nature of the court as a scene of representation existing not only for the benefit of the prince's power but for the self-fashioning courtiers as well. Rosello, however, was a political pragmatist who knew that there was little chance of righting the wrongs of the court but that there was great risk of loss of status if one did not participate in its workings. Although they warn about its dangers, the interlocutors of the dialogue call, not for the elimination or even for the reform of the court, but rather for a morally acceptable means of accommodation to its conversation. The sole available remedy for the pomp and poison of court life, as Montalbano explains to Rosello, is "patience" (*pacientia*), which is the "virtue" (*virtù*) at the origin of prudence itself.[66]

The practice of *pacientia,* as the exercise of prudent and stoical resignation to the blows of adverse fortune at court, is doubtless intended in the dialogue to be antithetical to the *sprezzatura* of Castiglione's ambitious courtier, who actively seeks mastery over both self and other. This concept seems clearly drawn from both the Stoic and Christian traditions of self-control and self-denial. Nevertheless, it would be difficult to define "patience" here as anything other than a species of dissimulation, appropriate to the circumstances of the early modern absolutist court. In employing patience at court, one was not deliberately to deceive the other courtiers, but neither was one to reveal oneself to them: Montalbano prescribes dissimulation through reservation as the sole remedy for the evils of courtiership. This weapon was already available in the arsenal of classical rhetorics—and Rosello was an accomplished humanist—but here it is given a new ethical meaning in the specific context of the sixteenth-century court. By avoiding the vices of the other courtiers (flattery, hypocrisy, and so on), the prudent practitioner of patience aims to maintain an uncontaminated moral sphere within the mind and heart, while accepting the necessary public compromises of court life in order to remain afloat there. *Pacientia,* unlike *sprezzatura,* was not intended by Rosello to provide any material advantage to those employing it in their courtly negotiations. It has a defensive design, which is to preserve one's secret moral rigor, despite the courtly *continuum* that subjects all participants in the conversation to the constant surveillance of others.[67]

Pacientia is needed, as the dialogue makes clear, chiefly because the prince's opinions are constantly shifting: "every prince is of a varying state of mind, nor does he long keep the same opinion."[68] Thus the patient courtier has to be prepared to adapt to ever-changing circumstances, without becoming just another sycophant or flatterer ready to speak whatever words are necessary in the pursuit of personal gain. In terms reminiscent of Aquinas, Montalbano explains that the prudent courtier is moved to act only out of the "necessity" (*necessità*) of following the mutations of princely fashion, not out of personal ambition.[69] "One accommodates oneself to the times, now yielding, now coming closer, as the occasion requires."[70] The courtier can in this way make allowances for the foibles of the prince's nature, as long as inner moral coherence is maintained. Rather than try to sway events, in other words, one had to accept them outwardly but resist them inwardly. Dissimulation appears as a polyvalent practice for Rosello, a mode of both accommodation and resistance that masks—if only to the sight of other courtiers—the insuperable split between the public political persona and the private one at court. Unlike Castiglione's supremely skilled practitioner of *sprezzatura,* Rosello's patient courtier never desires to "make a display of his or her virtue" (*far mostra della sua virtù),* employing it only as the need arises and otherwise keeping it out of sight, in the sanctuary of moral conscience.[71] If patience and prudence are keys to survival at court, as Montalbano argues, they cannot be allowed—like dissimulation itself in *Il Libro del Cortegiano*—to circulate within the court's economy of the visible.

The patient courtier places as high a premium on the twin cornerstones of dissimulation—secrecy and silence—as do Castiglione's worldly and ambitious courtiers. In polemically questioning whether an impatient person can "be taciturn and secretive," Montalbano implies that the truly patient courtier is in fact a taciturn and secretive person.[72] In opposing the universal rule of *sprezzatura,* then, Rosello adopts basically the same rhetorical devices as Castiglione had, but transforms dissimulation into a morally positive choice for the courtier with a conscience. This accommodation could easily be mistaken for hypocrisy or sheer opportunism, however, if it were not for Rosello's (unspoken) belief in justification through faith alone, one of the doctrines of the new Protestantism.[73] In emphasizing the importance of the autonomous moral conscience, even in the social and political pressure cooker of the court, Rosello's philosophy of patience offers a backhanded endorsement of thinly disguised religious dissimulation of the sort practiced by the Italian Nicodemites.[74] Indeed, the author dissimulates entirely his own religious beliefs in the text of the dialogue, all of whose authorities are taken from pagan antiquity: Rosello's dialogue on courtiers is itself an exemplum of the art of patience that it promotes.

Pacientia would, if it were to be generally applied as a rule of moral conduct in court life, put an end to the reign of *sprezzatura*. This, however, remained (as Rosello was only too aware) an unrealizable ideal in the contemporary Italian courts.[75] When Montalbano is asked to provide "a general rule of patience" *(una regola generale della pacientia)* for the courtier, he simply answers: "use the medicine of patience anywhere that it seems appropriate [to the courtier] to use it."[76] However effective a medicine for the courtier's symptoms, patience can never be a cure. Rosello's brief treatise justifies courtly *dissimulatio,* or tactical irony, but only insofar as it is necessary to the goal of resisting coercion to the universal rule of *sprezzatura;* in his dialogue there is no aesthetics of patience, only an ethics. The social discipline and *savoir-vivre* of the patient courtier is that of knowing how and when to sacrifice one kind of good (the seamless continuity of thoughts and words, moral conscience and public persona) for another, and greater, good. In order to remain in the courtly conversation, the patient courtier has to avoid endangering sociability by speaking freely but without being forced to violate intimate moral and religious beliefs. Patience is a "medicine," as Montalbano calls it, not because it heals the lacerated, distressed psyche of the dissimulating courtier, but because it allows the courtier to endure such wounds. At the end of the dialogue Montalbano concludes: "I likewise demonstrate that patience is, in every misfortune, a singular remedy, especially needed in courtly life—[if one does] not want to see go for naught in a moment, I will not say the long time spent in the courts before the courtier attains the desired goal, but so much toil, so much dissimulating, [and] infinite hopes."[77] The patient courtier, by practicing self-censorship and observing secrecy, preserves the rule of dissimulation in the care of the self at court, but only out of a profound disenchantment with the "world" and its values.

The Secret Theater of Wit

The poet-critic Torquato Tasso (1544–1595), "who was partly educated at the court of Urbino and himself played the courtier in Ferrara, once planned a dialogue in imitation of Castiglione's, set at the court of Urbino and including in its cast of characters Baldassare's soldier son Camillo."[78] This dialogue was never composed; however, in the dialogue *Il Malpiglio ovvero de la corte* (Malpiglio, or the court), Tasso took up some of the century's dominant themes regarding courts and courtiers. Although the term "dissimulation" never appears in the text of the dialogue, the description of the courtly practice given by the speakers corresponds to what others openly called by that same name.[79] "Feigning" (*infingere*) is regularly used by Tasso in this sense, and the definition given by one of the speakers in the dialogue—"to hide that which I am" (*il celar quel che io sono*)—leaves little room for doubt about what Tasso intended but possibly felt it unwise to say.[80] In the kind of open-ended dialogue favored by him, it is difficult to fix the author's position, which seems to fall somewhere in between those of the speakers, allowing him to hide his thoughts behind a dialogical screen. The sort of lateral thinking represented in such a dialogue, moreover, gives Tasso an excellent means to deal with a controversial topic such as courtly dissimulation—although he takes the further precaution of avoiding naming it as such. In 1584–1585, the period of composition of the *Malpiglio* (which first appeared in print in 1587), Tasso was still confined to the hospital of Sant'Anna in Ferrara, following his nervous collapse in 1579 at the festivities for the Duke Alfonso's marriage. Soon after his confinement in Sant'Anna, he wrote in a letter that "not because I hid some part of the truth should I be considered any the less a philosopher. . . . If I denied a thing to the priest and avowed it to the prince, I did not only what was necessary according to the new and extraordinary fashions, but also what was fitting."[81] How much of the danger that Tasso thought himself to be in was real, and how much was the product of his persecution complex, may never be known. What is certain is that his theory of courtiership synthesizes Castiglione's *sprezzatura* and Rosello's *pacentia* in order to adapt dissimulation to the context of Counter-Reformation absolutism as he understood it.

Like so many others of their time, the three interlocutors in *Il Malpiglio*—Vincenzo and Giovanlorenzo Malpiglio, plus a nameless visitor from Naples—have already read and admired *Il Libro del Cortegiano*. In fact, the youngest of the three, Giovanlorenzo Malpiglio, acknowledges that he "has almost memorized it."[82] Asked by the others to comment at length on the work of Castiglione, "the creator of courts," the Neapolitan visitor professes that the argument is still absolutely contemporary: "if by chance there is something in courtiers that alters and varies with time and occasion, it is not essential."[83] Having paid homage to *Il Libro del Cortegiano* in this way, however, he proceeds to revise the doctrine of *sprezzatura,* eventually arriving at a critical view of the work.

Castiglione's courtier openly (if paradoxically) makes a display of the art that conceals all art, but the participants in Tasso's dialogue readily agree that prudent reservation instead ought to be the virtue of the new courtier: "concealment becomes the courtier more than display."[84] When the younger Malpiglio protests that concealment is "so difficult," the unnamed Neapolitan visitor explains to him bluntly that "this concealment can nevertheless be shrewdly managed."[85] Following both Castiglione and Rosello, the Neapolitan further notes that dissimulation—defined as concealing (*ricoprendo*) and keeping silent (*tacendo*)—serves a double purpose in the closely watched arena of the court. Not only does it shield the courtier from the prince's displeasure but also from the other courtiers' envy: "by concealment, then, the courtier can avoid his prince's displeasure and also, it seems, protect himself from the envy of courtiers."[86]

Nowhere was this more invaluable than in the absolutist courts then flourishing in Italy.[87] Tasso's portrait of the ideal Counter-Reformation courtier resembles Castiglione's insofar as dissimulation is one of the most important virtues of both: "and if Castiglione's book was for the age in which it was written, yours ought to be valued in these days in which feigning is one of the highest virtues."[88] In the case of the court of Ferrara, however, despite the great value placed on pomp and display, *Il Malpiglio* contends that a courtier's success is chiefly determined by the exercise of prudence (*prudenza*), along with the shrewdness (*accortezza*) that is one of its essential ingredients.[89] Rosello had left patience to the discretion and moral conscience of the courtier, but Tasso insists that one has also to be psychologically shrewd (*accorto*) in order to dissimulate successfully at court. But the late-sixteenth-century courtier skillfully dissimulates not in order to attract admiration and to gain the prince's favor, as the doctrine of *sprezzatura* proposes, but rather as a means of conforming to the courtly conversation. For Tasso's interlocutors, "the courtier's prudence . . . consists in carrying out the prince's orders."[90] The days in which a favored courtier could expect to instruct the prince, or hope to influence administrative or political decisions, were over. Indeed, "princes usually hate greatness of mind. When a courtier has great intelligence, which sometimes happens, he ought to cover it up modestly, and not show it off with pride."[91]

In the eyes of the three interlocutors in the dialogue, dissimulation serves not to acquire the prince's favor, as Castiglione had argued, but to allow the courtier to coexist with the others in the courtly conversation. Admiration is acquired at court through *mediocrità,* or conformity to the mean, because that is the chief mode of display of prudence, and "prudence is the quality that overcomes all difficulties at court."[92] Every courtier, in dissimulating ability and ambition, and thus seeming to be equal with the others, is in fact demonstrating superior skills in the art of prudence. This is the paradox of courtly conduct in *Il Malpiglio*.[93] Every courtier may thus, by conforming to the mean, be like all the other courtiers, or at least seem not to be different from them. Envy and rivalry are to be avoided in this way, and equilibrium maintained in relations between the courtiers. The court is to be a common social space in which interpersonal conflicts may be subsumed and differences rationalized within the sphere of "proper" conduct. Thus self-effacement is a sign of supreme ability in the art of courtly dissimulation, for "this art of diminishing the praises one really deserves is more praiseworthy and honorable than any other."[94] To equate conformity with the mean, and the mean with prudence itself, means that all members of the court—with the prince at its center—have to participate in a general economy of dissimulation that guarantees the production of courtly consensus. Although the result of an elaborate artifice in which each courtier proves his or her superiority to the others by appearing to be no better than them, this consensus is the most important social and cultural trait of Tasso's ideal absolutist court.

The courtier's *raison d'être* is firmly grounded in knowing and accepting his or her place as a member of this court society while giving unquestioning obedience to the prince: "many times it is inappropriate for the courtier to seek the reasons for that which he is told to do, or want to know too much."[95] This willingness to obey the prince at any price marks a sea change from *Il Libro del Cortegiano*, of course. For, according to Castiglione, the courtier chooses to pay voluntary homage to the prince, and is free to leave if the latter is not worthy of such respect: this is unthinkable in *Il Malpiglio*. By the same token, the universal courtly artifice of *mediocrità*—generated through dissimulation—is not intended as a collective gift of grace to the prince organized by the courtiers who are bound to serve him. Any display of exceptional talent at court is instead to be seen as simply inappropriate and lacking in respect for its grave decorum (*gravità*). The young Giovanlorenzo objects on the grounds that "concealing oneself from one's prince is no argument of goodwill." But the far more experienced Neapolitan visitor quickly sets him straight: "it is nonetheless a sign of respect."[96] The courtier's self-control in the expression of thoughts and passions and interests thus displays due respect for—and homage to—the prince, keeping him from suffering either melancholy (at the thought of his own shortcomings) or envy of the courtier. For *Il Malpiglio,* the dissimulating mediocrity of the courtier is an act of service that can console the prince and keep him serene.

Tasso nevertheless sees a way to make courtly dissimulation as aesthetically compelling as it was for the courtiers in Urbino. The Neapolitan visitor points out that "the adaptation of ancient things to our own times is very praiseworthy when it is done in the right way."[97] This holds true for dissimulation as well; the participants in the dialogue note that it was first practiced in antiquity by Socrates. When the Neapolitan visitor wonders whether or not an honest man should dissimulate, the young Giovanlorenzo Malpiglio tells him to consider Socrates as an example of such a man.[98] Courtly dissimulation is an early modern form of Socratic irony, or, in other words, an adaptation of the Athenian philosopher's dissimulating dictum, "I know only that I know nothing." In the context of the absolutist court in Ferrara, the ancient Socratic saying is now transformed by Tasso into "I know only that I know what the other courtiers know." Keenly aware of the courtier's state of dependence on the prince and on the institution of courtiership, Tasso recognizes that the courtier must be incapable of speaking in any other way, and must embrace irony in order to play—and to stay—in the game of life at court.

At last it is possible to see Giovanlorenzo Malpiglio's objection that dissimulation is *così difficile,* or very difficult, as pointing to what Tasso really has in mind for his ideal courtier. The difficulty of sustaining the fiction underlying the absolutist court is all the more reason for the courtier to dissimulate: in Tasso's eyes, an aesthetics of courtiership is founded upon the very complexity of successful dissimulation at court. Any prudent courtier wishing to exercise *argutezza* or *avvedimento* every day in the courtly conversation must secretly command the art of Socratic rhetoric, all the while without seeming to have done so. This is an art of wit by no means easy to master, yet it is the essence of courtiership. The interest and value of dissimulation for Tasso lie, in short, not only in its pragmatic quality as a program of conduct, but in its high degree of rhetorical and aesthetic complexity, which could only occur within the *continuum* of the court. And only those courtiers of consummate skill are able to carry it out successfully or understand its meaning, although they may pass for mere faces in the crowd. The courtier's craft, as defined in *Il Malpiglio,* is admirable in both practical and aesthetic terms, precisely because it is so very difficult to be prudent at court.

Caught up in an intricate web of dissimulating irony and artful self-effacement, conversation at court—that ambiguous institution at once public and private—is transformed into a secret theater of *ingegno,* or wit, in which no one knows for certain who is performing and who is not.[99]

Violence and Confidence

Ferrara was also the city in which Lorenzo Ducci (dates of birth and death unknown) was active in the years between the end of the sixteenth and the beginning of the seventeenth century. A secretary in the service of Cardinal Giovan Francesco Biandrate di San Giorgio, he came to Ferrara in 1598 with his employer, not long after the city had become part of the Papal States. Ducci's role as private secretary to a "prince" of the Church clearly distinguishes him from the courtiers Castiglione and Tasso. The post of professional secretary was the fate of many *letterati* of lesser means in the second half of the Cinquecento, for it was one of the only available avenues to success.[100] Ducci's work as a secretary reflects the increasingly peripheral position of the courtier in general in regard to the decision-making process of the early modern state, as administrative and bureaucratic systems began to be consolidated. As the "instrument" of the "mind" and "will" of his employer (as Tasso put it in his *Il Segretario*), a private secretary such as Ducci was expected to be adept at all the rhetorical genres, from public speeches to business letters.[101] Author of a rhetorical treatise entitled *De elocutione libri duo* (On speech, books 1–2; 1600), a speech commemorating the fifth anniversary of Tasso's death (1600), and works on historiography (*Ars historica,* The art of history; 1604) and nobility (*Trattato della nobiltà,* A treatise on nobility; 1603), among others, Ducci is chiefly known today for his treatise on the court, the *Arte aulica* (1601, reprinted in Viterbo in 1615), which was translated into English as *Ars aulica or the Courtier's Art* in 1607 by Edward Blount, who also published path-breaking translations of Montaigne and Miguel de Cervantes in these same years.[102]

Composed only sixteen years after *Il Malpiglio,* Ducci's widely read treatise on courtiership shifts the discourse on the court and dissimulation away from both aesthetics and ethics, displaying the influence of the Tacitus revival then underway across Europe.[103] Ducci portrays the contemporary practices of the Italian courts in baldly pragmatic terms, without the use of the dialogue form or lists of rules of conduct: his book is a pocket-sized survival manual for the Counter-Reformation courtier that anticipates still more notorious works to come, such as the pseudo-Mazarin's *Breviarium politicorum* (The politician's breviary).[104] An ardent admirer of Tacitus, "that most excellent instructor of courtiers" (*ottimo maestro de' Cortigiani*), Ducci frankly acknowledges the necessity of simulation and dissimulation—terms that he often uses interchangeably to refer to dissembling—in the *continuum* of the courtier's existence. These devices represent civility itself, the opposite of "the natural."[105] The *Arte aulica* states in no uncertain terms, while toying with scholastic terminology, that the primary reason for the courtier's presence at court is self-interest. Ducci's is an admission that Castiglione and Tasso had gone to elaborate lengths to avoid: "it appeareth then that the ends or scopes that the Courtier hath are three, that is, his proper interest, and this is that which chiefly he endevoureth; next, the favour of the Prince, as the cause of his first end: and then, the service of the Prince, as the efficient cause of that favour."[106] Ducci appears unconcerned by the traditional ethical ban on the use of dissimulation in human affairs; even if a moral error, it is far from a mortal sin in his eyes, at least in regard to the courtier. Service at court justifies recourse to such techniques, which might be nonetheless inappropriate in everyday life: "That to the dutie of service so much is pardonable, as may for the pleasure and service of his Prince be done in some things, if not honorable, at least without such note of infamy, as in a person at full liberty could not be born out without passing censure or incurring blame."[107]

The courtier's existence is necessarily liable to ethical criticism, Ducci notes, for the fact that scrupulous courtiers can never hope to procure confidence from rulers.[108] The courtier is still supposed to be the mirror of the prince, "the very portrait of his properties and fashions," but this no longer occurs—as it had for Castiglione—through the mutual recognition of virtue and talent. Rather, as was the case for Tasso, the courtier is to seem to conform unquestioningly to the prince's desires, but in order to forward his or her own interests: "without all question is the Courtier to enable and conforme himselfe . . . he is to adapt and fit himselfe by all the meanes he may unto his will, and make himselfe, if it be possible, the very portrait of his [the prince's] properties and fashions."[109] In order to gain the prince's confidence and favor, in other words, Ducci's courtier must appear, like Rosello's and Tasso's, to "conform" to the will of the prince and seem to fully comply "without all question" to his whims. If the prince looks at the courtier, he should see only himself.[110] This might be nothing more than a charade of simulation and dissimulation, of course, for the courtier is under no obligation to be sincere. As noted in Guazzo's *La civil conversazione*, "in the presence of his lord, a courtier should either keep silent / or be quick to say something to his liking."[111] But, before speaking or acting, how can the courtier be sure of what the prince's likes and dislikes are? *Hoc opus, hic labor.*

Throughout the *Arte aulica*, Ducci reminds his readers that the primary goal is always only one, namely to gain the prince's confidence and to get to know his secrets, for in this way alone can the courtier win favor and advance at court while pleasing and serving the prince well. Both Rosello and Tasso, however, had warned that life at court was anything but easy; the competition between courtiers was intense, and all were fundamentally insecure in their relations with the prince. Any reader of *Il Libro del Cortegiano*, moreover, would have grasped that the golden rule of the courtier was never to underestimate the other courtiers, who certainly must all share the same ambitions and the same training in the fine art of dissembling. Indeed, Ducci remarks, "Many [courtiers] had rather use dissimulation and close stratagems against their enemies, either for their reputation in making slight regard of wrongs, or the commendations which they procure in pardoning injuries, or at least because by this meanes they make their enemie the lesse heedfull, whereby with the more ease they suppress him; & *quo incautior deciperetur, palam laudatum*, saith *Tacitus*."[112] This presents Ducci with a particularly thorny problem to resolve in the treatise. How are the prince's secrets to be discovered in this prevailing atmosphere of mutual distrust between ruler and courtiers, on the one hand, and between the envious courtiers themselves, on the other? The prince might dissimulate at will, trying to probe the courtier's thoughts "with amphibologies and figures and, in short . . . obscurely," without risk of exposure.[113] His ostensible purpose would be to discover a courtier with whom to entrust some part of his power, in the form of a shared secret. But the courtier cannot act in the same way as the prince: theirs is a wholly asymmetrical relationship. Thus the courtier's art, Ducci explains, consists in a confidence game: through role-playing and dissimulating intended to remove and extinguish all suspicion, the prince may be led to believe that his interlocutor in the courtly conversation is speaking freely and plainly, although the courtier is in fact closely guarding his or her true thoughts and desires. Ducci notes, not without a touch of cynicism, that "those who are held to be sincere and frank in nature, and who are thought to represent openly with their words what is in their hearts, are indeed those to whom we give credence."[114] This confidence game should lead the prince, in turn, to speak his own mind freely and frankly—and thus to fall into the courtier's carefully laid trap.

Any display of affectation would be fatal to this project, for it would reveal the courtier's ambition to the eyes of all at court and perhaps lead the prince, suspecting dissimulation, to shun his or her company: "But herein we must stand well advised to shunne a most dangerous rocke, that is, *curious and open affectation,* which may breed an opinion in the Prince of want of judgement, in knowing what's convenient, or else that which is more perillous, a doubt or suspect of dissimulation, and by consequence an effect of hatred or scorn, not alone with the Prince, but with the Courtiers also, who take no pleasure that any man should be over-diligent, or in appearance too-too passionate in the Prince's service."[115] As was the case for Castiglione's courtier, Ducci's must be highly self-disciplined, and able to keep well hidden the calculations that govern every gesture and every word. This confidence game is an endless one, demanding constant vigilance if affectation is to be avoided and the courtier's true intentions not exposed to public scorn:

> But these observations cannot be put in practice but by a witty, provident and wise Courtier, who if sometimes with an expression or shew of grief, or a light anger he join these admonishments it will greatly increase his credit, because such affections [*sic*] of freedome and plainnesse would wholly remove and extinguish all suspition of dissimulation, whereunto also will adde very much the avoiding of all affectation, and shunning this *decorum* and *seeming-wise-gravitie,* in your reprehensions. But above all, the most assured way to settle and gaine credit, is alwaies and in all your actions to shew your selfe such as you pretend.[116]

Within the courtly *continuum,* in which the conversation unfolds continuously from one day to the next, involving many pairs of eyes and ears, the success of the dissimulator depends upon being perfectly consistent. The courtier consequently requires a perfect memory, for to forget the dissimulator's script and allow even a single wrong word to slip out could prove catastrophic. In the *Arte aulica,* the courtier's being is entirely caught up in this dialectic of display and concealment, for the code of dissimulation and the code of courtly conduct are one and the same.[117]

According to Ducci, the prince has almost as much need to know the courtier's nature as the courtier has to know the prince's. Someone must, after all, assist in the business of state, for some power has to be delegated to others besides the prince alone.[118] The latter is entitled to employ dissimulation in sounding the courtiers for knowledge of their nature, as part of an ongoing search for those who might be entrusted with some service: "the other *Underminings* which are undertaken by dissimulation, and falsely, are only done to winne the knowledge of the *Courtiers* nature, albeit they are no lesse by a wise Prince to be handled with great dexteritie & art."[119] And the courtier, by the same token, has to sound out cautiously the prince, discovering his secret inclinations in order to know how to please him and to gain favor in his eyes. Here as elsewhere, the asymmetrical nature of the relation between prince and courtier is decisive in Ducci's analysis of the court, for in playing the confidence game the Counter-Reformation courtier who appears too curious about the secrets of the prince and the *arcana imperii* runs the risk of being taken for a spy.[120]

The *Arte aulica* departs even more radically from the model of *Il Libro del Cortegiano,* however, in its answer to the pressing question of how to "find the Prince's mind," or, for that matter, anyone else's mind at court. First and foremost, Ducci explains, this is to be done through the minute psychological study of others' behavior:

We say that the true meanes to attaine to the knowledge of the Princes nature and custome is by his actions: and yet not all, but those of choice, because these discover the inclination, as by the effect the cause is knowne; and although dissimulation, at first sight putting on a colourable habit, and occasion of the action, either different or contrary to the naturall propension and inclinement, it is yet notwithstanding impossible to conceale or hide the same, from a circumspect and wise Courtier, for that if watchfully he shall observe actions, it will easily appeare whether he worke naturally and by a contracted.habit, or else dissemblingly.[121]

However, it is difficult to deal with the truly cunning dissimulator, who would tend to be exceptionally wary and unwilling to expose his or her true thoughts in conversation. Despite this obstacle to in-depth psychological analysis of others, there are nonetheless options at hand, Ducci reassures his readers: "True it is that the cunning dissembler is cautelous and wary, and therefore doth not disrobe himselfe of his habit, but either by violence or confidence."[122] The courtier thus has to turn to one of three possible methods for uncovering the mind of any dissimulator: violence, confidence, or—Ducci adds—physiognomy.

The revival of interest in the ancient pseudo-science of physiognomy in the second half of the sixteenth century reflected the depth of concern over the popularity of those same dissimulating practices that Tasso discussed in his abovementioned letter, as well as the demand by secular and religious authorities for new means of penetrating to the core of the individual's interiority. In his treatise Ducci explicitly invokes the aid of the tradition of physiognomical interpretation in deciphering the mind of the dissimulator: "we say then that diverse are the meanes whereby the natures of men are known, amongst the which the art of *Physiognomy* doth helpe very much, by meanes wherof some have been able to penetrate and search into the inmost and most concealed affects of the minde of other men: And howbeit the arte seeme full of fallacies, yet when many signes concurre together signifying one and the same affect, then wise men will not that it be vaine to give credit, as settled upon naturall grounds."[123] Giambattista della Porta, in the 1599 edition of his *De humana physiognomia* (On human physiognomy), for example, had suggested that dissimulators (*dissimulatores*) were easy enough to recognize because they resembled monkeys: with a round face, small, deep and sparkling eyes, large eyebrows, wrinkles around the eyes, and a sleepy countenance, they were good-looking and soft-spoken.[124] However, Ducci himself admits that this is not much to go on when there is so much at stake for the courtier. In the last analysis, physiognomy and allied arts are "too much grounded upon Generals" to be of much practical use in the courtier's situation.[125] The really useful methods, as he noted above, are instead "violence or confidence."

There are, he observes, two sorts of violence that might be employed to expose "the true natural habit" of the mind hidden by dissimulation.[126] The first of these is the use of sheer force, such as torture, "by some mighty hand" to unmask the dissimulator. But this option, Ducci recognizes, is available mainly to princes and other potentates, and should not normally occur in relations at court.[127] There is, however, another possibility: "but there is an other kinde of violence, very profitable, and to be considered, that is, an excesse of the affections stirred up or moved."[128] If a strong enough emotional reaction can be provoked in the dissimulator, then it is possible that the shield of self-discipline might fall long enough for prying eyes to gaze at "the secrets of the heart, and discovereth that, which dissimulation kept most secret."[129] Such violence is not dangerous except to the one provoked "or stirred up" to an outburst of anger, jealousy, or some other strong passion or affection. This technique, however, may be employed with other courtiers but not with princes, whose wrath is to be avoided at all times. Violence is therefore effective in certain circumstances, but not in the discovery of the prince's own "true natural habit," which is the goal of every courtier.

Thus, in the last analysis, the most effective means available to the courtier is "the consideration of *Confidence*."[130] Inasmuch as the chief end of dissimulation is to disguise natural instinct, there have to be both persons with whom and places in which the prince would wish to be open and uncircumspect, in order to give free rein to the forces of nature lurking beneath the calm surface of self-control.[131] Ducci agrees with those who claim that it is unthinkable for dissimulation to be sustained indefinitely. The force of the passions cannot be forever dominated by reason and the will, and has to find a release sooner or later, even in the case of the sovereign. Usually the latter prefers to be himself with common folk and in secret places, the *Arte aulica* explains to its readers: the courtier must study carefully what the prince does and says at those particular moments, in order to divine his true thoughts.[132] Once certain of the prince's nature, one must conform to it and wholly fit oneself to "his true and naturall inclination" in order to gain the priceless benefit of the prince's confidence.[133]

This, however, may be far more complicated than at first appears to be the case. The full complexity of the confidence game as it is played out between prince and courtier may perhaps best be grasped in the following scenario, in which Ducci observes that the prince, in practicing dissimulation, displays a lack of desire for the very thing that he in truth desires most. In such a case it is imprudent, to say the least, for the courtier either (i) to pretend to conform to the prince's dissimulation (for the latter would secretly despise the courtier for it) or (ii) to endorse the very thing that the prince secretly is thinking or desiring (for the prince would intuit that his screen of dissimulation had been discovered). Fortunately, however, there is another and better option. Ducci explains in the treatise that, after grasping the natural inclination beneath the prince's dissimulation, the courtier must pretend that this is also the courtier's own instinct, while showing at the same time, however, that one's reason and will are trying mightily to resist it. This ploy should convince the prince, Ducci suggests, that his secret is safe and that the courtier is simply a kindred spirit, or a suitable "mirror" of his own mind:

But the Courtier must shew himselfe to be naturally inclined thereunto, although in reason he repugne the same, and be faine to force himselfe thereunto: because that which is truly naturall unto the Prince, shall so much the more be iudged a naturall inclination in him, though masked with a vaile of dissimulation. Hence it very likely would grow great good liking in the Prince, and the high way unto confidence would be made easie: besides, since needs he must lie open unto some, it is cleere, he will sooner discover himselfe unto one, to be of like affect, and much more if happily the Courtier be able to serve him in that inclination; wherefore we say it is necessary in termes of obedience and of dutifull regard towards the Prince dissembling, to conforme himselfe in some part to the coloured affect and fashion. But to make passage unto confidence, it is more profitable to give apparent signes of a true, or a truly dissembled inclining in himselfe, the which inclining must be like to that which he knowes truly to be naturall in the Prince, unto whose humour in my opinion this is the next way to be conformable.[134]

The courtly dynamic of double or parallel dissimulation described by Ducci in the above passage from the *Arte aulica* draws heavily, as his predecessor Tacitus had done, on the peculiar psychology implicit in the relationship between ruler and ruled under absolutism. The courtier's confidence game, in which secrets are discovered only in order to be concealed again through dissimulation, is thoroughly grounded in an analysis of human conduct *as it can be seen by others,* especially—but not exclusively—at court. As Gracián was later to remark, "Always behave as though others were watching. A man who looks after his actions sees that others see him, or will. . . . Even when he is alone he behaves as though all the world were watching, and knows that all will be revealed. He behaves as though he already had witnesses: those who, when they hear something, will be so later."[135] The art of courtiership consists not only in knowing oneself but in knowing others just as well; intimacy is not reserved solely for one's own mental and emotional experience, but—paradoxically—for that of others as well, whether they wish it nor not. This mutual psychological scrutiny (as well as all resistance to it) occurs in and through the courtly conversation, without which the courtiers would not even exist. The early modern court is therefore not just a locus of cultural production, or a political center of power, but a system of communication. If Ducci's courtier, in the above passage, crosses over the line from dissimulation into active feigning or simulating of "something that is not," this is due to his complete lack of concern for any moral—or aesthetic—justification for the courtier's choice of a mode of comportment. When, in the final chapter, Ducci reveals that throughout the treatise he has been discussing the ways of the courtiers at all Italian courts except the papal court in Rome, which is the one place in which transparency, sincerity, and honesty reign and dissimulation is absent, his contemporary readers must have realized that the author of the *Arte aulica* had followed his own advice on dissimulation in writing down his thoughts on the courtier, thanks to which he obtained the necessary ecclesiastical *nihil obstat* for the publication of this unsettling work.

"The Only Bond"

Eustache de Refuge (1564–1617), who served as a diplomat and counselor to Henry IV (assassinated in Orléans in 1610), published his *Traicté
de la Cour* (Treatise on the court) in 1616.[136] With the exception of the
court of Rome, the Italian courts had by this time lost much of their lus-
ter as a model for the rest of Europe, in which great nation-states had
come to dominate political and economic life: Madrid, Paris, and Vienna were, despite the ups and downs of their respective ruling dynasties, the courts to which all eyes were turned. But the discourse on
courtly dissimulation that had first gathered momentum in Italy continued well into the seventeenth century. Indeed, de Refuge drew very
heavily on Italian sources (among others) in composing his work on the
court: Castiglione, Guazzo, Ducci, and Canonieri were among those
from whom he borrowed, sometimes verbatim and often without acknowledgement. Tacitism was the intellectual fashion of the day, and de
Refuge was greatly indebted to the ancient Roman historian as well as
to the Italian *politici*. The treatise was well received, and was reprinted in
French at least a dozen times by 1661. Nicolas Faret's (1596–1646) even
more successful *L'Honneste-Homme ou, L'Art de Plaire à la Court* (The
respectable man, or the art of pleasing at court, 1630) in turn drew extensively on it.[137] Besides translations into Latin, Italian, and German,
the *Traicté de la Cour* was translated into English more than once in the
seventeenth century, and was even translated back into French from the
English.[138]

In his treatise, which is in large part concerned with the *accortise* and
dexterité of the successful courtier, de Refuge devotes a brief chapter to
dissimulation at court.[139] He shows himself to be, like Ducci, a pragmatist and a Tacitist, observing that "the most mixed, difficult and thorny
of all kinds of conversation is that of the court, into which ordinarily the
only people who throw themselves are those driven by ambition or by
desire to further their own interests."[140] And, like Ducci, de Refuge
openly grants that at court "interest is the only bond" for the courtiers.
Indeed, this admission was scandalous enough to be removed from the
subsequent edition of the treatise.[141] Although one has to accept the
predominance of self-interest in order to manage at court, he acknowledges, nonetheless one should try to avoid, as far as possible, becoming
as corrupt as the other courtiers. De Refuge offers his readers a synthesis of much of the previous courtly and polite discourse on dissimulation, including a virtually verbatim rehashing of Canonieri's *Il Perfetto*

Cortegiano (1609), which was a much more important and influential work for subsequent writers on conduct and the court than is generally recognized today.

After providing a general justification for the practice of reservation, de Refuge notes that "although dissimulation is necessary for all sorts of people, it is far more so for the courtier, in order to manage his ambition."[142] Dissimulation is one of the principal means for furthering the courtier's ambition, in short, but de Refuge has little that is new to add to the discourse. His composite portrait of the "discreet and wise" courtier was to have resonance, nonetheless, for the greatest seventeenth-century text to belong to the discourse on courtly dissimulation: "in short, to effect with few words the demeanor of an able and alert courtier, he must bend his wit to examine in detail the actions of others, as well as his own; he must remain ever vigilant and keep [his thoughts] to himself, so that he may see, understand and judge all things, while nevertheless speaking sparingly and covering his thoughts, desires, and designs with a pleasing and sincere countenance."[143] Discreet, wise, capable both of knowing others and of self-knowledge, vigilant, prudent, taciturn, pleasing to all, and expert in the arts of self-control and dissimulation. Who is this courtier, after all, if not the hero of Balthasar Gracián's *Oráculo manual y arte de prudencia*?

A Book about Nothing and Everything

Gracián came to prominence during the 1640s, when interest in Europe peaked concerning the discourse on dissimulation. He spent his entire life in Spain, most of it as a member of the Jesuit order, producing a steady stream of works in spite of efforts by his superiors to stop him. Gracián was well versed in the interrelated bodies of literature on the civil conversation, the court, reason of state, and Neostoicism, among others. What he wrote traversed this entire cultural field, from Castiglione and Machiavelli to Malvezzi and Bacon, in which the discourse on dissimulation was inscribed. His extraordinary publications were widely read at home and abroad, despite the disapproval of his Jesuit superiors and the precipitous decline of Spanish power in Europe, and were greatly influential for such French *moralistes* as La Rochefoucauld, the Chevalier de Méré, Saint-Evremond, Madame de Sablé, and Jean La Bruyère.[144] As Gracián's renown spread, his works were reprinted in many places—Anvers, Lisbon, Coimbra, Amsterdam, Brussels—in the original Spanish version, and were eventually translated into a number of European languages. *El Héroe* (1637) was the first, appearing in a French version in 1645 by Nicolas Gervaise meant to show his countrymen how the Spanish "enemy" thought. The first translation in Europe of Gracián's popular *Oráculo manual y arte de prudencia* (The oracle: A manual of the art of prudence, 1647)—the work with which I am concerned here—was, however, only published in 1670: it appeared in Italy as *L'uomo di corte* (The man of the court). In 1684 Amelot de la Houssaie published his French translation of the *Oráculo manual,* entitled *L'Homme de Cour* (The man of the court), and before the end of the century it was reprinted a dozen times and translated in turn into a number of other European languages.[145]

The *Oráculo manual* was written as a guidebook for surviving and succeeding in contemporary seventeenth-century high society. It was meant to be consulted like a pocket breviary, a "book for constant use" (as Arthur Schopenhauer later called it) in courtly or civil conversation. Gracián frequented the Spanish court only briefly, but he counted among his acquaintances some wealthy and influential members of the nobility, and knew the social world for whom the court was the supreme expression of civility. However, the first translators of his treatise agreed that the work belongs with the literature of the court and courtiers, as can be seen from the titles given to the Italian and French versions, and this seems to have been the way that most early modern readers understood the text. The *Oráculo manual* offers a collection of aphorisms on the contemporary art of prudence—three hundred in all, plus glosses— some of which are original and some of which are adopted from Gracián's prior publications, including *El Héroe* (The hero), *Agudeza y arte de ingenio* (Wit and the mind's art, 1642/1646) and *El Discreto* (The discreet man, 1646). The aphorisms are not arranged or ordered according to a scheme, defying any attempt to reconstruct the author's system of thought.[146] The portrait of the prudent and refined individual that emerges from reading this anthology is as contradictory, and as difficult to bring into sharp focus, as is the figure of its author—at once sharp-eyed lynx and saint, inky cuttlefish and brightly burning flame, crafty dissimulator and moral paragon, scheming parvenu and noble hero. It seems to be composed like a puzzle, made of fragments, discrete cases, aporias, oracular utterances, enigmas, paradoxes, impenetrable prose passages, and dazzling conceits, as if Gracián meant to show his readers that no single text, and no single court or courtier, could capture the totality of contemporary social experience. And as if he meant to display to his readers the kind of language—terse, laconic, elliptical—they would need to survive and, perhaps, to prosper.

These aphorisms are directed at anyone aspiring to the condition of "the disenchanted individual" *(el varón desengañado)*, who understands that in contemporary life "things pass for what they seem, not for what they are."[147] Such a worldly soul would necessarily be a "wise Christian and a courtly philosopher" *(cristiano sabio, cortesano filosofo)* without showing it.[148] Obviously, in Gracián's eyes, the early modern courtier has particular need of such disenchantment, for the courtier must inhabit the house of mirrors that is the Old Regime court. The author does not, however, explicitly treat the theme of the court in the *Oráculo manual,* any more than he limits the art of prudence to the courtier alone. His work encompasses many different perspectives, from that of the prince to that of the courtier to that of the gentleman, and many cultural trends: it is truly about everything, and—in its emphasis on dissimulation—nothing. Although undoubtedly encyclopedic in his knowledge of the literature on conduct and on the court, Gracián mentions no other works of this genre in the *Oráculo manual* (only aphorism 123, on the avoidance of affectation, seems to offer a clear allusion to Castiglione). In spite of what his seventeenth-century translators may have thought, the work is addressed to anyone wishing to become "the consummate person—wise in speech, prudent in deeds," who could gain entrance into "the singular society of the discreet" and achieve worldly success in a highly imperfect world.[149]

In some of the aphorisms of the *Oráculo manual* Gracián does directly address courtiers, whom he encourages during their careers to "frequent the homes of courtly heroes: theaters of heroism, not palaces of vanity. . . . Those who accompany them form a courtly academy of gallant discretion and wisdom."[150] At another point, however, he suggests that princes be treated with great care, presumably by those ministers and courtiers near to them: "most people do not mind being surpassed in good fortune, character, or temperament, but no one, especially not a sovereign, likes to be surpassed in intelligence. For this is the king of attributes, and any crime against it is lèse-majesté. Sovereigns want to be so in what is most important. Princes like to be helped, but not surpassed."[151] At first glance, these two aphorisms seem to contradict one another, but that would be to misunderstand Gracián's point. If the true courtier is discrete and helpful, it is thanks to the knowledge of how to efface all traces of ambition in front of the prince. Like Tasso's ideal courtier some sixty-odd years earlier, Gracián's is

supposed to dissimulate the use of wit (*ingenio*) at court, and accommodate to its rigid social hierarchy.[152] The court expresses the highest level
of the theater of human life, and the clever courtier is a protagonist of
that scene, but only by appearing not to be so. If such a deferential and
self-effacing attitude has its rewards, it is due in large part to the extraordinary powers accorded by Gracián to dissimulation.

According to this pocket breviary, dissimulation is a key to the art of
prudence; indeed, perhaps no other component is as crucial to its successful deployment in the courtly conversation. Metaphysical, theologi-
cal, and even moral issues regarding this practice are consequently cast
aside in the *Oráculo manual,* in favor of a pragmatic anthropology. As
discussed previously, Gracián thought that "the most practical sort of
knowledge lies in dissimulation."[153] Like Accetto, he was largely indifferent to the technical and rhetorical issues involved in the use of reservation and secrecy. Like Accetto, moreover, he drew on both Neostoicism and ascetic Christian traditions in urging his readers to exercise
over their impulses, desires, and thoughts an ever-vigilant self-control,
the foundation of all successful dissimulation. As Gracián remarks in
one particularly telling passage in the work: "cunning people set these
traps for prudence in order to sound matters out and fathom the minds
of their opponents. Prying out secrets, they get to the bottom of the
greatest talents. Your counter-strategy? Control yourself, especially your
sudden impulses."[154] The passions and drives of heart and mind can and
must be reined in by reflection and reason, two of the prime qualities of
the prudent person: "whenever possible, let reflection foresee the sudden movement of the passions; the prudent will do so easily."[155]

One has to know not only how to control passions raging on the
stormy sea of the heart, however, but also how to govern the expression
of those passions. Reservation and taciturnity are the golden rule for the
courtier seeking to succeed in the chess game of the courtly *continuum,*
for "reserve in all things has always been a great rule for living and for
winning, especially in the loftiest positions."[156] The court is a dangerously fickle place, Gracián notes, and to be caught outside of the general
consensus there could prove catastrophic: it is best to conform outwardly to the opinions of the rest of the courtiers. "Rowing against the
current makes it impossible to discover deceit and is extremely dangerous. Only Socrates could attempt it."[157] But Gracián does not have mar-
tyrdom in mind for his *varón desengañado.* His target audience for the
Oráculo manual consists primarily of worldly men and women intent on
furthering their careers at court and elsewhere. He therefore explains to

them that only the able use of silence and reticence, or of cunning in those situations in which speech is unavoidable, will allow the prudent person to survive the dangers of the court. One has to rein oneself in, and reserve oneself, but without seeming to do so: "[feelings] live in silent retirement and if sometimes they choose to show themselves, it is only to a few wise people."[158]

Following in the footsteps of many others, Gracián sees dissimulation as crucial to the courtier's advancement. It must, however, be kept secret from others and hence never put on display at court. Over and beyond the avoidance of affectation, which is necessary in order not to arouse suspicions among others, Gracián urges his readership to remember that dissimulation itself has to be dissimulated if it is to be effective: "the best artifice is to conceal it, for artifice is taken as deceit."[159] Any whiff of dissimulation would make one's designs that much more difficult to realize, as happened to Tiberius. But seventeenth-century absolutism depended upon a deep-seated culture of suspicion, leading princes and courtiers alike to doubt the sincerity of all participants in the courtly conversation. Gracián warns in the *Oráculo manual* that, in this situation of corrosive suspicion and mutual surveillance, even the most reserved and withdrawn courtier constantly risks seeing the most secret designs penetrated by the gaze of others: "reserve is threatened by others who feel you out, who contradict you to get a handle on you, or insinuate things that can make even the shrewdest give himself away. Neither say what you will do nor do what you have said."[160] Here as elsewhere in Gracián's writings, the border between simulation and dissimulation—tenuous as it is and difficult to sustain even under the best of circumstances—seems to dissolve at times, opening the door to charges of hypocrisy. Not that these would have deterred in the least the Spanish Jesuit from making dissimulation the still point of the endlessly turning social world.[161] Nevertheless, the *Oráculo manual* expresses genuine concern about the relentless pressure of existence in the treacherous courtly *continuum,* in which traps are likely to be laid for the unwary courtier in order to sound out the secret depths of the heart. Gracián's theory of dissimulation is rooted in a disenchanted vision of worldly and courtly existence as a perpetual rising and falling of reputations, and an endless shifting of opinions, made and unmade by the guardians and thieves of one's innermost secrets. As he warns his readers, "don't belong so much to others that you stop belonging to yourself."[162]

What distinguishes Gracián from other Tacitists who discoursed on courtly dissimulation is his profound awareness of the mobility and instability of not only the world of the court but of social interaction *tout court*. It is possible, with the help of fortune and the aid of prudence, to climb the ladder of courtly or worldly success; or, without them, to tumble off the top rungs (as happened to Count-Duke Olivares).[163] In any case, however, the court offers to his readers the most cogent model of the aspirations and anxieties of the age. Gracián's great renown in the seventeenth century was due not only to his remarkable accomplishments as a prose stylist but to his critical acumen concerning the transnational social and cultural configuration of absolutism. Beyond the immutable law of dissimulation, however, his portrait of the Old Regime is hard to fix in place. The complexity of its inner workings, and capacity for the rapid change of reputations and opinions, were such that this cosmopolitan society and culture could only be represented obliquely in his treatise. In the *Oráculo manual,* which is without reference to contemporary princes or courts, there are in fact virtually no proper names, place names, or philosophical authorities, just the seemingly disembodied utterances of an urbane, worldly-wise oracle. The text seems meant to appear as a neutral, atemporal, transcendental set of concepts and precepts belonging to everywhere and nowhere. Gracián's little book was made to travel across borders and across time, and it did just that.

For all of this, in it Gracián said nothing really very original about dissimulation at court or elsewhere; but he said what he had to say in a new and different way. The *Oráculo manual* marks a moment of rupture in the discourse on courtly dissimulation, for henceforth the treatise form is no longer preeminent, and the aphorism emerges as the preferred mode of writing about the court.[164] It is no coincidence that publishers' interest in *Il Libro del Cortegiano* began to decline sharply in these same years of the Seicento, although Castiglione's masterpiece remained a *sine qua non* more than a century after its initial publication.[165] Certainly later writers on the court brought little that was substantially new to the discourse on dissimulation and rarely tried to formulate a different set of rules for the courtier's behavior than those laid out in the works examined in this chapter. Like those marvelous inventions of the age, the telescope and microscope, Gracián's is a work that captures the infinitely great and the infinitely small, from the splendors of the court surrounding the absolute sovereign to the minutiae of ordinary everyday affairs. His aphorisms, dense and compact and enigmatic, are framed by silence, and seem to threaten either an overflowing surplus of meaning or its complete absence. In the *Oráculo manual* the paradox of courtly dissimulation—at once present everywhere and visible nowhere—is pushed to its outer limits, and the chain of texts on the court society that began early in the Cinquecento is brought to a fitting conclusion. In keeping with this paradoxical frame of mind, we might conclude that Castiglione died not once, but twice, in Spain.[166]

CHAPTER 4

The Government of Designs

Dissimulation and Reason of State

Las sombras de la razón de estado suelen ser mayores que el cuerpo,
y tal vez se deja éste y se abrazan aquéllas.
The shadows of reason of state tend to be larger than its body,
and sometimes one leaves the latter and embraces the former.

Diego de Saavedra Fajardo,
Idea de un Príncipe político cristiano

Donc le premier indice de ceste dissimulation, ie le prens de la
nature & condition des Roys, qui sont tous grans & insignes
dissimulateurs.
I find the first sign of this dissimulation in the nature and
condition of kings, who are all great and notorious
dissimulators.

Louis D'Orléans,
Le Banquet et après dinée du Conte d'Arete

Reason and the State

This chapter traces the transformation occurring over the course of the
sixteenth and seventeenth centuries in the discourse on dissimulation as
it concerns the doctrine of "reason of state." For the sovereigns of the
Quattrocento and their humanist counselors, there had seemed to be an
obvious (if often unobserved) bond between ethics and politics.[1] The
political theorists of absolutism, however, made the maintenance of the
state in a world of radical mutability the basis of the doctrine of *ragion di
stato, raison d'état, ratio status, ius dominationis,* or reason of state. They
were keenly aware of the social and political risks and consequences of

the disclosure of information (not to mention the potential uses of dis-information), as well as the need for its control by princes.[2] Reason-of-state theorists therefore tended to see "political" dissimulation as a legit-imate technique of information-control for princes to practice in the interest of state security and dynastic stability. The Italian Tacitist Carlo Pasquale wrote in 1581, as religious strife tore at the fabric of the great European states, that "not only Tiberius, but many other princes count dissimulation among those special virtues which it is necessary for them to have; and so they care for none of the other virtues as much."[3] The preservation of the state required extraordinary emphasis on secrecy—*secretum, la segretezza, le secret*—in the conduct of the prince's affairs. The success of Venice in thwarting its enemies on the European main-land, for instance, was often attributed by contemporaries to its secret services and organs of government that operated in secrecy.[4] Hence the importance of dissimulation for reason-of-state doctrine, which was destined to clash with Aristotelian political theory and the Augustinian ethics of transparency.

No doubt dissimulation was employed by the political elites of Eu-rope from antiquity onward. However, to constitute dissimulation as an object of knowledge—to put it into discourse—meant to alter its status irrevocably. In early modernity it was no longer an invisible and tacit practice of powerful political figures and heads of state that might pass unobserved by their rivals or subjects. Rather, dissimulation was open to revision, negotiation, and contestation within the field of reason-of-state doctrine, and thus became part of the public arena. Before turning to this doctrine, however, I would like to issue a few caveats. First, the origins of the doctrine of reason of state in the sixteenth century have been studied extensively, and there is no need to rehearse them here.[5] (The Florentine historian and political thinker Francesco Guicciardini was probably the first to introduce the term "reason of states" into early modern discourse: *secondo la ragione ed uso degli stati*).[6] Second, although the reciprocal links between Skepticism, Neostoicism, Tacitism, and doctrines of reason of state are of compelling interest, they can only be mentioned here in passing.[7] As Richard Tuck has pointed out, the new humanism of this era, in combining these different intellectual currents, contended that "the only secure basis for conduct was an acceptance of the force of *self-interest* and *self-preservation*."[8] This same rationale was the foundation of the early modern discourse on political dissimulation. Third, the body of political literature on the prince and reason-of-state doctrine is immense, and cannot be fully treated here. In what follows I

will therefore look only at some of the most influential and representative works of this tradition that concern themselves with the problem of
dissimulation.

Dissimulation in the treatises on reason of state is usually described
in what we by now know to be standard fashion—as a rhetorical technique of omission by reservation or reticence, a psychological art of
knowing others' minds as well as one's own, or an ascetic practice of
contraction and withdrawal. But the age-old accusations of hypocrisy
and deception, reaching back to Augustine, were never far from the
minds of readers of these works. This explains in part the vehemence
with which many people, although not all, reacted to the idea of dissimulation. Even today, after all, we still expect those who are speaking with
us to be "present" to us in the conversation, and not actively trying to
make themselves absent from it. Although it might be found in private
letters or diplomatic reports, for instance, dissimulation was understood
by the men and women of the age to operate above all in conversation.
The Old Regime period saw the flourishing of rhetorical genres intended to sway public opinion, but political dissimulation continued to
be envisaged chiefly on the level of a dialogical exchange between relatively few individuals (a king and his counselors or courtiers, for instance). It thus formed a threat to the notion of a common language of
the state, so prized in earlier periods of European history; many found it
troubling to think that some members of the absolutist state apparatus
might employ secret communicative protocols that could not be understood by other members of the polity. The discourse on dissimulation
thus participates in the growing specialization of political discourse in
early modernity, with secrecy and dissembling serving as interchangeable code words for it.

In the later sixteenth and seventeenth centuries, much of Europe was
racked by bloody religious strife, civil war, and conflict over economic
interests. Italy, on the other hand, grew increasingly stable after the
signing of the Treaty of Cateau-Cambrésis in 1559, which put an end to
the Italian Wars and consolidated Spanish and papal dominance on the
peninsula. Whereas the city-states of Italy had been founded upon republican principles of political legitimacy, however, the new absolutist
states with their vastly expanded role followed a logic of self-interest
sustained by force. Florence, of course, offered a perfect example of this
radical shift, passing from the Republic to the dynasty of the Medici
Grand-Dukes. Nevertheless, the system of absolutist governments that
gradually emerged in these years, ranging from the Spanish empire to

the kingdom of France to the northern and central Italian courts (such as the Farnese court in Parma and Piacenza, Savoy, Tuscany, and the Papal States), helped to lay the cornerstone of the modern state structure in Europe. The early modern centralized sovereign state came to possess growing powers to tax, to exercise a monopoly on the use of coercive violence through the army and the police, and to expand its territories in Europe and overseas; but perhaps equally important was its intensified social disciplining of an often-tumultuous populace.[9] In an era of invasions, religious conflicts, and popular revolts, many thought that the state could and should use every available means to control both foreign and domestic turmoil. At the center of all this was the court, and at the very center of the court—without whom, indeed, it would not exist in the first place—stood the prince.

As Norbert Elias and others have observed, the emergence of absolutism depended in part upon the development of new practices of control and self-control by the elites, of which dissimulation was one of the most controversial.[10] The French essayist Louis D'Orléans, in his 1594 attack on the politics of Henry IV, remarked: "how true is the maxim that kings greatly dissimulate. It is even truer that they ably use this tool of dissimulation, whenever states must be maintained or conquered or ravished."[11] Echoing the language of recent European political theory, D'Orléans here explicitly links statecraft and the practice of dissimulation.[12] The early modern prince, who used his power in order to "maintain or conquer or ravish" states, had to know how to deploy the "tool" of reservation. Thoughts and passions were to be disguised by the prince for the purpose of dominating those of others. It cannot be a coincidence that the genre of advice-to-the-prince books grew as the absolutist states flourished: for the sovereign had the most visible role to play—as well as the most invisible one, many suspected—in the establishment and expansion of the state's authority. For all such rulers, the doctrine of reason of state placed a premium not only on secrecy and political prudence but on the disciplining of the body politic: the aim was to exercise control not only over the behavior of subjects but over the expression of their political passions and ideas.[13] The following pages offer an overview of the development of this discourse on "political" dissimulation, starting with Machiavelli and concluding with his French apologists, as an essential component of the doctrine of absolutist statecraft.

Lion and Fox

As the sixteenth century progressed, interest shifted away from the art of politics as the humanists had understood it, and a new kind of reason—"the reason of states," as Guicciardini called it—was required to justify this event.[14] The doctrine of reason of state sought to legitimate and sustain absolutism, as well as to endow it with its own logic. Certainly Niccolò Machiavelli's *Il Principe* (The prince) was among the most important sources of the new philosophy of the state, serving as the starting-point for the discourse on political dissimulation. Granted, the issues raised by Machiavelli (1469–1527) in his treatise were rarely radically new, and remained rooted in a critique of earlier Florentine humanist thinking about the state. His analysis of "the art of the state, the art of preserving and reinforcing the state *of* the prince," moreover, was not intended to replace politics and civil philosophy as he understood them.[15] *Il Principe* describes the techniques and skill-sets necessary for a prince to gain and remain in power amid the turbulence of early sixteenth-century Italy, but depicts absolutism as neither necessary nor irreversible in the development of European history. Moreover, its author seems to care little for such important elements of the modern state as a professional standing army or the use of fiscal authority.[16] In this sense Machiavelli was, despite his creative insights into power, at a considerable distance from the theorists of reason of state who appeared later in the century and drew on his pathbreaking work.

One of the most famous and controversial passages for early modern readers of *Il Principe,* a text that first appeared in print in the winter of 1531–32 but which had been composed and circulated between 1513 and 1516 (although this date is still the subject of debate), is to be found in chapter 18, where Machiavelli deals with simulation and dissimulation as a part of his advice to the prince. This passage was taken by the other contemporary European societies—especially those of France and England—as proof that dissimulation was a particularly Italian art, especially but not exclusively in matters of state, as well as central to the doctrines of "Machiavellianism," which often had little to do with the text of *Il Principe*. The notoriety of Machiavelli in Elizabethan and Jacobean England has long been well documented.[17] The legends about him originated in France, however, at the time of Catherine de' Medici, and seem to have spread from there. The Frenchman Mathieu Coignet (1514/15–1586) was far from alone in complaining: "And the saide *Italians* unable to excuse the great faultes, cruelties, treacheries, coward-

nesse, treasons, and dissimulations of their nation, goe about to dis-
guyse these villanies with a name of *Italian Prudence*."[18] Although the
ostensible target of his critique were the so-called *politiques* of his own
country, Coignet was right to observe that, as seen in the previous chapters, "prudence" and "dissimulation" were often interchangeable terms
for Italian political thinkers. It allowed them to avoid at times the negative connotations belonging to the latter term without abandoning the
concepts that it designated.[19]

For Machiavelli, however, who might have been surprised (but
pleased) to learn that his little book had become the subject of a truly international controversy, dissimulation was just one technique in the arsenal of the prince's weapons for the defense of his state. The passage
given below, however, scandalized many of his early modern readers,
and left subsequent political theorists with these vivid similes of the lion
and the fox:

Know then that there are two ways to fight, with laws and with force. The first
is suited to humanity, the second to beasts: but because many times the former
is not enough, one must make recourse to the latter. . . . Since the prince well
needs to know how to be a beast, he must take the examples of the fox and the
lion: because the lion cannot defend itself from snares, and the fox cannot defend itself from wolves. One must be a fox and know the snares, *and* a lion to
frighten off the wolves. . . . He who best knows how to play the fox is best off,
but this must be kept well hidden, and the prince must be a great simulator and
dissimulator: and people are so simple, and so concerned with present necessi-
ties, that whoever wishes to deceive will always find those who will let themselves be deceived.[20]

Machiavelli here indicates that the prince must be a "great simulator and
dissimulator" in order to hide his skills as a "fox" from his own subjects.
He is not to do so out of amoral opportunism, however, but in order to
maintain the loyalty of subjects and thus to preserve the state. Although
it is "praiseworthy" for a prince to keep faith with his subjects and
neighboring states, the lessons of recent Italian history are clear, Machiavelli argues. Those who would make use of their cunning (*astuzia*), acting like "foxes" as well as "lions," will most likely defeat those who could
not or would not do so. However, although the use of force does not
need to be disguised, the use of cunning has to be kept hidden from
view, because it would weaken the prince's reputation among his subjects if he were to be perceived to act without regard for the moral standards of his society and religion. The secret of power is to know how to

keep secrets.[21] In other words, as one can infer from *Il Principe,* princes need to maintain their reputations not only in order to seek glory, which is the chief purpose of their rule, but in order to keep the support of their subjects, without whom no prince could survive for long. There is, according to Machiavelli, no possibility of a reign of pure domination and will to power supported by terror alone. The prince's prudent but secretive management of his own image will therefore be the source of much of his political strength and legitimacy.

In the same chapter 18, Machiavelli fires a salvo at organized religion that, once again, was destined to cause an outcry among his readers: "know this: a prince—especially a new prince—cannot observe all those things for which men are reputed to be good, for he is often obliged, in order to maintain the state, to act against faith, against charity, against humanity, against religion."[22] Here Machiavelli makes his argument even more forcefully. To sustain the level of popular support necessary *per mantenere lo stato,* the prince may justifiably resort to violence against his enemies but has to appear to possess the necessary qualities of piety and charity in regard to his own subjects. (Machiavelli had Pope Alexander VI in mind as a recent Italian example.) Simulation and dissimulation are therefore instruments that the prince employs chiefly in managing the internal affairs of state. The ideal early modern prince has to create for himself the image of a sovereign who adheres to the standard moral and ethical principles of his particular society. In this way he displays himself as an exemplary individual, one to whom his subjects would concede the position of head of state out of respect as well as fear. Too great a variance from those moral and ethical norms would weaken the prince dangerously, Machiavelli warns, if it were to become visible to too many others, and this is where the arts of secrecy and reservation come into play. The prince who wants to succeed as a fox has to become expert, in short, in the art of "impression management," incorporating dissimulation into his every word and deed.[23]

Dissimulation is given only this brief mention in *Il Principe,* and Machiavelli proposes neither a definition of his terms nor a hard-and-fast distinction between simulation and dissimulation. No doubt the public nature of this carefully manufactured princely exemplarity could also be considered a case of outright simulation. Toward the end of chapter 18, Machiavelli notes that "human beings in general judge more with their eyes than with their hands, because everyone may see, but few may feel; everyone may see that which you seem to be, but few may grasp that which you are; and those few do not desire to oppose the general opinion, supported by the majesty of the government."[24] Although this psychological insight is equally applicable to simulation and dissimulation as tools of the early modern prince, Machiavelli's reference to the faculty of vision is a particularly revealing one. To succeed in the princely art of impression management means, first of all, to try to see oneself as one is seen by others. The prince has to understand that the masks of simulation and dissimulation—whether in the form of active feigning or withdrawal into silence—serve only to manipulate the mass of his subjects. Some members of the political class, such as courtiers and counselors, may manage to see through even the most skillful subterfuge and to penetrate the most secret space of thought. Therefore the prince's projected public representation has to be chosen for maximum effect on the largest possible number of subjects (among those who mattered): the state is a theater of sovereign power and the prince its main player.[25] The prince's public image has to be maintained at all costs, because only the power of "general opinion," backed by the "majesty of the government," keeps the prince from being unmasked by the "few." The art of governing, in other words, consists not only in masking or silencing one's own thoughts and passions but also in divining those of others, in order to deflect and control them. Only in this manner can the prince, in order to preserve the illusions of others, know precisely in what way to simulate or dissimulate.[26]

The legitimation of simulation and dissimulation in *Il Principe* signals a key moment in the development of the early modern theory of the state. In defining the behavior of the true prince, private moral conscience does not appear as an issue for Machiavelli: traditional virtue dissolves into a dizzying array of possible poses and manufactured identities. If, on the one hand, the prince has to exercise self-control in speech and gesture, such artifice is acceptable insofar as it furthers the entirely legitimate aim of preserving his own power and, by extension, that of the state (since Machiavelli notoriously does not distinguish clearly between the two).[27] Thus "by emphasizing the need for a powerful state, Machiavelli focused the attention of political thinkers on power and the means to attain it."[28] Yet, on the other hand, without the imposition of any further moral or ethical limitations on the prince's behavior, these same arts of self-management could all too easily serve the ends of fraud and hypocrisy, as the chorus of Machiavelli's detractors was to insist over the centuries to come. In *Il Principe* he does, however, draw an implicit line between the use of simulation and dissimulation by the prince, on the one hand, and its use by any other member of the body politic, on the other. Only the prince, by virtue of the need to maintain the state for the benefit of all citizens, has the legitimate right to employ such techniques, and only within the "public" domain of affairs of state.[29] This is, in fact, the guarantee of their efficacy. This distinction between the prince and all other members of the polity in the matter of dissimulation will be formally instituted and articulated by later generations of reason-of-state theorists, and will endure well into the seventeenth century. In *Il Principe* Machiavelli anticipates only partially, then, the coming transformation of the theory of the state and of the sovereign. For although early modern princes would, for many years to come, continue to endorse and express many traditional Christian attributes, they would have to come to terms with the obligation to rule, sometimes with the aid of secrecy and silence, in the name of an increasingly impersonal state power.

Incommunicable States

Francesco Guicciardini (1483–1540) wrote, re-wrote, and revised a collection of maxims entitled simply *Ricordi* during the years 1512–1530. He reworked the text for the final time in the years 1528–1530, immediately following the sack of Rome and assorted other military and political disasters of that period. Although this work was originally intended to provide practical advice for the members of his family and a circle of close friends, it began to circulate in Rome in manuscript form sometime in the early 1560s, was subsequently published a number of times over the course of the late sixteenth century, starting with Jacopo Corbinelli's Paris edition of 1576, and saw translations into several other European languages. Guicciardini was a friend and admirer of Machiavelli, who declared in the spring of 1527 in a famous letter to Francesco Vettori: "I love Francesco Guicciardini; I love my country (more than my soul, or: more than Christ)."[30] Guicciardini was Machiavelli's peer as a political thinker, as well as a distinguished historian of Florence, an able politician and administrator who served as one of Pope Clement VII's chief counselors, and a scathingly critical observer of the struggle for political supremacy in contemporary Italy. His distinctly practical approach to questions of state power, violence, and self-interest differed from Machiavelli's, however, and made him an authority for subsequent generations of reason-of-state political theorists across Europe.[31] His brief book was not in the advice-to-the-prince genre, although it offered many observations about sovereigns, ministers, and others who practiced contemporary statecraft. Rather, it was a work intended for a wealthy and important Florentine clan whose members were inevitably involved in every level of political life, although in it Guicciardini also addressed a variety of other issues, from recent Italian history to economics, religion, and moral philosophy.

In his *Ricordi* Guicciardini, like Machiavelli, does not attempt to make a firm distinction between simulation and dissimulation. Nor is this surprising, for the work was not meant to be a systematic or methodical one, although Guicciardini obviously put a good deal of care into the arrangement of the *ricordi* (the term may be loosely translated as "maxims" or "counsels") over the course of various redactions. Like the Florentine secretary, he understood well that the prince had to keep his intentions secret from others much of the time, and that there were various ways to accomplish this. The critic Alberto Asor Rosa has claimed that if Guicciardini was the first Italian to give such great consideration to the theme of dissimulation, it was due to the political turmoil of those years, in which feigning had become an instrument of survival.[32] However, such a claim is based on the assumption of a direct mimetic relationship between text and historical event; it overlooks the fact that such practices had likely long been familiar to the political elites but had not been articulated as such. What is instead distinctive is the emergence of a full-fledged discourse on political dissimulation, which opens up a discursive space of representation of this particular practice. Moreover, Asor Rosa's claim that the *Ricordi* constructs a "system of defense" for those trying to survive in the difficult conditions of post–1527 Italy ignores Guicciardini's repeated praise of simulation, which constitutes not a defensive maneuver but an expression of "Machiavellian" will to power.[33]

In his *ricordo* 199, for example, Guicciardini remarks:

Always, when you wish to simulate or dissimulate an intention of yours to other people, do your best to prove to them with the most powerful and efficacious arguments you can find that you intend to do just the opposite. For when men believe you to be convinced that this is what reason requires, they are easily persuaded that your actions must follow the dictates of reason.[34]

Here Guicciardini describes simulation (mixing dissimulation together with it) in terms of interest and utility—two of his privileged conceptual categories—but avoids any suggestion of a stoical defensive posture. Instead, simulation is to use "powerful and efficacious arguments" that are the opposite of one's own secret intentions, in order to produce a practical result in the world of human affairs. Although this might prove effective in the political arena, it is difficult to see how such use of language could constitute in moral terms anything other than falsehood. In fact, in *ricordo* 37 Guicciardini uses similar language to urge his readers to employ any means whatsoever in order to keep others from discovering that which had to be kept secret: "always deny what you do not wish to be known, and affirm what you wish to be believed."[35] In his view, morally rigorous language is not appropriate in matters of secrecy; interest and utility always must take precedence if one is to have any hope of attaining one's political goals.

In *ricordo* 104, Guicciardini adds to his case for using simulation when truly necessary. For it would be especially efficacious, he notes approvingly with the sort of apparent moral laxity that outraged so many nineteenth-century readers of this work, when used by someone with a reputation for sincerity:

A quality greatly appreciated in men, and which all appreciate, is a free and loyal and, as we say in Florence, straightforward nature. On the other hand, simulation is condemned and hated yet it is much more profitable, and frankness is helpful to others rather than to oneself. But because it is undeniably a fine quality I would praise the man who in his daily life lives freely and openly and uses simulation only rarely and for some very important reason. Thus you will acquire the reputation of being free and frank and will enjoy the popularity of those so regarded; yet in matters of the greatest importance you will profit most by simulation, the more so since having the reputation of not being a simulator, your duplicity will the more easily be believed.[36]

Displaying considerable insight into human nature, Guicciardini points out that the innate desire to believe in others' sincerity makes the mind extremely vulnerable to manipulation and exploitation through simulation, so that it is almost child's play to deploy it from time to time "for some very important reason" on an unsuspecting public. Even if this particular tactic were to fail, however, it is still possible for the simulator to sway other people's minds. In fact, one of the greatest advantages of simulation is found in the sheer inability of others to distinguish the truth from a lie. As Guicciardini remarks in *ricordo* 105: "although a man may have a reputation for simulation and deceit, yet one sees that his lies are sometimes believed. It seems strange yet it is very true."[37] Machiavelli feared for the prince who was exposed as a liar, for he risked loss of reputation and, together with it, power. Guicciardini instead, with

considerable psychological acumen, doubts whether most are capable—
without access to privileged conduits of information—of consistently
resisting the power of the lie.

Another set of *ricordi,* however, deal with themes belonging more
properly to the discourse on dissimulation. It is here that Guicciardini
goes well beyond Machiavelli in representing the practice of covering
over one's thoughts and curbing one's tongue. Once again, unlike *Il
Principe,* the focus is not strictly political. In these maxims he addresses
not only princes and their ministers, but those who need to gain an advantage over others in their everyday affairs. First and foremost, control
of the passions and their expression is crucial to success in one's affairs.
Guicciardini notes in *ricordo* 133 that one should always dissimulate
anger or resentment, in order to gain an eventual advantage over those
provoking these emotions:

> Although few are capable of doing this, it is greatly prudent to know how to dis-
> simulate one's displeasure with others, if it can be done without harm or shame,
> for it often happens that in the future you have occasion to use those very peo-
> ple, which is hard to manage if they already know that you are dissatisfied with
> them.[38]

Anger as a hazard to the prince was to become a great theme of subsequent reason-of-state literature, and would be further extended and developed by later writers in the field. The seemingly Neostoic overtones
of this passage on controlling the passions, however, are turned aside by
Guicciardini, who focuses instead on the means of acquiring utility and
furthering one's own interest through self-control. Dissimulation is, for
him, an instance in which power is exercised through self-management,
and for possible political or personal gain, rather than for the sake of a
philosophical or moral position.

In *ricordo* 184, Guicciardini argues that reservation and circumspection are key elements of this sort of prudence, which can do much to
contrast the fickle winds of fortune. Everyone should represent as little
as possible of their thoughts and plans to others:

> I say that it is prudent to speak of one's own affairs only when absolutely neces-
> sary, and when speaking of them only to give such account of them as is needed
> to one's present conversation or purpose, always keeping to oneself everything
> possible. To do otherwise is more pleasant, but to do this is more useful.[39]

Guicciardini thus urges his readers to monitor carefully what they say,
and to keep secrets well hidden from others ("always keeping to oneself

everything possible"), for the sake of utility. No one can deliberately interfere in another's affairs if nothing is known about them. By no means an ascetic, Guicciardini sees no pleasure to be had in doing so, but he does see the benefit that incommunicability offers the dissimulator. Information about one's intentions, once set into circulation, could do harm to one in unforeseeable ways; therefore rational foresight demands reservation and circumspection whenever it is "absolutely necessary" to discuss one's affairs with others, and tight-lipped silence the rest of the time. Here is a defensive gesture of the very same sort that would distinguish so many subsequent descriptions of dissimulatory practices in politics and statecraft.

Once shared, secrets—and the power that derives from them—are surely lost forever, Guicciardini frets. The impulse to speak, which can reveal whatever one knows or desires, is so strong in humans that it tends to overcome any resistance from the will or from culturally imposed restraints. Not even the bonds of friendship, family or political loyalty, or innate good judgment and common sense, can be expected to protect a secret, once it has been given out. When it comes to the affairs of this world, trust is, needless to say, simply out of the question: "do not tell anyone what you do not want known, because men gossip for various reasons . . . and if you have needlessly told your secret to another you must not be at all surprised if he, who is less concerned than you are to keep it secret, does the same."[40] One can only rely on oneself to keep a secret; to yield it *sanza bisogno* to someone else would be an act of folly, displaying a fatally flawed grasp of human behavior. Guicciardini's readers are therefore asked implicitly to abandon any residual humanist notion of republican civic dialogue, and to look to themselves alone to close any and all "windows" into their intimate inner world of intentions and designs.

As befit the nature of his heteroclite text, Guicciardini also offers some direct advice to heads of state about dissimulation. In keeping with one of the themes of the *Ricordi*, he encourages princes and ministers, following the logic of the reason of state, to be particularly vigilant in exercising self-control and regulating self-expression. Indeed, in *ricordo* 88 he singles them out as persons who have no choice but to participate in the political culture of secrecy, providing his readers with a peerless—for its brevity and cogency—portrait of the function and end of political dissimulation:

A prince or anyone else involved in affairs of great moment must not only keep secret things that are better hidden, but also accustom himself and his ministers to keep silent even over very small and apparently unimportant matters, other than those which it is an advantage to make known. When neither those near you nor your subjects know your affairs, men will always be in suspense and as it were amazed, and your every smallest movement and action are noticed.[41]

This is the key text of the *Ricordi* for the discourse on political dissimulation. The sovereign and his ministers not only have to be educated to silence but to the micromanagement of every single gesture or action. Like the preference in civil conversation for the trivial, political dissimulation requires complete attention not only to great affairs of state but also to "very small and apparently unimportant matters." The trivial is a form of power, in short, because it can supply the means with which to cover over, or uncover, the secrets of statecraft. Thus the keen self-vigilance of the dissimulator is vital to the success of any project for political dissembling, for those "very small and apparently unimportant matters" may be very difficult to discern and yet dangerous to overlook. Moreover, this attention to the trivial increases the power of the prince, whose mastery over his own words and gestures must be manifest to all: subjects and rivals alike are forced to sift through the minutiae of "every smallest movement and action" in the hope of glimpsing his true intentions, hidden somewhere behind an impenetrable veil of dissimulation.

By the same token, the tyrant tries to penetrate the minds of his subjects in order to know their secrets and thus to strengthen his hold on power. In *ricordo* 103 Guicciardini warns his readers:

The tyrant does everything possible to uncover the secret of your heart. He will be affectionate, will hold long conversations, and have you observed by others whom he has ordered to become intimate with you. It is difficult to take precautions against all these snares, and hence if you do not want him to know your thoughts, think very carefully and avoid with the utmost diligence everything that may expose you. Make as much of an effort to hide your thoughts as he makes to find them out.[42]

This is clearly the obverse of the advice to the prince given in *ricordo* 88. Guicciardini had no love of tyrants, and his words here are meant to make dissimulators beware of the "snares" set for them by such rulers, who wish to be the only ones in possession of secrets. For the techniques used by the tyrant—interrogations in the guise of conversations, offers of false friendship in order to gain the confidence of the dissimulator, spies to expose the truths of one's intimate secrets—are, he admits, quite effective ("it is difficult to take precautions against all these"). If dissimulation may also be a form of resistance to power, it is nonetheless often weaker than what it opposes, that is, the tyrant's sheer

will to domination. As is the case for the prince seeking to shield his secrets from the inquiries of others, so dissimulators preparing to face the
withering pressure of the tyrant's gaze have to undergo thorough and
rigorous self-examination before they can attempt to hide the tracks left
by thoughts and feelings. One has "to think very carefully" in order to
dissimulate defensively in these circumstances, trying to see oneself
as the tyrant would, and "make as much of an effort to hide [one's]
thoughts as he makes to find them out." Because secrecy itself is a neutral category, it can serve either side (or both at once) in such an exchange. This highly intellectualized intersubjective game of cat-and-
mouse confirms that, for the *Ricordi,* much is at stake in the cultivation
of secrecy, including the very possibility of freedom from tyranny.
Whether secrets are "great matters of state" or just personal "thoughts"
or opinions, there will always be a struggle over truth in and through
language—or, to put it another way, in the scene of dialogical
exchange—when power is involved with dissimulation. Depending on
the circumstances of this exchange, the winner of this contest of wills
will succeed either in keeping something from being spoken or signaled,
on the one hand, or in forcing its disclosure in and through words and
signs, on the other. Guicciardini was prescient in foreseeing that the
political imperatives of dissimulation and the problematics of self-
representation would be linked together in this discourse in ways that
Machiavelli had not imagined, and in ways that subsequent generations
would not always find easy to accept.[43]

Asceticism and *Arcana Imperii*

Over the decades following his death, Machiavelli's writings percolated
throughout European political discussions, finding advocates and enemies in England, France, Spain, and the Low Countries. Indeed, there
gradually came into being an entirely new subgenre of political writing,
the anti-Machiavellian treatise.[44] Until well into the century, Ciceronianism continued to be the dominant paradigm for many humanists, as
did Aristotelian political theory for those who wrote about statecraft.
Two events occurred in 1559, however, that marked a watershed in the
fortunes of *Il Principe.* First, with the signing of the Treaty of Cateau-
Cambrésis, the *pax hispanica* came to the peninsula, and with it increasing awareness of the power of states such as Spain to impose internal
and external political equilibrium for the sake of self-interest. This was

also the year in which the reconstituted Roman Inquisition established an Index of Forbidden Books; one of the first authors to be banned was Machiavelli. Although the Index was not a particularly efficient institution of censorship by modern standards, those who desired to use Machiavelli's language of political realism in treating the "reason of the states" were henceforth deprived of his authority.

In his *Autobiografia* (1728–1729), Giambattista Vico remarked that the works of the ancient Roman historian Tacitus were fundamental in order to know humankind as it is (*l'uomo qual è*). Well into the eighteenth century, Vico was merely repeating a platitude of early modern thought that had its roots in the Tacitus revival of the late sixteenth and seventeenth centuries. A decade and a half after Machiavelli's works were placed on the Index, Justus Lipsius published his magisterial edition of Tacitus (1574). The rediscovery of the ancient Roman historian—as an intellectual model to emulate or villain to disparage— quickly became a pan-European phenomenon that transformed the theory of the state from the Netherlands and Germany to Italy and Spain. The history of Tacitism in early modern Europe has been ably discussed elsewhere.[45] Not only did Tacitism represent a transitional phase between humanism and historicism, but it allowed intellectuals to interrogate Machiavelli's controversial ideas indirectly, by commenting on the Roman historian's *Annals* and *Histories*. In particular, the Tacitists drew on his trenchant analysis of the reigns of emperors such as Tiberius, Claudius, and Nero to explain, justify, and criticize the behavior of the early modern prince, including the use of dissimulation.

Giovanni Botero (1544–1617) first published *Della Ragion di Stato* (The reason of state) in Venice in 1589.[46] The success of the book was such that it was reprinted and translated numerous times over the course of the following century, and many of its imitators employed the same title.[47] Botero was not a brilliantly creative political thinker like Machiavelli, but he was the first to formalize the maxims of the art of the state circulating widely at that moment in Europe and whose main points of reference were Machiavelli and Tacitus.[48] Although Botero took a Christian stance against both of these controversial authorities on government, he nevertheless drew on classical sources in an attempt to show that his doctrine was based on reason rather than faith alone.[49] Botero promoted the image of a prince who rules by divine right, but virtuously, in justice and liberality, and without recourse to fraud or tyranny. At the same time, however, he succinctly defined the state and its "reason" in the famous first lines of the work: "state is a stable rule over a people and Reason of State is the knowledge of the means by which such a dominion may be founded, preserved and extended."[50] What mattered, in the context of reason of state, was the "logic" of the state itself, not the justification of its origins or its ends. As a priest, a secretary to Charles Borromeo, and a participant in various diplomatic and Church missions, Botero was intimately connected to the power structure of Counter-Reformation Italy. His philosophy of reason of state identified the prince as a servant of the autonomous state and made the state's self-preservation its highest goal and greatest moral good.[51]

Political dissimulation was justified within this context for its functionality: it provided the prince with a useful means for the maintenance and expansion of the state's power and authority to rule over disciplined and obedient subjects. In book 2, chapter 7 of *Della Ragion di Stato,* Botero discusses secrecy as one of the cardinal points of the new philosophy of reason of state. Nothing could be more important to the success of the prince's negotiations, he observes: "the designs of princes work well and smoothly while they are hidden, but as soon as they come to light they lose their ease and effectiveness."[52] One could object that this point had already been made long ago in *Il Principe,* but Botero goes on to add, using Tacitus as his authority on the subject (and these lines from the *Annals* were to become a commonplace of European political writing for many decades to come):

And since counselors and ambassadors, secretaries and spies are those who deal most often with secret matters, they should be selected for their acute minds and for their taciturnity. Dissimulation is a great aid, and Louis XI of France thought it an important part of the art of ruling, while Tiberius was more proud of his skill in dissimulating, in which he excelled, than of anything else. By dissimulation I mean feigning to be ignorant of what you know, and to be uninterested in what affects you closely, as simulation is pretending and doing one thing in place of another. There is nothing more fatal to dissimulation than the impetuosity of wrath, and the prince must so control this passion that he never betrays himself by words or other signs of his thought or emotion.[53]

This passage from *Della Ragion di Stato* contains a number of important points for the nascent theory of reason of state. First of all, in it Botero synthesizes the reflections of Tacitus, Machiavelli, and Guicciardini on political dissimulation, confirming the convergence of the Tacitus revival with the fortunes of the two Florentine writers. Dissimulation benefits the ruler and his closest collaborators—counselors and ambassadors, secretaries and spies—because it requires a "closed" or "taciturn" (*cupo*) and acute mind, ideal for treating the secrets of state or *arcana imperii*.[54] The subtext here is surely the famous motto, *nescit regnare qui nescit dissimulare,* which Botero—like many others—attributes to Louis XI of France.[55] The use of the techniques of political dissimulation enables those involved in great affairs of state to guard their secrets and to keep them from view, thus gaining an advantage over rivals for power and compelling civil obedience. Botero employs the verb *mostrare* here to emphasize the visual aspect of such dissimulation; in public the prince is supposed to display, as it were, a lack of knowledge or interest, making dissimulation a representation of an absence. This defensive procedure, whose purpose is to block access by others to privileged information but without seeming to do so (for that might give away the fact that there was a secret to withhold in the first place), differs from the active feigning carried out in simulation.[56] One of the chief threats to the success of such dissimulation, Botero warns, comes from a sudden loss of self-control, as could occur in an *impeto dell'ira* (impetuosity of wrath), in which innermost passions and thoughts might impulsively be disclosed. The silence and diffidence of the prince and his cohorts are the visible signs of a force of will that imposes total control over the expression of the passions and thoughts, which—like the secrets of state—are not to be revealed *in parole, ò in altri segni d'animo, ò di affetto* (by words or other signs of thought or emotion): this is the morally neutral code of prudence.[57] As Elias contended centuries later, this political practice of prudence was likely influenced by the progressive rationalization of the inner life of the individual in early modernity, in which there were fewer and fewer possibilities of spontaneous self-expression.[58] How the moderation of the emotions was to be achieved remained a thorny issue, however, and others—such as the Neostoics—came up with more convincing answers than Botero was able to find.

In *Della Ragion di Stato* the Machiavellian synthesis of simulation and dissimulation disappears, or rather is transformed into Counter-Reformation terms. Simulation is morally unacceptable for the Christian prince, and, in the context of reason-of-state secrecy, dissimulation figures as a necessary act of asceticism and self-domination.[59] For the sake of the *arcana imperii,* the prince has to monitor continuously his own impulses. In detaching public image from private intention, and in applying the rule of secrecy to the expression of inner life as well, he submits to the imperative of the preservation of the absolutist state, whose chief end is to continue to exist in a world of radical mutability.[60]

The dialectic of secrecy and display is one of the principles both of the state and the prince charged with its preservation, and is part of the absolutist project for the disciplining of subjects as well as sovereigns. For Botero, far more so than for Machiavelli, dissimulation possesses a specifically psychological dimension—the governance of the passions, the body, and language—that accompanies its practical or technical value as an instrument of information control for the early modern ruler in the service of the state. At the same time, however, Botero's prince has to renounce *tempestività,* or timeliness, one of the essential qualities of the Machiavellian politician. To dissimulate means to temporalize, responding to events with a delayed reaction that permits the prince to keep his secrets safely out of sight. He of course continues to rely on what Gabriel Naudé was later to describe as "coups d'état," or extraordinary actions in the name of the state, but these must always be carefully contemplated ahead of time.[61] This psychological turn in the discourse on dissimulation in politics and statecraft was, however, to be only partially explored by Botero in his famous treatise. Further discoveries were to come from a scholar who was no stranger to the violent passions of the Counter-Reformation.

Homo Secessus: The New Psychology of the Prince

Justus Lipsius, the founder of modern Neostoicism and the first editor of Tacitus, was himself caught up in the civil war in the Netherlands. Over the course of his lifetime, Lipsius several times switched cities, universities, and religions, leading some contemporaries to consider him a peerless dissimulator.[62] In 1583 he began to work on the *Politicorum sive civilis doctrinae libri sex* (Six books of politics or civil doctrine), and the volume first appeared in print in 1589.[63] No one in Europe knew Tacitus better than Lipsius did, and his book offered readers a seductive synthesis of Neostoicism and clear-eyed political pragmatism. The book was an unqualified success, and was reprinted over fifty times between 1589 and 1760.[64] Lipsius's chief concern in the *Politica* was to translate into political terms the Neostoic theme of constancy, which he had first developed in his *De Constantia* (On constancy, 1584). How can rulers preserve the stability of the state in the midst of so many dangers?[65] Like other Tacitists, he steadfastly refused to separate fortune from prudence, making them interlocking concepts detached from the question of morality. Lipsius's work took a decidedly secular view of politics, depicting it as underlying the religious conflicts of the age and offering both a critique and defense of Machiavelli that was to prove influential with later essayists such as Bacon. Although the Machiavellians were under fierce attack from many quarters, and had been blamed for such atrocities as the St. Bartholomew's Day massacre in France, Lipsius wrote in the preface to the *Politica:* "I do not despise the intellect of Machiavelli alone, for it is sharp, subtle and fiery: and if he had only directed his Prince on the straight path towards that great temple of Virtue and Honor!"[66] This did not keep Lipsius's treatise from being placed on the 1590 Roman Index of Forbidden Books, or from being much admired by seventeenth-century freethinkers such as Gabriel Naudé.[67]

Lipsius notes at the beginning of the *Politica* that "I could truly say that all of it is mine, and nothing is. For although the selection and the arrangement are mine, the words and phrases I have gathered from different sources in the ancient writers, especially the historians, that is, in my opinion, from the very wellspring of Political Prudence."[68] His text is, in other words, a cento or palimpsest of citations from classical authors, arranged to suit Lipsius's arguments and connected by his commentary. He includes an *auctorum syllabus* naming more than one hundred sources, with the lion's share of the citations (about 25 percent) taken from the works of Tacitus himself.[69] Always the thorough scholar, Lipsius carefully marks in italics the citations included in the text and/or sets them off with white space. In what follows I treat the entire *Politica* as if it consisted of Lipsius's own words (while retaining his italics), given that his text's composite and heteroclite assemblage of classical, medieval, and early modern citations certainly expressed his own positions: it was simply prudent of him to have others speak for him at times in the text.

Having already established his stance toward Machiavelli in the preface, Lipsius protests in book 4, which is devoted to the prudence of the prince (or *prudentia a se*), that "the Italian fault-writer" has become the straw man for the distorted interpretations of both Catholic and Protestant political theorists. Those who criticize Machiavelli so severely, however, are blind to the true conditions of absolutist Europe, Lipsius complains:

They seem not to know this age and its men, and *to speak their opinion as if in Plato's Republic, instead of in the dregs of Romulus's.* For what kind of men are we living among? Cunning men, bad men: who seem *to consist entirely of fraud, deceit, and lies.* The princes themselves, with whom we have to do, are often of this category: and however much they play the lion, *they hide a cunning fox under their evil hearts.*[70]

The Flemish author obviously intends to make reference here to chapter 18 of *Il Principe*. There are dangers and evils everywhere in politics, he warns his readers, for most contemporary princes may play the lion but are in fact foxes practicing fraud. Unlike Machiavelli, however, Lipsius is not so bold as to suggest that dissimulation has no moral valence, and is just one among many instruments of statecraft available to the prince. The interests of the state take precedence over all else in the art of government, and in the prince's dealings familiar moral logic has to be suspended in favor of the autonomous logic of the state. However dubious it may appear to be, then, dissimulation nonetheless possesses a specifically political virtue. Thus dissimulation belongs to what Lipsius calls *prudentia mixta* (mixed prudence), the term by which he translates the Machiavellian notion of *virtù,* and can only be acceptable if defined in this way.[71]

Lipsius explains to his readers that the goal of the preservation of the state—the cornerstone of reason-of-state doctrine—justifies the prince's use of certain types of subterfuge at the appropriate time and place. He recommends, in short, fighting fire with fire:

> *By fraud and deceit states are overthrown,* the Philosopher remarks [Arist. Polit. 1304b20]. Do you want it to be forbidden to be saved by the same means? And for the Prince now and then *to play the fox, when dealing with a fox* [Adas 129]? Even if it serves public profit and well-being, which are always connected with the Prince's profit and well-being?[72]

Lipsius's justification of prince's choice of "the fox" in terms of practical reason or mixed prudence thus restates a key tenet of reason-of-state doctrine. Christian moral and ethical ideals of piety and probity have to be tempered by a realistic assessment of humanity's capacity for evil, at least in the realm of the politics of states. Dissimulation is praiseworthy in the prince—within the limits outlined by Lipsius—so long as it leads to the public good, which may be identified with whatever is good for the prince as a servant of the state (as opposed to personal gain), bad for his enemies, and may lead to security and stability for the state and its citizens. The prince, in short, is allowed to forsake virtue so long as he is governed by virtuous intentions in developing and imposing his authority for the good of the body politic.[73]

In the *Politica* dissimulation is—together with diffidence—described as belonging to the first of three modes of mixed prudence, which Lipsius terms "light deceit," or *levis fraus:* "Light deceit I call the kind WHICH DEPARTS ONLY SLIGHTLY FROM VIRTUE, AND CONTAINS NOT

MORE THAN A LITTLE DROP OF MALICE, which category I take to contain Distrust and Dissimulation."[74] Unlike treachery and injustice, both of which belong to the third mode of mixed prudence and are to be condemned outright, light deceit is legitimate for the prince and is not very far from virtue itself. It is obviously not, however, to be identified as a moral virtue: Lipsius is one of the few thinkers in the reason-of-state tradition to consider dissimulation a slightly malicious form of deception. Lipsius explains in the *Politica* that this recommended sort of political dissimulation unfolds in two temporally distinct phases. First, the prince has to strive to overcome what Guicciardini first warned of, namely the natural tendency to be credulous and to believe unquestioningly what others might choose to tell him. This first step, then, requires rulers to treat everyone and everything with distrust or diffidence.[75] The prince, Lipsius remarks, has to believe only the evidence of his own eyes, and exercise doubt and caution in all else:

I might almost say that *he believes in nothing but that which presents itself clearly before his eyes.* . . . So let the Prince keep his real thoughts to himself, and find safety behind the shield of *believing nothing, and being wary of everything.* Do they seem to be friendly and trustworthy? Watch out. [76]

Courts and palaces are filled with feigners, dissemblers, spies, and other dangerous persons. In order to serve the state wisely, the sovereign must transform himself into a disciplined skeptic who trusts almost no one and believes in almost nothing. Dissimulation has to develop, then, in the absence of belief; it can be born only from and successfully sustained by an attitude of radical doubt.[77]

Lipsius thus portrays the prince who practices mixed prudence as an almost tragically solitary and withdrawn figure, or *homo secessus.* Surrounded by the pomp and circumstance of court and retinue, and standing at the imaginary pinnacle of the Old Regime state, the prince finds himself subject to the laws of prudence. As sovereign, he has a double duty not only to disbelieve (in) others but to disguise his own disbelief in order to continue to keep the upper hand over those around him: "that is: believe only a few in fact, but in appearance many."[78] Lipsius's instructions on how to do this touch on many of the usual commonplaces of the discourse on dissimulation. The prince must master his passions and thoughts, curb his tongue, and use his countenance as an impenetrable screen of impassivity. Dissimulation, Lipsius warns (citing Cicero), "[is that] which *opens our face, but closes our mind.*"[79] Moreover, he notes, dissimulation would fail if it were to be discovered and seen through (*si transluces*) by those against whom it is directed; therefore it has to be used with moderation and tact in order not to attract suspicion.[80] Dissimulating his innermost thoughts and feelings to all except the most trusted of counselors, the prince's face must in public be a mask that cannot be interpreted, betraying nothing about the self-disciplined mind that lies behind it. It is to seem the same—equally unreadable and enigmatic—to all men, although in truth the prince must perforce trust a few of them with his thoughts. On this point Lipsius's prince resembles Tacitus's portrait of Tiberius, who, as was famously reported in the *Annals,* was renowned for—and most proud of—his ability to dissimulate in this manner.[81] But the early modern prince, according to the *Politica,* is not a crafty and brutal tyrant like Tiberius, and does not feel himself to be morally deficient for curbing the expression of his passions. He turns to dissimulation only as a means of rational self-defense—as a counter to adverse fortune—legitimated by the moral and political obligation to preserve the state whenever and wherever it is threatened. Since he commits no act of injustice and does not corrupt others in dissimulating, his use of this technique of *levis fraus* may be considered only slightly malicious.

In the *Politica,* Lipsius's reading of *Il Principe* emphasizes—as Machiavelli had done only implicitly—the limits of dissimulation in anything other than affairs of state. After defending its integral role in the prince's dealings inside and outside the palace, he remarks acidly:

> Some upright soul is certainly going to dislike these ideas, and will exclaim: *Feigning and dissimulation must be removed from every part of life.* Which I agree with as regards the private life, but totally deny with respect to the public life. Those will never rule well who will not veil: *and there is no choice for those to whom the entire commonwealth is entrusted.*[82]

The state has its own logic and its own morality, which is not the same as that of private persons, and therefore the prince is obliged to govern well, which means to cover well, that is, to dissimulate. Political prudence is nothing other than this duty and cannot be judged by the same standards of ethics and morals that apply in everyday life.[83] Only a miniscule but very powerful group of highly trained and principled persons, namely European heads of state, will ever need to practice this sort of prudence in the name of public utility, and will avoid the overuse of force as a result. Therefore, Lipsius concludes, it is an error to condemn political dissimulation as pernicious in an age in which so many "foxes" are on the prowl.

However, the underlying Neostoicism of his position forces the author to recognize that the prince who dissimulates does so at a significant personal price. For this austere practice of self-mastery demands the mortification of the passions, which can no longer freely find expression in language and gesture. Reason was not meant to play this repressive role in Neostoic doctrine, according to which surging emotions were to be controlled by other emotions that were beneficial to the individual.[84] Lipsius points out, with psychological insight not to be found in *Il Principe*: "*In order to realize their plans, they have to feign many things against their will, and to dissimulate although they hate to do so.*"[85] Thus the Flemish humanist returns, via Cicero, to the problem of conscience that seemed to so many early modern readers to have been overlooked altogether by Machiavelli. The prince serves the state and submits to its "reason," in the name of the common good, but only at the cost of a wounded and lacerated moral conscience that causes "grief" (*cum dolore*) in the practitioner of political dissimulation, who stands with one foot in each of two spheres. There are, on the one hand, public affairs, which follow a utilitarian logic, and there is, on the other hand, the autonomous mental and emotional world of the individual, who attempts to give it coherence through the moral and ethical codes of Christianity. The prince hesitates to abandon these standards of natural and divine law, as well as his own natural inclinations, even as he finds himself increasingly under pressure to finesse them for the sake of the state.[86] Such emphasis on the psychology of the conflicted mind of the prince adds new depth to this strand of the discourse on dissimulation, and will become a central component of the latter for a century to come. Lipsius's portrait of the prudent ruler in the *Politica* is surely nothing like Machiavelli's portrait of Pope Alexander VI, who ruthlessly exploited the division of public and private personae with blithe indifference to prevailing standards of conduct. Willingly or unwillingly, Lipsius's Counter-Reformation prince plays the fox in the service of the autonomous state, but at the same time—like Hamlet, Prince of the Danes—mourns the incommensurable distance that has sprung up between his thoughts and his actions.[87]

Secrets like Knives

Scipione Ammirato (1531–1601) was one of the most influential of the Italian reason-of-state theorists. After spending his early years in a

variety of Italian cities, including Rome (where he met Botero), he settled in Florence in 1569 and remained there for the rest of his life. He
worked for the Grand Dukes of Tuscany for the greater part of his career, chiefly as an official historian, essayist, and rhetor, for which the
dukes provided him with housing and a regular salary. His *Discorsi sopra
Cornelio Tacito* (On Tacitus), on which he worked for at least a decade,
was published in 1594, and the book soon became "an international classic" with numerous translations.[88] In reading Tacitus, Ammirato—like
Botero and Lipsius before him, and like many who were to follow
him—fragmented the ancient texts into a series of citations that were
then reordered in order to express his own thoughts. Unlike Botero and
Lipsius, however, Ammirato did not see Tacitism as a surrogate form of
Machiavellianism. On the contrary, his *Discorsi* present the works of the
Roman historian as an antidote to *Il Principe,* and this approach was to
prove widely popular during the long Tacitus revival.[89] Moreover, Ammirato's doctrine of reason of state defined such "reason" as violating
neither natural nor divine law; it was the reason of the greater public
good (such as public safety) and thus, in departing from the ordinary
moral order in extraordinary circumstances, the modern prince did not
come into conflict with Christianity.[90]

In his *Discorsi* Ammirato presents himself as an anti-Machiavellian
from the outset, leaving no stone unturned in his efforts to confute the
main theses of *Il Principe* (whose author he never mentions by name in
the text). Nonetheless, his views, like those of Botero or Lipsius, do not
diverge radically from those of the Florentine secretary on some key
points, such as the legitimacy of dissimulation for the prince. In the
fourth discourse of the first book of the work, entitled "Esser molto utile
il far vista di non vedere" (On the great utility of being seen not to see),
Ammirato offers numerous examples of legitimate dissimulation in
statecraft, chiefly taken from Tacitus and military history. The author
observes, first of all, that no one should be scandalized by arguments for
the legitimacy of dissimulation, inasmuch as God himself dissimulates
the sins of men so that they may repent of them.[91] Less divine dissimulators should "be seen not to see"; they should act as if dumb or slightly
stupefied when faced with a situation in which their own thoughts or in-
tents risk sudden exposure. Ammirato notes that in politics "there are
obtuse dissimulations, to use this highly meaningful term in this regard."[92] Dissimulation of this obtuse sort allows for a delayed reaction
to new information, so that the prince may digest it and gain time to
consider how to deal with it. Needless to say, this is a far cry from

Machiavelli's blunt call for the prince to be a great simulator and dissimulator who cynically manipulates the masses. For Ammirato's *dissimo-
lazioni milense* constitutes neither a lie nor an equivocation, but merely a
means to buy time; and if others should conclude from this that the
prince does not see and believe in his blindness, he is under no obligation to set them straight.[93] Thus this practice, at least in the eyes of the
author, is morally acceptable to a Christian reason-of-state doctrine.

Ammirato limits himself to commenting on only a few cases, and
concludes that "from that which has been said, everyone can see how
one should proceed skillfully in the matter of dissimulation."[94] In a brief
manuscript fragment not included in the *Discorsi* but belonging to this
same period, Ammirato justifies military dissimulation (and simulation)
in the same terms that he elsewhere reserves for reason of state. Whether
it involves a question of preserving the state, or of its involvement in an
armed conflict, recourse to secrecy and the cloaking of one's intentions
and positions are wholly legitimate for him.[95] In his later political treatise *Della Segretezza* (On secrecy, 1599), Ammirato begins by reflecting
on Plutarch's *De garrulitate* (On talkativeness) before sketching a brief
doctrine of secrecy that seems to be a correlate of the doctrine of dissimulation, although this term itself is never mentioned. Dedicated to
Giovanni de' Medici, the treatise is intended for "those who deal with
princes, and for others too."[96] In it Ammirato defends the widespread
culture of secrecy that had sprung up in Counter-Reformation Italy,
noting that "keeping silent, veiling, covering over, and hiding are terms
similar" to secrecy.[97]

Ammirato gives some attention in the treatise to both republics and
principalities, but although he ostensibly considers secrecy an issue of
reason of state, he says relatively little about current political theory or
the state of affairs in Europe. Secrecy is simply part of prudence, and
"the duty of the prudent man is to know how to say what he ought to
say, and to keep silent that which he ought to keep silent."[98] There can
be no hard-and-fast rule of secrecy, in other words, only a constant attention to what should be said or left unspoken: Ammirato appropriately calls this "the decorum of the secret." Like all definitions of decorum, this definition leaves it up to one's discretion to decide when,
where, and with whom to exercise secrecy.[99] The decorum of the secret
is equally applicable to princes and their subjects: secrecy is a central
concern of political life, but it is not limited only to the palace and is just
as necessary in the piazza. Like other operational keywords such as "prudence" or "decorum," however, secrecy eludes codification, and *Della*

Segretezza is not intended to be a how-to manual for successfully keeping secrets, whether political or personal. One thing, however, seems clear to Ammirato. In politics there are high stakes involved in secrecy, far higher even than loss of favor for the courtier or loss of face for the polite person in the civil conversation. Under absolutism the decision to keep a secret through silence is an act of the greatest prudence because it is always preferable to the risks entailed in speaking or writing: language is a trap. An excess word, *un mot de trop,* could prove fatal, especially in affairs of state—and not only for the prince. Ammirato addresses a chilling warning to courtiers and ministers alike about the danger of violating the discipline of state secrecy: "and I say: let no one allow secrets that he has heard from the prince to escape from his mouth, because they will arm themselves with many knives that will pierce his heart."[100] Any violation of the rule of secrecy, in other words, can never be kept secret or become a secret in its own right: indeed, in the statecraft of the Old Regime this is one of the very few things that cannot be dissimulated.

Shadowy Statecraft

Peace came to the northern Netherlands (or United Provinces) in 1609, marking the beginning of the Twelve Years' Truce there. Despite its vast overseas territories and colonial sources of wealth, the Spanish empire in Europe was mortally wounded, although its death throes would drag on for decades. There would be no universal Catholic empire, much less the unification of the continent under a single sovereign. Two decades later, the long Italian peace (1559–1628) was shattered by the War of the Mantuan Succession, although, prior to this, Spain and Savoy had fought a limited war from 1613 to 1617 over succession to the Duchy of Monferrat. After 1631 the popes began to take advantage of the decline of Spanish power on the peninsula, and Italy once again became the scene of many minor (but financially draining) wars. Reason of state remained the most prominent political doctrine, but attitudes began to shift somewhat in the areas of Italy under Spanish control, as more than one political writer suggested that princes must also know how to accommodate themselves to their subjects and to the best interests of those subjects. The self-interest of princes was no longer necessarily synonymous with what was good for the state or the society governed by that state.[101] Dissimulation continued to be seen as an instrument of reason of state, but as the question of personal freedom stirred among the Baroque elites (discussed in chapter 2), it also was adopted as a means for individuals to construct another "reason" of their own. Diego de Saavedra Fajardo's *Idea de un Príncipe político cristiano representada en cien empresas* (Idea of a political christian prince, represented in one hundred emblems), completed in 1640 and an exemplary work among seventeenth-century writings on reason of state, displays the anxieties of those trying to come to grips with the relationship between reason of state and subjectivity.[102]

Diego de Saavedra Fajardo (1584–1648) was a nobleman and diplomat who represented the Spanish crown in important embassies in Italy, Germany, France, Switzerland, and elsewhere during the course of his career. He played a leading role in the diplomatic and political maneuvering of the Thirty Years' War, and was the chief Spanish delegate at the conference leading to the Peace of Westphalia in 1648. Author of numerous historical and political works, Saavedra lived in Rome from around 1612 to 1633, serving the Spanish ambassador to the papal court and perfecting his knowledge of great princes and their secrets. Devout and erudite, he—like so many others of this era—knew and admired the writings of Tacitus and the Tacitists. Saavedra's *Idea de un Príncipe político cristiano* was composed during his travels and first published in Germany (Munich) in 1640, during a period of intense diplomatic activity. The work, an anti-Machiavellian defense of Christian reason of state more often referred to as the *Empresas políticas,* was widely translated and reprinted in Europe well into the eighteenth century.[103] Dedicated to ten-year-old Prince Balthasar Charles, Saavedra's book was meant to instruct and advise him in the arts of Christian statecraft that he would need one day as ruler of the Spanish empire; its author could not have known that the young prince was to die in only a few years' time. The text contains one hundred and one essays (*empresas*), one hundred of which comment on an emblem with a Latin motto. Several essays treat dissimulation to some degree (including nos. 18 and 22), but three of them—nos. 43, 44, and 45—deal specifically with the prince's use of dissimulation, and constitute a veritable primer of dissimulation in seventeenth-century absolutist statecraft.

The first of these three emblems, "Ut sciat regnare" (43: That he may know how to reign), displays a lion's skin, with a tangle of serpents in place of a mane, hanging under a canopy in an unadorned room. Iconographically speaking, there is nothing original about Saavedra's choice of elements for this emblem. It refers here to the *impio y feroz*—impious and ferocious—chapter 18 of Machiavelli's *Il Principe,* which employed, on the one hand, the well-worn metaphors of the lion and the fox and, on the other, the text of Matthew 10.16, *Estote ergo prudentes sicut serpentes et simplices sicut columbae* (be prudent as the serpent and candid as the dove). The Latin motto for the essay, Saavedra acknowledges, was taken from the famous dictum so often attributed to Louis XI, *nescit regnare qui nescit dissimulare*.[104] He explains the genesis and significance of the emblem as follows:

Because sometimes it is suitable to cover force with cunning, and indignation with benignity, the lion's head is crowned in this emblem, not with the arts of the fox, which are vile, fraudulent, and unworthy of the generosity and magnanimous heart of the prince, but rather with serpents, symbols of empire as well as prudent and vigilant majesty, and hieroglyphs [composed] of the sacred letters of prudence; because this cunning in protecting one's head, in closing one's ears to the siren's song, as well as in other things, aims for self-defense rather than harm to others.[105]

Saavedra reviews Lipsius's original classification of the three modes of deceit, before rejecting the conclusion that "light" deception may be justified on the part of the prince, for these three modes are notoriously difficult to define and tend to shade into one another. Deception ought to be avoided at all costs, for it is ultimately based on malice and lying, both of which are a stain on the royal reputation that can never be removed or disguised. Dissimulation is legitimate only when it is intended "for self-defense rather than harm to others." Saavedra therefore recommends that the prince practice dissimulation only on the following terms:

Dissimulation and cunning can only be licit when they neither deceive nor leave the prince's reputation stained. . . . This occurs when prudence, respecting its own preservation, makes use of cunning to hide things, according to the different circumstances of time, place and persons, so that the heart and tongue, and the mind and words, may always agree. That dissimulation ought to be avoided which employs deceptive means and lies with things themselves, i.e. that which would make another understand that which is not, not that which merely pretends not to understand that which is. Thus one may well use indifferent and equivocating words, putting one thing in place of another with a different meaning, not in order to deceive, but rather to secure oneself or prevent deception, or for other legitimate ends.[106]

Throughout the work, Saavedra clearly insists on the importance of a moral and ethical dimension of dissimulation, in accordance with his Augustinian approach to truth-telling ("so that the heart and tongue, and the mind and words, may always agree"). The value of this morally legitimate defensive procedure is, for the prince, to be found in the security that it affords to his mental and emotional world, which others constantly threaten to penetrate and exploit in some way. It also offers a weapon with which to fight against the deceptions of others, while nonetheless remaining in conversation with them and continuing to co-exist with them. Within the conflict-driven sphere of politics, dissimulation supplies a valuable and morally acceptable means of reducing violence: the prince does not always crush his opponents with force but confuses them with his cunning.

Saavedra contends that this art of self-management is especially necessary when dealing with other princes that practice fraud, like Machiavelli's fox:

These arts and designs are very necessary when dealing with cunning and fraudulent princes; because in such cases they may use diffidence and secrecy, dissimulation in their countenance, and vagueness and equivocation in their speech. In trying not to be ensnared by such princes, nor to allow their schemes and deceptions to occur, what is one doing by employing similar arts—without offending or mocking public faith—if not being doubly on one's guard?[107]

The prince has to rein in every impulse to self-expression, "silence being the principal tool of government" (as Ammirato had pointed out years before). Without resorting to falsehood, he may nonetheless dissimulate the truth when necessary for the good of the state: "a prince must not lie, but is allowed to keep silent or to hide the truth." The culture of secrecy, with its imperative of silence, is thus at the very heart of Saavedra's reason-of-state doctrine. The prudent use of reservation and reticence should shield the prince from the great dangers that surround him at the center of the state, for many want to possess information that he alone should have. Where there is an art of secrecy, however, the *Empresas políticas* recognizes that there also has to be an art of memory. Although secrecy ought not corrupt the virtues of the ruler, who should remain pure and simple at heart, yet he must never forget—except at great risk to himself—the potential for fraud in others: "let the prince's mind be innocent and simple, but aware of others' arts and frauds." In other words, he must never forget that the culture of secrecy is not exclusive to him alone, but is subscribed to by many others. How does the prince know when, and in what circumstances, to apply the rule of dissimulation? Here Saavedra does not differ markedly from his predecessors, for only experience and knowledge can supply the answer on a case-by-case basis.[108]

Unlike some reason-of-state theorists, Saavedra pays a good deal of attention in the *Empresas políticas* to the specific rhetorical techniques involved in successful dissimulation ("indifferent and equivocating words," "putting one thing in place of another with a different meaning"). For the Spanish diplomat is keenly aware that the prince has little margin for error, even in the most apparently trivial actions. Among the various techniques of dissimulation mentioned in the treatise, one of the most original is to be found in the prince's use of frankness. Sometimes the most successful dissimulation of all, Saavedra notes paradoxically, comes in speaking to enemies with *una candidez real,* or royal candor. If bent on interpreting the prince's words as deceptive, as they normally would tend to do, his listeners instead may become confounded by such sincerity. In thinking that they have failed to understand what the prince was really thinking, although in fact he had told them exactly what he had in mind, his enemies will not arm themselves against him as they otherwise might have done. Thus, in an illusionistic Baroque twist, veracity and sincerity could become the vehicles of a legitimate act of disinformation: "the truth is a generous deception." However, princes already renowned for their prudence cannot get away with this, because whatever they might say or do will always be taken for an illusion.[109] Saavedra observes that some princes pretend to be simple and modest individuals in order to dissimulate more effectively in precisely this manner, as Domitian did (Tacitus, *Histories* 1.4) and as Guicciardini recommended. Even this, however, is no easy task in the contemporary world. "The greatest prudence lies in knowing how to be ignorant at the right time. There is nothing more convenient or more difficult than in moderating one's knowledge."[110]

The final section of this first *empresa* examines the extent to which dissimulation is practiced in contemporary European politics. Saavedra laments the current state of affairs, which is reflected in ongoing wars, quarrels between states and their leaders, repeated treaty violations, and so on. The problem, as he sees it here, is that no one wants to be duped by others, and consequently everyone has come to believe that everyone else is dissimulating at all times. Such general skepticism regarding the veracity of others leads to a truly Baroque conundrum:

Such is the malice of present-day politics that it not only penetrates these arts, but slanders the purest simplicity, causing great damage to the truth and to public peace, for nothing is interpreted rightly. . . . Serious errors arise when people search works and words for different meanings than those that they seem to have. Thus, having found out opinions and intentions in this way, they arm themselves with arts, one against the other, and all live in perpetual distrust and suspicion.[111]

This "perpetual distrust and suspicion"—reminiscent of Tacitus's descriptions of the ruling class of imperial Rome under Tiberius—has resulted in the paralysis of understanding between contemporary politicians and statesmen, making it impossible to disentangle the political from the psychological aspect of the problem. Every time a hermeneutics of suspicion is employed to find out "opinions and intentions," for instance, in the king's council chamber or in the reading of a diplomatic memorandum, its practitioners move further away from the possible recovery of the truth. The spread of universal doubt has increasingly led, Saavedra complains, to the invention of meanings that simply are not there in reality: "nothing is interpreted rightly." What appears at first glance to be an immense theater of illusion (the "theater of the world") is in truth often no more than mere self-deception. Thus Saavedra's Tacitism allows him to explore—as Lipsius had done before him—the intricate and complex relationship between public and personal conduct, which had been accorded less relevance by the logic of "pure" reason-of-state doctrine.[112]

Saavedra, whose words here reveal a moderate Baroque mind at work, laments the fact that "the man who is cleverest in his suspicions is the furthest from the truth, because he shrewdly penetrates more deeply than that which is ordinarily thought; and we create as a certainty for others that which in ourselves is a deception of the imagination."[113] Far from being the victim of a shadowy world of conspiracy among dissimulators, the early modern head of state is a prisoner of his own paranoid imagination. The current political situation, in which the Machiavellians had the upper hand and fraud and suspicion were rampant, has, Saavedra notes, encouraged leaders to embrace illusions and to overlook the visible evidence of the truth. "The shadows of reason of state tend to be larger than its body, and sometimes one leaves the latter and embraces the former."[114] In this way, Saavedra observes with acute psychological insight, contemporary princes harm themselves in a way far worse than their enemies could ever have done to them. By clinging stubbornly to a state of self-delusion, the only thing these princes can grasp are the mere simulacra of the truth.

Thus Saavedra tempers the praise that he had given dissimulation earlier in the essay and concludes with a counterargument, as might Montaigne, Bacon, or Malvezzi. He observes that diffidence (*la difidencia*) is valuable as a component of prudence, but in politics good faith is still needed, "without which there are neither friendships nor firm relationships nor contracts, and the rights of peoples will remain weak and the world will remain in the grasp of deception."[115] Without a measure of good faith or trust in others, the political system of absolutism is, Saavedra perspicaciously argues, destined to slide into moral bankruptcy. It is necessary to accept that in negotiations "one does not always act with a second intention." As many others before him had warned, the practice of dissimulation has to be discontinuous, functioning only in specific circumstances. But none prior to Saavedra had so eloquently raised the specter, in the sphere of politics, of a universal order in which nothing was but what was not. Like the opening of Pandora's box, the discovery of the rule of dissimulation was harmful to the "world" itself.[116]

The second of these three *empresas*, "Nec a Quo nec ad Quem" (44: Neither where nor whom), represents a serpent writhing in the grass, its body so tangled and twisted that it is impossible to know which way it is going. The prince resembles the serpent, Saavedra notes, because the direction of his thoughts cannot be guessed by others.[117] Returning to the themes treated in the previous essay, Saavedra adds: "princes should hide their counsels with such secrecy that sometimes not even their ministers can penetrate them."[118] Tiberius and Philip II of Spain were both masters of the art of hiding their true thoughts from others, even from their closest counselors, in order to get them to act in a way that they otherwise might not have been willing to do. This constitutes entrapment, but not fraud, if done for the good of the state and without resorting to falsehood. Dissimulation is valuable to the prince precisely because it is the enemy of publicity, which always threatens the *arcana imperii* with disclosure and, consequently, menaces the prince with a loss of power. (Little wonder that publicity would eventually become the protagonist of bourgeois culture, whose nucleus was to form around "public opinion.")[119]

As was the case in the previous *empresa*, the most important defensive use of dissimulation for a prince is to counter the dissimulation of others. More than a third of the citations in the work are taken from Tacitus, and here a sudden flurry of them (nine in this section alone) accompanies Saavedra's interpretation of the serpent emblem:

The most suitable art and cunning for the prince, and the most permissible and necessary type of dissimulation, is that which calms and composes the face, speech and actions against those who try to deceive him with dissimulation but do not know that they have been discovered. In this way the prince gains time, the better to penetrate and punish or mock the deception, making this dissimulation less suitable for the aggressor. Once discovered, the latter begins to be afraid, and it seems to him that he cannot be safe if he is not raising deceptions around his head.[120]

This scenario can only have reminded Saavedra's readers of Tacitus's unforgettable description of the emperor Tiberius. Supreme self-control, accompanied by a zero degree of self-expression, a penetrating gaze and a great secret to maintain: these are the elements that Saavedra's prince took from the text of the ancient Roman historian, although with a quite different motivation than that of the tyrant Tiberius. In the above passage from the *Empresas políticas*, the prince and his adversary seem each to stand behind one-way mirrors that reflect one another, each believing himself to be invisible to the other, and each trying to see through the other's defense. The task of the prince is to find out what lies behind his adversary's mirror, in order to create fear and insecurity in the "aggressor" and eventually punish or expose him (which amounts to the same thing), even perhaps with the same ferocity that Tiberius would have used.

In the *Empresas políticas* this scenario is intended for princes, who stand alone atop the absolutist system; but what about other members of the state apparatus, who did not always have the power to punish this sort of aggression? Ministers of state may defend themselves from a corrupt and duplicitous prince, Saavedra explains, through a dissimulated simplicity or lack of understanding similar to Ammirato's "obtuse" dissimulation. "This dissimulation or feigned simplicity is very necessary in ministers who attend to princes who are overly cunning and duplicitous, and who make a study of keeping their arts impenetrable."[121] As in the case of the banquet at which Britannicus was poisoned by Nero (Tacitus, *Histories* 4), this sort of dissimulation is most necessary when the prince's malicious design is clear to all. As Tacitus recounts the episode in the *Histories,* some senators at the banquet imprudently fled in horror at the sight of the victim in his death throes, thus revealing to the tyrant that they knew it to be an assassination, but others stayed and pretended to believe Britannicus's death a natural one: "this dissimulation is more necessary in the errors and vices of the prince, because he abhors those who witness or know about them."[122] For it is dangerous to do otherwise, that is, to let on that one has grasped the true nature of the fraud. Tyrants like Tiberius hate to be found out, Saavedra explains in another one of his deep psychological insights, because "[they] desire an absolute dominion over minds, not subject to the intelligence of others."[123] Absolute power was perhaps a fiction, as Machiavelli had argued, but it could not in any case be absolute if the tyrant's schemes were known to others around him. The tyrant desires to be a true *homo clausus,* hidden like an oyster in its shell, for to lose one's secrets means to risk losing power over one's subjects, who have to live instead in perpetual fear, doubt, and uncertainty concerning the tyrant's state of mind.[124]

The third *empresa,* "Non maiestate securus" (45: Safety is not in majesty alone), displays a lion resting with its eyes open. The link between the three emblems in the series must have been apparent to Saavedra's readers, who were likely versed in the art of interpreting emblems. In the first we find a lion's skin with a mane of serpents, in the second a serpent, and in the third a lion; the latter two are, as it were, the components of the first emblem. The lion rarely sleeps, Saavedra claims, and when doing so its eyes remain open as if it were still awake. He explains to his readers the reason for this unusual behavior: "Cunning and dissimulation are, in the lion, sleeping with open eyes. The intent is not to deceive, but rather to dissimulate the distraction of his senses."[125] When dissimulating sleep, in other words, the lion astutely disguises his obliviousness of all that surrounds him, with eyes that seem to see but do not. This cleverly protects him even at a moment of supreme defenselessness. Likewise the contemporary prince has to be seen to see, even in his moments of *enajenación* (distraction), because without his vigilant gaze he too is vulnerable to the frauds that others might—thinking him to be unconscious—try to practice on him.

The paranoia of the early modern prince, expressed in his lack of confidence in others and his fear of being entrapped by them, is thus intimately linked to the overarching themes of reason of state and mutability. Saavedra eloquently recounts the intense contemporary conflicts between the English and the Dutch over sea power, the French and the Spanish over the Low Countries, the Venetian Republic and the Ottoman Empire over the eastern Mediterranean, and so on. The struggle for the maintenance and preservation of the state is in part, he asserts, the natural result of constantly shifting international power relations. There is only impermanence in Saavedra's Baroque vision of contemporary history; every state is destined one day to die and decompose. Yet this is not the whole story of the current European political scene. For, as he observes, "few or none speak the truth, because one does not speak what one fears; and thus [the prince] must not sleep confident in his power. Let him undo art with art, and force with force. The magnanimous heart should anticipate dangers with dissimulation and caution, and should resist them with valor and strength."[126] The foreign and domestic "dangers" faced by the state may be resisted with force, of course, as reason of state requires. But far more difficult to resist or to undo is the "art" of others, which produces specters and ghosts of truth: only caution and dissimulation on the part of the prince can preempt the loss of his power to this far more insidious and phantasmagoric threat.

These three *empresas* offer overlapping, and sometimes contrasting, points of view on the early modern discourse on political dissimulation. In spite of his belief in the legitimacy of its use by princes in self-defense and in certain carefully delimited circumstances, Saavedra abruptly concludes that dissimulation is actually much more appropriate for ministers of state. Here he turns to the notion of sacral kingship, which had come to play such a key role in absolutism.[127] Princes possess a hidden divinity that is offended by recourse to dissimulation, he explains, for the latter is ordinarily grounded in the basest impulses of "fear and ambition." "Ordinarily dissimulation is the daughter of fear and ambition, and neither one of these should be found in the prince; when dissimulation is called for, let it be called for by prudent silence and gravity."[128] In an apparently paradoxical final flourish, given his strenuous arguments in defense of princely dissimulation, Saavedra asserts at the end of this third essay that the prince who acts with genuine simplicity, naturalness, and ingenuousness—like Tacitus's Petronius—will in fact be most greatly loved by his subjects, because in the last analysis everyone hates artifice, and a good reputation is the reward of the honest prince. Saavedra thus reverts to the model of the Christian prince, in line with the principles first outlined in Botero's *Ragion di Stato,* after treading on dangerously Machiavellian territory. Yet his readers are left suspended between the two poles of Saavedra's treatment of dissimulation, for these three essays have made it abundantly clear that such Christian qualities—however admirable and desirable—were not enough for anyone to survive as a prince in early modern Europe. Saavedra's advice to the young prince Balthasar Charles is as difficult to grasp as the elusive "shadows" of reason of state.

An Aesthetics of the Everyday

In 1624 Cardinal Richelieu came to power in France, advocating a truly Catholic state that would oppose Spanish universal hegemony. As Richard Tuck comments, "while *ragion di stato* on behalf of Catholic imperialism was present from the very beginning of his rule, only in the 1630's [after the Day of Dupes] do we find blatant statements of the fundamentally anti-constitutional and even anti-moral views of the Tacitist humanists—and the most blatant of them all was never allowed publication." The author of those views was the French ecclesiastic Louis Machon (ca. 1600–ca.1672), who was from the Lorraine and supported Richelieu's plan to annex the province.[129] A member of the cardinal's circle and an apologist for his absolutist politics, Machon was also an advocate for Machiavelli at a moment in which the controversy between pro- and anti-Machiavellians showed few signs of waning. Machon's massive treatise, *Apologie pour Machiavel,* was begun at the request of Richelieu, and Machon worked on the text for more than twenty-five years, beginning around 1641.[130] One version was finished in 1643, but a second version was completed only in 1668.[131] Due to the changed political circumstances in France after the death of Richelieu, the work was left unpublished. It nonetheless offers one of the most ambitious and unusual analyses of the problems posed by dissimulation for reason-of-state doctrine in the middle decades of the seventeenth century.

Machon's stated aim, in his treatise, is to reconcile Machiavelli's writings with the Holy Scriptures and the corpus of patristic literature.[132] His arguments are numerous and complex, but the thrust of the work is to show that the early modern prince was free to engage in the sort of behavior promoted in *Il Principe* insofar as he "is an imitator of a God who himself employed illusion and deception in the interests of salvation."[133] Given the size of Machon's work, I will limit my treatment of the *Apologie pour Machiavel* to the sections that comment directly on dissimulation. The reading of Machiavelli that it offers is, in any case, nothing short of scandalous. Machon ransacks the classical and Christian sources, and seriously distorts the text of *Il Principe,* in an attempt to give his argument authority; few anti-Machiavellians ever took greater liberties with the work of the Florentine secretary in attacking it than does Machon in defending it.

Machon first turns his attention to the maxim *dissimuler, pour bien regner* (adapted from the familiar motto *nescit regnare qui nescit dissimulare,* with reference to chapter 18 of *Il Principe*). The opening pages of this section supply a psychological disquisition on the ways in which humans constantly deceive themselves and ignore their own true nature. Nowadays everyone accuses everyone else of being *dissimulé,* Machon complains, when in fact those doing the accusing have failed to recognize the truth about themselves. Indeed, he contends, the discourse on dissimulation has thus far been dealt with much too harshly by those who should have known better. For Machiavelli, on the other hand, dissimulation seemed instead a self-evident rule for the early modern prince, and one that he did not need to bother to explain to his readers:

Our author did not amuse himself with long discourses to justify this maxim or, in advising it, to show its necessity. He thought it so important and inseparable, not only from affairs of state, but also from private and personal affairs, that he always held it up as a general rule that could not be challenged or condemned, if not by those whose intrigues are as slight as their judgment, and whose affairs and commerce among men are equally lacking, to say nothing of their scarce intellect and reason in dealing with their books and their writings.[134]

This is, quite obviously, not what Machiavelli said in the text of *Il Principe*. Although it is true enough that he did not make any attempt at a moral justification of dissimulation, at no point did Machiavelli suggest that the prince's *virtù*, which included the arts of dissimulation, was an art for courtiers or for the masses. It was, as he understood it, an exquisitely political art of secrecy; but for Machon it is much more than this. Thus at the very outset of this singular defense of dissimulation—for the text is an apology, and there is no question of a multifaceted essay exploring contradictory points of view à la Montaigne—Machon begins openly to link the logic of reason of state to the moral, ethical, and civil comportment of the individual in "private and personal affairs."

Drawing on the well-developed discourse of honest dissimulation, he points out that nature has made humanity with a heart hidden from the view of others. The heart is like "a secret cabinet" whose curtains are made of dissimulation: "nature has made in the soul a secret cabinet where the most important thoughts are hidden and kept until prudence finds the appropriate moment to bring them to light and to carry out their counsels. . . . Dissimulation serves as the curtains for this cabinet, and the prudence to hide them [these thoughts] is its most lovely attire."[135] Dissimulation is an inherently natural component of subjectivity, in other words, rather than an undesirable artifice of a decadent era. Moreover, its practice demands the moderation of the passions and the exercise of constraint in self-expression, both virtues that signal triumph over the turbulent and disorderly inner life of the human being:

Whoever knows how to dissimulate and give himself patience is worth more and can do much more than whoever has only strength and courage, being a certainty that whoever is master of his passions, and can moderate them and rein them in, will have a greater effect, along with greater and more glorious exploits, than those who can conquer cities by the force of arms alone.[136]

The language of this passage must have been familiar enough to any contemporary reader even casually acquainted with the debate over dissimulation. Self-mastery, through the moderation and disciplined control of the passions, is more valuable than the exercise of sheer force in gaining an advantage over others, according to the author of the *Apologie,* and will bring greater glory to those who have the will to conquer themselves.

Without the practice of dissimulation in everyday life, Machon argues extravagantly, "in truth men would kill each other, and they would be at each other's throats every day; there would be only rage, fury, vengeance, murders and cruelties among them; they would oppose themselves, and thus, for an imaginary vice that is nonexistent, they would ruin everything that is theirs of virtue, justice, religion, the sacred and all that should be loved devotedly."[137] Without the stabilizing presence of dissimulation, in other words, all civilized values would be destroyed and humanity itself would be thrown into chaos. In Machon's perspective, dissimulation is first and foremost the practice of nonviolence, serving to neutralize the natural tendency to aggression of all humans: it is, as it were, the embodiment of the civilizing process, the bond that holds together not only the political life of the state but society itself. Indeed, the domain of civility relies entirely on dissimulation to hold together the civil conversation like a kind of glue: "all of my life, like that of other men, is nothing but constraints and ceremonies . . . [yet] is it not dissimulation, is it not to practice in effect the very thing that others want me to condemn with my tongue and my words? What would become of this world without dissimulation?"[138] Both society at large, and the "world" of good manners and etiquette, therefore are— like all persons who belong to them—fully inscribed in the logic of dissimulation.

But what of reason of state? Citing Tacitus as his authority, Machon acknowledges that political dissimulation is both natural and necessary to the prince.[139] Without "covering his eyes" the prince would leave not only himself, but his state, all too vulnerable to the maneuvering of his enemies. Necessary for the prince's control over information about the affairs of state, dissimulation is a matter of public security; the *arcana imperii* have to be kept out of the hands of those who constitute a threat to the state and its subjects.[140] Furthermore, the prince, as an actor in *le théâtre des affaires publiques,* or theater of public affairs, must be prepared to change his mask with each change of scene. The protean nature of the prince and his ministers is justified in the *Apologie* by the mu-

tability of political affairs and by the necessity of defending the state under rapidly changing conditions, for "the good and the health of the
state are the center and the end toward which all of their counsels and all
of their actions should tend, at which they cannot often arrive except by
shifting and dissimulating their designs and their undertakings."[141] Machon has clearly absorbed the lessons of the discourse on reason of state
but has placed himself in a quite difficult position, for once the concept
of dissimulation is admitted as the cornerstone of individual and collective human existence, it is difficult for him to set the political practice of
dissimulation apart from its other modes.

Despite his intimate acquaintance with the works of Machiavelli,
Lipsius, and others in the same tradition of the *politiques*, Machon is unable in the *Apologie* to sustain coherently the distinction that he originally sought to make between the prince's use of dissimulation and that
of his subjects. "Civil or moral" and "political" dissimulation seep into
each other like the colors on a sheet of marbled paper. "Let us confess
that grace and dissimulation are so necessary, not only to princes
and their ministers, but to all sorts of men, both in general and in particular, that without [them] it is entirely impossible to be able to act securely among men, and to ward off their malice."[142] What started out as
a political treatise thus shifts ground entirely, and makes dissimulation
the universal law of all human intercourse. In essence, what had originally been treated—by Machiavelli, Lipsius, et al.—as one among many
techniques available to the prince now becomes, in Machon's hands, the
full-fledged equivalent of prudence itself, one of the most important of
all moral and political concepts of the early modern era.

In the *Apologie* Machon often ranges quite far from Machiavelli, ostensibly the subject of his apology, but never further than in the following passage:

Holding nothing more certain than that dissimulation is the mainstay of kings,
states, goods, families and the seasoning of all human action, and its practice is
so necessary in all things, that I dare to put forward to you that, in order never
to forget it in my petty intrigues and in looking after my own particular interests, I had written in very large letters above the upholstery in the *ruelle* alongside my bed—"Dissimulation is the mainstay of affairs"—so that, in going to
bed and in rising I would not forget it in my undertakings, as the salt of prudence, the basis of all our designs, and the consolation for things that are not
granted to us.[143]

It is not easy to imagine what life in Machon's bedroom might have
been like. Although an ecclesiastic, he was not so ascetic as to be without

a comfortable bed and fashionable space for sleeping (with its *ruelle*); yet his motto, inscribed over the bed, is reminiscent of nothing so much as the prayers written over the inner doorway of a monastic cell, exhorting its inhabitant to think of "last things" like salvation and damnation. For this is what dissimulation becomes, in the last analysis, in the *Apologie pour Machiavel,* an invisible thread connecting all human affairs, offering both the means to achieve one's ends and consolation for one's failures to do so. Earthly existence is, in turn, connected by dissimulation to the heavens. Inasmuch as God himself is a skillful and mysterious dissimulator, those who practice this art on earth are imitators of the divine and follow the foreordained plan for the universe itself.[144]

Louis Machon's bedroom, with its unique motto inscribed on the wall-hanging, embodies the transformation in the role of political dissimulation that had occurred in Europe by the middle decades of the seventeenth century. Although still practiced in the "privy chamber" of the prince, dissimulation had also acquired legitimacy in the wider world of courtiers, secretaries, bureaucrats, and other members of the state apparatus. Indeed, all subjects of the absolutist state are entitled to use it as "the mainstay of affairs," according to Machon's treatise: dissimulation has become a secularized practice of self-management taking the place of traditional Christian self-discipline. The author of the *Apologie* understands only too well that his bedroom—a locus of intimacy (but not yet the private sanctuary of the individual, unlike in later bourgeois society), a liminal zone between "inside" and "outside"—is the place where he has to begin the daily task of (re)producing himself according to the imperatives of this world of "intrigues" and "particular interests." Dissimulation belongs to the quotidian reality of "affairs," "things," "actions," and not that of "the most important thoughts," Machon protests—but without its presence, paradoxically, these intimate thoughts would not be able to occur in the first place. Outside of the bedroom, and perhaps even in it (*en me couchant*), one has always to wear the mask imposed by the universal rule of dissimulation, which may be forgotten only at the greatest risk to one's own success in the world or safety in matters of state. Precisely as for the prince, it forms the basis of all of one's projects for the present and the future. In observing daily the motto hanging by his bedside, Machon attempts to reformulate and discipline his own existence in order to be analogous, at least in matters of dissimulation, to that of his sovereign liege and his social superiors. Small wonder, then, that his manuscript was left unpublished.[145]

Certainly an anthropology of dissimulation as well as a "sociology of aspirations" are at work here.[146] However, the more universal the rule of dissimulation becomes in the *Apologie,* the more it begins to appear in another light, namely as an aesthetics of the person(a). The intriguing description of Machon's bedroom included in the treatise speaks clearly on this point. If the entire social and political "world" of the Old Regime is in fact dissimulated, as Saavedra too had feared, then its members must select daily for themselves a whole set of masks, insofar as without the proper mask at the proper moment they would cease to exist for that world, which is the only one that matters for them.[147] These masks may be individually imposed by social conventions of various sorts; taken one by one, they may be stifling in their conformity to the norm. We know from Lipsius, for instance, that the pain of having to wear them constantly may have been great indeed. But, according to the *Apologie,* it is up to the individual to invent the sequence in which they will be deployed, and this relation that one has to oneself—in the ordering of a series of masks, from the polite to the moral to the political—constitutes a fundamentally creative activity, an aesthetics of existence in the age of absolutism.[148] At the same time, however, the legitimation of the "rule" of dissimulation, and its dislocation from the field of reason of state to the daily life of individuals, accentuates the crisis of conscience and consensus in early modern Europe. In this sense, as Denise Aricò has pointed out, "dissimulation is a cultural procedure representing perhaps the most painful aspect of the newly codified psychology of seventeenth-century humanity."[149]

The "Perfect Government" of Designs

The steady stream of political treatises dealing with dissimulation continued well into the seventeenth century. Many offered justifications of the practice in terms of reason of state; some were published in places where censorship was lax, and some never appeared in print, although they circulated in manuscript form.[150] Of all these works, which cannot be discussed here, one had a particularly unusual appeal for early modern readers: the *Breviarium politicorum* (The politicians' breviary), attributed to Cardinal Mazarin (1602–1661) and published for the first time in 1684 in Cologne. During the reign of Louis XIV the work was reprinted more than ten times in various cities in France and elsewhere but was never translated into French. It did, however, appear in Italian in 1695, with the title *Epilogo dei Dogmi Politici secondo i dettami rimastine dal Cardinal Mazzarino,* supposedly at the insistence of an unnamed great "Italian prince."[151] Perhaps not coincidentally, the only surviving copy of the Latin manuscript (dated 1683) was found in the Biblioteca Comunale dell'Archiginnasio in Bologna until 1950, when it mysteriously disappeared.[152]

Among the great statesmen of the *grand siècle,* Mazarin was renowned for his subtlety, political acumen, and supreme expertise as a negotiator. The slender volume claiming to be his work thus offered curious contemporary readers a glimpse of the secrets of one of the most powerful figures of the age, as well as of someone reputed to be a master dissimulator. Even if Mazarin was not the true author of the *Breviarium* (which seems likely), the enthusiastic reception of the work indicates that it painted a plausible portrait of him; whoever wrote the work was, in any case, intimate with the culture of secrecy to which the cardinal subscribed.[153] And it is well known that Mazarin was an indefatigable writer of his *Carnets,* which—perhaps like this "breviary"— were never meant to be published.[154] Given that there is no definite proof of his authorship, however, in the pages that follow I will consider *Mazarin* (which is to say, "pseudo-Mazarin") to be responsible for the work.

The printer's preface to the 1698 Italian-language text of the *Breviarium* confirms the accuracy of Machon's intuitions about the rising tide of dissimulation across seventeenth-century society. The printer announces that *Mazarin*'s work is destined to be read by "the leading crowned heads of Europe, as well as their noble subjects, princes of low rank, and private gentlemen," and to be used "for the perfect government of one's subjects, and, above all, of one's own self."[155] Politics is not simply reason of state, and everyone plays the game, whether at court or at home. If this is to be a breviary for politicians and statesmen, "to which this labor of mine is particularly addressed," as the printer announces, it also offers practical advice for the public as well.[156] Machon's defense of dissimulation was long on philosophy and short on practical concerns: *Mazarin*'s is quite the opposite. It figures as a primer, a how-to manual, containing hundreds of practical tips on how to deal with servants, superiors, family members, friends, money, jokes, clothing, reading, writing, sleeping, eating, loving, and so on, in a dizzying succession of "human and civil actions."[157] The treatise offers an authoritative portrait of early modern men and women doggedly (re)creating themselves on a daily basis, in the sort of self-fashioning aesthetic activity that Machon had foreseen. And if Machon's periods were seemingly endless, *Mazarin* instead preferred a laconic, dense, and fragmentary narrative prose, restricting himself to brief clauses and paragraphs that succeed one another abruptly, often leaving the reader to piece together the author's intended meaning from a few enigmatic and ambiguous words.

The text begins with the following observation, drawn directly from the Stoic tradition: "the most sincere philosophy of the ancients may be reduced to just two maxims, which are the following: 'endure' and 'abstain.'" *Mazarin* then adds, however, his own updated version of these same principles: "likewise today there are just two maxims, namely: 'simulate' and 'dissimulate'; or rather, 'know yourself' and 'know others as well.' The latter two, if I am not wrong, support the first two."[158] This perhaps may be the most concise formulation ever given to the discourse on dissimulation—but what it says has little to do with reason-of-state doctrine or any other political theory. It instead brings the *Breviarium* far closer to what Naudé called *la divination morale*, namely the art of penetrating and recognizing thoughts, which, although vitally important to politicians and statesmen, is also pertinent to a wide variety of early modern individuals in other walks of life.[159]

The plan of the work seems simple enough: first these two contemporary maxims are interpreted and explained in separate sections, and then the rest of the text is devoted to various and sundry "human and civil actions" touching on the themes of simulation and dissimulation. Of the two maxims, *Mazarin* devotes almost five times as much space to the meaning of "know others well" as he does to the meaning of "know yourself." The *Breviarium* is meant, in short, to be an essay in applied psychology. In the end, however, this hardly matters, for the author freely mixes advice on simulation and dissimulation in the two sections. And neither the one nor the other is restricted to the maneuvering of princes and ministers. The advice that the maxims offer is useful not only to the great and powerful, in other words, but to those who aspire to succeed at virtually any undertaking. *Mazarin*'s justification of dissimulation in politics, statecraft, and everyday life is nakedly pragmatic, lacking even the slightest attempt to defend it in terms of the logic of reason of state. One dissimulates because it is extremely expedient to do so, in order for one's affairs to prosper. There is no need to appeal to a greater moral or political good (that is, the stability and security of the state) that would justify recourse to such dire measures. The *Breviarium politicorum* is a work that explains how to succeed in the business of getting ahead in the world, but the avenue to success that it promotes is by no means an easy one.

Mazarin's advice touches on many of the standard topics of the discourse on dissimulation. The first thing to do is to examine one's own heart, in order to see "if you have some stirring of anger, fear, or some other passion in you."[160] The expression of these passions has to be brought under control, and the only feelings that are to "walk freely across your face . . . are humaneness and other such feelings."[161] All other "desires are to be kept strictly shut up [in your heart], and you should not hesitate to feign opposite ones."[162] Next come habits, gestures, and the general appearance of the body; one has to shrewdly scrutinize oneself for defects that could reveal closely held secrets. However, without a thorough initial psychological self-analysis, attempts to neutralize one's external appearance are destined to fail. In fact, even very closely trimmed fingernails might reveal that one is too superficially concerned with looks rather than with what lies behind them. As *Mazarin* sneers, "[these individuals] mortify themselves externally, without taking the least care to mortify themselves internally."[163] The dissimulator is simply to be modest and grave in carriage and comportment, for this suggests a well-balanced inner regimen. At the same time, *Mazarin* warns in touching upon one of the commonplaces of the discourse on dissimulation, it is necessary to see everything without having been seen to see: "observe everything with a keen eye, and have a wise way of looking that shows your curiosity to be satisfied, because such people pass for prudent, astute, and alert."[164]

According to the *Breviarium,* dissimulation is especially useful in disguising feelings of anger, that supreme enemy of self-control. If some outrage has been committed, it is of course an error to react with "signs, words, or gestures of indignation" that might reveal one's inner state.[165] In fact, "if you are offended, the best choice is dissimulation; because one clash gives rise to new clashes, and peace is lost."[166] "Give your enemy ample opportunity to realize on his own that he has offended you," *Mazarin* urges his readers, "but do not point it out to him yourself, so that he should not perceive your anger."[167] One may also answer an insult with irony or humor, of course, and sometimes this is the only option. In a piece of advice directed at the statesman, the author remarks: "you will [dis]simulate your emotions if you see false religions enter into your dominion, which are adversaries to your rule. Do not appear in public. . . . During such a time do not frequent or converse with anyone, for inevitably the external appearance of your face will reveal happiness, indignation, or other emotions to others."[168] This is, however, a fine line to draw. The danger with such dissimulation—displayed as an absence of anger—is that one's enemies might take heart to think that they have managed to wound the dissimulator very deeply. As *Mazarin* notes, "to hide oneself from view is not always appropriate when adverse events occur, in order not to lead others to think, through one's dissimulation, that they know what really happened to you."[169] The politician or statesman always has to calculate the most profitable way to represent the passions, sometimes hiding them and sometimes putting them on public display, depending upon what can be gained from each.

If such forced insensibility meshes seamlessly with earlier notions of dissimulation, *Mazarin* also suggests some unusual ways to practice this art that seem particularly well suited to life in the seventeenth-century palace, in which privacy was often a rare and sought-after commodity. He recommends that the windows of one's living quarters have the following arrangement: "the shutters of your windows should open onto the interior of your rooms; and what frames the window-glass should be painted black, so that from the outside no one can tell if the windows are open or closed."[170] These windows are a fitting metaphor for the master dissimulator: for no one can tell if his mind and heart are "open or closed" either. This impenetrable wall of privacy, sealing off oneself from the prying gaze of others, is equally useful in matters of reading and writing, especially in the crowded chambers of the royal ministers. *Mazarin* explains that

if you have to write in a place where many people pass by, prop up an already written page, as if you had to copy it. It should be visible to everyone; but the sheets on which you are actually writing should be lying in front of you, so well covered that others can only see the line that you are transcribing at that moment, legible to anyone coming up to take a look. Cover up what you have written with a book, or another sheet of paper, or with some other propped-up papers, like the first.

If, while you are reading, someone glances at what you are doing, turn over several pages quickly in order to keep your mind from being discovered. Or rather, it would be well to have many books piled in front of you, in order to prevent that person from knowing what you are really reading.[171]

These and other similar practical suggestions in the treatise seem meant to keep one's thoughts from being externalized and divulged to all in violation of their essential intimacy. By scattering books about on a desk, or covering up one's letter while leaving others in plain view, the dissimulator closes the shutters on a window into the mind. By peering at the wrong book or pile of papers, the inquisitive and the curious might fail to fathom what the dissimulator is thinking: without resorting to the use of deliberately articulated falsehood, this defensive gesture serves to protect the secret inner cabinet of the self from any unauthorized entry. Writing and reading are necessary tools of the politician, *Mazarin* allows, but nevertheless may endanger the secrecy necessary to success in politics. Ciphers and codes are, however, also risky, because if they appear "illegible" they would "arouse suspicion, and interception"; it is therefore advisable to have secrets written in another's hand and with another's pen—namely those of a trusted secretary.[172]

Mazarin's political maxims call for the dissimulator "to have full knowledge of everyone"; the task is to investigate others' secrets without revealing one's own.[173] Again, this is easier said than done, but *Mazarin* devotes much of his work to proposing practical means for carrying out this investigation. Among these is physiognomy, rarely treated in the discourse on dissimulation (although Ducci does mention it in his *Arte aulica*) but very popular throughout Europe in this period. This pseudo-science has the distinct advantage, from a moral perspective—not that this is any concern of *Mazarin*'s—of avoiding the use of simulation and other traps for the unwary. "Astute men are for the most part," he notes, "those that display an affected sweetness, have a little hill in the middle of the nose, and penetrating eyes."[174] Instead "those who are for the most part liars by nature form two small depressions in their cheeks when they laugh."[175] All that is needed is a lynx-like and well-trained eye to know the very depths of these individuals, whose secrets are written on their faces. *Mazarin* also provides readers with a moral typology of humanity that may assist them in grasping the true identity of others. There are forgers, liars, sneaks, frauds, simulators, fools, false friends, flatterers, braggarts, thieves, melancholics, cheaters, gamblers, spies: a rogues' gallery of early modern scoundrels, each of whom may be recognized by certain behavioral traits known to the informed observer.

Others are far more difficult to expose, the *Breviarium* admits, and the dissimulator is free to use any suitable artifice that might assist in this undertaking. Some of these artifices are entirely ordinary: "to grasp another's intentions, it will benefit you to suborn someone with whom he is in love, and by this device you will discover his greatest secrets."[176] Many others depend largely on simulation and outright falsehood: "You can test a false friend this way. Send someone to give him the news that you find yourself on the brink of ruin, and that the documents upon which your position [in the world] depended turned out to have been false. If he listens to all of this as if none of it were his concern, then he never was your friend."[177] Still others are even more irregular. "Sometimes," *Mazarin* suggests, "you can act as a doctor, mixing certain ingredients into the food that overexcite your tablemates and make them talk too much."[178] Or, he adds, "every so often one may have intercepted letters addressed to one's subordinates, in order to read them carefully and [even] answer them."[179] In short, the *Breviarium politicorum* takes the traditional moral, ethical, and political justifications for dissimulation and turns them on their heads. Each brief chapter of the work bears a title that is a well-worn *topos* of moral philosophy—"know yourself," "don't let yourself be deceived," "avoid others' envy," "be circumspect," "acquire prudence," "gain and grant honor," "hear and speak one's own praises," "possess the mind's inner peace," "avoid vanity," "seek the truth"—subsequently belied by the author's purely instrumental and often brutal pragmatism.

With *Mazarin*'s breviary for statesmen and "private gentlemen" the early modern discourse on political dissimulation finally comes full circle. The *Breviarium* returns to Machiavelli's scandalous "Italian" blend of simulation and dissimulation, short-circuiting a century and a half of strenuous efforts to distinguish between the two. The printer's 1698 protestation—"use this [prudence], not to deceive others, but to prevent others' deceits, and . . . as an antidote to fraud, which is so rife these days"—must have rung hollow indeed for *Mazarin*'s readers.[180] Reason of state was, in any case, gradually losing its allure as a means to justify absolutism. By the year of the cardinal's death, Descartes was long in his grave, Thomas Hobbes had published his *Leviathan* years before, John Locke would soon complete his *Essay on Tolerance,* and Baruch Spinoza's subversive ideas had begun to circulate (and would only a few years later, in 1670, culminate in the revolutionary *Tractatus theologico-politicus*): the early radical enlightenment was underway.[181] Of course, Cardinal Mazarin was among the most powerful men in Europe in the years during which he, or perhaps someone close to him, composed this work. He could say what he wished, at least in a purportedly anonymous tract of practical moral and political philosophy like this one: or could he?

This breviary, which takes Machon's motto ("Dissimulation is the mainstay of affairs") off the wall of a bedroom in Paris and puts it into the pocket of both the mighty and the merely ambitious, essentially demonstrates that absolutist politics was completely subject to the rule of dissimulation. Dissimulation was not, in other words, a tool of a centrally located sovereign who was accountable for all of the activities of state power. Rather, it was power itself, reproducing itself endlessly in every interchange at all levels of human affairs. The most able practitioners of this art were the most powerful members of their society, or would become such, but they were nonetheless—as in the case of the laws of civility—governed by a design far greater than themselves.[182] This design was not due to a divinity, for God is nowhere to be found in the *Breviarium*. Nor was it to be attributed to the all-powerful sovereign, who is in these pages an immensely remote and nebulous figure. The actions of these persons—and all other members of the Old Regime as well—were instead informed and disciplined by dissimulation to such a degree that it produced their subjectivity as such (as *Mazarin*'s work tries to show).

This, however, left absolutism at an impasse. For if the rules of dissimulation, as articulated by the *Breviarium,* were not restricted solely to the prince but openly observed by many other members of society who acted as "politicians" (to use *Mazarin*'s term) in their own right, then increasingly the subjects of absolutism would be led to see dissimulation to be inherent in the very workings of the state and would reject the latter's claims on their allegiance as just another instance of duplicity.[183] The *arcana imperii* would, like the secrets of the heart, always be hidden from scrutiny; there could be no more sincerity in the affairs of state than in everyday life. Yet Machiavelli had presciently warned that this was precisely what could not be allowed to happen, for the prince had to "appear" to possess all of the moral and spiritual qualities that were expected of him in the common view of the multitudes ruled by him. Otherwise the sovereign would lose his reputation as an exemplary person and, with it, control over both his subjects and his dominions. No one else, according to Machiavelli, was meant to act as a fox or as a lion; and an entire society of foxes, like that envisaged in the *Breviarium,* could only end with its members turning on one another. The Old Regime states would eventually be shaken to their roots by this crisis of sincerity, as European political theory turned its focus to consensus and contract.[184]

To Rule and to Live

Giovanni Battista Ricciardi (1623–1686), scion of a noble Pisan family, taught philosophy at the University of Pisa, wrote comedies and verse, and befriended the painter Salvator Rosa, with whom he shared his interest in Neostoicism. In 1672 Ricciardi published in Perugia an unusual drama, perhaps composed some years earlier, entitled *Chi non sa fingere non sa vivere, ovvero le cautele politiche* (Who does not know how to dissemble does not know how to live, or political prudence).[185] In this three-act play, set in Renaissance Naples, King Alfonso learns from an anonymous letter that members of his immediate entourage are plotting against his throne.[186] To discover the conspirators he lays an elaborate trap for them, centered around an act of (dis)simulation: he will accuse Enrico, his closest and dearest confidant at court, of high treason, confiscate his property and expel him from the kingdom. Enrico, who had loyally brought King Alfonso the anonymous letter to read, is his willing co-conspirator in the counterplot. The sudden turn of events when Enrico falls from grace creates confusion among the ladies of the court—Portia and Elena—who are vying for Enrico's affection, and who are put to the test by the latter through a series of amorous ruses. The king spies on his courtiers, waiting to see who will try to move against him with Enrico out of the way, and eventually uncovers the plotters, revealing himself only after the others have unintentionally shown him their true thoughts. However, thanks to switched letters, Alfonso wrongly comes to think that he is being betrayed by his beloved Enrico (who at the outset he had specifically asked to simulate treachery), and turns against him. This results in a climactic scene in which the two, disoriented by multiple layers of simulation and dissimulation, cannot understand one another any longer. Ultimately their friendship is saved by a fortunate coincidence, and all ends well: the two ladies are married off, the traitors are executed, and Enrico returns to his proper place at court by the side of the king.

Ricciardi's play is a mise-en-scène of some of the chief commonplaces of the early modern discourse on dissimulation. Early in the first act of the play, Enrico's two servants, Florante and Trespolo, have the following exchange:

> *Florante:* If for no other reason than that one wears a mask all the time, it seems to me.
>
> *Trespolo:* It doesn't seem to me that, outside of Carnival, I've seen any masks, and yet my eyes aren't on the soles of my shoes. . . .
>
> *Florante:* It's not that you don't see, but—as it happens—you don't reflect on what you do see.
>
> *Trespolo:* Go hang yourself.
>
> *Florante:* Let's see if you don't end up saying the same thing that I do. . . . Tell me, doesn't wearing a mask mean to try to be something that one isn't, in order not to be recognized by people?[187]

There are at least three overt references to the debate over simulation and dissimulation here. Florante's first remark seems a direct citation of Paolo Sarpi (see line from a letter of Sarpi's, quoted as the epigraph to the section on Accetto, in chapter 2), his second remark appears to refer to Gracián and perhaps to Accetto, and the third to the classic definition of simulation and dissimulation repeated by hundreds of treatise-writers from the Middle Ages onward ("one simulates that which is not, one dissimulates that which is"). The anonymous letter to King Alfonso, warning of the plot to overthrow him, instead employs the language of Botero, Lipsius, Saavedra, and other reason-of-state theorists: "when you read this, do not give any sign of being upset, and do not get it into your head to have me held by your guards, because the conspirators are close to you, and it is more important for your safety that they not come to know of this note than for you to find out who I am."[188] Alfonso tells Enrico that "I had to master myself forcefully, [dis]simulating in order to hold back the stream of blood that, in the turbulent flood of my emotional tumult, was flooding quickly across my face. I pretended to read other things, and, masking my face with a sardonic laugh, I spoke indifferently with the knights nearest to me."[189] No reason-of-state theorist from Machiavelli and Guicciardini onward could have described more concisely either the need for a sovereign to act with self-control and wear a mask, or the dangers for dissimulation of sudden anger or other powerful emotions. Furthermore, as the king explains to his confidant, taking another page from reason-of-state doctrine, "many times one must tolerate [dissimulate] the evil that would be exacerbated by a violent application of the remedy for it," for "it is necessary to save external appearances, so that justice does not seem like tyranny."[190]

The ruse practiced by Alfonso and Enrico to catch the conspirators involves the kind of royal trickery of which Ducci, for one, had warned courtiers to beware. The former tells the latter that "after much thought, and after looking at all the pros and cons of the matter, I have decided to feign casting you out of my grace, and, giving show of having a very good reason to do so, but not saying what it is, because I cannot have anyone discover it to be feigned, I will confiscate all of your possessions."[191] The trap is set to be sprung, but, in an anticlimax, by the end of the second act the culprits have already been found out. Ricciardi's chief concern from this point on is to explore the ways in which simulation and dissimulation contaminate human relationships under absolutism. Although some allusions to counterfeiting in love may be found, these *fingimenti amorosi* are of much less interest to the playwright than those that have a political purpose. Adopting the Neostoic perspective first proposed by Lipsius, Ricciardi shows us a sovereign who, by late in the third and final act, finds himself unable to know who to trust any more (scenes 18–19). The price to be paid for willfully setting this game in motion is the utter solitude of the head of state. Although the king eventually restores his relationship with his chosen confidant Enrico, the warning is clear: in the government of hidden political designs, the imperative of secrecy renders the absolute ruler subject to the implacable logic of reason of state; he is alone and unable to trust even his closest companion, because he must believe that the behavior of others is not as it seems. Although the play has a happy ending for the virtuous Alfonso and his loyal subjects, we see that simulation and dissimulation, so very difficult to control, threaten to disrupt not only the possibility of companionship and intimacy with others but the possibility of belief in anything other than the maintenance of the state itself.[192]

At the end of the play the king concludes, consonant with reason-of-state doctrine, that "the great and powerful should learn that, in matters of uncertainty that are important to the state, the truth is found through feigning."[193] In this truly Baroque vision of the illusory nature of human experience, the truth is so weak that unaided it is often unable to reveal itself for what it is. We are left to rely instead upon the remedy of dissimulation to achieve what Naudé called *déniaisement,* or to "by indirections find directions out," as Polonius put it (*Hamlet* II.i). King Alfonso's trusted vassal Enrico observes, citing that famous commonplace of reason of state, that "in short, fiction is the mother of truth: who does not know how to dissemble does not know how to rule."[194] And this would appear to be the moral of the play, if not for one thing: oddly, the title is never referred to, or even alluded to, at any point in the text. Although in the dialogue between the characters there are only the vaguest echoes of Accetto's treatise, where we first encountered the formula *chi non sa fingere non sa vivere* (who does not know how to dissemble does not know how to live), the motto of political dissimulation has been clearly replaced by the motto of honest dissimulation as the title of the play. Perhaps Ricciardi felt it incumbent to avoid in the title any overt reference to Machiavellianism, which was associated with the motto *nescit regnare qui nescit dissimulare* (who does not know how to dissemble does not know how to rule) in the minds of many, and with which reason-of-state doctrine was still inextricably entangled, nearly a century and a half after the Florentine secretary's death. Yet, of course, the characters in the play make recourse to that notorious epigram, as well as to the vocabulary of reason of state. The play's subtitle, "or of political prudence," suggests an equivalence rather than an opposition between knowing how to rule and how to live: Ricciardi, in short, makes these two mottos synonymous. The fine arts of governing (*regnare*) and living (*vivere*) are, in essence, interchangeable, and determined by the same universal law of dissimulation. Although the plot of the play is concerned with the uses of feigning in statecraft and politics, these techniques, and the wary approach to experience that they demand, appear in the author's eyes equally necessary in the everyday affairs of the early modern individual. The subtle semantic shift from *regnare* to *vivere*, from ruling to living, that Ricciardi effects in the title of his play thus anticipates Mazarin's conclusions concerning the uncontrollable spread of dissimulation in Baroque Europe.[195] Finally, the title itself of the work constitutes a perfect model for the practice of dissimulation: for it may or may not contain the only known reference in print made in Italy before the twentieth century to the greatest, most enigmatic and elusive of all early modern theories of dissimulation and the culture of secrecy, Torquato Accetto's *Della dissimulazione onesta*.

CHAPTER 5

The Writing on the Walls

Fingere e dissimulare se bene al tempo d'hoggi sono stimate virtù,
e tengono notabili qualità fra le comuni opinioni; perdono
nondimeno questi tali i loro veri amici.

These days feigning and dissimulating are considered virtues,
and are esteemed by popular opinion for their special
qualities; nevertheless those (who practice them) lose their
true friends.

Pio Rossi, Il convito morale (1639)

Penelope's Tears

Even in those Old Regime states in which the rule of dissimulation was
most deeply rooted, there were the stirrings of change by the middle
years of the seventeenth century. Anti-court sentiments ran high in
many places, although the courts continued to grow in size and influence. Six major rebellions rocked Europe in the decade of 1640–1650,
weakening the foundations of reason-of-state doctrine. Although the
transnational standards of civility seemed secure among the dominant
groups, the private sphere began to develop rapidly in some of the most
economically advanced parts of Europe (such as Holland), leading to
the first challenges to the seemingly immutable conventions of the
"good society." However, these different secular developments seemed
too widely scattered to pose any real threat to the prominence of dissimulation in Old Regime culture, politics, and society. Organized
religion—whether Catholic or Protestant—had long resisted the allure

of this discourse, of course, with the exception of marginalized groups of religious dissidents and persecuted cults. Although regularly practiced (more than once a year) chiefly by the Catholic elite throughout most of the seventeenth century, as the historian R. Po-Chia Hsia has argued, confession stood as the spiritual "other" of dissimulation for, in the ritual of the confessional, conscience was supposed to be subjected to a rigorous examination, represented fully and sincerely, and subsequently disciplined to conform with religious norms.[1]

The saintly Charles Borromeo instructed confessors not to administer the sacrament of confession to "those who present themselves without the necessary internal and external preparation" for this potentially uncomfortable and decidedly austere exercise in self-scrutiny, contrition, and penitence.[2] Unlike Catholicism, however, there was no church of dissimulation and no universally recognized breviary for the fellowship of initiates. One was initiated into its doctrines by belonging, or aspiring to belong, to the loosely woven network of institutions that constituted the backbone of the Old Regime: for, as we have seen, the tacit knowledge or practice of dissimulation was considered necessary to many segments of that society, whether statesmen or courtiers or urban patricians. By the second half of the Seicento both Ricciardi and the author of the *Breviarium politicorum* understood, however, that the distinction in the discourse on dissimulation between moral, civil, and political spheres could not long hold, with the result that its power began to be undermined as the precepts of the culture of secrecy became increasingly diffused across the social spectrum.

The reception of the discourse on dissimulation was far from uniform, and although its principles found wide acceptance in the culture at large, there were also numerous challenges to them. As the seventeenth century advanced, individuals scattered around Europe began to explore avenues of approach to a moral ideal—namely sincerity—that figured as the secular "other" of dissimulation. Although Montaigne, among prominent Catholics, had promoted the ideal of sincerity many years before, and although its principles had long been part of Protestant theology, sincerity was still a relatively unfamiliar concept for many members of Counter-Reformation societies.[3] The redoubtable Pio Rossi complained in 1639 in his *Convito morale*, a collection of essays on contemporary moral life, that "sincerity and frankness are very rare in the intentions of men."[4] He added to his lament in the 1657 edition of the work: "sincerity is wandering, roaming, and banished from the world."[5] The artists and intellectuals who endorsed this ideal of sincerity were often not intimately connected to the patronage networks of the state, the court, or the church, and embraced sincerity as the secular version of the confessional, free of rigid ceremonial and convention.[6] Such freedom, however, generally came at the cost of being excluded from the power centers of the Old Regime.

Accetto complained in *Della dissimulazione onesta* that, because envy and greed were rampant in contemporary Italy, one had to be quite cautious in displaying one's own happiness or good fortune.[7] In order to avoid attracting the potentially dangerous envy of others, it was important to know how to keep one's innermost joys from being exposed to view. But the same held for any display of emotion, no matter how pleasant or unpleasant. The transparent individual was simply far too vulnerable to ruthless manipulation or exploitation by others seeking to gain an advantage in the superheated competition for social and economic advancement. In chapter 8 of his slender treatise, Accetto takes the Homeric figure of Odysseus as an ideal model of the opaque dissimulator, singling out the passage in the *Odyssey* in which the wanderer returns at last to Ithaca and pays a visit in disguise to his wife Penelope (19.204–212).[8] Unlike the cunning Odysseus, the loyal Penelope has no means to hide her heart from her unknown guest. At the wanderer's words, tears flow like melted snow down her cheeks, offering visible and tangible signs of her inner purity. Odysseus, on the other hand, hardens his eyes to display no emotion at all, as if they were made of "horn or iron," although he is deeply moved by what he sees and hears. For Accetto, those who have to accommodate to the rules of life under the Old Regime are left no choice but to imitate Odysseus: one's tears will have to flow, but only "inwardly" and invisibly. In the seamless continuity between her thoughts, words, and gestures, Penelope embodies sincerity itself, while Odysseus represents instead the impassive model of passion without expression. From Accetto's point of view, to act like Penelope in public means, inevitably, to risk losing face, and a great deal more besides; whereas to act like Odysseus means to know how to keep oneself—that is, one's true self—secret and therefore secure.

One of the key indices for tracking the shifting ground beneath absolutism is to be found, then, in the growth of the early modern discourse on sincerity.[9] As the previous chapters have argued, anyone in the least ambitious had to know how to maintain silence, to wear a mask and to exercise self-dominion in the public domain. However, some did dream of other and better modes of existence, without the endless self-surveillance and wholly instrumental image-management needed to make one's way in the only world that mattered. One such mode—the sincere expression of the self—required a reversal of prevalent attitudes toward truth-telling as they pertained to moral (if not religious) experience. Perhaps Penelope's tears could be openly displayed under certain circumstances, among one's own innermost circle of friends, or between lovers, where the unwelcome gaze of outsiders would not intrude into this hard-won intimacy. Perhaps moral virtue and the expression of the self were not to be kept isolated from one another but were instead to coincide publicly, as Augustine had argued long ago. To do so would, however, overthrow one of the very cornerstones of the Old Regime culture of secrecy. The dichotomy between the conduct of a virtuous life for oneself and the instrumental rationality of public life, which presupposed a pragmatic accommodation to religious, political, and social hierarchies, grew increasingly difficult to balance in the later Seicento.

At the epicenter of the most powerful European absolutist state of the era, Madeleine de Scudéry (1607–1701) recounted, in a "conversation" taken from one of her popular novels and entitled "De la Dissimulation et de la Sincerité" (On dissimulation and sincerity), a day on which a group of friends began "without knowing it to speak of dissimulation, which courtiers are more often accused [of practicing] than the rest of the society."[10] When one of the interlocutors in the conversation—Dom Pedro (not surprisingly, he is a Spaniard)—attempts to defend dissimulation as a masterpiece of prudence, another responds polemically: "can you praise a thing directly opposed to sincerity, which makes life sweet for honest people and without which the world's business would be nothing other than continual deception?"[11] In the rest of the conversation, the participants speak mainly about the value of sincerity as an effective counter to the influence of dissimulation both at court and elsewhere. There is no mention of the trend-setting capital city, Paris, but the dialogue makes it clear that the fashion of the times was turning against the discourse on dissimulation, which could not take into account the new social relations (and new forms of etiquette) then emerging with the growth of the French metropolis, by then the largest urban center on the continent.

Although they raise questions about the effect of sincerity in a number of different contexts—should one say everything that one thinks when in polite society? can friends or lovers be completely sincere? are kings exempt from frankness?—the men and women in this circle of friends can find no way to dismiss Mathilde's argument that "sincerity necessarily brings with itself all the beauty of truth, all the charms of frankness, and all the sweetness of trust. It ordinarily produces a certain opening of the heart that can be seen in one's eyes. . . . It is the enemy of every artifice and all dissimulation."[12] This *ouverture de coeur* was one of the great themes of the discourse on sincerity throughout the early modern period, and in "De la Dissimulation et de la Sincerité" it received its apotheosis.[13] Sincerity was essential for overcoming artifice and allowing the spontaneous and public expression—like Penelope's tears—of passions and emotions, without risking social death through the ridicule of others.

Madeleine de Scudéry knew the royal court well, where intrigue and dissimulation reigned, but led an independent existence in the city of Paris.[14] Loyal to her king and God, she was a far from marginal member of the social and political world of the Old Regime, and an unlikely candidate to destabilize the rule of dissimulation. Her dialogue nevertheless synthesizes some of the main points of an ongoing controversy that was to grow more intense with the cultural turn toward the Enlightenment.[15] As the title of her brief text suggests, the discourses on dissimulation and sincerity were not only diametrically opposite but were now destined to accompany one another on the forward march of early modern culture. Only a century later, with the end of the monarchy in France, was the Gordian knot connecting this semantic couple finally cut.[16]

Cherasco: The *Saletta del Silenzio*

I wish to return now to my original point of departure in northwestern Italy. Here there survives a remarkable visual record of not only the endurance of the discourse on dissimulation, but the pressure under which it began to be placed at the close of the Seicento. The town of Cherasco, which sits on a strategically positioned hill overlooking the juncture of the Stura di Demonte and Tanaro river valleys in southern Piedmont, was in the seventeenth and eighteenth centuries sometimes a summer residence and place of refuge for the court of Turin. Its rigorously geometrical Baroque town plan and complex modern fortifications must have made it seem both familiar (Turin was also laid out on a grid) and secure to court officials. The main streets of the old walled town were lined with the palaces of the prosperous local nobility, who hosted the Savoy family and the court when they visited there. During the terrible plague of 1630–31 that accompanied the War of the Mantuan Succession, for instance, Duke Victor Amadeus I and Duchess Christine of France, followed by court and retinue, fled Turin and came to stay in the town; according to local chroniclers, no one died of the epidemic. During the siege of Turin by French forces in 1706, the Shroud of Turin was brought for safekeeping to Palazzo Salmatoris in Cherasco for three days.[17] There it was placed in the recently frescoed *Saletta del silenzio,* an unique work by the local architect and painter Sebastiano Taricco (1641–1710).

Taricco was an important and successful Piedmontese artist by the standards of his day. Like other local painters, he likely traveled outside of the region early in his career, and his work displays the influence of the classicizing Bolognese art of Guido Reni and Domenichino. Lacking international credentials, however, Taricco spent much of his career laboring in and around Cherasco and nearby provincial towns, where he was also active as an architect and designer. For instance, he was responsible for the scenery and props for a spectacular religious processional in Cherasco in 1688 (for which he also served as director). Although Taricco was recognized as a leading citizen of Cherasco, and even served for a time as the town's mayor, he eventually set his sights on the capital of Piedmont. Turin was, as a regional cultural center, rather less cosmopolitan than Florence, Milan, or Rome in this period, however, and artists there had to rely largely on the church and the court for commissions. Although he did little for the court, Taricco managed to obtain work in Turin, returning to Cherasco periodically for other locally commissioned artistic projects, and thus served as a link between the capital city and the provinces in the closing years of the seventeenth century.[18] His daughter Domenica Taricco studied painting with her father and also became an artist, after taking holy vows and entering the convent of S. Andrea in Chieri.

In the *Saletta del silenzio* (The chamber of silence), one of Taricco's last known works, he produced a fresco cycle representing two of the key themes of the discourse on dissimulation: secrecy and silence. The presence in Cherasco of Taricco's frescos shows that, as late as the beginning of the eighteenth century, these themes were still circulating on the periphery of Italian absolutism.[19] In fact, the cycle was commissioned for a space that was not only located on the *piano nobile,* but directly faced the top landing of the main staircase of the palace. With the doors open and the room illuminated, some of the frescos on the south wall (especially the image appearing in fig. 9) may be seen by anyone ascending the staircase.[20] Visitors to the adjacent *Sala della pace* (The hall of peace), where the peace treaty ending the War of the Mantuan Succession was signed in 1631 by some of Europe's leading statesmen, including Cardinal Mazarin, may enter it by passing through the *Saletta* first.

The four walls of the small chamber, as well as the ceiling, were entirely covered by the artist with emblems, symbols, ancient deities, biblical figures, and portraits of moral philosophers associated with the twin themes of silence and secrecy. (One of the four tondos in the ceiling has been destroyed, but the rest of the fresco cycle has been restored and currently appears to be in good condition.)[21] Taricco certainly must have used Cesare Ripa's best-selling *Iconologia* and other standard emblem books in planning the iconographical program of this work. The figure of Angerona bears more than a passing resemblance to Ripa's emblem of secrecy, Andrea Alciato's emblem of silence in his famous *Emblemata* shows and explains the same Harpocratic gesture ("let him press his lips, and with his finger mark his silences"), and the scrawny lion looks rather like the one in Saavedra's *Empresas,* but the artist also must have drawn on other, as yet unidentified, erudite sources treating these same themes.[22] It is certainly possible that a local savant was also involved in the selection and arrangement of the imagery and the accompanying epigraphs or mottos in Latin and Italian. Such a decorative program reflects, in any case, considerable familiarity with the cultural imperatives of dissimulation, secrecy, and silence, although the precise motive for the commission remains obscure.

Above the painted colonnade in the *Saletta del silenzio* are found eight emblematic images arranged in groups of two, unaccompanied by text, and placed at opposite corners of each wall. These represent: (1a) an intact pomegranate and (1b) a crocodile; (2a) a key and (2b) a necklace with a seal; (3a) a split pomegranate and (3b) a hand holding a left index finger to a disembodied pair of lips (see fig. 9); and (4a) a hooked fish with rod and line and (4b) a net. These are arrayed above a series of historical, biblical, and mythological figures: Seneca, Xenocrates, Isocrates, Pythagoras, Epaminondas, Simonides, Solomon, Judith, Tacita, and Angerona, each accompanied by a Latin epigraph concerning silence, taciturnity, or secrecy. There are also two unidentified male figures on the south wall framing the doorway: one is crowned with a laurel wreath and bears a Latin epigraph; the other has his right index finger pressed to his lips and a seal clutched in his left hand (fig. 3). Above the room's apertures—two doors, one window and one *trompe l'oeil* perspective—are four more emblems, each accompanied by a Latin or Italian motto, representing a white lily about to bloom (fig. 4), an

FIGURE 3. Fresco detail (south wall), man with seal in hand. Sebastiano Taricco, *Saletta del silenzio* (1706), fresco, Palazzo Salmatoris, Cherasco, Italy. Reproduced by permission of the City of Cherasco. Photograph by author.

FIGURE 4. Fresco detail (east wall), lily with epigraph *Tanto più odoroso quanto più chiuso*. Sebastiano Taricco, *Saletta del silenzio* (1706), fresco, Palazzo Salmatoris, Cherasco, Italy. Reproduced by permission of the City of Cherasco. Photograph by author.

hourglass, a beehive, and a prowling lion, respectively. On the ceiling are more emblems: a smoking brand on a heap of ashes, a turtle, and a half-open oyster displaying pearls (fig. 5), each accompanied this time by an Italian motto concerning silence.[23] Finally, in the center of the ceiling is found an emblem representing a white goose in flight with a stone held firmly in its beak (fig. 6), accompanied by the motto *tuta silentio* (silence preserves [one] from harm); this image, discussed in chapter I, refers to the Latin version (*De garrulitate*) of Plutarch's *Moralia*, 510A–B.[24]

This uniquely rich complex of emblems, most of which are readily interpretable on their own terms, does not narrate a story or sequence of actions; rather, the viewer is offered a symbolic account of the modes and functions of secrecy and silence. As the epigraph brandished by the unnamed figure on the south wall states, not without irony, "it is excellent to demonstrate [by] things."[25] In the *Saletta del silenzio* the early modern virtues of secrecy and silence, which would otherwise remain undetectable, appear to the viewer as tangible and visible. No references

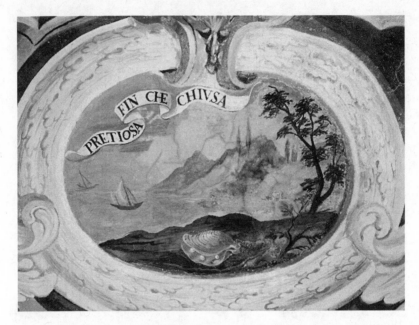

FIGURE 5. Ceiling tondo, emblem of open oyster with epigraph *Pretiosa fin che chiusa*. Sebastiano Taricco, *Saletta del silenzio* (1706), fresco, Palazzo Salmatoris, Cherasco, Italy. Reproduced by permission of the City of Cherasco. Photograph by author.

are made to the sovereign, the court, or polite society, although the eclectic synthesis of symbols, *topoi,* and figures taken both from antiquity and from the Renaissance is typical of the classicizing culture of the age. Not surprisingly, there is no mention of dissimulation in any of the epigraphs or mottos, yet its governing themes of complete self-control, reticence, taciturnity, and withdrawal are everywhere in evidence.

Drawing on the *mare magnum* of emblem literature, the *Saletta del silenzio* provides the viewer a compendium of allusions to this same thematics of the secret: the lily, of which "the more closed [it is], the richer the scent"; the beehive, which holds a "hidden accumulation"; the still-smoking brand, which "lives with its reserve covered over" (that is, is hidden by ashes); the oyster, with its pearls, is "precious as long as it is closed"; the turtle is "only monstrous" when it shows itself; and so on. The emblems set above the frescoed colonnade, without texts accompanying them, point in this same direction, while elaborating specifically on the theme of silence. The hooked fish is mute (*muto come un pesce,* or "silent as a fish," is an old Italian proverb) and has been caught because it opened its mouth; the seal—sitting on a red cloth—is virtually identi-

FIGURE 6. Detail of ceiling fresco, emblem of goose in flight with epigraph *Tuta silentio*. Sebastiano Taricco, *Saletta del silenzio* (1706), fresco, Palazzo Salmatoris, Cherasco, Italy. Reproduced by permission of the City of Cherasco. Photograph by author.

cal to the one held by the figure of the goddess Angerona on the west wall; the key suggests a locked door, or a door that—like the human mouth—can be closed as well as opened; and the net indicates the traps spread for the careless and the unwary. The crocodile was believed to have been venerated by the Egyptians as an animal without a tongue, and thus serves here as a hieroglyph of silence.[26] The belief (which also appears in Saavedra's *Empresas*) that lions sleep with their eyes open, and hence are the epitome of vigilance, was an ancient commonplace; in a variation on this theme, Taricco's lion covers its tracks in order that its location not be disclosed.[27] The two pomegranates, one closed and the other split open (fig. 7), are set at opposite corners of the chamber, and point to the same dialectic of concealment and disclosure to which many of the other emblems clearly allude.

On the basis of these compelling images and the decorative program to which they belong, it seems that on earth there is really no wiser course of action than to choose secrecy and silence. The figures of the ancients, arrayed along the walls at eye level, all strive to remind the viewer in one way or another of the same high moral theme. Two pagan deities, identified by an accompanying epigraph, make a gesture calling

FIGURE 7. Fresco detail (south wall), emblem of split pomegranate. Sebastiano Taricco, *Saletta del silenzio* (1706), fresco, Palazzo Salmatoris, Cherasco, Italy. Reproduced by permission of the City of Cherasco. Photograph by author.

for silence: Angerona, "goddess of silence venerated by the Romans," presses a seal to her lips (fig. 8), and Tacita, "Roman goddess and guardian of secrets," holds her right forefinger directly in front of her mouth, as Harpocrates is usually shown to do. The mortal men and women represented here also display their wisdom concerning the twin virtues of secrecy and silence. The Platonic philosopher Xenocrates brandishes a banner stating "I regret some things that I have said, but I never regret having kept silent," while the poet Simonides displays a motto claiming that "it harms no one to keep silent, but [for something] to be spoken may bring harm."[28]

The Stoic philosopher Seneca's epigraph urges the viewer to "speak very little with others, and very much with oneself," and the ascetic soldier-statesman Epaminondas, renowned for never having uttered a falsehood, is accompanied by the words: "Listening makes you smart, talking makes you sorry."[29] Two Old Testament figures join Taricco's eclectic blend of figures, mottos, and symbols ransacked from the heritage of antiquity. Solomon warns that "a flattering mouth works ruin,"

ANGERONA · DEA
SILENTÝ À ROMANIS
VENERATA

FIGURE 8. Fresco detail (west wall), Angerona, Roman goddess of silence.
Sebastiano Taricco, *Saletta del silenzio* (1706), fresco, Palazzo Salmatoris,
Cherasco, Italy. Reproduced by permission of the City of Cherasco. Photograph
by author.

and Judith, holding the severed head of Holofernes in one hand while keeping her index finger to her lips with the other, implores: "I desire that you search not into what I am doing"[30] (see the image on this book's cover). The rhetorician Isocrates admonishes the viewer to "watch over words as carefully as you put down money," and the great early Greek philosopher of silence, Pythagoras, urges us to "keep silent or offer something better than silence."[31] All of these epigraphs would seem to dovetail neatly with the emblems painted high overhead: they not only suggest that secrecy and taciturnity are inseparably intertwined, but constitute one of the most valuable kinds of practical human knowledge—the knowledge of when and how *not* to speak one's heart or mind.

The name traditionally given to Taricco's fresco cycle is, therefore, somewhat misleading. Silence, as represented in the *Saletta del silenzio,* is not limited to the traditional ideal of cautious restraint in the use of speech, perhaps best embodied by Guazzo's theory of civil conversation, for which "knowing how to keep silent gathers no less admiration than skillful speech, because if the latter displays eloquence and doctrine, the former bears signs of gravity and prudence."[32] Just as we have been given two ears and two eyes, but only one tongue, so the use of words should be moderate and circumspect in the best of circumstances, according to this tradition.[33] Although this is all well and good from Taricco's perspective, there is nonetheless a striking insistence in the Cherasco frescos on the representation of silence *together with* secrecy: these two intertwining terms cannot be effectively isolated from each other, at least not in the context of early modern Europe. This is, of course, entirely consonant with the discourse on dissimulation examined in the previous chapters of the present book. Themes of enclosure, covering, veiling, disguise, invisibility, and impenetrability are prominent on the walls of the *Saletta*, embodied in images such as the oyster hiding its pearls, the closed lily giving off its scent, the turtle withdrawing into his shell, the ashes covering the embers, and the beehive's rich reserve of honey that cannot be seen.

Among the epigraphs culled from antiquity and painted onto the walls of Palazzo Salmatoris by Taricco we can, as has already been suggested, detect a similar thematics. Some of these nuggets of ancient wisdom reinforce the age-old adage that "silence is golden," but others, from Tacita's guardianship of secrets to Judith's desire to act unseen by others, suggest something else: a cultural imperative to defend, and to act in, secrecy. No particular political, ethical, or civil motive for this endorsement of the early modern culture of secrecy can be found in

FIGURE 9. Fresco detail (south wall), emblem of silence. Sebastiano Taricco, *Saletta del silenzio* (1706), fresco, Palazzo Salmatoris, Cherasco, Italy. Reproduced by permission of the City of Cherasco. Photograph by author.

Taricco's frescos, and there is no evident reference to the patron who must have commissioned the work (although we may legitimately suspect that such a reference is hidden somewhere within the decorative program of the room). Supported by the combined cultures of antiquity and modernity, dissimulation has simply replaced prudence as the most effective, most relevant, and most pragmatic approach to dealing with the infinite contingencies of existence.[34] Anyone well versed in the cultural precepts of the Old Regime would undoubtedly have recognized many of these emblems and epigraphs, and inferred that this was a representation legitimizing the culture of secrecy and calling on the viewer to submit to its discipline (fig. 9).

What might have been the original purpose of this decorative program? The fact that the Shroud of Turin was housed in the *Saletta del silenzio* during its brief stay in Cherasco in 1706 does not indicate that Taricco's fresco cycle, which must have been completed not long before the shroud was brought to the Palazzo Salmatoris, was inspired by a religious theme.[35] As the most precious relic of the Savoy dynasty, the shroud undoubtedly was a source of wonder for devout subjects of the realm, and the setting of the *Saletta del silenzio* may have suggested an aura of wordless awe. Or perhaps Palazzo Salmatoris instead offered the most satisfactory security arrangements in town.[36] It seems to be beyond doubt that Taricco's decorative program for this room was not, in any event, directly motivated by religious concerns. Nor were his frescos intended to be puzzles for an erudite public, meant to keep viewers guessing at their true meaning. The significance of each individual emblem was, then as now, readily accessible to anyone steeped in the *cultura classicista* of the period. Although the arrangement of the frescos may possess some recondite allegorical significance, many viewers must have understood without difficulty the overall message that they were meant to convey. One of the most remarkable aspects of this fresco cycle is, in point of fact, its serene embrace of the twin themes of secrecy and silence, in spite of all of the questionable cultural baggage that they must have brought with them by this point in history. In the *Saletta del silenzio* there is to be found none of the tense, even paranoid atmosphere of the *Breviarium* or Ricciardi's *Chi non sa fingere non sa vivere*.

We can infer from this work's notable iconographical serenity, moreover, that the artist clearly did not think its themes controversial for contemporary viewers in Cherasco: there is no trace of a critique to be found here. On the contrary, in displaying and exalting the positive moral and practical value of secrecy and silence, Taricco emphatically endorses dissimulation as a legitimate foundation stone of Old Regime culture and society. In other words, the painter attempts—in a gesture not without irony—to dissimulate nothing in the *Saletta del silenzio*. No masks appear in the frescos, perhaps because of the negative connotations so often attached to them in the traditions of moral philosophy and emblem literature. The faces of the human and divine figures on the walls nevertheless maintain the same disciplined lack of expression (almost mask-like in their impassivity) that characterizes innumerable portraits of the early modern elite: in the guise of biblical, mythical, and historical personages, the latter are present in the paintings. This is another indication that the program of the *Saletta del silenzio* is intended primarily to support the existing culture of secrecy. Here at the periphery of the power structures of Europe, Taricco insists somewhat anachronistically that, if practiced with great enough moral rigor, dissimulation can still be a desideratum for those who belong—or aspire to belong—to the insider circles of the Old Regime.

Although the Piedmontese artist privileges concealment over disclosure, the latter nonetheless has a place in the *Saletta del silenzio*. A small opening for the discourse of sincerity is also encoded in the room's decorative program, as if to acknowledge the trend by then well under way in the leading countries of Europe: there were to be no important treatises on dissimulation written or published in the eighteenth century, just a few scattered dissertations and articles. Taricco seems more than willing to suggest that, despite the dominance of the virtues of secrecy and silence, these are not the only ones to which one may legitimately aspire. At the proper moment, with the proper persons, and under the proper circumstances, openness and frankness may be used, even if to subvert the rule of dissimulation: the choice depends upon the decorum of the situation. Diametrically opposite the ripe red pomegranate set in the west corner of the north wall is found a split or open pomegranate (at the east corner of south wall). The emblem of the split pomegranate, exposing its lustrous seeds to the light, is highly polysemous. Although it may represent a warning about the risks of disclosure, one of its many other traditional meanings is that of the open heart that reveals itself freely to others.[37]

In other words, the split pomegranate is a multivalent symbol of sincerity and openness—the bright red seeds, visible through the broken skin of the fruit, represent a heart devoid of secrets and full of trust. The split pomegranate embodies the act of the intimate revelation of personal truths, calling on the viewer not only to be sincere but to assist others in what would elsewhere be called *prudentia cardiognostica,* or the analysis of one's sincere intentions.[38] One must willingly show oneself, and one's secrets, to others in order to be believed to be truly sincere: as Mlle de Scudéry reminds us, sincerity "ordinarily produces a certain opening of the heart that can be seen in one's eyes." In this sense the split pomegranate stands for the very opposite of the secrecy embodied by the still-closed pomegranate, whose inner treasures are hidden from view, like those of the oyster. The split pomegranate is not only more mature than in its previous stage of development, when it still encloses its seeds, but, in terms of temporal logic, marks a necessary climactic stage in the tree's annual reproductive cycle. Might Taricco's double perspective on the pomegranate refer to the contrast between the discourses of dissimulation and sincerity then emerging across Europe?

There are other hints of this same tension between concealment and disclosure in the *Saletta del silenzio.* The emblem of the key (on the east wall) is a case in point. The emblem accompanying the key is a seal, and so the fresco must be intended to refer chiefly to the key's ability to conceal. If a key serves to lock a door or a chest, however, then it must logically also serve to unlock it: only the particular circumstances can determine which is to be its function. On the north wall of the room, the Pythagorean dictum "Keep silent or offer something better than silence" is equally ambiguous. If the Greek philosopher makes the choice of silence a clear sign of virtue, his words nevertheless suggest that something better is possible. What could this be? The only authentic improvement that can be made on the absence of speech (which always possesses the potential for deception and falsehood) is the naked truth itself. In the context of the *Saletta del silenzio,* this cannot be truth in the metaphysical sense of *logos,* that is, something that stands on its own principles and may be discovered by anyone through the rigorous exercise of reason. Rather, it must be the intimate moral truth of the individual—the frankly disinterested expression of the innermost experience of heart and mind. The dominant thematics of secrecy and silence in the Cherasco frescos emphasize that a mode of communication based on sincerity is of limited use in Old Regime societies, for all the reasons with which readers are by now familiar. But this alternative cannot simply be dismissed any longer, and the potential force of its discourse must at least be acknowledged.

Last Words

The frescos in the *Saletta del silenzio* confirm that, from the core to the periphery of the Old Regime, select elements of the discourse on dissimulation persisted into the eighteenth century. For the culture of secrecy, however, the writing was on the wall. The growing appeal of the new ideals of sincerity progressively weakened and marginalized the discourse on dissimulation as the century wore on, and we find fewer and fewer traces of it in the written record. With the privilege of historical hindsight, it is not difficult to understand why discussions of dissimulation were anathema both for the Enlightenment and, later on, for Romanticism—the new directions in which more and more members of European societies had begun to move, albeit for many different reasons. This is not, of course, to suggest that dissimulation was no longer practiced. That could hardly be the case in the eighteenth century, whether in Venice, Paris, Madrid, or Vienna. The age of dissimulation had not, by any means, come to an end; but around the beginning of the new century it ceased to be a central concern for moral and political theorists, whose attention turned elsewhere.

We can, perhaps, crudely map this cultural turn by looking now at one last document in the long history of impassioned debate over dissimulation. A little more than a half-century after Taricco painted his fresco cycle in Cherasco, the second edition of Diderot's and D'Alembert's, *Encyclopédie* was published in 1759 in Lucca, probably the only place in Italy where such a politically and culturally unorthodox work could have appeared at this time.[39] The difference between these two cultural artifacts—a provincial Italian fresco cycle and one of the pathbreaking publications of the French Enlightenment— is marked in regard to their treatment of dissimulation. The *Encyclopédie*'s article on dissimulation, contributed by the German-born but French-speaking man of letters Johann Heinrich Samuel Formey (1711–1797), contrasts most unfavorably the self-centered solitude of the dissimulator or the tyrant to "the sweetness of society" *(la douceur de la société)* found among those who freely share their thoughts and feelings with each other.[40] The author, well versed in the careful distinctions developed by previous writers on the topic, observes that "the dissimulator keeps close watch on others, in order to prevent them from becoming able to know him."[41] Formey's sympathies, however, lie elsewhere, and his essay on dissimulation soon veers into an enthusiastic treatment of sincerity. He explains, with more than a touch of Leibnizian optimism, that "the first trait that is [instead] required in the character of a man suited to furthering society's happiness is frankness and sincerity."[42] Formey invokes the fellowship of the early Christian communities as a good example of such a society, in which the members were "of one heart and one soul."[43] This could certainly not be said of those early modern societies in which dissimulation had long been considered a key to worldly success, if not to the happiness of those who know how to use it best.

Dissimulation is in fact dismissed by Formey in the *Encyclopédie* for failing to contribute to "the happiness of society in general." Although political dissimulation may have a role in "great affairs" of state, Formey admits, in the exchanges between individuals that can lead to mutual happiness one has to "show those with whom we negotiate that we seek to join their advantage to our own."[44] Consensus, candor, and trust are, in other words, the most important elements in the *discretum* of everyday affairs. Formey notes that the use of secrecy is all too often necessary against those who would interfere with our legitimate undertakings in the pursuit of happiness: for the secret offers us a means to fight back against those who try to take away that which is most rightfully ours, namely happiness. In an ideal world, however, the use of secrecy would become rare indeed if everyone's projects were above reproach and hence without the need for invisibility.[45] It is "candor," not dissimulation, that draws others to our side and convinces them to share the same interests that we have. In essence, the happiness of society depends on the ability of its members to cooperate freely and openly in pursuit of their commonly held interests which can, like contracts, be discussed and scrutinized publicly. This will in turn lead, without the need for repression, to a reduction in conflict between the individuals and groups that constitute society.

Formey concludes his entry for the *Encyclopédie* with three points that reiterate the main arguments of the present book. First, he argues, "one should not esteem the character of those who, without choice or distinction, are reserved and secret." In other words, anyone who applies the rule of dissimulation to daily life, rather than to some extraordinary situation in which there is no other choice, is to be viewed with a very jaundiced and critical eye: if Formey insists upon this point, it may well be because he perceives that such a behavioral model is, or has been, widespread in Europe, especially among the educated classes resistant to Enlightenment ideals. Second, one should "not have secrets except concerning those things that truly merit them." By arguing that recourse to secrets should be made only in exceptional circumstances, and never as a rule, Formey seems to target the cornerstone of the practice of dissimulation itself, identified broadly with the Old Regime, to which the *Encyclopédie* was fundamentally antagonistic. Third, one's conduct should be such "that there is only the least possible need for secrets." All persons should live, in other words, in as transparent and open a manner as possible: the new code of sincerity, candor, and frankness will put an end to the silent and secret shadow world in which the truths of the self have been hidden for so long, and restore those truths to the "sweetness of society."[46] Formey's words, projecting an unlimited faith in a future without the need for dissimulation, confirm that a powerful solvent was eating away at the culture of secrecy, which in fact was destined to endure in France for only another thirty years.

With all of his usual perspicacity, Gracián notes in the *Oráculo manual* that "it is a maxim of prudent people to abandon things before being abandoned by them."[47] So it is with my book, which has at last come to its end.

Notes

This book's epigraph is taken from Salvator Rosa, *Il teatro della politica: sentenziosi afforismi [sic] della prudenza,* ed. Giorgio Baroni (Bologna: Commissione per i testi di lingua, 1991), 16, aphorism 128. Rosa likely drew on an ancient source for this aphorism, possibly Plutarch (*Consolatio ad Apollonium* 6) or Plutarch's own source, Pindar (*Pythian* 8).

Preface

1. René Descartes, *Oeuvres de Descartes,* eds. Charles Adam and Paul Tannery, vol. 10 (Paris: J. Vrin, 1996) 213.4–6: "Ut comœdi, moniti ne in fronte appareat pudor, personam induunt, sic ego hoc mundi teatrum conscensurus, in quo hactenus spectator exstiti, larvatus prodeo."

2. Fernand Hallyn, *Descartes: dissimulation et ironie* (Geneva: Droz, 2006) 9–15, provides a useful treatment of Descartes and dissimulation.

3. "Bene vixit, bene qui latuit": the motto is derived from Ovid (*Tristia*) with reference to the Epicurean dictum "láthe biôsas" or "live in hiding."

4. Louis D'Orléans, *Le Banquet et après dinée du Conte d'Arete, où il se traicte de la dissimulation du Roy de Navarre, & des moeurs de ses partisans* (Paris: Guillaume Bichon, 1594) 49: "mais l'homme estant un animal secret & cache, & qui comme les huistres se retire chez soy, & n'ouvre que quand il luy plait, & a qui il luy plaist, & de qui les pensees ne peuvent estre transparentes par la lumiere plus vive, & plus ardents rayons du Soleil, cest pourquoy il est aussi difficile d'en juger, qu'il est difficile de juger dun faux ou dun bon diamant au milieu des obscuritez de la nuict, ou dune belle ou laide peinture au milieu des tenebres."

5. See Sebastiano Taricco, *La Saletta del silenzio* (1706), Palazzo Salmatoris, Cherasco, Italy, ceiling tondo with emblem displaying an open oyster and the motto *Pretiosa sin che chiusa* (precious while closed).

6. D'Orléans 4: "Et quand je pense à l'homme, en l'estomach duquel se cachent tant de choses incogneües, i'acompare son edifice a un bastiment Royal. Pource qu'entre tant de sales, de chambres, & antichambres, tant de montees & tant de galleries, il y a un cabinet, qui est le cabinet du coeur, que le Prince qui est Dieu, s'est reservé pour son secret, & duquel il porte la clef, & dont il n'y a que luy seul qui sache les entrees & les issues & l'abondance des tresors, que sa Divinité supreme y a secrettement [*sic*] enfermez." [When I think of man, in whose insides so many unknown things are hidden, I compare his construction to a royal building, because among so many rooms, chambers and antechambers, ramps and galleries, there is a cabinet, which is the cabinet of the heart, that the prince (who is God) has reserved for his secret, and for which he holds the key, and for which he is the only one who knows all of the entrances and exits and the abundance of treasures that his supreme divinity has secretly hidden therein.]

7. Jean-Pierre Cavaillé, *Dis/simulations. Jules-César Vanini, François La Mothe Le Vayer, Gabriel Naudé, Louis Machon et Torquato Accetto: Religion, morale et politique au XVIIe siècle* (Paris: Champion, 2002).

8. Cavaillé, *Dis/simulations* 7–9: "une pratique réflexive de la dis/simulation"; "une écriture de la persécution et de la censure"; "une poétique et . . . une pratique subjective et subjectivante du secret."

9. Cavaillé, *Dis/simulations* 344: "à travers lesquelles une pleine, forte et douloureuse individualité insiste, résiste et d'abord, simplemente, existe." [through which a full, strong and painful individuality insists, resists and, first of all, simply exists.]

10. Cavaillé, *Dis/simulations* 9.

11. Cavaillé, *Dis/simulations* 17.

12. Cavaillé, *Dis/simulations* 24: "l'espace intérieur des consciences."

13. Cavaillé, *Dis/simulations* 31: "une chose est garder un secret, une autre mentir."

14. Cavaillé, *Dis/simulations* 332: "[Machon] lève au moins un peu le voile de la dissimulation, dans la mesure même où il ne parvient pas à dissimuler."

15. Cavaillé, *Dis/simulations* 341: "il faut entendre, dans le texte qui tait, le cri de la plaie." See also his reading of the works of Salvator Rosa: "Rosa montre de manière éclatante que sous le contrôle des apparences intériorisé, désiré et subi à la fois, couve la rébellion des esprits et bouillonne une rage rentrée" (38). [Rosa shows in a striking manner that, behind the control of appearances, at once interiorized, desired and sustained, there brews the rebellion of minds and boils a barely checked rage.]

16. Cavaillé, *Dis/simulations* 371–372: "la tension entre le souci de publication de la vérité et celui de sa protection par l'élaboration de procédures dis/simulatoires justifiables, est un élément fondamental de la culture occidentale."

17. Cavaillé, *Dis/simulations* 381–382.

18. Peter Burke, *The Art of Conversation* (Ithaca, NY: Cornell University Press, 1993) 92–93.

19. See, for instance, Jonathan Dewald, *The European Nobility, 1400–1800* (New York: Cambridge University Press, 1996), who examines the aristocratic elites, with an emphasis on cultural issues, on pp. 149–176.

20. Amedeo Quondam, "Elogio del gentiluomo," in Giorgio Patrizi and Amedeo Quondam, eds., *Educare il corpo, educare la parola nella trattatistica del Rinascimento,* Biblioteca del Cinquecento 80 (Rome: Bulzoni Editore, 1998) 18: "l'economia comunicativa del corpo e della parola nella lunga durata del Classicismo è regolata da categorie omologate e omologanti assolutamente universali (cioè condivise per convenzione) che profilano una genealogia del comportamento secondo virtù: affabilità, benevolenza, convenienza, cortesia, creanza, decoro, discrezione, dissimulazione, garbo, gentilezza, grazia, liberalità, magnanimità, magnificenza, perfezione, piacevolezza, politezza, prudenza, sprezzatura, eccetera eccetera. Categorie di un paradigma stabile nel tempo e diffuso nello spazio: formidabile macchina di omologazione virtuosa." [During the *longue durée* of Classicism, the economy of communication for both body and speech is regulated by absolutely universal—that is to say, shared by convention—categories that are both standardized and standardizing. These establish a genealogy of behavior according to the virtues: affability, benevolence, suitability, courtesy, manners, decorum, discretion, dissimulation, tact, courteousness, grace, generosity, magnanimity, magnificence, perfection, pleasantness, politeness, prudence, nonchalance, etc. These are the categories of a paradigm that is stable over time and widely spread through space, constituting a formidable mechanism of homologation through the virtues.]

Chapter 1

Michel de Montaigne, *The Complete Works: Essays, Travel Journal, Letters,* trans. Donald M. Frame (New York: Knopf, 2003) 614; Montaigne, *Les Essais,* ed. Pierre Villey, 3rd rev. ed., 3 vols. (Paris: Presses Universitaires de France, 1999) 2:18.

Pio Rossi, *Il convito morale per gli etici, economici e politici* (Venice: Guerigli, 1657) 201.

1. Alessandro Anguissola, "Della dissimulatione," 1612, MS M.III.6., Biblioteca Nazionale di Torino. Nicola Raponi, "Alessandro Anguissola," *Dizionario biografico degli italiani,* vol. 3 (Rome: Istituto della Enciclopedia Italiana, 1961) 315–316, provides a basic biography. See also Paolo Maria Arcari, *La ragion di stato in un manoscritto inedito di Alessandro Anguissola,* 2nd ed. (Rome: Nuove Grafiche, 1939) 7–50, for further biographical information.

2. Girolamo Cardano, *Arcana politica, sive de prudentia civili liber singularis* (Louvain: Elzevir, 1635) 196, nevertheless assured his readers that "necessaria est valde simulatio; praecipue cum potentioribus: ideo in aula maxime in usu est, atque cum Satrapis et Principibus." [Simulation is necessary especially with the powerful; for this reason, it is used particularly at court and with satraps and princes.]

3. The Biblioteca Casanatense in Rome possesses two copies of an anonymous late sixteenth-century text, "Avvertimenti utili per quelli che vogliono entrare in corte" (MS 2096, fols. 324–330 and MS 2371, fols. 1–13). In this work, which appears to have been circulated but not printed, the author argues that "la dissimulazione è l'anima della Corte" [dissimulation is the soul of the court]. The term "dissimulation" systematically replaced "simulation" in the second, later version of the manuscript cited here (MS 2096, fol. 325v–325r). Repeatedly attributed to the Count of Verrua, this manuscript was first published in the *Miscellanea di storia italiana edita per cura della Regia Deputazione di storia patria*, series 1, vol. 1 (Turin: Stamperia Reale, 1862) 321–352. In a parallel fashion, a work on political theory that was published in two successive—and highly successful—collections prepared by Comin Ventura, *La Prima Parte del Thesoro Politico* (Milan: Girolamo Bordone, 1600), and *La Seconda Parte del Thesoro Politico* (Milan: Girolamo Bordone and Pietromartire Locarni, 1601), contains a text that appears under different titles with different attributions: anonymous, "De' Fondamenti dello Stato," 1600; and Scipione da Castro, "Instruttione [*sic*] a Prencipi per sapere ben governare li Stati," 1601. This treatise warns the prince to flee dissimulation in the 1600 volume, but changes its advice a year later, urging the prince to flee simulation instead, in what is otherwise a nearly identical text. For the altered passage, see p. 345 of the 1601 edition, which begins "ma sappia il Principe che molto gli conviene fuggir la superstitione, & la simulatione, come due scogli sommamente pericolosi." For more on the publication history of this unusual work, see Jean Balsamo, "Les Origines parisiennes du *Tesoro politico* (1589)," *Bibliothèque d'Humanisme et Renaissance* 57.1 (1995): 7–23. Some forty years after the publication of the *Tesoro politico*, Torquato Accetto would note dryly that "la simulazione non facilmente riceve quel senso onesto che si accompagna con la dissimulazione." [Simulation does not easily receive the honest meaning that comes with dissimulation.] This is the title of chapter 4 in Torquato Accetto, *Della dissimulazione onesta* [1641], ed. Salvatore S. Nigro (Turin: Einaudi, 1997) 19.

4. Baltasar Gracián, *The Art of Worldly Wisdom: A Pocket Oracle*, trans. Christopher Maurer (New York: Doubleday, 1992) 45 (I have altered the translation); Gracián, *Oráculo manual y arte de prudencia*, in *Obras Completas*, ed. Arturo del Hoyo (Madrid: Aguilar, 1960) 173 (aphorism 80): "vívese lo más de información, es lo menos lo que vemos: vivimos de fe ajena. Es el oído la puerta segunda de la verdad y principal de la mentira. La verdad ordinariamente se ve, extravagantemente se oye; raras veces llega en su elemento puro, y menos cuando viene de lejos; siempre trae algo de mixta de los afectos por donde pasa."

5. Accetto 22: "la dissimulazione è una professione, della quale non si può fare professione."

6. Richard Tuck, *Philosophy and Government 1572–1651* (New York: Cambridge University Press, 1993) 132. See also Shakespeare, *Henry VI, Part 1*, 3.1.140ff.

Bishop of Winchester: Well, Duke of Gloucester, I will yield to thee;
Love for thy love and hand for hand I give.
Gloucester: [Aside] Ay, but, I fear me, with a hollow heart.—

See here, my friends and loving countrymen,
This token serveth for a flag of truce
Betwixt ourselves and all our followers:
So help me God, as I dissemble not!

7. Gracián, *Art of Worldly Wisdom* 102 (I have altered the translation); *Oráculo manual* 200 (aphorism 181): "sin mentir, no decir todas las verdades. No hay cosa que requiera más tiento que la verdad, que es un sangrarse del corazón. Tanto es menester para saberla decir como para saberla callar."

8. Valentin Groebner, *Who Are You? Identification, Deception and Surveillance in Early Modern Europe,* trans. Mark Kyburz and John Peck (New York: Zone Books, 2007) 217. Groebner's book reproduces the abovementioned image on p. 40.

9. See Celio Calcagnini, *Descriptio silentii,* in Salvatore S. Nigro, ed. and trans., *Elogio della menzogna* (Palermo: Sellerio, 1990) 33–47, for an early sixteenth-century treatment of the theme of silence as a supreme good.

10. Accetto 52: "qualche uomo di eccellente virtú, alcuna volta sta quasi sepellito vivo."

11. Accetto 52: "senza lasciar vestigio, come il fumo nell'aria."

12. Justus Lipsius, *Epistola de fructu peregrinandi et praesertim in Italia* (1578), first printed in *Epistolarum selectarum: centuria prima* (Leiden: Christophe Plantin; London: George Bishop, 1586); adapted and translated by Sir John Stradling as *A Direction for Travailers* (London: R. Bourne for Cutbert Burbie, 1592) C4: "an open face, few words, an inaccessible mind."

13. Norbert Elias, *The Civilizing Process,* trans. Edmund Jephcott (Oxford: Blackwell, 1994) 63, 480–484. See also Elias, *The Court Society,* trans. Edmund Jephcott (Oxford: Blackwell, 1983) 104–106.

14. Stuart Clark, *Vanities of the Eye: Vision in Early Modern European Culture* (New York: Oxford University Press, 2007) 9–10.

15. Accetto 22: "Degli eccellenti dissimulatori che sono stati, e sono, non si ha notizia alcuna."

16. Curiously enough, the term "dissimulation" does not appear in Shakespeare's corpus.

17. Giovanni Pontano pointed out in his *De Prudentia* (published in 1505, but composed in the 1490s) that prudence was "neque solertiam, neque sagacitatem, neque astutiam" [neither cleverness nor acuteness nor cunning]. See Pontano, *Opera omnia soluta oratione composita,* vol. 1 (Venice: Aldus Manutius, 1518–19) fol. 194*v*. The text of the *De Prudentia* found in Pontano's collected works contains a section entitled "De Simulatione, & Dissimulatione" (fol. 202*r*). See, on the concept of prudence, Mario Santoro, *Fortuna, ragione e prudenza nella civiltà letteraria del Cinquecento* (Naples: Liguori, 1967); Victoria Kahn, *Rhetoric, Prudence and Skepticism in the Renaissance* (Ithaca, NY: Cornell University Press, 1985); Eugene Garver, *Machiavelli and the History of Prudence* (Madison: University of Wisconsin Press, 1987) 3–13; John Martin, *Myths of Renaissance Individualism* (New York: Palgrave Macmillan, 2004) 48–53; Sophie Gouverneur, *Prudence et subversion libertines: la critique de la raison d'État chez*

François de la Mothe le Vayer, Gabriel Naudé et Samuel Sorbière (Paris: Honoré Champion, 2005) 75–76; and Jeremy Robbins, *Arts of Perception: The Epistemological Mentality of the Spanish Baroque, 1580–1720* (New York: Routledge, 2007) 97–100.

18. Santoro 53.

19. David Summers, *The Judgment of Sense: Renaissance Naturalism and the Rise of Aesthetics* (New York: Cambridge University Press, 1987) 266–267. The Latin inscription in the painting reads "Ex praeterito praesens prudenter agit ni futuram actionem de-turpet." Like so much of early modern classicist culture, this motto was a commonplace that was destined to be endlessly recycled. For instance, in the first edition of his *Il convito morale per gli etici economici, e politici* (Venice: Guerigli, 1639) 390, Pio Rossi remarked: "Che 'l prudente deve ricordarsi delle cose passate, servirsi delle presenti, e prevedere le future." [The prudent person must remember past things, use present things, and foresee future things.]

20. Aristotle, *The Nicomachean Ethics,* ed. and trans. Hippocrates G. Apostle (Dordrecht and Boston: D. Reidel, 1975) 111 (1143A).

21. Robbins 99.

22. John Martin, "Inventing Sincerity, Refashioning Prudence: The Discovery of the Individual in Renaissance Europe," *The American Historical Review* 102.5 (1997): 1323–1326.

23. Accetto 19. Accetto thus rewrote the early modern motto (whose origins are unknown)—*qui nescit dissimulare nescit regnare*—by shifting it from the political to the personal and by substituting the more generic *fingere* for *dissimulare.* See Ursula Geitner, *Die Sprache der Verstellung: Studien zum rhetorischen und anthropologischen Wissen im 17. und 18. Jahrhundert* (Tübingen: Max Niemeyer Verlag, 1992) 75, who cites a widely read German political treatise by Christian Georg Bessel, *Schmiede des politischen Glücks* (Hamburg: Johann Naumann, 1666) 105: "Die Italiäner extendiren die Nothwendigkeit dieser Stell=und Verstellungs Kunst noch weiter, sagende: 'chi non sa fingere, non sa vivere,' wer nicht zu simuliren weiss der weiss auch nicht zu leben." [The Italians extend even further the meaning of this art of simulation and dissimulation, saying: whoever does not know how to dissemble does not know how to live.] I have not modernized Bessel's German here.

24. Louis Machon, *Apologie pour Machiavel en faveur des Princes et des Ministres d'Estat* (Paris, 1643; Bibliothèque Nationale MS 19046–7) 636: "quand on veult faire une vertu de la dissimulation, on l'appelle prudence."

25. The Roman expression "aliquem reddere Harpocratem" did not, in any case, refer directly to the cult. Hesychia was a goddess of quiet to whom was consecrated the refusal to speak: see Henri Estienne, *Thesaurus Graecae linguae* (Geneva: Henricus Stephanus, 1572), in which *hesychazo* is defined as "quietum reddo," "taceo," or "sileo" (as cited by Monica Fintoni, "Teorie della dissimulazione tra XVI° e XVII° secolo," unpublished doctoral thesis, Università degli Studi di Trieste, 1996, 18n–19n).

26. Giulio Cesare Capaccio, *Il Principe, tratto da gli Emblemi dell'Alciato, con duecento, e più Avvertimenti Politici e Morali* (Venice: Barezzo Barezzi, 1620) 18,

avvertimento XI: "Gran segno di pazzia è la loquacità; che perciò essendo detto a Mamarato in una conversatione, per qual cagione mostrasse questa pazzia di tacere? Disse; e come volete voi, che un pazzo possa tacere? Per questo consecrarono la Statua di Harpocrate, che col deto si suggellava i labbri. Zenone dicea, che l'huomo hà due orecchie per udire molto; & una bocca per parlar poco." [Talkativeness is a great sign of madness. When M(. . .) was asked in a conversation for what reason he showed this madness of keeping quiet, he answered: "do you think that a madman can keep quiet?" For this reason they consecrated the statue of Harpocrates, who sealed his lips with a finger. Zeno said that man has two ears to listen often, and one mouth to speak rarely.]

27. Vincenzo Cartari, *Le imagini de i dei de gli antichi* [*sic*], eds. Ginetta Auzzas, Federica Martignago, Manlio Pastore Stocchi, and Paola Rigo, anastatic reprint of 1571 ed. (Vicenza: Neri Pozza Editore, 1996) 334: "ad Arpocrate fu dedicato il persico perché questo arbore ha le foglie simili alla lingua umana et i suoi frutti rassimigliano il core, come che la lingua manifesti quello che è nel core ma non lo debba però fare se non vi considera ben sopra." See Linda Bisello, *Sotto il 'manto' del silenzio. Storia e forme del tacere (secoli XVI–XVII)* (Florence: Olschki, 2003) 50–62.

28. Calcagnini, *Descriptio silentii*, in Nigro, *Elogio* 34.

29. John Lemprière, *Lemprière's Classical Dictionary* (1792; London: Bracken Books, 1984) 54. Agenoria was another name for the goddess of silence.

30. See Cartari 332: "Ma Macrobio vuole che Angerona con la bocca legata e suggellata mostrasse che chi sa patire e tacere dissimulando gli affanni vince quelli al fine, e se ne gode poi vita lieta e piacevole. Plinio e Solino scrivono che questa dea fu così fatta per dar a vedere che non bisogna parlare de' secreti misteri della religione per divulgarli; come volle anco Numa far conoscere, quando introdusse di adorare certa dea da lui nomata Tacita, secondo che Plutarco scrive, che bisogna tacere le cose de i dei." [Macrobius claims that Angerona, whose mouth was bound and sealed, showed that whoever knows how to suffer and keep silent by dissimulating one's travails triumphs over them in the end, and then enjoys a happy and pleasant life. Pliny and Solinus write that this goddess was made in this way in order to show that one should not speak of the secret mysteries of religion and divulge them. When he introduced the cult of a certain goddess whom he called Tacita, according to Plutarch Numa too sought to show that one must not speak of the things of the gods.]

31. Lemprière 421. See Mario Andrea Rigoni, "Una finestra aperta sul cuore," *Lettere italiane* 26.4 (1974): 434–458, and Lina Bolzoni, *La stanza della memoria: modelli letterari e iconografici nell'età della stampa* (Turin: Einaudi, 1995) 154–164, for an extensive treatment of the theme of the Socratic window in the breast. For a brief discussion of this same theme in early modern Spanish culture, see Hansgerd Schulte, *El Desengaño: Wort und Thema in der Spanischen Literatur des Goldenen Zeitalters*, Freiburger Schriften zur Romanischen Philologie 17 (Munich: Wilhelm Fink Verlag, 1969) 168.

32. Carl Ittig, *De simulatione et dissimulatione* (Leipzig: Literis Immanuelis Titii, 1709) 24–26 (chap. 13), makes this point.

33. See also Accetto 29–30 (chap. 8), who comments on this same passage.

34. Virgil, *Aeneid* IV. 305–306: "dissimulare etiam sperasti, perfide, tantum/ posse nefas tacitusque mea decedere terra." See also *Aeneid* IV. 288–291: "Mnesthea Sergestumque vocat fortemque Serestum,/classem aptent taciti sociosque ad litora cogant,/arma parent et, quae rebus sit causa novandis,/ dissimulent." [He (Aeneas) calls Mnesthus and Sergestus and brave Serestus, bidding them make ready the fleet in silence, gather the crews to the shore, and order the armament, but hide the cause of his altered plans.] Pontano, folio 202*r*, notes that "apud Virgilius Aeneas spem vultu simulat, altum tamen corde dolorem premit" (this is a paraphrase of *Aeneid* I.209).

35. Rodolfo De Mattei, *Dal premachiavellismo all'antimachiavellismo* (Florence: Sansoni, 1969) 15–18, makes this point in his chapter on "Il problema della liceità del *mendacio*." See, in particular, *Republic* III.389C–D, *Republic* III.414B– C, *Republic* V. 459D–460A, and *Laws* II.63D.

36. See Fintoni 1: *eironeia* was the Greek term used to indicate the attitude of that individual known to the Romans as a *dissimulator*. On *docta ignorantia,* see Stefano Velotti, *Sapienti e bestioni: saggio sull'ignoranza, il sapere e la poesia in Giambattista Vico* (Parma: Pratiche, 1995).

37. *Symposium,* trans. Michael Joyce, in Plato, *Collected Dialogues,* eds. Edith Hamilton and Huntington Cairns, Bollingen Series 71 (Princeton: Princeton University Press, 1961) 566. See Desiderius Erasmus, *Collected Works,* vol. 34: *Adages II.vii.1 to III.iii.100,* trans. R. A. B. Mynors (Toronto: University of Toronto Press, 1992), adage III.iii.1, for a discussion of the *praeposterus Silenus* or "reverse Silenus," which includes the majority of humanity.

38. Aristotle, *Nicomachean Ethics* 68.

39. Aristotle, *Nicomachean Ethics* 75. I have altered the translation.

40. See Stefano Guazzo, *La civil conversazione,* ed. Amedeo Quondam, vol. 1 (Modena: Franco Cosimo Panini, 1993) 84, whose source was Diogenes Laertius (VIII.10).

41. Seneca, *De tranquillitate animi,* in *Dialoghi morali,* ed. Carlo Carena and trans. Gavino Manca (Turin: Einaudi, 1995) 298 (XVII.3). See, for instance, La Rochefoucauld, *Maximes et reflexions diverses,* ed. Henry A. Grubbs, Jr. (Princeton: Princeton University Press, 1929), for a typical anti-Senecan polemic. Grubbs notes (115n) that "La Rochefoucauld considered the Roman philosopher Seneca the typical false philosopher. The frontispiece of the first four editions of the *Maxims* showed a child labeled 'L'Amour de la Vérité' removing a mask from a bust of Seneca, and underneath the inscription 'Quid vetat?'—'why not unmask him?'"

42. Plutarch, *De garrulitate,* in *Moralia,* trans. W. C. Hembold, vol. 6 (Cambridge, MA: Harvard University Press, 1939) 439–441. See Guido Casoni, *Emblemi politici* (Venice: Paolo Baglioni, 1632) 89–91, for an emblematic treatment of this theme, repeated in Sebastiano Taricco's frescos in the *Saletta del silenzio* (1706, in the Palazzo Salmatoris in Cherasco), discussed in chapter 5.

43. De Mattei 19.

44. See Mark Morford, "Tacitean *Prudentia* and the Doctrines of Justus Lipsius," *Tacitus and the Tacitean Tradition,* eds. T. J. Luce and A. J. Woodman

(Princeton: Princeton University Press, 1993) 129–151; Ronald Mellor, *Tacitus* (New York: Routledge, 1993) 137–152; Kenneth C. Schellhase, *Tacitus in Renaissance Political Thought* (Chicago: University of Chicago Press, 1976) 101–161; José Antonio Maravall, "La corriente doctrinal del tacitismo político en España," *Cuadernos Hispanoamericanos* 238–240 (1969): 645–667; André Stegmann, "Le Tacitisme: programme pour un nouvel essai de définition," *Machiavellismo e antimachiavellismo nel Cinquecento. Atti del convegno di Perugia, 30.9–1.10.69,* special issue of *Il pensiero politico* 2.3 (1969): 117–130; and the still valuable Jürgen von Stackelberg, *Tacitus in der Romania* (Tübingen: Max Niemeyer Verlag, 1960), esp. 94–148, 159–219.

45. Tacitus, *The Histories,* trans. Clifford H. Moore, and *The Annals,* trans. John Jackson, vol. 3 (Cambridge, MA.: Harvard University Press, 1937) 125–127: "nulla aeque Tiberius, ut rebatur, ex virtutibus suis quam dissimulationem diligebat: eo aegrius accepit recludi quae premeret." These same lines are employed by Paolo Sarpi, for instance, in his portrait of Pope Paul III in the *Istoria del concilio tridentino,* as cited in Rosario Villari, *L'elogio della dissimulazione: la lotta politica nel Seicento* (Bari: Laterza, 1987) 22. See two works by Vasily Rudich, *Political Dissidence under Nero: The Price of Dissimulation* (New York: Routledge, 1993) and *Dissidence and Literature under Nero: The Price of Rhetoricization* (New York: Routledge, 1997), both of which scrutinize the widespread practice of *dissimulatio* in imperial Rome: "But it was in the Julio-Claudian Empire that the practice of *dissimulatio* acquired paramount importance, becoming a prerequisite not only of political success, but even of physical survival. *Dissimulatio* was a complex and contradictory state of mind within one and the same person, a resultant of conflicting forces—intellectual, emotional, and instinctive" (*Political Dissidence* xxii).

46. Carlo Pasquale, *C. C. Tacitus ab excessu divi Augusti Annalium libri quatuor priores, et in hoc observationes* (Paris: Roberto Colombel, 1581) 235, as cited and translated in Tuck 43–44. The text can also be found in Carlo Pasquale, *Gnomae, seu, axiomata politica: et Taciti Annalibus excerpta,* in *C. Cornelii Taciti et C. Velleii Paterculi scripta quae exstant* (Paris: Pierre Chevalier, 1608) 706: "non solum Tiberius, verum etiam plurimi principum connumerant dissimulationem inter praecipuas eas virtutes, quas ipsos habere necesse est: atque adeo et caeteris omnibus nullam aeque diligunt: idque hactenus ut eam principi necessariam esse affirment." See also von Stackelberg 118–119.

47. Andrea Collodio contended, in a defense of Tacitus, that Tiberius's dissimulation was built upon a wall of hidden intentions, shadowy meanings, and equivocal gestures. See Collodio, *Disputatio Politica Ad C. Corn. Taciti Annal. lib. I. De Tiberii Dissimulatione ad per illustrem ac nobilissimum D. D. Romanum Garzonium. Patronum Optimum* (Lucca: Ottaviano Guidoboni, 1616), 4v: "Nam ut omittam eius ingenium ad simulationem factum, quo pridem ductus ad dissimulandum, mox arcanos sensus ambiguis verborum integumentis obducere, reconditasque; & penitus abstrusas animi notas obscuro quodam orationis implicatae pigmento fucatas exponere assuerat." [Over and beyond his innate skill at simulation, for which he was led at other times to dissimulate, he quickly grew

accustomed to enclosing recondite meanings in ambiguous coverings of words and to expressing the deeply hidden traits of the mind masked over by those sorts of dark shades that belong to involuted speech.]

48. Gracián, *El Héroe* (1637), in *Obras completas* 30 (Primor XVII): "afectó Tiberio el disimular, pero non supo disimular el disimular."

49. Tertullian, *Patience,* in *Disciplinary, Moral and Ascetical Works,* trans. Rudolph Arbesmann, Emily J. Daly, and Edward A. Quain, The Fathers of the Church 40 (New York: The Fathers of the Church, Inc., 1959) 220 (chap. 15.4–5).

50. Johann P. Sommerville, "The 'New Art of Lying': Equivocation, Mental Reservation and Casuistry," *Conscience and Casuistry in Early Modern Europe,* ed. Edmund Leites (New York: Cambridge University Press; Paris: Éditions de la Maison des Sciences de l'Homme, 1988) 160–161.

51. "Nonne dissimulavi? nonne silui? nonne quievi? et venit super me indignatio." This biblical passage is included in Accetto 61 (chap. 22), as is a discussion (pp. 39–40, chap. 13) of the respective stories of Noah and his sons (Genesis 9:18–23) and Joseph (Genesis 45:1–3). See Perez Zagorin, *Ways of Lying: Dissimulation, Persecution, and Conformity in Early Modern Europe* (Cambridge, MA.: Harvard University Press, 1990) 15–37, for a valuable discussion of biblical sources for the early modern discourse on dissimulation. Other relevant scriptural passages not discussed by Zagorin are found in Galatians 13, Romans 9 ("let love be without dissimulation"), and John 3:1–2. As Zagorin points out (16n), *hypokrisis,* in the original Greek text of the New Testament, was translated as *simulatio* in the Vulgate and as "dissimulation" in the 1611 Authorized Version. The latter appeared within a year of Anguissola's revisions of his manuscript on dissimulation.

52. St. Jerome, *Commentarium in Epistolam ad Galatas Tres Libri,* in *Patrologiae Latinae Cursus Completus,* ed. Jacques Migne, vol. 26 (Paris: Migne, 1844–1855) cols. 363–367, as cited in Zagorin 17: *utilem vero simulationem et assumendam tempore.*

53. De Mattei 19–21.

54. St. Augustine, *Epistolae ad Galatas Expositionis Liber Unus,* in *Patrologiae Latinae Cursus Completus,* vol. 33, cols. 112–113; *Letters,* trans. Wilfred Parsons, vol. 1 (Washington, DC: Catholic University of America Press, 1951–1956) 93–98, as cited in Zagorin 18.

55. St. Augustine, *De Mendacio,* trans. M. S. Muldowney, 51–110, and *Contra Mendacium,* trans. Harold B. Jaffee, 121–179, both in *Treatises on Various Subjects,* ed. Roy J. Deferrari, The Fathers of the Church 16 (Washington, DC: Catholic University of America Press, 1952). The passage cited here is from *De Mendacio* 60.

56. St. Augustine, *"Confessions" and "Enchiridion,"* trans. and ed. Albert C. Outler, The Library of Christian Classics 7 (Philadelphia: The Westminster Press, n.d.) 350. These words did not, however, prevent the sixteenth-century religious reformer Ortensio Lando from interpreting the *Enchiridion* in a heterodox manner. Lando claimed that, according to Augustine, the function of the human heart was to *simulare, et dissimulare;* Mario Rosa, "Chiesa e stati

regionali nell'età dell'assolutismo," in *Letteratura italiana*, ed. Alberto Asor Rosa, vol. 1 (Turin: Einaudi, 1982) 262. See Sisto da Siena, *Bibliotheca Sancta* (Venice: Johann Gryphius, 1566) for a list of scriptural and patristic passages concerning lying.

57. Michel Foucault, *Fearless Speech*, ed. Joseph Pearson (Los Angeles: Semiotext(e), 2001) 11–20.

58. See Charles Lefebvre, "Dissimulation," *Dictionnaire de droit canonique*, ed. R. Naz, vol. 4 (Paris: Librairie Letouzey et Ané, 1949) 1296–1308, and Giuseppe Olivero, *Dissimulatio e tolerantia nell'ordinamento canonico*, Università di Catania: Pubblicazioni della Facoltà di Giurisprudenza 18 (Milan: A. Giuffré, 1953) 43–63.

59. St. Thomas Aquinas, *Summa Theologiae* 2a2ae, q. 110, art. 3 (41:160–161), as cited in Zagorin 30.

60. Zagorin 31.

61. Peter von Moos, "*Occulta cordis:* contrôle de soi et confession au Moyen Âge," *Médiévales* 29 (automne 1995): 131–132, and Bisello, *Sotto il 'manto' del silenzio* 28–49.

62. Machon 642. For a more recent attempt to classify early modern practices of dissimulation, see Wolfgang G. Müller, "Dissimulation as a Theme and Rhetorical Device in Kyd's *Spanish Tragedy*," *Arbeiten aus Anglistik und Amerikanistik* 10.1–2 (1985): 21–22.

63. See Dante Alighieri, *Purgatorio* XXII.90–91, where Statius explains to Dante and Virgil "ma per paura chiuso cristian fu'mi, / lungamente mostrando paganesmo."

64. Important works abound in this field: among many others, see Zagorin, *Ways of Lying* and his subsequent "The Historical Significance of Lying and Dissimulation," *Social Research* 63.3 (1996): 863–912; Albano Biondi, "La giustificazione della simulazione nel Cinquecento," *Eresia e Riforma nell'Italia del Cinquecento* (De Kalb: Northern Illinois University Press, 1974) 7–68; and Carlo Ginzburg, *Il Nicodemismo. Simulazione e dissimulazione nell'Europa del '500* (Turin: Einaudi, 1970).

65. Martin Berbeeck, *Compendium manualis controversiarum huius temporis de fide ac religione* (Luxembourg: Hubert Reulant, 1625) 542–543: "aliud est negare fidem, quod non licet, aliud est tacere, dissimulare, occultare."

66. Here I refer readers to the brilliant Cavaillé, *Dis/simulations*.

67. See Amedeo Quondam, *La conversazione: un modello italiano* (Rome: Donzelli Editore, 2007) 133–219.

68. Guazzo 1:85. Quondam points out in his editor's notes that this is derived from Seneca, *De Moribus (qui nescit tacere, nescit et loqui)*, although it is attributed by other early moderns to Pythagoras instead. Salvatore Rosa, *Il teatro della politica. Sentenziosi afforismi [sic] della prudenza*, ed. Giorgio Baroni, Scelta di curiosità letterarie inedite o rare dal secolo XIII al XIX, Dispensa 281 (Bologna: Commissione per i testi di lingua, 1991) 42, repeats this aphorism verbatim, confirming the enduring influence of works like Guazzo's for Old Regime culture.

69. Cf. Remo Bodei, *La geometria delle passioni. Paura, speranza, felicità: filosofia e uso politico,* rev. ed. (Milan: Feltrinelli, 1992) 181–211, and Jean-Jacques Courtine and Claudine Haroche, *Histoire du visage: exprimer et taire ses émotions, XVIe–début XIXe siècle* (Paris: Rivages, 1988) 35–38.

70. Burke, *Art of Conversation* 139–140: "speech like other forms of behaviour at court was subject to increasingly strict control, best documented at the model courts of Madrid and Versailles. Like the soldier, the courtier was increasingly expected to demonstrate self-control or discipline, or to use the language of the time, *continentia* and *coercitio.*"

71. La Bruyère, *Les Caractères* (*De la Cour,* 2 (1)), ed. Robert Garapon (Paris: Garnier, 1962) 22: "un homme qui sait la cour est maître de son geste, de ses yeux, et de son visage; il est profond, impénétrable; il dissimule les mauvais offices, sourit à ses ennemis, contraint son humeur, déguise ses passions, dément son coeur, parle, agit contre ses sentiments."

72. Henri Estienne, *Deux Dialogues du nouveau langage françois italianizé,* as cited in Pauline M. Smith, *The Anti-Courtier Trend in Sixteenth Century French Literature,* Travaux d'Humanisme et Renaissance 84 (Geneva: Droz, 1966) 209: "Recipé trois livres d'Impudence (mais de la plus fine, qui croist en un rocher, qu'on appelle Front d'airain), Deux livres d'hypocrisie, Une livre de Dissimulation, Trois livres de la science de flatter, deux livres de Bonne mine. Le tout cuict au jus de Bonne grace par l'espace d'un jour et d'une nuict. . . . Apres il faut passer ceste decoction par une estamine de Large conscience. . . . Vela un breuvage souverain, pour devenir courtisan en toute perfection de courtisanisme."

73. The term "prince" in this book will refer in a gender-neutral fashion to a dynastic sovereign.

74. Maurizio Viroli, *From Politics to Reason of State: The Acquisition and Transformation of the Language of Politics, 1250–1600* (New York: Cambridge University Press, 1992) 7. For a somewhat different approach, see Robert Birely, *The Counter-Reformation Prince: Anti-Machiavellianism or Catholic Statecraft in Early Modern Europe* (Chapel Hill: University of North Carolina Press, 1990) 45–71.

75. Bolzoni xix–xx.

76. Groebner 217.

77. Groebner 29.

78. Groebner 83.

79. Anna Maria Battista, *Politica e morale nella Francia dell'età moderna,* ed. Anna Maria Lazzarino Del Grosso (Genoa: NAME, 1998) 119.

80. Cavaillé, *Dis/simulations* 16 and Hallyn 198.

81. Martin, *Myths of Renaissance Individualism* 48.

82. See Clark 1–8.

Chapter 2

Gracián, *Oráculo manual* 183 (aphorism 118); all translations are mine unless otherwise indicated.

1. See Jon R. Snyder, "Norbert Elias's *The Civilizing Process* and the Critique of Conduct," in *Educare il corpo, educare la parola nella trattatistica del Rinascimento,* eds. Giorgio Patrizi and Amedeo Quondam, Biblioteca del Cinquecento 80 (Rome: Bulzoni, 1998) 289–307. Useful critical perspectives on Elias may also be found in Anna Bryson, *From Courtesy to Civility: Changing Codes of Conduct in Early Modern England* (Oxford: Clarendon Press, 1998) 8–16, and Harry Berger, Jr., *The Absence of Grace: Sprezzatura and Suspicion in Two Renaissance Courtesy Books* (Stanford: Stanford University Press, 2000) 39–45.

2. Alain Corbin, Jean-Jacques Courtine, and Georges Vigarello, eds., preface, *Histoire du corps, 1: De la Renaissance aux Lumières* (Paris: Éditions du Seuil, 2005) 11.

3. See, for instance, Peter Burke, *The Fortunes of the "Courtier": The European Reception of Castiglione's "Cortegiano,"* The Penn State Series in the History of the Book (University Park: Penn State University Press, 1996) 39–80.

4. Berger 45. For the debate over Elias's theory of the civilizing process, see Eric Dunning and Stephen Mennell, eds., *Norbert Elias,* 4 vols. (Thousand Oaks, CA: SAGE Publications, 2003), esp. part 7 ("Critiques and Counter-Critiques").

5. Giordano Bruno, *De magia; De vinculis in genere,* ed. Albano Biondi (Pordenone: Biblioteca dell'immagine, 1986) 189, as cited and translated by Fintoni 155: "sul piano della civil conversazione gli oratori, i cortigiani e quelli che comunque sanno gli usi del comportamento vincolano con più efficacia quando operano con clandestina dissimulazione dell'artificio . . . giacché non piccola componente dell'arte è usare l'arte dissimulandola."

6. Guazzo, 1:xi (Quondam's introduction). See Alain Montandon, "Pour une Histoire des traités de savoir-vivre italiens: esquisse bibliographique," *Traités de savoir-vivre en Italie. I trattati del saper vivere in Italia,* ed. Alain Montandon (Clermont-Ferrand: Association des Publications de la Faculté des Lettres et Sciences Humaines de Clermont-Ferrand, 1993) 309–334, for an invaluable bibliography of early modern editions and translations of these three treatises.

7. Giovanni Della Casa, *The Refin'd Courtier, or a Correction of Several Indecencies Crept into Civil Conversation,* trans. Nathaniel Walker (London: R. Royston, 1663). This abridged version of Della Casa's *Il Galateo* was reprinted for the last time in 1804.

8. Giovanni Della Casa, *Galateo ovvero de' costumi,* ed. Carlo Cordié (Milan: Mondadori, 1993) 4: "io incomincerò da quello che per avventura potrebbe a molti parer frivolo: cioè quello che io stimo che si convenga di fare per potere, in comunicando ed in usando con le genti, essere costumato e piacevole e di bella maniera." On the "good society," see Elias, *Court Society* 94–99. On the concept of the social in the *Galateo,* see Alain Pons, "Le Thème de la communication dans le *Galatée* de Giovanni della Casa," in *Savoir Vivre I,* ed. Alain Montandon (Meyzieu: Césura Lyon Édition, 1990) 12.

9. Montandon, "De l'Urbanité: entre étiquette et politesse," in Alain Montandon, ed., *Étiquette et politesse* (Clermont-Ferrand: Association des Publications de la Faculté des Lettres et Sciences Humaines de Clermont-Ferrand, 1992)

16. He points out (17) that this same relationship is defined by Adorno in *Minima moralia* as that between convention and tact.

10. See Vittorio Dini, *Il governo della prudenza: virtù dei privati e disciplina dei custodi* (Milan: FrancoAngeli, 2000) 118: "Si entra così in un territorio veramente decisivo per il mondo della prima età moderna: quello della dissimulazione e della simulazione, della conversazione, del parlare, del tacere, della menzogna. Un mondo per il quale la retorica classica . . . è nei fatti, nella pratica, del tutto ampliata a pratica e teoria del comportamento." [Thus we enter into a truly decisive territory for the early modern world: that of dissimulation and simulation, conversation, speech, silence and falsehood. A world for which classical rhetoric . . . has in fact and in practice expanded into a practice and theory of behavior.]

11. Elias, *Court Society* 48, 99–101.

12. Accetto 32: "Or, passando all'utile che nasce dalla dissimulazione ne' termini morali, comincio dalle cose che piú bisognano, dico dall'arte della buona creanza, la qual si riduce nella destrezza di questa medesima diligenza. E leggendosi quanto ne scrisse monsignor della Casa, si vede che tutta quella nobilissima dottrina insegna cosí di ristringer i soverchi disiderii [*sic*], che son cagion di atti noiosi, come il mostrar di non veder gli errori altrui, acciò che la conversazione riesca di buon gusto." I have modified here the translation provided in Brendan Dooley, ed. and trans., *Italy in the Baroque: Selected Readings* (New York: Garland Publishing, 1995) 375.

13. Montandon, "De l'Urbanité" 12.

14. Giorgio Patrizi, "Il valore della norma: etichetta come comunicazione e rappresentazione tra *Cortegiano* e *Galateo*," in Montandon, *Étiquette et politesse* 39.

15. Bernardino Pino da Cagli, *Del Galant'huomo overo Dell'Huomo Prudente, et Discreto* (Venice: Sessa, 1604) fol. 6v.

16. Pino da Cagli fol. 42v: "GALANT'HUOMO [*sic*] altro non vuol dire, che huomo saggio, discreto, & prudente, il quale in ogni luogo, in ogni tempo, & con ogni persona, prudentemente si governa, & è si accorto nelle parole, & ne' fatti, che si scuopre sempre degno di loda . . . l'intentione e 'l fermo proponimento nostro è di mostrare, come in ogni atto humano l'huomo possa esser detto galant'huomo."

17. In the *Advancement of Learning*, Francis Bacon refers to "conversation" as the study of social behavior and appearances, and designates it a branch of "civil knowledge." See Adriana McCrea, *Constant Minds: Political Virtue and the Lipsian Paradigm in England, 1584–1650* (Toronto: University of Toronto Press, 1997) 91. See also Burke, *Art of Conversation* 98–102.

18. Montaigne, *Works* 38–39; *Essais* 1:48–49: "non seulement chasque païs, mais chasque cité a sa civilité particulière, et chasque vacation. . . . [C]'est . . . une très utile science que la science de l'entregent."

19. See Marc Fumaroli, *Le genre des genres littéraires français: la conversation* (Oxford: Clarendon Press, 1992) 11–12: "la conversation devient ainsi une diplomatie générale de la vie en société: elle atteint l'exemplarité dans les 'académies,'

où elle prend les proportions d'une encyclopédie orale et vivante. Mais elle trouve place aussi dans le cercle de famille et dans les autres petits forums où l'on s'instruit sans pédantisme, selon une pédagogie réciproque et ininterrompue." Fumaroli adds that "cet idéal bienveillant et souriant de cohésion sociale . . . est spécifiquement catholique et italien, bien que son prestige contagieux ait gagné toute l'Europe."

20. I am indebted here to Patrizi, "Il valore della norma" 32–42. Baldassare Castiglione, *Il Libro del Cortegiano* (Milan: Garzanti, 1981); *The Book of the Courtier,* trans. Charles S. Singleton (New York: Anchor Books, 1959), in contrast, refuses to fix the rules for such conversations, which he terms "il conversare cottidiano": "e di questo credo veramente che sia difficile dar regola alcuna per le infinite e varie cose che occorrono nel conversare . . . però chi ha da accommodarsi nel conversare con tanti, bisogna che si guidi col suo giudicio proprio e, conoscendo le differenzie dell'uno e dell'altro, ogni dì muti stile e modo, secondo la natura di quelli con chi a conversar si mette" (*Cortegiano* 143 [II.17]). [And, truly, I think it difficult to give any rule in this, because of the infinite variety of things that can come up in conversation. . . . Hence, whoever has to engage in conversation with others must let himself be guided by his own judgment and must perceive the differences between one man and another, and change his style and method from day to day, according to the nature of the person with whom he undertakes to converse (*Courtier* 109).]

21. For the "trivial," see Patricia Fumerton, *Cultural Aesthetics: Renaissance Literature and the Practice of Social Ornament* (Chicago: University of Chicago Press, 1991) 1–2.

22. See Mario Biagioli, "Etiquette, Interdependence, and Sociability in Seventeenth-Century Science," *Critical Inquiry* 22 (1996): 193–238.

23. Jacques Revel, "Les Usages de la civilité," *Histoire de la vie privée, 3. De la Renaissance aux Lumières,* eds. Philippe Ariès and Georges Duby (Paris: Seuil, 1986) 194.

24. Elizabeth C. Goldsmith, *Exclusive Conversations: The Art of Interaction in Seventeenth-Century France* (Philadelphia: University of Pennsylvania Press, 1988) 10–12. Goldsmith cites Richard Sennett's observation that the modern world, on the contrary, thinks that "social relationships of all kinds are real, believable and authentic the closer they approach the inner psychological concerns of each person" (37).

25. Cf. von Moos 136–137. On the *je ne sais quoi,* see Paolo d'Angelo and Stefano Velotti, *Il 'non so che': storia di un'idea estetica* (Palermo: Aesthetica Edizioni, 1997) and Richard Scholar, *The "Je-Ne-Sais-Quoi" in Early Modern Europe: Encounters with a Certain Something* (New York: Oxford University Press, 2005).

26. Eduardo Saccone, *Le buone e le cattive maniere: letteratura e galateo nel Cinquecento* (Bologna: Il Mulino, 1992) 129, speaks of "l'attenzione, acuta, rivolta dal Della Casa al rilevamento di tensioni, in particolare nella società, e alla possibilità di trovar loro delle soluzioni." [Keen attention (was) paid by Della Casa to surveying tensions, particularly in society, and to the possibility of finding solutions for them.]

27. Della Casa, *Galateo* 59 [par. 24]: "se alcuno sarà tutto in assetto di raccontare un fatto, non istà bene di guastargliele né di dire che tu lo sai: o, se egli anderà per entro la sua storia spargendo alcuna bugiuzza, non si vuole rimproverargliele né con le parole nè con gli atti crollando il capo o torcendo gli occhi, sì come molti soglion fare, affermando sé non potere in modo alcuno sostener l'amaritudine della bugia; ma egli non è questa la cagione di ciò, anzi è l'agrume e lo aloe della loro rustica natura e aspera, che sì gli rende venenosi e amari nel consorzio degli uomini che ciascuno gli rifiuta."

28. See Javier Laspalas Pérez, "El problema de la insinceridad en cuatro tratados de cortesía del Renacimiento," *Aportaciónes a la historia social del lenguaje: España siglos XIV–XVIII*, eds. Rocío García Bourrellier and Jésus M. Usunáriz (Madrid: Iboamericana; Frankfurt: Vervuert, 2005) 44.

29. Giorgio Patrizi, "*Galateo* di Giovanni della Casa," in Asor Rosa, ed., *Letteratura italiana* 2:474, notes that "il giovane educato ai precetti del *Galateo* è raggiunto, in ogni circostanza del proprio agire, dal dovere di una totale 'comunicabilità.'" [In every circumstance concerning his own actions, a young person imbued with the precepts of the *Galateo* has the duty to achieve total "communicability."]

30. Della Casa, *Galateo* 24–26 [par. 13]: "diligentemente è da guardarsi di non cadere in queste sciocchezze."

31. Castiglione, *Courtier* 172 (I have extensively modified Singleton's translation here); *Cortegiano* 223 [II.75]: "è simile a questo modo una certa dissimulazion salsa ed acuta, quando un omo, come ho detto, prudente, mostra non intender quello che intende."

32. Heinrich Lausberg, *Elemente der Literarische Rhetorik,* 2nd ed. (Munich: Max Hüber Verlag, 1971) 142: "Die Ethik hat Schwierigkeiten, die handlungstaktische Ironie gutzuheißen. Es kommt sogar Verwerfung der Höflichkeitsformen vor." [Ethics has difficulties in considering active tactical irony as good. It is even found to be a fault of forms of courtesy.] See also Müller 21–41. The relevant passage from the *Book of the Courtier* is found in 2.72–74 (220–223).

33. Castiglione, *Courtier* 139 (I have modified Singleton's translation here); *Cortegiano* 181 [II.41]: "voglio ancora che 'l nostro cortegiano si guardi di non acquistar nome di bugiardo." See book 2.49 for the full text of Bibbiena's remarks: "for in such cases a man can without blame invent as much as he pleases; and if he speaks the truth, he can adorn it with some little falsehood, in varying degree, according to the need" (*Courtier* 148); "perché in tal caso è licito fingere quanto all'uom piace, senza colpa; e dicendo la verità, adornarla con qualche bugietta, crescendo o diminuendo secondo 'l bisogno" (*Cortegiano* 192).

34. Cf. Foucault, *Fearless Speech* 144: "practical books containing specific recipes and exercises one had to read, to reread, to meditate upon, to learn, in order to construct a lasting matrix for one's own behavior."

35. Guazzo 1:60: "'l simulare è un termine ampio, il quale si stende a molte cose e a diversi fini."

36. Guazzo 1:60: "E non solamente fra nemici, ma spesso fra conoscenti il fingere in cosa che non apporti loro danno si concede, come se essendo io

invitato a veder una comedia o altro spettacolo, m'infingerò, per non andarvi, indisposto; o se, per non esser conosciuto la notte, mi torcerò la vita o mi contrafarò a guisa d'un zoppo." [And not only among enemies, but often among people who know one another it is permitted to feign something that harms no one. For instance, if I am invited to view a comedy or some other spectacle, I may feign illness in order not to go; or if I do not wished to be recognized at night, I may twist my body or disguise myself as a cripple.]

37. Guazzo 1:60: "senza alcuno interesse, et senza intenzione d'offender altrui."

38. Guazzo 1:67: "Io non niego già che non vi siano alcuni luoghi e tempi nei quali il dir bugia non solamente non è ascritto a vanità né a vizio ma è stimato (presso al mondo) per discreta e lodevole accortezza, mentre sia dirizzata a qualche onesto fine." [I do not deny that there are some places and moments in which telling a lie is not only neither an act of vanity nor a vice, but is considered by the world to be discreet and praiseworthy shrewdness, as long as it is directed toward some honest end.]

39. Guazzo 1:67.

40. Guazzo 1:60: "ma se in atto di creanza, io faccio di berretta ad un mio conoscente senza amarlo, non debbo perciò esser chiamato vizioso, perché io mi son mosso ad onorarlo più per segno di cortesia et di civiltà che d'amore."

41. La Rochefoucauld 35 (maxim 87): "Les hommes ne vivraient pas longtemps en société, s'ils n'étaient les dupes les uns des autres."

42. Quondam's note, in Guazzo 2:121n.

43. See chapter 5 of this book for a selection of such mottos on silence. See also Chapter 1 of this book, especially pp. 10–18, for more on the theme of silence in antiquity.

44. Guazzo 1:84: "la principal virtù è il saper contenere la lingua." See Quondam, in Guazzo 2:186n–189n, for an array of classical, biblical, and humanist sources for this section of the work.

45. See, for instance, Guazzo 1:84, 1:106, and Quondam's note, in Guazzo 2:186n.

46. Guazzo 1:50: "è . . . segnalata virtù il saper tacere, et frenare la sua lingua." Quondam adds, in Guazzo 2:186n, that this precept comes from the *Catonis disticha*, although it also has a biblical resonance (Proverbs 10:19).

47. Guazzo 1:84: "certamente chi ha a caro che stiano occulti i suoi pensieri, non gli scuopra ad altri, ma sia secretario di se stesso." See Tomaso Costo and Michele Benvenga, *Il segretario di lettere,* ed. Salvatore S. Nigro (Palermo: Sellerio, 1991), for a fascinating compendium of sixteenth- and seventeenth-century ideas about the "secretary," one of the focal points of reflection on manners in the period. See also Alessandro Fontana and Jean-Louis Fournel, "Piazza, Corte, Salotto, Caffè," in Asor Rosa, ed., *Letteratura italiana* 5:656n.

48. Guazzo 1:84.

49. Guazzo 1:84: "non meno d'ammirazione porta seco il saper tacere che 'l ben parlare, perché sì come questo scuopre l'eloquenza e la dottrina, così quello dà segno di gravità e prudenza." As Quondam observes, both "gravity" and

"prudence" are inextricably linked in early modern culture to the theme of silence and, ultimately, to the thematic couple "simulation/dissimulation" (Guazzo 2:187n–189n).

50. Pino da Cagli fol. 20r: "nel parlare, & nel tacere a tempo, si scopra la vertù, & la Natura del Galant'huomo."

51. Pino da Cagli fol. 8r–8v: "sarà adunque il Silentio, o la Taciturnità nel Galant'huomo, o, nel Huomo prudente, quando accorgendosi, di non potere col parlare vincere l'Aversario, con cui tal hora contenda, o, rigettare qualche calunnia d'invidioso Ragionatore, riserverà il parlare a più commodo tempo, & prudentemente tacerà mentre con migliore Occasione possa spiegare il proprio concetto, accio che sia meglio inteso, & l'Avversario rimanga più chiaramente confuso."

52. Giovanni Macchia, *Le Théâtre de la dissimulation,* trans. Paul Bédarida (Paris: Gallimard, 1993) 65.

53. Pino da Cagli fol. 9v: "Nel qual modo di prudenza, & di senno appariscono due cose degne di consideratione, l'una quando si tace senza parlare; col non rispondere a chi invita, o propone, come fece Thalete: l'altra quando non si risponde al proponente, o all'invitante, ma a qualcun'altro per maggiore confusione, o negletto di quello . . . & questa seconda cosa ben considerata, ha del piacevole, & del aere ancora, quando si fa con quel giuditio, che è proprio del Galant'huomo per restare a sommo, o (come si suol dire) a galla senz'offesa della persona di cui si ragiona, & senza sospetti d'essere stimato mordace."

54. Pino da Cagli fol. 24v: "questa vertù detta pazienza, è parte di fortezza, & di prudenza, & è propria del Galant'huomo, perche con essa nel maggior colmo degli affanni suoi, si prudentemente & con tale valore d'animo si governa, che come in un gorgo d'acqua ben notando, rimane a sommo come galla, & come habbiamo già detto non si sommerge."

55. Pietro Andrea Canonieri, *Il Perfetto Cortegiano et dell'Ufizio del Prencipe verso 'L Cortegiano* (Rome: Zannetti, 1609) 112ff. In his preface "Alli Lettori," moreover, Canonieri provides a remarkably thorough bibliography of literature on the court and on the civil conversation, including Castiglione, Della Casa, Guazzo, Guevara, Vannozzi, Lipsius, Garzone, Tacitus, Nifo, Evitascandalo, Sigismondi, Calcagnino, and many others. The entire list is reprinted in Gianfranco Borrelli, *Ragion di stato e leviatano: conservazione e scambio alle origini della modernità politica* (Bologna: Il Mulino, 1993) 137n.

56. Canonieri 112: "la dissimulazione è necessaria ad ognuno."

57. Canonieri 112: "non ogni dissimulazione è buona, & onesta. Quella solamente è tale, che ha buono, & onesto fine, & che servate le debite circostanze, non nega la verità, & non va contra il giusto. Così fatta dissimulazione è parte, e termine di prudenza, & si fa per il più col tacere, & per queste cause."

58. Canonieri 113: "per non scoprire un'intenzione, che scoperta non conseguirebbe il suo fine"; "per non mostrare, che vediamo i pensieri d'altri, o il mal animo, ch'altri hanno contra noi, o contra quelli che noi amiamo, ovvero il buon'animo, ch'altri porta a coloro che sono nostri nemici"; "per non publicar quello, che altri commette alla nostra fede"; "per non mettere in luce un fatto, dalla notizia del quale ne possa succedere scandalo"; "per non dare a vedere, che

noi conosciamo i difetti d'alcuno, ovvero qualche mala sua opera, perché gli huomini diffetosi & colpevoli quando sono conosciuti per tali, odiano chi li conosce"; "per non far segno, che noi sappiamo un'offesa fattaci, o che noi ci la riputiamo offesa, o che la stimiamo tanto"; "per non metterci in necessità di operare in danno, & ruina nostra di contendere, & rispondere quando non lo richieda o la cosa, o la persona, o il luogo, o il tempo"; "per non fare danno, o vergogna a noi stessi, o ad altri, & per far benefizio, & onore a noi stessi, o ad altri."

59. Canonieri 114: "non si manchi al maggior rispetto, & che non facciamo a noi stessi peggio."

60. Canonieri 114: "questa dissimulazione ricerca più artifizio, perché il parlare non si può fuggire, e noi vogliamo salvarci così dal pericolo di dire bugia, come da quello di dire il vero"; "la risposta adunque ha da essere simile alla retirata [*sic*], che si fa senza fuggire, e senza combattere salve le robbe e le persone."

61. Canonieri 114: "non negare il vero. Non dir quello, che non si deve. Et lasciare ne i suoi primi termini l'animo di chi domanda."

62. Canonieri 115: "[è] lecito di notare chi domanda d'impertinenza"; "li rispetti delle persone, & le qualità delle circostanze."

63. Canonieri 115: "fare credere, che noi vediamo le cose, che non vedemo, e che sentiamo quelle cose, che non sentimmo"; "& è quando per le ragioni, & fini predetti ci astenemo dal dimostrare, o allegrezza, o mestizia, o speranza, o timore, o altro affetto, che sia in noi."

64. Canonieri 115: "in tutto il viver dell'huomo, & in tutte le sue operazioni"; "infinite cose nocive."

65. Canonieri 290.

66. Bonifacio Vannozzi, *Della Supellettile degli Avvertimenti Politici, Morali, et Christiani*, vol. 3 (Bologna: Eredi di Giovanni Rossi, 1613) 494. This third volume was printed in 1613, and the section on dissimulation is found on pp. 492–495.

67. Vannozzi 3:492 (par. 2054): "guardisi dunque ciascuno, mentre tace con la lingua, di non parlare co' cenni, o movimenti del corpo, del riso, e altri gesti della persona; perché questi indizi, son bene spesso bastanti a scoprir'i pensieri interni, & i segreti dell'animo: vi vuol dunque cautela, & accortezza grandissima a . . . far che la dissimulatione non venga nè conosciuta, nè scoperta."

68. See Jeroen Duindam, *Myths of Power: Norbert Elias and the Early Modern European Court*, trans. Lorri S. Granger and Gerard T. Moran (Amsterdam: Amsterdam University Press, 1994) 179–180.

69. On Castiglione, see Burke, *Fortunes* 117–118.

70. François Senault, *De l'Usage des passions* (Rouen: Par la Société, 1656).

71. Gracián, *Art of Worldly Wisdom* 4–5; *Oráculo manual* 153 (aphorism 8), "no hay mayor señorío que el de sí mismo, de sus afectos."

72. Gracián, *Art of Worldly Wisdom* 31; *Oráculo manual* 166 (aphorism 55), "Sea uno primero señor de sí, lo será después de los otros."

73. Gracián, *El Héroe*, in *Obras completas* 8 (Primor 2): "lega quedaría el arte si, dictando recato a los términos de la capacidad, no encargase disimulo a los ímpetus del afecto."

74. Bodei 154. He describes the exacting price of such intelligence in the following manner: "Vivere in luoghi dominati da regole di sottigliezza . . . e conoscere . . . la molteplicità cangiante del reale aiuta l'individuo a distinguere sfumature determinanti, a conoscere la varietà dei fenomeni e dei caratteri, a diventare 'uomo di mondo,' aperto alla ricchezza e ai pericoli dell'esperienza. Contribuisce a insegnargli come muoversi in ambienti dominati da esigenze e regole specifiche e mutevoli, a conquistare cioè l'*imperium* su se stesso e il controllo sulle passioni mediante un parallelo sviluppo dell'intelligenza e del senso della giusta distanza da sé e dagli altri." [Living in places dominated by rules of subtlety . . . and knowing the shifting multiplicity of the real helps the individual to distinguish determining nuances, to know the variety of phenomena and individual characters, to become a 'man of the world,' open to the wealth and the dangers of experience. This helps to teach him how to move in settings dominated by specific yet changeable needs and rules, that is to say, to establish an *imperium* over himself as well as control over the passions through the parallel development of his intelligence and his sense of the proper distance from himself and from others.] See also Thomas Pavel, *L'Art de l'éloignement. Essai sur l'imagination classique* (Paris: Gallimard, 1996).

75. Timothy J. Reiss, *Mirages of the Selfe: Patterns of Personhood in Ancient and Early Modern Europe* (Stanford: Stanford University Press, 2003) 466, and Bodei 144.

76. Giovanni Macchia, introduction, *I moralisti classici da Machiavelli a La Bruyère* (Milan: Adelphi, 1988) xlx.

77. John Michael Archer, *Sovereignty and Intelligence: Spying and Court Culture in the English Renaissance* (Stanford: Stanford University Press, 1993) 25, 39–40.

78. Gracián, *Oráculo manual* 151 (aphorism 3): "aun en el darse a entender se ha de huir la llaneza, así como ni en el trato se ha de permitir el interior a todos" (my translation).

79. Gracián, *Art of Worldly Wisdom* 1; *Oráculo manual* 151 (aphorism 1): "más es menester para tratar con un solo hombre en estos tiempos que con todo un pueblo en los pasados."

80. For an overview of the early modern metaphor of "the theater of the world," see Martin Euringer, *Zuschauer des Welttheaters: Lebensrolle, Theatermetapher und gelingendes Selbst in der Frühen Neuzeit* (Darmstadt: Wissenschaftliche Buchgesellschaft, 2000).

81. Pino da Cagli fol. 12*v*.

82. Gracián, *Art of Worldly Wisdom* 54–55; *Oráculo manual* 177–78 (aphorism 98), "son las pasiones los portillos del ánimo. El más plático saber consiste en disimular . . . a linces del discurso, jibias de interioridad. No se la sepa el gusto, porque no se le prevenga, unos para la contradición, otros para la lisonja." On Gracián's complex concept of prudence, see *Diccionario de conceptos de Baltasar Gracián,* eds. Elena Cantarino and Emilio Blanco (Madrid: Ediciones Cátedra, 2005) 205–211.

83. Éric Marquer, "Vers une moralisation du secret aux XVIe et XVIIe siècle," in *D'un Principe philosophique à un genre littéraire: les 'secrets,'* ed. Do-

minique de Courcelles (Paris: Honoré Champion, 2005) 483, points out that for Gracián dissimulation is never a matter of nature but of art.

84. Accetto 35: "le volpi son tra noi molte e non sempre conosciute."

85. Nigro notes (in Accetto xxv) that Accetto "non fa che tradurre la categoria classica di onestà ('quod decet, honestum est et quod honestum est, decet' [Cicero, *De Officiis*, I, 27.93]) e 'l'onesta mediocrità' del *Cortegiano* [II.41] di Castiglione ('grandissimo e fermissimo scudo contra la invidia') nella dizione ossimorica, già agostaniana, della 'honesta fraus' dei *Politicorum sive civilis doctrinae libri* (1589) di Giusto Lipsio." [Accetto merely translates the classical category of honesty . . . as well as the "honest mediocrity" of Castiglione's *Courtier* ("a very great and solid shield against envy") in the oxymoronic diction, reminiscent of Augustine, of the 'honest fraud' of Justus Lipsius's *Politicorum sive civilis doctrinae libri* (1589).]

Nigro adds, in a note, that Augustine had spoken critically of "honesta mendacia" in the *De Mendacio*. A good early seventeenth-century example of the currency of the term is found in Canonieri 112: "La dissimulazione è necessaria ad ogniuno, massime nelle Corti, ma non ogni dissimulazione è buona, & onesta. Quella solamente è tale, che ha buono, & onesto fine." [Dissimulation is necessary for everyone, especially at court, but not every dissimulation is good and honest. Only that dissimulation that has a good and honest end can be so.]

This passage from Canonieri is reported nearly verbatim in Vannozzi 3:492, who does acknowledge his source on this occasion (par. 2055). Canonieri, for his part, cites Vannozzi's text at the end of *Il Perfetto Cortegiano*. But the use of the term "honest dissimulation" likely reaches back at least to the humanists themselves (see Pontano's *De Prudentia*). See also Jennifer Richards, *Rhetoric and Courtliness in Early Modern Literature* (New York: Cambridge University Press, 2003) 20–42, for further analysis of "honesty" in the civil conversation.

86. Marin Cureau de la Chambre, *The Art How to Know Men*, trans. John Davies (London: Thomas Dring, 1665) 222; Cureau de la Chambre, *L'Art de connoistre les hommes*, 2nd rev. ed. (Paris: Jacques d'Allin, 1663) 327–328: "et entre les actions, les exterieures se peuvent cacher sous des apparences contraires, et les Interieures qui sont les Pensées et les Passions, peuvent estre facilment dissimulés." Cureau de la Chambre promises (328) to speak of this "plus amplement au Traité de la Dissimulation," which, however, he never seems to have published.

87. See, for instance, Giovanni Bonifacio's treatise on physiognomy and the language of the body, *L'arte de' cenni* (Vicenza: Francesco Grossi, 1616) 7: "Tanto più quest'arte de' cenni merita d'esser commendata, & abbracciata quanto in lei non ha così facilmente luogo la simulatione, come la vediamo havere nel nostro comune parlare. È vero che anco con cenni, e con gesti, si può simulare, e finger quello che non si ha nell'animo." [This art of signs deserves to be all the more commended and embraced inasmuch as in it simulation does not occur so easily as it does in our everyday speech. It is true that one can simulate even with signs and gestures, feigning that which one does not have in mind.]

88. Virgilio Malvezzi, *Il Tarquinio superbo* (1634), in *Opere historiche e politiche* (Geneva: Pietro Chouët, 1656) 40: "non è bene sempre dire tutto quello che si

ha nel cuore, ancorché fosse bene quello che si ha nel cuore: si deve por freno talvolta al parlar libero, quando è già corrotto il viver libero."

89. Accetto 33: "tanto è nostro quanto è in noi medesimi." Accetto speaks of Job's "conscienzia" on p. 62.

90. Bodei 144.

91. Gracián, *Art of Worldly Wisdom* 50–51; *Oráculo manual* 176 (aphorism 89): "Comprehensión de sí: en el genio, en el ingenio, en dictámenes, en afectos. Non puede uno ser señor de sí si primero no se comprehende. Hay espejos del rostro, no los hay del ánimo: séalo la discreta reflexión sobre sí."

92. Accetto 17: "onde a questo modo non si può far inganno a se medesimo, presupposto che la mente non possa mentire con intelligenza di mentire a se stessa, perché sarebbe vedere e non vedere . . . dal centro del petto son tirate le linee della dissimulazione alla circonferenza di quelli che ci stanno intorno."

93. Accetto 37: "prima dunque ciascun dee procurar non solo di aver nuova di sé e delle cose sue, ma piena notizia, ed abitar non nella superficie dell'opinione, che spesse volte è fallace, ma nel profondo de' suoi pensieri, ed aver la misura del suo talento e la vera diffinizione di ciò ch'egli vale."

94. Accetto 59–60: "si ammira, come grandezza degli uomini di alto stato, lo starsi ne' termini de' palagi, ed ivi nelle camere segrete, cinte di ferro e di uomini a guardia delle loro persone e de' loro interessi; e nondimeno è chiaro che, senza tanta spesa, può ogni uomo, ancorch'esposto alla vista di tutti, nasconder i suoi affari nella vasta ed insieme segreta casa del suo cuore."

95. For the *editio princeps*, see Pontano, *De Prudentia* (1505).

96. Pontano fol. 202r. Nigro, in Accetto 28n, identifies this as the beginning of the tradition of citing this passage from the *Aeneid* in treatments of dissimulation.

97. Well over a century later, Accetto called dissimulation "il decoro di tutte l'altre virtù" (67), or the decorum of all the other virtues.

98. Von Moos 133–135.

99. Franco Bacchelli, "Science, Cosmology, and Religion in Ferrara, 1520–1550," in *Dosso's Fate: Painting and Court Culture in Renaissance Italy,* eds. Luisa Ciammitti, Steven F. Ostrow, and Salvatore Settis, trans. Jon R. Snyder, Issues and Debates 5 (Los Angeles: The Getty Research Institute for the History of Art and the Humanities, 1998) 341. Calcagnini's text was never published in the sixteenth century; his literary executor, Antonio Musa Brasavola, did not include it in Calcagnini's posthumous *Opera aliquot* (Basel: G. Froben, 1544).

100. Celio Calcagnini, "Simulatae virtutis defensio," Bacchelli 350n–351n: "Omnia succedunt facili pede, dummodo cauta/mente gerat, quaecunque facit sub nocte tegenda;/atque ita praecipiunt sacrati dogmata Christi:/'Aut peccata cave aut tegi sub nocte sopora.'"

101. Calcagnini, in Bacchelli 350n–351n.

102. Calcagnini, *Descriptio silentii,* in Nigro, *Elogio* 44. The text translated by Nigro appeared in the 1544 *Opera aliquot* and is cited by the erudite Vannozzi in his *Della Supellettile* 3:516: "Celio Calcagnino [*sic*] solamente loda l'uso del mascherarsi; & si vede, ch'egli il fà più tosto per ostentazion d'ingegno, che per

dir cosa, che habbia del vero." [Celio Calcagnino (*sic*) only praises the practice of wearing a mask; and it is clear that he does so in order to display his wit rather than to say something that has some truth to it.] Vannozzi's remarks are reported nearly verbatim by Rossi, *Convito* (1639) 283.

103. Erasmus 34:405n.

104. Erasmus 34:262.

105. Erasmus 34:262.

106. Erasmus 34:264, 267.

107. Erasmus 34:264.

108. Jorge Arditi, *A Genealogy of Manners: Transformations of Social Relations in France and England from the Fourteenth to the Eighteenth Century* (Chicago: University of Chicago Press, 1998) 121, notes that Erasmus in his *De civilitate* insists that "the private experience of oneself . . . be made an object of self-identity."

109. Girolamo Cardano, *Proxeneta, seu de prudentia civili liber* 201 [chap. 53]: I refer here to the 1635 edition. The first edition was *Proxeneta, seu de humana sapientia liber, recèns in lucem protractus* (Leiden: Elzevir, 1627). The edition of the text included in the *Opera omnia*, vol. 1 (Lyon: Hugetan and Ravaud, 1663; facsimile reprint, Stuttgart-Bad Canstatt: F. Fromm Verlag [Günther Holzboog], 1966) 355–474, is identical to the 1635 edition. An unabridged modern Italian translation has appeared as *Il Prosseneta, ovvero della prudenza politica* (Milan: Silvio Berlusconi Editore, 2001).

110. Cardano 201–203. There is also another mode of dissimulation, he adds, for those who "cannot stay calm and keep quiet," in which one says and does things other than those called for in the conversation. This is "more secure" than silence but more "turbulent" (202). See also Gianfranco Borrelli, "Tecniche di simulazione e conservazione politica in Gerolamo Cardano e Alberico Gentili," *Annali dell'Istituto storico italo-germanico in Trento* 12 (1986): 87–145.

111. Cardano 201–202.

112. Cardano 201–202. Remarks such as these make it difficult to agree entirely with Anthony Grafton, *Cardano's Cosmos: The Worlds and Works of a Renaissance Astrologer* (Cambridge, MA: Harvard University Press, 1999) 189, who sees the *Proxeneta* as "a manual for successful life at court."

113. Cardano 201.

114. Carlo Gregori, "L'elogio del silenzio e la simulazione come modelli di comportamento in Gerolamo Cardano," *Sapere e/è potere: discipline, dispute e professioni nell'università medievale e moderna—il caso bolognese a confronto. Vol. III: dalle discipline ai ruoli sociali*, Atti del 4° convegno, Bologna 13–15 aprile 1989, ed. Angela De Benedictis (Bologna: Comune di Bologna/Istituto per la Storia di Bologna, 1990) 77–79. Cardano's thoughts on political dissimulation may be found in his *De Sapientia*, sec. 3, in *Opera Omnia*, 1:536–537.

115. Montaigne, "Of Presumption," *Works* 596; "De la Praesumption," *Essais* 2:366: "Car, quant à cette nouvelle vertu de faintise et de dissimulation qui est à cette heure si fort en credit, je la hay capitallement: et, de tous les vices, je n'en trouve aucun qui tesmoigne tant de lácheté [*sic*] et bassesse de coeur." I have altered slightly this translation.

116. Montaigne, "Of Presumption," *Works* 596–597; "De la Praesumption," *Essais* 2:366–67: "Un coeur genereux ne doit point desmentir ses pensées; il se veut faire voir jusques au dedans. Ou tout y est bon, ou au moins tout y est humein [*sic*]. . . . Ce seroit une grande simplesse à qui se lairroit amuser ny au visage, ny aux parolles de celuy qui faict estat d'estre toujours autre au dehors qu'il n'est au dedans, comme faisoit Tibere." Raymond Martin and John Barresi, *The Rise and Fall of Soul and Self: An Intellectual History of Personal Identity* (New York: Columbia University Press, 2006) 121, note that Montaigne invented the word "sincerity" as well as being its first great apostle.

117. Martin, "Inventing Sincerity" 1336.

118. Margot Kruse, "Justification et critique du concept de la dissimulation dans l'oeuvre des moralistes du XVIIe siècle," in *La Pensée religieuse dans la littérature et la civilisation du XVIIe siècle en France,* eds. Manfred Tietz and Volker Kapp, Biblio 17 (Tübingen: Papers on French Seventeenth-Century Literature, 1984) 150–153.

119. Montaigne, "Of Presumption," *Works* 598; "De la Praesumption," *Essais* 2:368–369: "Or, de moy, j'ayme mieux estre importun et indiscret que flateur et dissimulé . . . je n'ay pas l'esprit assez souple pour gauchir à une prompte demande et pour en eschaper par quelque destour, ny pour feindre une verité, ny assez de memoire pour la retenir ainsi feinte, ny certes assez d'asseurance pour la maintenir; et fois le brave par foiblesse." I have altered the translation.

120. Martin, "Inventing Sincerity" 1335.

121. Montaigne, "Of the Useful and the Honorable," *Works* 730; "De l'Utile et de l'honneste," *Essais* 3:6: "Les hommes doubles sont utiles en ce qu'ils apportent; mais il se faut garder qu'ils n'emportent que le moins qu'on peut." I have altered this translation.

122. Montaigne, "Of the Useful and the Honorable," *Works* 732; "De l'Utile et de l'honneste," *Essais* 3:8: "Je ne veux pas priver la tromperie de son rang, ce seroit mal entendre le monde; je sçay qu'elle a servy souvant profitablement, et qu'elle maintient et nourrit la plus part des vacations des hommes." I have altered this translation.

123. Montaigne, "Of Presumption," *Works* 598; "De la Praesumption," *Essais* 2:368.

124. Montaigne, "Of the Useful and the Honorable," *Works* 731; "De l'Utile et de l'honneste," *Essais* 3:7: "l'innocence mesme ne sçauroit ny negotier entre nous sans dissimulation, ny marchander sans manterie."

125. Montaigne, "Of Presumption," *Works* 597; "De la Praesumption," *Essais* 2:367: "Il ne faut pas tousjours dire tout, car ce seroit sottise; mais ce qu'on dit, il faut qu'il soit tel qu'on le pense, autrement c'est meschanceté."

126. One of the most enthusiastic of Montaigne's early readers was the French priest Pierre Charron, whose *De la Sagesse* (Bordeaux: Simon Millanges, 1601) sold extremely well across Europe, although quickly placed on the Index. Charron's treatise on moral and political philosophy, influenced by Neostoic currents of thought, "incorporates virtually verbatim great chunks of Lipsius's *Politicorum* and Montaigne's *Essais* (the former with, and the latter without, acknowledgement): it was quite openly an attempt to put their ideas into a more

philosophically systematic framework and to extend them in various ways"
(Tuck 84). His treatment of dissimulation, however, was brief and unsystem-
atic: see Charron, *De la Sagesse,* ed. Barbara de Negroni (Paris: Librairie
Arthème Fayard, 1986). The outspoken Charron agreed with Montaigne that
dissimulation was "un humeur couarde et servile" (3.10.6, 656). (In fact, the latter had used an identical phrase in "De la Praesumption," although Charron did
not acknowledge this.) And he concurred with Lipsius that this profession led
only to "une grande inquietude . . . de vouloir paroitre autre, que l'on n'est"
(3.10.7, 657). There were only two classes of individuals for whom dissimulation
was excusable, namely princes and women. The former could cover his thoughts
for reasons of state, whereas the latter could do so "pour la bienseance, car la li-
berté trop franche et hardie leur est messeante et gauchit à l'impudence"
(3.10.10, 657). Frankness in women was unbecoming, but—questions of civility
aside—they were in any case, Charron misogynistically contended, natural dissimulators who did not need to be taught their art, which was "comme naturelle
en elles" (3.10.10, 657).

127. See McCrea 71–101. Two biographical studies of Bacon are Perez
Zagorin, *Francis Bacon* (Princeton: Princeton University Press, 1998) and Lisa
Jardine and Alan Stewart, *Hostage to Fortune: The Troubled Life of Francis Bacon*
(New York: Hill and Wang, 1999).

128. For example, one such reader was the Italian moralist Pio Rossi (1581–
1667), general of the Congregazione dei Monaci Eremitani di S. Gerolamo d'I-
talia, author of a moral lexicon, *Il convito morale per gli etici, economici e politici*
(first published in 1639), and renowned for his devotion to the monastic life.
Rossi was sensitive to the theme of honest dissimulation, and he produced two
brief and unoriginal texts on the topic, both of them recycling the work of others. His 1639 entry on "Dissimulation" bears traces of the influence of Canonieri
and Vannozzi (the latter had, for the most part, repeated Canonieri *verbatim*);
the 1657 entry on "Dissimulation" is entirely different, and is an outright copy of
sections of the abovementioned essay by Francis Bacon (as noted by Fintoni
196n–197n). Traces of Vannozzi are to be found elsewhere in the 1639 edition of
the *Convito:* compare Vannozzi 3:168 (par. 750) to Rossi 426. For more detailed
information on Rossi, see Albano Biondi, "Il *Convito* di Don Pio Rossi: società
chiusa e corte ambigua," *La corte e il 'Cortegiano': 2—un modello europeo,* ed.
Adriano Prosperi (Rome: Bulzoni, 1980) 93–112, and Éva Vígh, *Barocco etico-
retorico nella letteratura italiana* (Szeged: JATE Press, 2001) 217–246. Another
seventeenth-century reader of Bacon was von Knichen, who, using a Latin
translation, summarized lengthy sections of the essay on simulation and dissimulation (508D–509C).

129. Francis Bacon, "Of Simulation and Dissimulation," in *The Essayes or
Counsels, Civill and Morall,* ed. Michael Kiernan, The Oxford Francis Bacon 15
(Oxford: Clarendon Press, 2000) 21. All citations refer to this edition of the es-
say, found on pp. 20–23.

130. Bacon 21–22 (the italics are Bacon's). On this same approach to secrecy
as both political and moral, see also Scipione Ammirato, *Della segretezza*
(Venice: Filippo Giunti, 1599). On Ammirato (1531–1600), see Eric Cochrane,

Florence in the Forgotten Centuries 1527–1800 (Chicago: University of Chicago Press, 1973) 95–161, and the editors' introduction to Ammirato, *Opere,* vol. 1 (Galatina: Congedo Editore, 2002).

131. See McCrea 95–96. For a different reading of Bacon's essay, see Martin Dzelzainis, "Bacon's 'Of Simulation and Dissimulation,'" *A Companion to English Renaissance Literature and Culture,* ed. Michael Hattaway (Oxford and Malden, MA: Blackwell, 2003) 233–240.

132. Nigro, "Usi della pazienza," in Accetto xxx, has discovered a possible trace of Accetto's treatise in the verses of *Gioa re di Giuda,* an oratorio by Metastasio first performed in Vienna in 1735, which contains several apparent allusions to the language of the treatise (although they may have been mediated by another, as yet unidentified text). As Nigro has suggested, these traces indicate that Metastasio had possibly studied the treatise (or another text that relayed its arguments), understood its meaning—and therefore dissimulated his reading of it. See also Nigro, *"Della dissimulazione onesta* di Torquato Accetto," in Asor Rosa, ed., *Letteratura italiana* 2:973–990.

133. For an excellent treatment of the seventeenth-century French debate over honest dissimulation and the influence of Montaigne, see Gouverneur 226–250. Cf. Louis Van Delft, "La notion de 'dissimulation honnête' dans la culture classique," in *Prémices et floraison de l'Âge classique: mélanges en l'honneur de Jean Jehasse,* ed. Bernard Yon (Saint-Étienne: Publications de l'Université de Saint-Étienne, 1995) 253–267.

134. Nigro, "Usi della pazienza," in Accetto xxiv: "la dissimulazione teorizzata da Accetto non ha nulla di originale." As Ulrich Schulz-Buschhaus observes, although Gracián's *El Héroe* appeared in 1637, four years before Accetto's treatise, comparative study shows that the Spanish text did not directly influence it in any detectable way; "Über di Verstellung und die ersten 'Primores' des *Héroe* von Gracián," *Romanische Forschungen* 91.4 (1979): 415.

135. Accetto 10: "mi ricordo il danno che avrebbe potuto farmi lo sfrenato amor di dir il vero."

136. See Villari 13.

137. Villari (36–37) speaks of "l'estrema violenza della repressione." See also Denise Aricò, "Anatomie della 'dissimulazione' barocca (in margine all'*Elogio della dissimulazione* di Rosario Villari)," *Intersezioni* 8.3 (1988): 565–566.

138. See Thomas J. Dandelet and John A. Marino, eds., introduction, *Spain in Italy: Politics, Society and Religion, 1500–1700* (Leiden and Boston: Brill, 2007) 1–18, and Anthony Pagden, *Spanish Imperialism and the Political Imagination: Studies in European and Spanish-American Social and Political Theory 1513–1830* (New Haven: Yale University Press, 1990) 65–69.

139. Accetto 54: "non è permesso di sospirare, quando il tiranno non lascia respirare." Malvezzi, in *Il Tarquinio superbo* (57, in his *Opere historiche e politiche*), similarly remarked: "muore col dir libero il viver libero, & è odioso al Tiranno, perché è necessario alle Republiche; non si può dire padrone di se, che ha soggetta altrui la lingua" [*sic*]. [The life of freedom dies when free speech dies, and is hateful to the tyrant, because it is necessary to republics. One cannot be called master of oneself if one's tongue is subject to another.]

140. Accetto 57: "alcuni . . . sono pronti ad ogni qualità di vendetta, e per un cenno che non sia fatto a lor modo, vogliono penetrare negli altrui pensieri e dolersene come di offese pubbliche."

141. Accetto 25: "con difficultà si viene al consiglio della dissimulazione; perché . . . riesce molto dura questa pratica, la qual contiene l'esser d'assai e talora parer da poco."

142. Accetto 67: "in questa vita non sempre si ha da esser di cuor trasparente."

143. Nigro, in Accetto 59n–60n. In chap. 21 Accetto cites Lipsius's translation of a fragment from Euripides (which appeared in the discussion of dissimulation in the *Politicorum*), as well as Lipsius's citation of a passage from Lucretius, which opened the *De Constantia*.

144. Accetto 26: "metter freno agli affetti, acciò che non come tiranni, ma come soggetti alla ragione, ed a guisa di ubbedienti cittadini, si contentino ad accommodarsi alla necessità." I am indebted, in my account of Neostoicism, to Bodei 202–207.

145. Accetto 45: "il maggior naufragio della dissimulazione è nell'ira, che tra gli affetti è 'l piú manifesto . . . e di piú fa precipitar le parole . . . che . . . manifestano quanto è nell'animo."

146. Accetto 46: "è maggior diletto vincer se stesso, in aspettar che passi la procella degli affettii, e per non deliberare nella confusione della propria tempesta."

147. Indeed, as Accetto explains to his readers (33) "onesta ed util è la dissimulazione, e di piú, ripiena di piacere; perché se la vittoria è sempre soave . . . è chiaro che 'l vincer per sola forza d'ingegno succede con maggior allegrezza, e molto piú nel vincer se stesso, ch'è la piú gloriosa vittoria che possa riportarsi. Quest'avviene nel dissimulare" [Dissimulation is honest, useful and, furthermore, full of pleasure; for if victory is always sweet . . . it is clear that victory through the sole strength of intelligence occurs with greater happiness, and much more so in triumphing over oneself, which is the most glorious victory that anyone can achieve.]

148. Accetto 58: "la quiete interna, ch'è bene inestimabile ed appartiene all'innocenzia." Elsewhere in the same text he describes this as "un'altezza d'animo, ed una quiete, che conduce al piacer ed alla gloria immortale" (60).

149. Accetto 59.

150. Accetto 19: "un velo composto di tenebre oneste e di rispetti violenti." Nigro explains (in Accetto 19n): "per ossimoro le *tenebre* sono *oneste* e i *rispetti* sono spinosamente *violenti* (cioè imposti a se stessi con violenza)." Thus the translation of *rispetti* into English needs to convey a sense of self-restraint, or self-inflicted violence, that precedes a show of respect: I have opted for "deference" in this case.

151. Accetto 67: "il non credere a tutte le promesse, il non nudrire tutte le speranze." In *Il Tarquinio superbo* (76), Malvezzi remarks: "chi sospetta sempre, non è mai ingannato; Gli huomini prudenti non credono, se non quello, che vedono, e di quello, che vedono, dubbitano anche sovente. Non è errore l'haver sospetto, ma si bene l'appalesarlo. Che può nuocere all'huomo il non

credere, quando si profitta delle cose, come se le credesse; e vi stà avvertito, come se non le credesse? Mostrare di credere sempre, e dubbitar sempre, è de' megliori ammaestramenti, che si possino insegnare per vivere sicuro." [Whoever is always suspicious is never deceived. Prudent men only believe what they see, and they often doubt even that which they see. It is not an error to be suspicious, only to be evidently suspicious. How can not believing harm someone, either when acting on things as if he believed them, or when staying on the alert as if he did not believe them? One of the most important precepts that can be taught, which will allow us to live safely, is, Always seem to believe, but always doubt.]

152. Accetto 37.

153. Accetto 59: "ogni ingegno accorto vagliasi degli abissi del cuore, ch'essendo breve giro, è capace d'ogni cosa."

154. Gracián, *Art of Worldly Wisdom* 101 (I have extensively modified Maurer's translation); *Oráculo manual* 199 (aphorism 179): "pecho sin secreto es carta abierta. Donde hay fondo, están los secretos profundos, que hay grandes espacios y ensenadas donde se hunden las cosas de monta. Procede de un gran señorío de sí, y el vencerse en esto es el verdadero triunfo."

155. Accetto 35–36: "Ma le volpi sono tra noi molte e non sempre conosciute, e quando si conoscono, è pur malagevole l'usar l'arte contra l'arte, ed in tal caso riuscirà più accorto chi più saprà tener apparenza di sciocco, perché, mostrando di creder a chi vuol ingannarci, può esser cagion ch'egli creda a nostro modo; ed è parte di grand'intelligenza che si dia a vedere di non vedere, quando più si vede, già che così 'l giuoco è con occhi che paion chiusii e stanno in se stessi aperti."

156. Compare Rossi, *Convito* (1639) 141: "Col far vista di non vedere, si scansa il pericolo, che soprastà dal vedere; ma col far vista di vedere in altro modo di quello che è, si conseguisce quanto si pretende." [The danger that comes from seeing is avoided by making oneself seen not to see; but by making oneself seen to see in another way than one really does, one can obtain whatever one wants.]

157. Accetto 67: "non sei altro che arte di pazienzia, che insegna così di non ingannare come di non essere ingannato."

158. Bodei 149, 153–154.

159. Fintoni 73.

160. Accetto 33: "si sent[e] non poco dolor quando si tace quello che si vorrebbe dire, o si lascia di far quanto vien rappresentato dall'affetto." Cf. Charron 604: "Or qui faict profession de ce beau mestier, vit en grande peine, c'est une grande inquietude, que de vouloir paroistre autre, que l'on n'est, et avoir l'oeil a soi, pour la craincte que l'on a d'estre descouvert. Le soin de cacher son naturel est une [gêne], estre descouvert une confusion." [Whoever professes to follow this fine line of work lives in great affliction; it is a great source of anxiety to want to seem to be other than one is, and to watch oneself out of fear of being discovered. To (have to) take care to hide one's true nature is troublesome, and to be discovered is a (cause of) confusion.]

161. Macchia, *Théâtre* 62–63.

162. Giovanfrancesco Lottini, *Avvedimenti civili* (Florence: Bartolomeo Sermartelli, 1574) 138 (Avvertimento 313): "non è possibile, che alcuno sia dissimile da se stesso per lungo tempo."

163. Cf. Rossi, *Convito* (1639) 312: "è difficil cosa nasconder'un vitio naturale in maniera che non ne apparisca qualche segnale. Quasi tutti quelli c'hanno voluto dissimulare in poco tempo si sono scoperti. Cosi intravenne a Filippo, cosi a Domitiano Imperatore, cosi a Silla, a Tiberio, a Nerone: finalmente a Teodato Re de gli Ostrogoti." [It is difficult to hide a natural vice in such a way that no sign of it should appear. Almost everyone who has sought to dissimulate has soon been discovered. This happened to Philip, to the emperor Domitian, to Sulla, to Tiberius, to Nero: and, finally, to Theodoric, king of the Ostrogoths.]

164. Accetto 21: "il dissimular sempre mi par che non si possa metter in pratica di buona riuscita." Elsewhere in the same text (38), Accetto adds: "dico breve, perché facilmente si muterebbe in letargo, se troppo si praticasse questa negligenza." [I say "brief" because this sort of negligence could easily turn into lethargy if it were to be practiced too much.]

165. Martin, "Inventing Sincerity" 1308–1342.

166. Gaëtane Lamarche-Vadel, *De la Duplicité: les figures du secret au XVIIe siècle* (Paris: La Différence, 1994) 81.

167. Accetto 26: "nella considerazione del tempo passato, per non contradir al presente e poter far giudicio dell'avvenire."

168. José Antonio Maravall, *The Culture of the Baroque*, trans. Terry Cochran, Theory and History of Literature 25 (Minneapolis: University of Minnesota Press, 1986) 188.

169. Ultimately, for Accetto, this state of "inner peace" has a distinctly religious quality to it. Citing the Book of Job (3:26)—"Nonne dissimulavi? nonne silui? nonne quievi?"—Accetto reminds his readers that diligence will be rewarded in the end.

170. Accetto 25: "dal conoscer gli altri nasce quella piena autorità che l'uom ha sopra se stesso quando tace a tempo, e riserba pur a tempo, quelle deliberazioni che domane per avventura saranno buone, ed oggi sono perniziose."

171. Accetto 4.

172. Accetto 63: "È tanta la necessità di usar questo velo, che solamente nell'ultimo giorno ha da mancare."

Chapter 3

Vannozzi 3:168.

1. Marcello Fantoni, *La corte del granduca: forma e simboli del potere mediceo fra Cinque e Seicento,* Biblioteca del Cinquecento 62 (Rome: Bulzoni, 1994) 14.

2. See Cesare Mozzarelli, "Aristocrazia e borghesia nell'Europa moderna," *Storia d'Europa. Vol. 4: L'età moderna,* eds. Maurice Aymard and Perry Anderson (Turin: Einaudi, 1995) 327–362.

3. Fantoni 30.

4. Duindam 194–195. This paragraph summarizes Duindam's argument in pp. 192–195.

5. Duindam III. The bibliography of studies of the court over the past three decades is immense; for the interdisciplinary work of the "Europa delle Corti" group, see the still-valuable Carlo Ossola, ed., *La corte e il 'Cortegiano.' 1—la scena del testo* and Adriano Prosperi, ed., *La corte e il 'Cortegiano.' 2—un modello europeo* (Rome: Bulzoni, 1980).

6. Berger (4) argues that such a problem was too widespread in early modern Europe for one country (Italy) to be considered its principal locus.

7. Philibert, *Le Philosophe de Court,* ed. Pauline M. Smith (Geneva: Librairie Droz, 1990) 171: "L'Italien en ses actes ne semble point precipitant, ains froidement et atrempément semble considerer toutes les circonstances, et comme taster le gué, qui est de prudence . . . au reste, il n'est ja besoing de dire comment ilz cachent, celent et repriment leurs affections, de leur patience et dissimulation. Brief, ilz naissent au païs Courtisans."

8. Castiglione's work was the dominant influence on all European courtly literature until the end of the 1620s, although references to it occur throughout the seventeenth century. See Carlo Ossola's remarks on the editorial history of Castiglione's book in *Dal 'cortegiano' all' 'uomo di mondo': storia di un libro e di un modello sociale* (Turin: Einaudi, 1987) 42–98. Bryson (122) comments: "it is clear that Castiglionean principles survived in France and England long after the wane of enthusiasm for Italian culture."

9. Burke, *Fortunes* 158–162.

10. Burke, *Fortunes* 153.

11. See, for instance, Smith's *Anti-Courtier Trend.* Manfred Hinz, *Die menschlichen und die göttlichen Mittel: Sieben Kommentare zu Baltasar Gracián* (Bonn: Romanistischer Verlag, 2002) 205–243, analyzes the reception of Castiglione's treatise in Spain.

12. Daniel Javitch, "*Il Cortegiano* and the Constraints of Despotism" (1983), *The Book of the Courtier: The Singleton Translation,* ed. Daniel Javitch (New York: W. W. Norton, 2002) 319–328, esp. 328, supports the latter of these two interpretations. See also Giancarlo Mazzacurati, *Il Rinascimento dei moderni. La crisi culturale del XVI° secolo e la negazione delle origini* (Bologna: Il Mulino, 1985) 149–235.

13. Castiglione, *Courtier* 1; *Cortegiano* 3: "fui stimolato . . . a scrivere questi libri del *Cortegiano;* il che io feci in pochi giorni." See José Guidi, "Les Différentes rédactions du *Livre du Courtisan,*" in *De la Politesse à la politique: Recherches sur les langages du 'Livre du Courtisan,'* eds. Paolo Grossi and Juan Carlos D'Amico (Caen: Presses Universitaires de Caen, 2001) 19–30.

14. Castiglione, *Cortegiano* 26; *Courtier* 18.

15. Zagorin, *Ways of Lying* 7. See also his "Historical Significance of Lying" 25.

16. As cited in Lorenzo Ornaghi, "La 'bottega di maschere' e le origini della politica moderna," *Famiglia del Principe e famigila aristocratica,* ed. Cesare Mozzarelli (Rome: Bulzoni, 1988) 9–23.

17. Giulio Ferroni, "Sprezzatura e simulazione," in Ossola, *La Corte e il 'Cortegiano'* 1:120.

18. See Ossola, *Dal 'cortegiano'* 45. For the notion of the *continuum*, I am indebted to Patrizi, "Il valore della norma" 38–39.

19. A search of the text reveals that the term *dissimulazione* appears (in some form) a total of nineteen times, although only a handful of these are truly significant. By comparison, both "prudence" (fifty-four times) and "secrecy" (thirty-three times) appear with considerably greater frequency.

20. Berger 155–156; and Emmanuel Bury, *Littérature et politesse: L'invention de l'honnête homme (1580–1750)* (Paris: Presses Universitaires de France, 1996) 67–68.

21. Castiglione, *Courtier* 43–44; *Cortegiano* 128 (I.26): "Trovo una regula universalissima, la qual mi par valer circa questo in tutte le cose umane che si facciano o dicano più che alcuna altra, e ciò è fuggir quanto più si po, e come un asperissimo e pericoloso scoglio, la affettazione; e, per dir forse una nova parola, usar in ogni cosa una certa sprezzatura, che nasconda l'arte e dimostri ciò che si fa e dice venir fatto senza fatica e quasi sensa pensarvi. . . . Però si po dir quella esser vera arte che non pare esser arte; né più in altro si ha da poner studio, che nel nasconderla: perché se è scoperta, leva in tutto il credito e fa l'omo poco estimato. E ricordomi io già aver letto esser stati alcuni antichi oratori eccellentissimi, i quali tra le altre loro industrie sforzavansi di far credere ad ognuno sé non aver notizia alcuna di lettere; e dissimulando il sapere mostravan le loro orazioni esser fatte simplicissimamente, e più tosto secondo che loro porgea la natura e la verità, che 'l studio e l'arte; la qual se fosse stata conosciuta, arìa dato dubbio negli animi del populo di non dover esser da quella ingannati."

22. See Eduardo Saccone, "*Grazia, Sprezzatura, Affettazione* in the *Courtier*," *Castiglione: The Ideal and the Real in Renaissance Culture,* eds. Robert W. Hanning and David Rosand (New Haven: Yale University Press, 1983) 54–58; now reprinted in Eduardo Saccone, *Le buone e le cattive maniere: letteratura e galateo nel Cinquecento* (Bologna: Il Mulino, 1992) 35–56. See also Walter Barberis, introduction, *Il Libro del Cortegiano* (Turin: Einaudi, 1998) xxxii–xxxviii, on the influence of Cicero in the literature on the court, and Richards, *Rhetoric and Courtliness in Early Modern Literature* 43–64, on the same issue.

23. Revel 194.

24. See Accetto 50–51: "La dissimulazione è una industria di non far vedere le cose come sono. Si simula quello che non è, si dissimula quello ch'è." Cf. Zagorin, *Ways of Lying* 3.

25. See Annick Paternoster's interesting argument in "Il teatro della retorica non-apparente. La struttura del dialogo nel *Cortegiano*," *Lingua e stile* 26.1 (1991): 35–55.

26. Here I refer to Reiss 471: "the preceding chapters have shown that the idea that a private, self-reflexive subject could think, act and exist in isolation [before Descartes] had no tradition behind it." See also Charles Taylor, *Sources of the Self: The Making of the Modern Identity* (Cambridge, MA: Harvard University Press, 1989), and "The Person," in *The Category of the Person: Anthropology,*

Philosophy, History, eds. Michael Carrithers, Steven Collins, and Steven Lukes (New York: Cambridge University Press, 1985) 257–281.

27. See Gouverneur 468–469.

28. See chapter 4 for further discussion of Machiavelli's and Guicciardini's respective arguments that reasons of state not only permit but require the prince to practice deception. On Machiavelli's presence in *Il Libro del Cortegiano,* see Rinaldo Rinaldi, "Scrivere contro: Machiavelli in Castiglione," in *De la Politesse à la politique* 31–49: "il discorso di Castiglione sembra avvicinarsi e finalmente sovrapporsi al discorso di Machiavelli, con un moto progressivo che finisce per far coincidere ogni margine di queste due forme originariamente lontanissime" (48–49). [Castiglione's discourse seems to grow closer to, and finally juxtapose itself with, Machiavelli's discourse, in a progressive manner that ends up making every aspect of these two forms, which were originally very far apart, coincide instead.]

29. Castiglione, *Courtier* 138: "this seems to me to be not an art, but an actual deceit; and I do not think it seemly for anyone who wishes to be a man of honor ever to deceive"; *Cortegiano* 179–180 (II.40): "Questa a me non par arte, ma vero inganno; né credo che si convenga, a chi vuol esser omo da bene, mai lo ingannare."

30. Giorgio Patrizi, "*Il Libro del Cortegiano* e la trattatistica sul comportamento," in Asor Rosa, ed., *Letteratura italiana* 3.2:856.

31. Quondam's introduction, in Castiglione, *Cortegiano* xliii. See also the classic remarks by Norbert Elias, *Court Society* 104–105: "This courtly art of human observation is all the closer to reality because it never attempts to consider the individual person in isolation, as a being deriving his essential regularities and characteristics from within. Rather, the individual is always observed in court society in his social context, as a *person in relation to others.* Here, too, the completely social orientation of court people is manifested. But the art of human observation is applied not only to others but to the observer himself. A specific form of *self-observation* develops. 'Let a favorite observe himself closely,' as La Bruyère says. This self-observation and the observation of other people are complementary. One would be pointless without the other. We are not concerned here with a religious self-observation that contemplates the inner self as an isolated being to discipline its hidden impulses, but with the observation of oneself with a view to self-discipline in social life."

At the end of Lucio Paolo Rosello's *Dialogo della vita de' cortegiani, intitolato 'La patientia',* in his *Due dialoghi* (Venice: Comin da Trino, 1549), one courtier remarks to another (23*v*): "Ma eccovi che il principe con la sua corte si lieva per andarsene al suo viaggio. Stiamo di gratia a considerare le faccie di ciascun, e vedremo ne la faccia gli affetti de l'animo in questi Cortegiani esser tutti di mestitia pieni, o molto dissimili da questo apparecchio esteriore, che tanta allegrezza con la sua pompa dimostra." [There departs the prince with his court to undertake a journey. If we observe the face of each one of them, we will see there the passions of these courtiers, who are in truth all full of sadness, or very dissimilar from this external device, which displays with its pomp so much happiness.]

32. Quondam's introduction, in Castiglione, *Cortegiano* xli.

33. Frank Whigham, "Interpretation at Court: Courtesy and the Performer-Audience Dialectic," *New Literary History*, 14.3 (Spring 1983): 626. Republished in revised form in his *Ambition and Privilege: The Social Tropes of Elizabethan Courtesy Theory* (Berkeley and Los Angeles: University of California Press, 1984).

34. Whigham 629. Quondam remarks, along these same lines, that all knowledge in the court is instituted "dal primato assoluto del 'vedere/essere visto'" (*Cortegiano* xliii).

35. Whigham 630.

36. Cf. Alessandro Piccolomini, *De la instituzione* [*sic*] *di tutta la vita de l'uomo nato nobile e in città libera* [1543], cited in Nigro, "Dar passione agli invisibili," *Elogio* 16–17: "Da questa verità per due contrarie strade si può l'uomo dipartire: per l'una eccedendo nel troppo, con far le cose maggiori ch'elle non sono; e per l'altra con eccesso nel poco, facendo le cose minori del vero. Questo estremo dissimulazione, overo ironia; e quell'altro vantamento si può domandare." [From this truth man may take two contrary roads; by the one he makes things out to be greater than they are, and thus lapses into excess by saying too much; by the other he makes things out to be less than they are, and thus lapses into excess by saying too little. The latter may be considered extreme dissimulation, or irony, and the former boasting.]

37. Castiglione, *Courtier* 169; *Cortegiano* 220 (II.72): "assai gentil modo di facezie è ancor quello che consiste in una certa dissimulazione, quando si dice una cosa e tacitamente se ne intende un'altra."

38. See Dilwyn Knox, *Ironia: Medieval and Renaissance Ideas on Irony* (Leiden: E. J. Brill, 1989) 42–43. George Puttenham, in chap. 18 of *The Arte of English Poesie* (1589), saw this kind of irony as governing the entire tropological system of the court: "the courtly figure *Allegoria*, which is when we speake one thing and thinke another, and that our wordes and our meanings meete not. The use of this figure is so large, and his vertue of so great efficacie as it is supposed no man can pleasantly utter and perswade without it, but in effect is sure never or very seldom to thrive and prosper in the world, that cannot skillfully put in use, in somuch as not onely every common Courtier, but also the gravest Counsellour, yea and the most noble and wisest Prince of them all are many times enforced to use it, by example (they say) of the great Emperour who had it usually in his mouth to say, *Qui nescit dissimulare nescit regnare*. . . . This figure therefore which for his duplicitie we call the figure of [*false semblant or dissimulation*] [is] the chief ringleader and captaine of all other figures, either in the Poeticall or oratorie science." Now in Brian Vickers, ed., *English Renaissance Literary Criticism* (New York: Oxford University Press, 2003) 247.

39. Lausberg 141: "Die *dissimulatio* besteht in der Verheimlichung der eigenen Partei-Meinung." [*Dissimulatio* arises in the dissembling of one's own personal opinion.]

40. Castiglione, *Courtier* 172; *Cortegiano* 223 (II.75): "è simile a questo modo una certa dissimulazion salsa ed acuta, quando un omo, come ho detto, prudente, mostra non intender quello che intende."

41. Accetto 59: "è parte di grand'intelligenza che si dia a veder di non vedere quando più si vede già che così 'l giuoco è con occhi che paion chiusi e stanno in se stessi aperti." See Rossi, *Convito* (1639) 141: "Col far vista di non vedere, si scansa il pericolo, che soprastà dal vedere; ma col far vista di vedere in altro modo di quello che è, si conseguisce quanto si pretende." [The danger is avoided by being seen not to see, which is superior to seeing; by making a show of seeing in another way than one really does, however, one gets what one is asking for.]

42. Lausberg 142: "Das Gegenteil der Dissimulation und Simulation ist die redaktische Offenheit (*confessum; sinceritas*), deren gedankliches und sprachliches Ausdrucksmittel die *perspicuitas* ist." [The opposite of dissimulation and simulation is discursive openness (*confessum; sinceritas*), whose means of expression in thought and speech is the figure of *perspicuitas*.]

43. Lausberg 142. See also Müller 21–41.

44. Puttenham, in Vickers 247.

45. I am indebted throughout this section to Ferroni 119–147.

46. Sissela Bok, *Secrets: On the Ethics of Concealment and Revelation* (New York: Pantheon Books, 1982) 6.

47. Ammirato, *Della segretezza* 15, observes that "l'ufficio di prudente huomo è di saper dire, e tacere, quel che di dire, & tacer si conviene." [The task of the prudent man is to know how to say, and not to say, that which is fitting to be said and not to be said.] Ammirato thus equates secrecy—as Castiglione had done—with not only the ability to keep silent but also the ability to speak up in the courtly conversation at the proper moment and in the proper manner. Secrecy has, according to Ammirato, its own "decorum" [*decoro*] or "appropriateness" [*convenevolezza*], since the person who could keep secrets at court was the person who knew not only when but *how* to speak, in a dialectic of concealment and display. See also Ammirato, *Della segretezza* 29: "Ma par che senta tuttavia alcun rampognarmi, che io ragiono più di parlar, che di segretezza, come se si potesse trattar della liberalità senza far menzione di avarizia, o di prodigalità, & tale è tra la taciturnità. & loquacità l'arte del saper parlare, & tacere, ma a questa non habbiamo un solo vocabolo, che ce la rappresenti." [It nonetheless seems to me that there are those who would rebuke me for speaking more about speech than about secrecy, as if one could speak of generosity without mentioning greed or prodigality; and this is so with the art of speaking and keeping silent, which lies between taciturnity and loquacity, but for which we do not have a single term that stands for it.]

48. See Ammirato, *Della segretezza* 21, who makes the same point.

49. Quondam's introduction, in *Cortegiano* xxxix.

50. Whigham 625, speaks in terms of "showing" versus "being."

51. Compare Bembo's complaint in book 2 (*Cortegiano* 241, II.29): "Ho pensato talor da me a me che sia ben non fidarsi mai di persona del mondo, né darsi così in preda ad amico, per caro ed amato che sia, che senza riserva l'omo gli comunichi tutti i suoi pensieri come farebbe a se stesso; perché negli animi nostri sono tante latebre e tanti recessi, che impossibil è che prudenzia umana possa

conoscer quelle simulazioni, che dentro nascose vi sono. Credo adunque che ben sia amare e servire l'un più che l'altro, secondo i meriti e 'l valore; ma non però assicurarsi tanto con questa dolce esca d'amicizia, che poi tardi se n'abbiamo a pentire." [(*Courtier* 125): I have sometimes thought to myself it would be well for us never to trust anyone in the world, or give ourselves over to any friend (however dear and cherished he may be) so as to tell him all our thoughts without reserve as we would tell ourselves; for there are so many dark turns in our minds and so many recesses that it is not possible for human discernment to know the simulations that are latent there. Therefore, I think it is well to love and serve one person more than another according to merit and worth; and yet never be so trusting of this sweet lure of friendship as to have cause later to regret it.].

52. Burke, *Fortunes* 58.

53. See Smith, *The Anti-Courtier Trend,* and Lionello Sozzi, "La Polémique anti-italienne en France au XVIe siècle," *Atti dell'Accademia delle Scienze di Torino,* 106 (1972): 99–190.

54. Philibert 160: "aux imperfections d'un chacun, quand cela ne nous porte prejudice."

55. Philibert 160: "c'est doncq' une chose fort louable de moderer noz affections, en sorte qu'elles n'aparoissent pas aux autres, et ainsi dissimuler et nous acommoder à un chacun, car c'est un aysé moyen pour atirer la benevolence des hommes, de laquelle vient l'honneur et la bonne reputation."

56. Daniel Javitch, *"The Philosopher of the Court:* A French Satire Misunderstood," *Comparative Literature* 23 (1971): 113ff., as cited in Smith's introduction to Philibert 20n.

57. Philibert 162–163: "quand la finesse d'aucuns dissimulateurs seroit subjete à reprehension, si ne devrions-nous pas pour cela blasmer generalement la dissimulation, car gens malins font mal leur profit de toutes choses . . . il ne fault point donques blasmer ceste facilité d'esprit qui fait que l'homme, selon le plaisir des autres, se change et transforme."

58. Philibert 168: "voylà comment vivent les vrays Courtisans, rompans leurs propres afections pour suyvre nostre vertu et plaire aux hommes. Voylà la vraye fontaine dont sortira ceste bonne grace qui gist principalement (comme nous voyons) en modestie et temperance. . . . Le Gentilhomme Courtisan n'est point subjet à soy: s'il fault rire, il rit; s'il faut se contrister, il pleure."

59. Giuseppe Vedova, *Biografia degli scrittori padovani,* vol. 2 (Padua: Minerva, 1832–36) 173–174. Rosello may have been the subject of an investigation by the Inquisition in Parma in 1549, the year of publication of the *Dialogo de la vita de' cortegiani intitolato 'La patientia'.* Rosello's house was searched, and many of his books were sequestered, by the Inquisition in Venice in 1551. For information concerning Rosello and his plagiarism of Calcagnini's *De patientia* (1544) in this text, see Debora Vagnoni, "Il plagio del *De patientia* di Celio Calcagnini nel secondo dei *Due dialoghi* di Lucio Paolo Rosello," in Roberto Gigliucci, ed., *Furto e plagio nella letteratura del classicismo* (Rome: Bulzoni, 1998) 347–355.

60. See Zagorin, *Ways of Lying* 70, and Ginzburg, *Il Nicodemismo.*

61. Zagorin, *Ways of Lying* 83–99.

62. Rosello 16*v:* "quanto a'i costumi, che voi dite, mi paiono rei costumi saper ingannare co' gesti e parole il compagno, finger di amarlo, e portargli odio mortale, haver tante faccie, quanti sono gli huomini, che s'incontrano, e tutte finte, e finalmente non esser mai di sincero animo, & haver congiurato contra la verità, cosa a la natura tanto noiosa e spiacevole."

63. See Smith, *Anti-Courtier Trend.*

64. Rosello 23*v:* "questo apparecchio esteriore, che tanta allegrezza con la sua pompa dimostra."

65. Rosello 17*v:* "aprendo e chiudendo gli occhi veggiamo l'ombre de le cose, ma non puotiamo palpare le cose istesse, che non vi sono."

66. Rosello 17*v*–18*r*, 21*r*.

67. For Jean-Louis Fournel, in "Place et Palais," *50 Rue de Varennes* 1 (1985): 47, the poverty of Rosello's doctrine of dissimulation is found precisely in its defensive stance: "quant au problème du jugement moral de la dissimulation, tel qu'on peut le retrouver dans les polémiques sur le nicodémisme au seizième siècle ou sur le libertinage au siècle suivant, il s'agit alors d'une conception défensive du secret, d'une pure et simple dissimulation qui ne peut en aucun cas être productive ni être une matrice de nouvelles pratiques politiques. Ce secret là est sans avenir: secret du pauvre, du rebelle, de l'hérétique ou 'luxe d'aristo-crate.'" [As for the problem of the moral judgment of dissimulation, such as it can be found in the polemics over Nicodemism in the sixteenth century or liber-tinism in the following century, it concerns a defensive notion of the secret, of a pure and simple dissimulation that can in no case be productive nor be a matrix of new political practices. Such a secret has no future: it is the secret of the poor man, the rebel, or the heretic, or it is an aristocratic "luxury."]

68. Rosello 19*v:* "ogni principe è di animo vario, ne sta longamente di un parere."

69. Rosello 20*r.*

70. Rosello 20*v:* "s'accomoda a' i tempi, hora cedendo, hora avicinandosi, come l'occasione ricerca."

71. Rosello 22*r.*

72. Rosello 21*r*–21*v:* "come sarà tacito e segreto un'impaciente?" See also Rosa, "Chiesa e stati regionali" 264.

73. See Zagorin, *Ways of Lying* 83 and "The Historical Significance of Lying" 30, on justification by faith alone in Nicodemism.

74. On the Nicodemite practices see, among many others, Biondi, "La giu-stificazione della simulazione" 7–68.

75. Paolo Simoncelli, *Evangelismo italiano del Cinquecento: questione religiosa e nicodemismo politico* (Rome: Istituto Storico Italiano per l'età moderna e con-temporanea, 1979) 379–381.

76. Rosello 22*r:* "usissi la medicina de la pacientia ovunque pare che faccia di mestiero usarla."

77. Rosello 23*v:* "Io parimente dimostro che la pacientia in ogni infortunio rimedio singolare specialmente a la vita cortegiana si richiede, non volendo in

un tratto perdere, non dirò il longo tempo ne le corti consumato, prima che venga il cortegiano al desiato frutto, ma le molte fatiche, il tanto dissimulare, le infinite speranze."

78. Burke, *Fortunes* 120.

79. Another Ferrarese man of letters, Gianbattista Giraldi Cinzio, in his anti-courtier *Discorsi intorno a quello che si conviene a giovane nobile nel servire un gran principe* (1565), distinguished between "simulation," "dissimulation," and "accommodation" in describing the courtier's conduct (cited in Burke, *Fortunes* 121). Nigro, in Accetto 27n, adds: "per quanto Tasso non usi il termine 'dissimulazione,' a lui è ben presente la distinzione concettuale tra 'simulazione' e 'dissimulazione.'" [Although Tasso does not use the term "dissimulation," he knows well the conceptual distinction between "simulation" and "dissimulation."] Nigro cites a letter from Tasso to Marcello Donati, stating that the poet subsequently wished to change the terminology in the dialogue, "perché mi spiacerebbe ch'altri pensasse ch'io formi il cortigiano simulatore" [because I would not want others to think that I'm preparing a courtier to simulate]. See also Ossola, *Dal 'cortegiano'* 133.

80. Torquato Tasso, *Il Malpiglio ovvero de la corte,* in *Tasso's Dialogues: A Selection with "The Discourse on the Art of the Dialogue,"* trans. Carnes Lord and Dain A. Trafton (Berkeley and Los Angeles: University of California Press, 1982), 180/182. This bilingual edition supplies both the Italian and English versions, and page numbers for both versions are provided in the following cites, separated by a virgule.

81. See Lord and Trafton's introduction, *Tasso's Dialogues* 6, where this letter of Tasso's (found in the *Lettere,* 2.74–75) is translated and a brief biography is provided.

82. Tasso 154/155: "lo ha quasi a mente."

83. Tasso 154/155: "ma s'alcuna cosa è forse la qual si cambi e si vari co' secoli e con l'occasioni, non è di quelle che son principali nel cortigiano."

84. Tasso 174/175: "appari il cortigiano più tosto d'occultare che di apparere."

85. Tasso 174/175: "[Giovanlorenzo Malpiglio:] A me pare così difficile l'apparere quel ch' io non sono, come il celar quel ch'io sono . . . [Forestiere napoletano:] Questo nascondersi nondimeno si può fare con alcun avvedimento."

86. Tasso 178/179: "dunque occultando il cortigiano schiva la noia del principe, e occultando ancora par ch'egli possa celarsi da l'invidia cortigiana."

87. Tasso 182/183: "e di queste particolarmente che sono in fiore."

88. Tasso 180/181: "e se l'altro del Castiglione fu per quella età ne la qual fu scritto, assai caro dovrà essere il vostro in questi tempi, in cui l'infingere è una de la maggior virtù."

89. Tasso 190/191.

90. Tasso 172/173: "la prudenza . . . del cortigiano consisterà ne l'essercitare i commandamenti del principe."

91. Tasso 174/175: "ogni maggioranza d'ingegno suole essere odiosa al principe: laonde, quando ella sia nel cortigiano . . . dee può tosto esser coperta con modestia che dimostrata con superba apparenza."

92. Tasso 178/179: "la prudenza è quella virtù che supera ne le corti tutte le difficultà."

93. The entire passage reads as follows: "dunque la prudenza è quella virtù che supera ne le corti tutte le difficultà, o la cognizione de le cose naturali; ma questa è propria del filosofo, quella del cavaliero: i quali, se pur son cortigiani, non debbon molto ricercar a gli altri ne le lettere o ne l' armi, perché, facendosi eguali in queste cose, superano con la prudenza, ch'è la principal virtù de le corti" (Tasso 178).

94. Tasso 182/183: "questo [eccesso] co 'l quale si scemano le proprie laudi, oltre tutti gli altri merita lode e onore."

95. Tasso 172/173: "molte volte è disdicevole ch'egli spii le cagioni di quel che gli è commandato, o che voglia più saper di quel che gli conviene."

96. Tasso 176/177: "il nascondersi al principe non è argomento di bene-volenza"; "è nondimeno segno di riverenza."

97. Tasso 182/183: "l'adattar le cose antiche a' tempi nostri è laudevol molto, purché si faccia acconciamente."

98. "[Forestiere Napoletano:] Ma può egli infingere il verace? [Giovan-lorenzo Malpiglio:] Veggaselo Socrate e Giotto" (Tasso 180).

99. For a more complete study of the problem of the secret and its spatial transformations at court (theater-boxes, secret passageways, hidden windows), see Fournel 37–50.

100. Although Tasso wrote a brief treatise entitled *Il Segretario* (1587), he never actually held such a post. On the role of the secretary, see Douglas Biow, "From Machiavelli to Torquato Accetto: The Secretarial Art of Dissimulation," in *Educare il corpo* 219–238.

101. For the development of the role of the secretary in Italy before the mid-sixteenth century, see Marcello Simonetta, *Rinascimento segreto: il mondo del se-gretario da Petrarca a Machiavelli* (Milan: FrancoAngeli, 2004).

102. Simona Foà, "Lorenzo Ducci," *Dizionario biografico degli italiani,* vol. 4 (Rome: Istituto della Enciclopedia Italiana, 1992) 740–41. On Blount, see Leah Scragg, "Edward Blount and the History of Lylian Criticism," *Review of English Studies* 46.181 (1995): 1–10.

103. Canoniero 163–167 provides a summary of Ducci's argument about the court.

104. Manfred Hinz, "Il cortigiano ed il 'tacitismo,'" in *Traités de savoir-vivre italiens. I trattati del saper vivere in Italia,* ed. Alain Montandon (Clermont-Ferrand: Association des Publications de la Faculté des Lettres et Sciences Hu-maines de Clermont-Ferrand, 1993), 198, has brilliantly observed that Ducci's is the first treatise in Italy to break decisively with Ciceronianism; instead of sup-plying rules on how to construct a conversation, Ducci's work points toward the coming seventeenth-century shift toward collections of aphorisms, à la Gracián, which avoid the systematic presentation of protocols for behavior.

105. Lorenzo Ducci, *Arte aulica, nella quale s'insegna il modo, che deve tenere il Cortigiano per divenire possessore della gratia del suo Principe* (Ferrara: Vittorio Bal-dini, 1601) 27. All references are to this edition. I have in some cases (where indi-

cated) used the English translation by Edward Blount, *Ars aulica, or the Courtier's Arte* (London: Printed by Melch. Bradwood for Edward Blount, 1607).

106. Ducci, *Ars aulica* 11; *Arte aulica* 11:"tre dunque par che siano i fini del Cortigiano. L'Interesse proprio, e questo è quello, per cui opera principalmente. La gratia del Principe, come causa del suo primo fine; e 'l servitio pur del Principe, come efficiente della gratia."

107. Ducci, *Ars aulica* 195; *Arte aulica* 135: "poiché molte cose sono permesse, e compatite alla necessità del servitio, un modo che non hanno turpitudine operate da una elettione interamente non libera, o vero non tale, che facilmente non possa abolirsi con la grandezza de gl'acquisti, che molte volte si fanno con l'amore del Principe."

108. Ducci, *Ars aulica* 195; *Arte aulica* 135. Rossi, *Convito* (1639) 342, repeated a commonplace of the age when he remarked: "il parlar veridico stà nella Corte mal'a morte." [Truth-telling is deadly at court.]

109. Ducci, *Ars aulica* 111; *Arte aulica* 79–80: "senza dubbio deve conformarsi il Cortigiano professando Armi, se'l prencipe è di natura armigero; lettere e dottrina se si diletta di sapere; bontà, e Religione, se è divoto; . . . insomma egli è necessario conformarsi quanto più si può alla sua volontà, e farsi, se è possibile, un ritratto de' costumi di lui."

110. In his *Ricordi,* Guicciardini remarked: "chi sta in corte de' principi e aspira a essere adoperato da loro, stia quanto può loro innanzi agli occhi, perché nascono spesso faccende che, vedendoti, si ricorda di te e spesso le commette a te; le quali, se non ti vedessi, commetterebbe a un altro." [Whoever is at the court of princes, and aspires to be employed by them, should be in their sight as much as possible, because affairs often arise in such a way that, if the prince should see you, he will remember you and often entrust them to you; and these, if he were not to see you, he would entrust to someone else.] See Francesco Guicciardini, *Ricordi* (par. 94), in *Opere,* ed. Vittorio de Caprariis (Milan: Riccardo Ricciardi Editore, 1953) 116–117. The translation is mine.

111. Guazzo 1:262: "il corteggian 'nanti al signore o taccia,/o sia presto a dir cosa che gli piaccia." See Laspalas Pérez, "El problema de la insinceridad," 46–53.

112. Ducci, *Ars aulica* 262–263; *Arte aulica* 179: "con tutto ciò piacciono più a' molti la dissimulatione, e le occulte macchine contra li nemici; ò per la riputazione che conserva la poca stima delle offese, ò per la lode, che s'acquista nel perdonar l'ingiurie, overo perche in questa maniera si rende men cauto il nemico, onde maggiore è la facilità in opprimerlo; & *quo incautior deciperetur palam laudatum,* dice Tacito; a non so che proposito." The citation from Tacitus is from the *Histories* 1.64: "and, to the end that he might more unwarily be deceived, praised him openly."

113. Ducci, *Arte aulica* 123: "con anfibologie, e figure; & in somma tanto oscuramente" (my translation).

114. Ducci, *Arte aulica* 117: "certo a coloro si presta fede, che sono stimati di natura libera, & aperta, & da quali si rappresenti fuori quello parlando, che dentro si rinchiude nel cuore" (my translation). Compare Ducci, *Arte aulica,*

101–102: "Quanto meno i Ragionamenti di trattenimento paiono necessarij; tanto è più faticosa l'arte di ben valersene; la quale nondimeno deve grande-mente essere osservata, e posta in prattica per l'utilità, che ne segue, percioche questi aprono più la strada alla confidenza, che non forse quelli di negotio. La ragione è perche essendo essi introdotti per elettione, e per gusto, partoriscono sovvente nel progresso tal dolcezza, e suavità nel Prencipe, che volentieri gli repete, & à poco à poco rimettendo della severità sterile viene con la famigliarità a proportionare più allo Stato suo la conditione del cortigiano, e co'l tempo di-sporsi à participargli molte cose, e successivamente habilitarlo alla notitia dei suoi più occulti pensieri: celati à gl' altri, ò noti per occasione del carico loro, non per mera elettione, e però forse non interamente participati."

Ars aulica 142–143: "By how much these conferences seem least necessary, by so much the skill and art to profit by them is the more laborious, the which notwithstanding must bee exactly kept and put in practice for the benefit which followeth thereof, because happily these open more the way to *Confidence,* than those of *State.* The reason is, because these being induced & brought in by choice and for pleasure, bring forth many times by their continuance, such de-light and sweetnesse to the Prince, that willingly he reiterates the fame, and by little and little, laying aside Princely severity, begins by this familiarity to pro-portionate the Courtiers condition nearer to that of his state, and so in time breeds a disposition to participate and impart unto him many things, and so successively doth enable him to take knowledge of his most secret thoughts; ei-ther hid from others, or only known by reason of their offices, not by free elec-tion of good liking, and therefore it may not be so fully imparted."

115. Ducci, *Ars aulica* 88–89; *Arte aulica* 65: "Mà in ciò ei bisogna star molto considerato in fuggire un pericolosissimo scoglio; questa è l'affettatione, laquale può partorire nel Principe opinione di poco giuditio, nel conoscere il convene-vole, ò quello che più è pernitioso dubbio, e sospetto di simulatione, e per con-sequenza effetto d'odio, ò derisione non solo appresso di lui; mà de Cortigiani ancora, à quali non può per più rispetti esser caro, che alcuno si mostri diligente troppo, e nell'apparenza appassionato nel servire il Principe."

116. Ducci, *Ars aulica* 169–170; *Arte aulica* 119: "Ma queste osservationi non ponno essere messe in prattica, se non da uno accorto, e molto sagace Corti-giano, il quale se talhora con espressione d'apparente ira accompagnerà simili uffici, accrescerà grandemente la fede, poiche questo affetto come aperto, e libero, interamente rimuove, & estingue il sospetto della simulatione; à che giova similmente il fuggire l'affettatione, & il riprendere con gravità, e decoro: Ma sopratutto via sicurissima d'acquistar fede è mostrarsi tale in tutte l'attioni sue chee 'l Prencipe faccia concetto, di persona ingenua, e libera."

117. Hinz, "Il cortigiano ed il 'tacitismo'" 195. See also Hinz, *Rhetorische Strategien des Hofmannes: Studien zu den italienischen Hofmannstraktaten des 16. und 17. Jahrhunderts* (Stuttgart: J. B. Metzler, 1992) 367–385.

118. Among the imposing number of panoramic studies of the courtier's role in the absolutist courts, see Duinden 81–95, and the essays collected in Davide Bigalli, ed., *Ragione e 'civiltas.' Figure del vivere associato nella cultura del Cinque-*

cento europeo, Filosofia e scienza nel Cinquecento e nel Seicento, Serie 1, Studi 28 (Milan: FrancoAngeli, 1986).

119. Ducci, *Ars aulica* 178–179; *Arte aulica* 125: "gl'altri [Tentativi] che con falsità, e simulatione s'introducono a fine solo di venire in cognitione della natura del Cortigiano, benche da un savio Principe siano ragionevolmente anch'essi fatti con molta destrezza, & arte."

120. See Ducci, *Arte aulica* 78–79: "facilmente gli sarà aperta la via di conoscerlo dentro, e di fuori: Avvertendo nondimeno di fare in modo, che di Cortigiano tal volta non paia divenuto esploratore: e si ricordi, che *tam nescire quaedam, quam scire oportet.*" *Ars aulica* 109: "The way will be very plaine to know him aswel [*sic*] within as without. Taking care notwithstanding to doe this in such sort, that for a *Courtier* you be not taken as a *spie,* and withall remember, that *tam nescire quaedam, quam scire oportet:* It is as fit not to know some things as to know them."

121. Ducci, *Ars aulica* 103–104; *Arte aulica* 75: "Diciamo che 'l vero mezzo da conoscere la natura, e costumi del Principe sono l'attioni sue; non tutte, ma l'elettive, percioche queste scuoprono l'inclinatione, come dall'effetto si notifica la causa; & se bene la simulatione, vestendo in prima vista habito diverso, è cagione d'attioni; o diverse, o contrarie alla naturale propensione; è nondimeno impossibile, che si celi, & asconda à un sagace, & avveduto Cortigiano; poiche se vigilantemente osserverà l'attioni facilmente verrà in luce, se si operi naturalmente, e per habito contratto; ò per simulatione."

122. Ducci, *Ars aulica* 106; *Arte aulica* 76: "vero è, ch' il buon simulatore è cauto; e perciò non si spoglia di quell'habito, se non per violenza o per confidenza."

123. Ducci, *Ars aulica* 101–102; *Arte aulica* 73: "diciamo dunque varij essere i modi di conoscere la natura degl'Huomini, percioche molto aiuta l'Arte della Fisonomia, per mezzo della quale alcuni hanno saputo penetrare negl'intimi, è più celati affettti dell'animo altrui, & se bene quell'arte pare fallace, nondimeno quando concorrono insieme più segni notanti, un medesimo affetto, vogliono i savij, non esser vana la fede, che se le presta, come stabilita in fundamenti naturali." On physiognomy, see Martin Porter, *Windows of the Soul: The Art of Physiognomy in European Culture 1470–1780* (Oxford: Clarendon Press, 2005) 27, who argues that "in early modern eyes . . . 'physiognomy' was a central, if not an all-pervasive, phenomenon of their encounters with the universe."

124. Giambattista Della Porta, *Della fisonomia dell'uomo,* ed. Mario Cicognani (Parma: Ugo Guanda, 1988) 577 (5.30). This edition is based on the 1610 Italian translation of the text.

125. Ducci, *Ars aulica* 103; *Arte aulica* 75: "fondate troppo sù generali."

126. Ducci, *Ars aulica* 106–107; *Arte aulica* 77: "l'habitudine naturale."

127. Ducci, *Ars aulica* 106; *Arte aulica* 76: "da qualche mano potente."

128. Ducci, *Ars aulica* 106; *Arte aulica* 76–77: "ma ci ha un'altra violenza al proposito nostro molto fruttuosa, e considerabile, questa è l'eccesso degl'affetti irritati."

129. Ducci, *Ars aulica* 106; *Arte aulica* 77: "l'intrinseco del Core, e palesa quello, che la simulatione tiene ricoperto."

130. Ducci, *Ars aulica* 107–108; *Arte aulica* 77: "la consideratione della confidenza."

131. Ducci, *Arte aulica* 77–78: "percioche essendo il fine prossimo della simulatione il ricoprimento del natural istinto: quando i luoghi affidano promettendo segretezza per essere dalla notitia degl'Huomini lontani: facilmente allettano il simulatore ad allargare il freno all'impeto della natura: per l'istessa ragione con persone ottuse, e di poco intelletto, è più indiligente nella cautela: anzi perche con piacere si fanno l'attioni naturali, si spoglia, o almeno s'alleggerisce dell'habito della simulatione." *Ars aulica* 107–108: "for that the chiefest end of dissimulation being to maske or shadow naturall instinct, when the places give assurance, promising secrecie by their remotenesse from the knowledge of men they do easily entice the dissembler to give the raines & liberty to the force of nature; and by the same reason, to discover himselfe to muddy persons of little understanding, and lesse accustomed to their caution: or rather because naturall actions, are done with more ease & pleasure, they put off, or at least ease themselves of that habit of dissimulation."

132. I provide here the crucial passage under discussion in Ducci, *Arte aulica* 75–78: "al Cortigiano per la commodità che tiene, s'offerisce strada più sicura; Diciamo che 'l vero mezzo da conoscere la natura, & costumi del Principe sono l'attioni sue; non tutte, mà l'elettive, percioche queste scuoprono l'inclinatione, come dall'effetto si notifica la causa; & se bene la simulatione, vestendo in prima vista habito diverso, è cagione d'attioni'; o diverse, o contrarie alla naturale propensione; è nondimeno impossibile, che si celi, & asconda à un sagace, & avveduto Cortigiano; poiche se vigilantemente osserverà l'attioni facilmente verrà in luce, se si operi naturalmente, e per habito contratto; ò per simulatione; percioche essendo l'istessa sempre la natura, e gl'habiti per consuetudine acquistati, l'attioni sono uniformi, e simili frà se medesime: mà la simulatione, da cui la natura non è vestita, mà ricoperta; non può avere tanto vigore, che alcuna volta non tralacca fuori di esse qualche raggio della vera, e naturale inclinattione, e questo è così vero, che mai non fu visto, me possibile sarà vedere sì eccellente simulatore, che non sia dà che domesticamente tratta con lui, & accuratamente considera l'attioni sue, facendone insieme paragone scoperto, e senza inganno conosciuto; Percioche l'Arte della simulatione nasce da un habito contrario, e violento alla natura, la quale non può essere, che molte volte co'l vigor proprio da quel grave giogo sottrahendosi non operi liberamente, & attioni contrarie à quelle, che opera la simulatione. Vero è, ch'il buon simulatore è cauto; e perciò non si spoglia di quell'habito, se non per violenza, o per confidenza; per violenza intendo forzato da qualche mano potente à dire, o operare il vero; cosa che non può cadere in un Principe verso un Cortigiano; mà ch hà un'altra violenza al proposito nostro molto fruttuosa, e considerabile, questa è l'eccessa degl'affetti irritati; percioche turbandosi alcuna volta la ragione; induce dimenticanza della cautela; apre l'intrinseco del Core, e palesa quello, che la simulatione tiene ricoperto; oltre che la facilità, o difficoltà istessa di cadere in questi eccessi, scuopre qual sia l'habitudine naturale: poiche da questa nasce l'esser più, ò meno pronto e facile alla perturbatione di tali moti: Mà di grandissima importanza è la

consideratione della confidenza, laquale consiste particolarmente ne luoghi, e nelle persone: e nelle persone, o per benevolenza, con laquale sono congiunte: ò per opinione che si porti della loro ineptitudine all'intendere, e penetrare: e anco à manifestare quello, che conoscano: Ne luoghi: percioche essendo il fine prossimo della simulatione il ricoprimento del naturale istinto: quando i luoghi affidano promettendo segretezza per essere dalla notitia degl'Huomini lontani: facilmente allettano il simulatore ad'allargare il freno all'impeto della natura: Per l'istessa ragione con persone ottuse, e di poco intelletto, è più indiligente nella cautela: anzi perche con piacere si fanno l'attioni naturali, si spoglia, o almeno s'allegerisce dell'habito della simulatione, L'istesso & molto più fà verso persone del cui amore molto confida. . . . Deve dunque il Cortigiano, che brami penetrare nell'animo del suo Principe: malgrado della simulatione; haver notitia dell'attioni di lui ne luoghi più riposti: sapere quali siano i Ragionamenti, che tiene con più sorte di persone communi confidenti particolarmente, con quelli, che per l'età, o tardità d'ingegno, lo possano, come s'è detto, render sicuro: percioche dal complesso dell'attioni, e Ragionamenti osservati, & insieme paragonati: e considerata la conformità, o difformità frà loro: facilmente gli sarà aperta la via di conoscerlo dentro, e di fuori: Avvertendo nondimeno di fare in modo, che di Cortigiano tal volta non paia divenuto esploratore: e si ricordi che *Tam nescire quaedam, quàm scire oportet.* In somma la destrezza deve condire, & accompagnare tutta questa opera: la qual destrezza non si può insegnare, mà è necessario haverla per natura, benche dalla esperienza delle cose venga molto affinata."

Arte aulica 104–110: "But because . . . there is a more secure passage offered, we say that the true meanes to attaine to the knowledge of the Princes nature and custome is by his actions: and yet not all, but those of choice, because these discover the inclination, as by the effect the cause is knownen; and although dissimulation, at first sight putting on a colourable habit, and occasion of the action, either different or contrary to the naturall propension and inclinement, it is yet notwithstanding impossible to conceale or hide the same, from a circumspect and wise Courtier, for that if watchfully he shall observe actions, it will easily appeare whether he worke naturally and by a contracted habit, or else dissemblingly; because nature being ever the same, and habits being gotten by custome, the actions must needes be uniforme and alike within themselves. But dissimulation wherewith nature is not invested, but over-shadowed cannot be of that force, but that some beame or raie of the true and naturall inclination at one time or other will pierce and passe the same, and this is so true, that as yet there hath never beene seene, nor is it possible, ever to see so excellent a dissembler, who hath not beene discovered and unmasked by him who familiarly shall deale with him and carefully consider his actions by due comparing them together. Because the arte of dissembling groweth of a forced and contrary habit unto nature, it cannot be, but many times of his proper force withdrawing itself from under so heavy a yoake it will worke actions quite contrary to those of dissimulation. True it is that the cunning dissembler is cautelous and wary, and therefore doth not disrobe himselfe of his habit, but either by violence or confidence: by *Violence,* I meane forced by some mighty hand to say or worke the truth, a thing which cannot fall out betweene the Prince and the Courtier. But there is an other kinde of violence, very profitable, and to be considered, that is, an excesse of the affections stirred up or moved: the cause is, *reason* being some-times troubled induceth forgetfulnesse of that caution, openeth the secrets of the heart, and discovereth that, which dissimulation kept most secret, besides the promptnes or difficulty itselfe of falling into these excesses laieth open what is the true naturall habit, because from hence it groweth that he is more or lesse prone or apt to perturbations upon such like motions. But the consideration of *Confidence* is of most speciall importance, the which particularly consisteth in *places* and *persons*, and in the persons is considered the benevolence wherewith they are made firme, or the opinion of their incapacity to understand and pene-trate, as also to make manifest that which they know in the *places*, for that the chiefest end of dissimulation being to maske or shadow naturall instinct, when the places give assurance, promising secrecie by their remotenesse from the knowledge of men they do easily entice the dissembler to give the raines & lib-erty to the force of nature; and by the same reason, to discover himselfe to muddy persons of little understanding, and lesse accustomed to their caution: or rather because naturall actions, are done with more ease & pleasure, they put off, or at least ease themselves of that habit of dissimulation. . . . The *Courtier* then who earnestly desireth to found his Princes minde must, mal-gree dissimu-lation, have notice of his actions in his most retired places, know what talke he hath with common persons, particularly confidents, and with those that either by age or want of wit may make him more secured, because by the collection of the actions and talke observed and compared together, and the conformity or disagreement betweene them well considered, the way will be very plaine to know him aswel within as without. Taking care notwithstanding to doe this in such sort, that for a *Courtier* you be not taken as a *spie*, and withall remember, that *tam nescire quaedam, quam scire oportet:* It is as fit not to know some things as to know them: To conclude, all these actions must be tempered and accom-panied with dexterity, the which cannot be taught, but must be naturall, though by experience in many things, it be much refined."

133. Ducci, *Ars aulica* 114; *Arte aulica* 80: "la naturale inclinatione di lui."

134. Ducci, *Ars aulica* 115–116; *Arte aulica* 81–82: "Mà deve il Cortigiano mostrare d'esservi inclinato per natura, benche con la ragione, repugni, e faccia forza à se medesimo; Percioche tanto più naturale inclinatione sarà giudicata in lui, quella che è veramente naturale al Principe, se ben co'l velo della simulatione ricoperta; e da questo ne seguirà verisimilmente molto compiacimento nel Principe, e si faciliterà l'adito alla confidenza, poiche dovendosi alcuno scoprire, chiara cosa è, che più volentieri svelerà l'occulto suo, à cui egli conosce simile d'affetto, e molto più se per sorte il Cortigiano fosse habile à servirlo in quella inclinatione; però diciamo esser necessario per termine d'ossequio, e di venera-tione verso il Principe simulante, conformarsi in qualche parte al simulato af-fetto, ò costume; ma per porgere adito alla confidenza, esser profitevole dar segni chiari della vera, ò come vera simulata propensione in se medesimo; la quale propensione sia simile à quella che veramente conosce naturale nel Prencipe; al cui humore questa è al mio giuditio la via d'accomodarsi."

This crucial passage may be found in its entirety in Ducci, *Arte aulica* 79–82: "Diciamo dunque che la natura del Principe ò è chiara, & aperta: & come si suol dire, senza fuco, e fallacia, o ella è involta, e ricoperta dalla simulatione: se è aperta, facile è la regola in ciò da osservarsi; perciò che ove si vede inclinare quello senza dubbio deve conformarsi il Cortigiano. . . . In somma egli è necessario conformarsi quanto più si può alla sua volontà, e farsi, se è possibile un ritratto de' costumi di lui. . . . Più difficile assai è l'accomodarsi a gl'humori dissimulati, perciò che accomodandosi a quello che con simulatione si professa dal Prencipe chiara cosa è, la conformità non cadere sopra la naturale inclinatione di lui e però non penetrare molto al vivo, ma consistere in affetto superficiale: Dall'altra parte se si vuol far professione del costume del Prencipe con simulatione occultato; non può questo da lui esser gradito, senza pregiuditio proprio, sapendosi che nissuno approva, & loda in altrui, quello che veramente abborisce [*sic*] in se medesimo, (parlo in materia di costumi) e certo molto vano sarebbe il pensiero di colui, che sperasse dar gusto con l'intemperanza, à che mostrasse grandemente d'amare la continenza, ò co'l desiderio di vendetta, à chi, o veramente o in apparenza, si scoprisse facilissimo all'oblivione delle ingiurie: In somma il Prencipe simulante non può scopertamente gradire alcuno, che si mostri habituato in quello che egli ricuopre con la simulatione, senza manifestare la verità dell'intrinseco suo & far conoscere la falsità dell'apparenza: Mà per il contrario non si conforma veramente al Principe, chi non s'accomoda alla vera, e realmente naturale inclinatione: onde frà queste difficoltà pare, che la via di mezzo sia di non scoprirsi apertamente, e con professione habituato nella cosa contraria alla simulatione del Principe, mostrandosi per essempio incontinentemente: con uno il quale professi grandemente la temperanza; poiche questo parrebbe ragionevolmente un dispregio di lui; & un havere in poca stima il disgusto, che se gli può dare con opere, & habiti contrarij all'apparente dispositione sua; overo si daria sospetto di conoscere la simulatione, cosa che sicuramente gl'acquistarebbe odio; mà deve il Cortigiano mostrare d'esservi inclinato per natura, benche con la ragione, repugni, e faccia forza à se medesimo; Percioche tanto più naturale inclinatione sarà giudicata in lui, quella che è veramente naturale al Principe, se ben co'l velo della simulatione ricoperta; e da questo n seguirà verisimilmente molto compiacimento nel Principe, e si faciliterà l'adito alla confidenza, poiche dovendosi alcuno scoprire, chiara cosa è, che più volentieri svelerà l'occulto suo, à cui egli conosce simile d'affetto, e molto più se per sorte il Cortigiano fosse habile à servirlo in quella inclinatione; però diciamo esser necessario per termine d'ossequio, e di veneratione verso il Principe simulante, conformarsi in qualche parte al simulato affetto, ò costume; ma per porgere adito alla confidenza, esser profitevole dar segni chiari della vera, ò come vera simulata propensione in se medesimo; la quale propensione sia simile à quella che veramente conosce naturale nel Prencipe; al cui humore questa è al mio giuditio la via d'accomodarsi."

Ars aulica III–116: "wherefore we say, that the nature of the Prince, either is plaine and open, and as they say, *absque fuco, & fallacia,* or it is encombred and shadowed with a skreene of dissimulation. If it be open, the rule is easie therein to be observed, because to what he is seene to incline, to the same without all question is the Courtier to enable and conforme himselfe . . . he is to adapt and fit himselfe by all the meanes he may unto his will, and make himselfe, if it be possible, the very portract of his properties and fashions. It is by oddes a thing more difficult to fit himselfe to dissembled humors: because framing himselfe to that which fainedly the Prince professeth, it is most cleare that such conformity doth not light upon his naturall inclination, and therefore doth not search unto the quicke, but resteth upon a superficiall affectation: On the other side, if he will make profession of the Princes fashions with a close dissimulation, it cannot bee pleasing unto himselfe without his own preiudice, knowing that no man praiseth or commendeth that in another, which he doth truly hate in himselfe (I speake in matter of cariage and behaviour) and surely he should feed himselfe with a vaine hope, that should thinke to be pleasing by intemperance, to him that maketh shew to be devoted unto continency: or by a desire of revenge to him, who either openly or covertly declares himselfe easie to forget all iniuries. To conclude, the Prince dissembling, cannot openly bee delighted with any one, that shall make shew to have a habit in that, which colourably he is faine to cover, without manifesting the truth of his inward meaning, and making the false appearance to be knowne. But on the contrary, he doth not truly conforme himselfe unto the Prince who doth not wholly fit himself to his true and naturall inclination. Wherefore in these difficulties, it seemes the indifferent way is not to discover himselfe openly or by a professed habit to be contrary to the dissimulation of the Prince; (for example) shewing himselfe incontinent, with one that professeth temperance. For that this might in reason seeme a despising of him, and to have in slight esteeme the disgust or displeasure which he by these actions and contrary courses might give to the Princes open and apparent disposition: or else might breed suspect of his knowledge of the disguise or counterfeiting; a thing, which questionles might win him hatred. But the Courtier must shew himselfe to bee naturally inclined thereunto, although in reason hee repugne the same, and be faine to force himselfe thereunto: because that which is truly naturall unto the Prince, shall so much the more be iudged a naturall inclination in him, though masked with a vaile of dissimulation. Hence it is very likely would grow great good liking in the Prince, and the high way unto confidence would be made easie: besides, since needs he must lie open unto some, it is cleere, he will sooner discover himselfe unto one, to bee of like affect, and much more if happily the Courtier be able to serve him in that inclination; wherefore we say it is necessary in termes of obedience and of dutifull regard towards the Prince dissembling, to conforme himselfe in some part to the coloured affect and fashion. But to make passage unto confidence, it is more profitable to give apparent signes of a true, or a truly dissembled inclining in himselfe, the which inclining must bee like to that which he knowes truly to be naturall in the Prince, unto whose humour in my opinion this is the next way to be conformable."

135. Gracián, *Art of Worldly Wisdom* 166–167; *Oráculo manual* 227 (aphorism 297): "Obrar siempre como a vista. Aquel es varón que mira que le miran o que le mirarán. . . . Aun cuando solo, obra como a vista de todo el mundo, porque sabe que todo se sabrá; ya mira como a testigos ahora a los que por noticia lo serán después."

136. Eustache de Refuge, *Traicté de la Cour* (Paris, 1616).

137. Nicolas Faret, *L'Honneste-Homme ou, L'Art de Plaire à la Court* [*sic*] (Paris: Toussaincts du Bray, 1630). See also Faret, *L'Honnête Homme ou L'Art de Plaire à la Cour,* ed. Maurice Magendie (Geneva: Slatkine Reprints, 1970). The term "honnête homme" is notoriously polysemous, and is often left untranslated.

138. See Burke, *Fortunes* 122. For the English editions, see Eustache de Refuge, *A Treatise of the Court, or Instructions for Courtiers. Digested into Two Books,* trans. John Reynolds (London: Aug. Matthewes for William Lee, 1622), and *Arcana Aulica: or Walsingham's Manual of Prudential Maxims, for the Statesman and the Courtier* (London: James Young, 1652). I prefer to use my own translations of de Refuge. See Claus Uhlig, "Moral und Politik in der europäischen Hoferziehung," *Literatur als Kritik des Lebens,* eds. Rudolf Haas, H.-J. Müllenbrock, and Claus Uhlig (Heidelberg: Quelle und Meyer, 1975) 27–51, for more information on Ducci's influence in France and England.

139. Cf. Javier Laspalas Pérez, "Cortesía y sociedad: las 'Artes' de vivir' de Gerolamo Cardano y Eustache de Refuge," *Cuadernos de Historia Moderna. Anejos* 3 (2004): 39–57.

140. Eustache de Refuge, *Traicté de la Cour, ou Instructions des courtisans,* 3rd rev. ed. (Paris: Abraham Saugrain, 1619) 1–2: "entre toutes les sortes de conversations, la plus meslee et ensemble la plus difficile & espineuse est celle de la Court. En laquelle n'ayant ordinairement autres qui se jettent que ceux qui sont poussez ou d'ambition ou de désir de faire leurs affaires." This edition contains a new preface by the author and illustrations, but still appeared anonymously.

141. De Refuge, *Traicté de la Cour* (1616) 12: "l'interest est le seul lien." This phrase appears in the aforementioned 1616 edition but was removed from the 1619 edition.

142. De Refuge, *Traicté de la Cour* (1619) 160: "et bien que la dissimulation soit necessaire à toutes sortes de personnes, si l'est elle davantage à un homme de Cour, pour conduire son ambition."

143. De Refuge, *Traicté de la Cour* (1619) 163–164: "Bref, pour recueillir en peu de mots la contenance d'un homme accort, faut qu'il ait l'esprit tendu pour examiner par le menu les actions d'autruy, & les siennes, qu'il se tienne toujours sur ses gardes & a soy, qu'il voye, entende, et juge tout, mais qu'il parle peu, couvrant ses pensées, ses volontez & ses desseins, avec neantmoins un visage ouvert, & agreable à tous."

144. Jürgen von Stackelberg, *Französische Moralistik im europäischen Kontext* (Darmstadt: Wissenschaftliche Buchgesellschaft, 1982) 79–94.

145. Kruse 156. See also Arturo del Hoyo, ed., "Vida y obra de Gracián," in Gracián, *Obras completas,* clvi. The original edition of the work was printed in Huesca in 1647 by Juan Nogués under the name "Lorenzo Gracián, Infanzón" because the author did not have the necessary permits from the Jesuit order, to which he belonged: see Benito Pelegrín's "Nota antibiográfica," in Gracián, *Oráculo manual y arte de prudencia,* ed. Benito Pelegrín (Zaragoza: Guara Editorial, 1983) 12–14. On the many early modern editions and translations of the text, see Peter Burke, *Fortunes* 123–124.

146. See Cantarino and Blanco, *Diccionario de conceptos de Gracián*. Representative overviews of Gracián's approach to prudence and to the court may be found in *Baltasar Gracián IV Centenario (1601–2001)*, eds. Aurora Egido et al. (Zaragoza: Instituto de Estudios Altoaragoneses, 2003); *Baltasar Gracián: Estado de la cuestión y nuevas perspectivas*, eds. Aurora Egido and María del Carmen Marín Pina (Zaragoza: Institución "Fernando el Católico," 2001); *"Levante sus primores la agudeza": Baltasar Gracián (1601–2001)*, ed. Guillermo Serés, spec. issue of *Ínsula*, nos. 655–656 (July–August 2001); and Aurora Egido, *Las caras de la prudencia y Baltasar Gracián* (Madrid: Editorial Castalia, 2000).

147. Gracián, *Art of Worldly Wisdom* 55; *Oráculo manual* 178 (aphorism 99): "las cosas no pasan por lo que son, sino por lo que parecen." For an expanded exploration of the theme of "el desengaño," see Hansgerd Schulte, *El Desengaño: Wort und Thema in der spanischen Literatur des Goldenen Zeitalters*, Freiburger Schriften zur Romanischen Philologie 17 (Munich: Wilhelm Fink Verlag, 1969).

148. Gracián, *Art of Worldly Wisdom* 55 (I have altered the translation); *Oráculo manual* 178 (aphorism 100): "varón desengañado: cristiano sabio, cortesano filósofo. Mas no parecerlo; menos afectarlo. . . . Vive desautorizada la ciencia de los cuerdos."

149. Gracián, *Art of Worldly Wisdom* 3–4; *Oráculo manual* 152 (aphorism 6): "el varón consumado, sabio en dichos, cuerdo en hechos, es admetido y aun deseado del singular comercio de los discretos." Aphorism 1, announcing that "all has reached perfection," has to be understood ironically.

150. Gracián, *Art of Worldly Wisdom* 6; *Oráculo manual* 154 (aphorism 11): "frecuenta[r] el antento las casas de aquellos héroes cortesanos que son más teatros de la heroicidad que palacios de la vanidad. . . . El cortejo de los que los asisten es una cortesana academia de toda buena y galante discreción."

151. Gracián, *Art of Worldly Wisdom* 4; *Oráculo manual* 153 (aphorism 7): "bien se hallará quien quiera ceder en la dicha y en el genio, pero en el ingenio ninguno, cuanto menos una soberanía; es éste el atributo rey, y así, cualquier crimen contra él fué de lesa majestad. Son soberanos y quieren serlo en lo que es más. Gustan de ser ayudados los príncipes, pero no excedidos."

152. See also aphorism 37, which seems addressed to the courtier.

153. Gracián, *Art of Worldly Wisdom* 54; *Oráculo manual* 177 (aphorism 98): "el más plático saber consiste en disimular."

154. Gracián, *Art of Worldly Wisdom* 117; *Oráculo manual* 206 (aphorism 207): "Traza la ahena astuta intención estas tentaciones de prudencia para descubrir tierra o ánimo; válese de semejantes torcedores de secretos, que suelen apurar el mayor caudal. Sea contraardid el reporte, y más en las prontitudes."

155. Gracián, *Art of Worldly Wisdom* 87; *Oráculo manual* 193 (aphorism 155): "si es posible, prevenga la prudente reflexión la vulgaridad del ímpetu; no le será dificultoso al que fuere prudente."

156. Gracián, *Art of Worldly Wisdom* 120 (I have altered the translation); *Oráculo manual* 207 (aphorism 212): "el retén en todas las materias fué gran regla de vivir, de vencer, y más en los empleos más sublimes."

157. Gracián, *Art of Worldly Wisdom* 24 (I have altered the translation); *Oráculo manual* 163 (aphorism 43): "Querer ir contra el corriente es tan imposible al desengaño cuanto fácil al peligro. Sólo Sócrate podría emprenderlo."

158. Gracián, *Art of Worldly Wisdom* 25; *Oráculo manual* 163 (aphorism 43): "[El sentir] retírase al sagrado de su silencio, y si tal vez se permite, es a sombra de pocos y cuerdos."

159. Gracián, *Art of Worldly Wisdom* 124; *Oráculo manual* 209 (aphorism 219): "el mayor artificio sea encubrirlo, que se tiene por engaño."

160. Gracián, *Art of Worldly Wisdom* 101; *Oráculo manual* 199 (aphorism 179): "Los riesgos de la retentiva son la ajena tentativa, el contradecir para torcer, el tirar varillas para hacer saltar aquí el atento más cerrado. Las cosas que se han de hacer no se han de decir, y las que se han de decir no se han de hacer."

161. Robbins 149–152.

162. Gracián, *Art of Worldly Wisdom* 19; *Oráculo manual* 160 (aphorism 33): "No hay de ser tan de todos que no sea de sí mismo." See August Buck, "Die Kunst der Verstellung im Zeitalter des Barocks," in *Studien zu Humanismus und Renaissance: Gesammelte Aufsätze aus den Jahren 1981–1990,* eds. Bodo Guthmüller, Karl Kohut, and Oskar Roth, Wolfenbütteler Abhandlungen zur Renaissanceforschung 11 (Wiesbaden: Otto Harrassowitz, 1991) 505.

163. Eleonora Belligni, *Lo scacco della prudenza: Precettistica politica ed esperienza storica in Virgilio Malvezzi* (Florence: Olschki, 1999) 179, remarks on Gracián's limitless admiration for Malvezzi, the great Italian analyst of the Count-Duke's career.

164. Louis van Delft, *Le moraliste classique* (Geneva: Droz, 1982) 240.

165. Burke, *Fortunes* 124.

166. Upon hearing the news of Castiglione's death in 1528, Charles V was reported to have said: "I tell you that one of the finest knights in the world has died" *(yo vos digo que es muerto uno de los mejores caballeros del mundo).*

Chapter 4

Diego de Saavedra Fajardo, *Empresas políticas,* ed. Sagrario López Poza (Madrid: Ediciónes Cátedra, 1999) 532.

D'Orléans 65.

1. Viroli (7) has argued that, according to humanist political theory, "politics held the monopoly of reason: ruling in justice, shaping just laws, framing and preserving good political constitutions were, in fact, regarded as the most genuine achievements of reason. The practices of the art of the state could claim no rational justification." In the Italian city-states of the Quattrocento, politics was identified with reason in civic life, and the virtues of justice, legality, and constitutionality were linked to their perceived rational nature. As the Italian peninsula was transformed into a web of principalities in the sixteenth century and the republican ideals entered into crisis, however, "the only way to provide some sort of justifica-

tion for the art of the state was to invent another reason and assert the impossibility of ignoring it. Waging an unjust war, treating citizens injustly, using public institutions for private purposes . . . were no longer practices that contravened the principles of reason, but practices accomplished on behalf of a new notion of reason: the reason of the states." The doctrine of "reason of state" was thus a critique of the conventional language of politics (which relied on the rational nature of justice and legality) and a justification of the state "as a product of mere force."

2. Bireley 203.

3. Pasquale, *C. C. Taciti ab excessu divi Augusti Annalum libri quatuor priores, et in hoc observationes* 235, as translated by Tuck, 43–44. For the Latin text, see chap. 1n46.

4. On the Venetian obsession with the maintenance of state secrets, see Paolo Prieto, *I servizi segreti di Venezia. Spionaggio e controspionaggio: cifrari, intercettazioni, delazioni, tra mito e realtà* (Milan: Il Saggiatore, 1994) 51–74.

5. The single most useful reference here is Gérald Sfez, *Les Doctrines de la raison d'État* (Paris: Armand Colin, 2000). English-language studies include Bireley, *Counter-Reformation Prince,* and Tuck, *Philosophy and Government 1572–1651.* An extensive bibliography of earlier critical studies can be found in Gianfranco Borrelli, "Bibliografia saggistica sulla letteratura della 'Ragion di Stato,'" *Archivio della Ragion di Stato* 1 (1993): 15–92.

6. Tuck (39) cites this phrase, which appeared in Guicciardini's *Dialogo del Reggimento di Firenze,* 1521–1525. Sfez (9) instead assigns its first appearance in the singular to a 1547 text by Giovanni Della Casa.

7. See Tuck 31–64.

8. Tuck 62.

9. Bireley 237. Michel Foucault, of course, argues in his 1975 classic, *Discipline and Punish: The Birth of the Prison,* trans. Alan Sheridan (New York: Vintage Books, 1979) 135–169, that the "disciplines" emerged in the eighteenth century with the Enlightenment and the reinvention of the prison, the school, the army, and so on.

10. Tuck 62: "the self could only be preserved by a kind of emotional horticulture, in which certain passions were allowed to blossom and others kept firmly under control. At the political level, the same kind of discipline was required of a potentially unruly and disruptive population."

11. D'Orléans 68: "or comme ceste maxime est veritable, que les Roys sont fort dissimulez, il est encores plus veritable qu'ils usent dextrement de cest outil de dissimulation, toutefois et quantes qu'il faut, ou maintenir, ou conquerir, ou ravir des Estats." Tuck (83) reports that "at some point after 1589 (it is not clear when) a former Leaguer named Louis D'Orléans, who had become reconciled to the new government of Henry IV, dedicated a manuscript series of observations on Tacitus to the king, and a second series to the Dauphin." This reconciliation clearly could not have occurred by 1594.

12. Giovanni Botero, *Della Ragion di Stato: Libri Dieci, con Tre Libri delle Cause della Grandezza e Magnificenza delle Città,* rev. ed. (Venice: Gioliti, 1598 [1589]; anastatic reprint, Bologna: Arnaldo Forni, 1990) 1 (I.1): "Stato è un

Dominio ferma sopra popoli; e Ragione di Stato è notitia di mezzi atti a fondare, conservare, e ampliare un dominio così fatto."

13. Borrelli, *Ragion di stato e leviatano* 144.

14. Viroli 7–8.

15. Viroli 131, 177. On this point, see also Roberto Esposito, *Ordine e conflitto. Machiavelli e la letteratura politica del Rinascimento italiano* (Naples: Liguori, 1984).

16. Tuck 21.

17. See especially Giuliano Procacci, *Machiavelli nella cultura europea dell'età moderna* (Bari: Laterza, 1995) 213–251, a revised version of his *Studi sulla fortuna di Machiavelli* (1965); Peter S. Donaldson, *Machiavelli and Mystery of State* (New York: Cambridge University Press, 1988) 36–110; Mario Praz, *The Flaming Heart* (New York: W. W. Norton, 1973) 90–145; and Felix Raab, *The English Face of Machiavelli: A Changing Interpretation, 1500–1700* (London: Routledge Kegan Paul; Toronto: University of Toronto Press, 1964).

18. Mathieu Coignet, *Politique discourses upon trueth and lying. An instruction to princes to keepe their faith and promise*, trans. Edward Hoby (London: Ralfe Newberie, 1586) 36; Coignet, *Instruction aux princes pour garder la foy promise, contenant un sommaire de la philosophie Chretienne et morale, & devoir d'un homme de bien. En plusieurs discours politiques sur la vérité et le mensonge* (Paris: Jacques de Puys, 1584) 52–53: "et lesdicts Italiens ne pouvans excuser les grandes fautes, cruautez, perfidies, couardises, trahisons & simulations de leur nation, taschent desguiser telles meschancetez du nom de Prudence Italienne." Coignet, a nobleman who held a number of important public offices, published this one book in his lifetime. Chapter 5, entitled "De la simulation et dissimulation" (leaf 14), condemns both practices in the strongest possible terms. Coignet is nonetheless constrained to admit (15) that "ce n'est toutefois à chacun, ny en tout temps, ny de toutes choses, dire ce qu'on pense. Car c'est prudence ne descouvrir ce que pour bonne cause ne voulons estre conneu. . . . Toute simulation qui se fait pour tromper autruy, est reprouvee: mais si c'est pour cacher un bon conseil, de peur qu'on ne l'empeche, elle n'est à blamer, & n'est toujours requis que manifestions ce qu'avons en l'entendement. Ce qui a meu aucuns Empereurs & Rois de dire, que qui ne sçait dissimuler, ne sçait regner." [It is not always for everyone to say what one thinks, neither in all times nor about all things. It is prudent not to reveal what for good reason we do not want known. . . . All counterfeiting, if performed in order to deceive someone, is to be reproached: but if it is done in order to hide a good counsel, fearing that others would obstruct it, then the counterfeiting is blameless, for we are not always required to display what we have in our minds. This has led certain emperors and kings to say that "he who does not know how to dissimulate does not know how to rule."] I have preferred my translation here to Hoby's (which appears on p. 10 of the *Politique discourses*).

19. On Machiavelli's reputation in France, see Procacci 125–212. Machon (636–637) notes that "quand on veult faire une vertu de la dissimulation, on l'appelle prudence; et quand on veult en faire un vice on lui rend son premier nom, avec

un petit motif, et quelque accent d'aigreur, de plainte, et d'accusation." [When one wants to make a virtue of dissimulation, one calls it prudence; and when one wants to make a vice of it, one resorts to its original name, with a minor theme and a few notes of spite, complaint, and indictment.]

20. Niccolò Machiavelli, *Il Principe,* in *Le grandi opere politiche,* eds. Gian Mario Anselmi and Carlo Varotti, vol. 1 (Turin: Bollati Boringhieri, 1992) 102–103: "Dovete, adunque, sapere come sono dua generazioni [i.e., due modi] di combattere: l'uno con le leggi, l'altro con la forza: quel primo è proprio dello uomo, quel secondo è delle bestie: ma perché el primo molte volte non basta, conviene ricorrere al secondo; pertanto, a uno principe è necessario sapere bene usare la bestia e l'uomo. . . . Sendo, dunque, uno principe necessitato sapere bene usare la bestia, debbe di quelle pigliare la golpe e il lione; perché il lione non si defende da' lacci, la golpe non si defende da' lupi. Bisogna, adunque, essere golpe a conoscere e' lacci, e lione a sbigottire e' lupi. Coloro che stanno semplicemente in sul lione, non se ne intendano. Non può, pertanto, uno signore prudente, né debbe, osservare la fede, quando tale osservanzia li torna contro e che sono spente le cagioni che la feciono promettere. . . . Quello che ha saputo meglio usare la golpe, è meglio capitato. Ma è necessario questa natura saperla bene colorire, ed essere gran simulatore e dissimulatore: e sono tanto semplici gli uomini, e tanto obediscano alle necessità presenti, che colui che inganna, troverrà sempre chi si lascerà ingannare."

21. Michel Senellart, "Simuler et dissimuler: l'art machiavélien d'être secret à la Renaissance," *Histoire et secret à la Renaissance: Études sur la représentation de la vie publique, la mémoire et l'intimité dans l'Angleterre et l'Europe des XVIe et XVIIe siècles,* ed. François Laroque (Paris: Presses de la Sorbonne Nouvelle, 1997) 99.

22. Machiavelli, *Il Principe* 1.103: "ed hassi ad intendere questo, che uno principe, e massime uno principe nuovo, non può osservare tutte quelle cose per le quali gli uomini sono tenuti buoni, sendo spesso necessitato, per mantenere lo stato, operare contro alla fede, contro alla carità, contro alla umanità, contro alla religione." The rest of this passage reads: "A uno principe, adunque, non è necessario avere in fatto tutte le soprascritte qualità, ma è bene necessario parere di averle. Anzi ardirò di dire questo, che, avendole e osservandole sempre, sono dannose; e parendo di averle, sono utili, come parere pietoso, fedele, umano, intero, religioso, ed essere; ma stare in modo edificato con l'animo, che, bisognando non essere, tu possa e sappi mutare el contrario."

23. Cf. Erving Goffman, *The Presentation of the Self in Everyday Life* (Garden City, NY: Doubleday, 1959) 208–237.

24. Machiavelli, *Il Principe* 1.104: "gli uomini, in universali, iudicano più agli occhi che alle mani; perché tocca a vedere a ognuno, a sentire a pochi. Ognuno vede quello che tu pari, pochi sentono quello che tu se'; e quelli pochi non ardiscono opporsi alla opinione di molti che abbino la maestà dello stato che li difenda."

25. Stephen Greenblatt, "Invisible Bullets: Renaissance Authority and Its Subversion," *Glyph: Textual Studies,* No. 8: 57 (1981), reprinted in *Shakespearean Negotiations: The Circulation of Social Energy in Renaissance England* (Berkeley

and Los Angeles: University of California Press, 1988) 21–65, famously contends that theater and absolutism were indissolubly linked in Elizabethan England.

26. Throughout the early modern period, defenders of *Il Principe* argued that Machiavelli was, like Tacitus, unmasking the secrets of political power rather than recommending that they be put into practice. The advice to the prince—Lorenzo de' Medici, who probably never read the copy of the book that Machiavelli sent him—may also be read as advice to others who must decipher the prince's words and deeds.

27. Sfez 17–18.

28. Bireley 32.

29. Although Aquinas, in his *Summa Theologica,* drew a distinction between public and private affairs (Bireley 15), the use of the term "public" here is anachronistic. However, by the late sixteenth century it was not uncommon for writers to refer to the public sphere of power. See, for instance, Lipsius's *De Constantia,* or the remarks by the man who was perhaps Lipsius's most important disciple, Jean de Chokier, in his *Thesaurus Politicorum Aphorismorum* (Rome: Bartolomeo Zanetti, 1611) 209, in a passage entitled "privata vita expers esto dissimulationis": "atque haec dicta sint in civilibus sive publicis, et arcanis Principum rebus; in queis, salva semper virtutis reverentia, simulatione uti licet: contra quam in privatis, internisve rebus." [And this may be said in what concerns the sphere of the civil or the public, and in that of the Prince's secrets; in which, maintaining respect for virtue, it is legitimate to employ simulation, as opposed to private or domestic affairs.]

30. Machiavelli, letter of April 16, 1527, as cited in Alberto Asor Rosa, *"Ricordi* di Francesco Guicciardini," *Letteratura italiana* 2.29: "io amo messer Francesco Guicciardini; amo la patria mia (più che l'anima, o: più di Cristo)."

31. Tuck 38–39. See, for instance, Guicciardini's well-known *ricordo* 48: "non si può tenere stati secondo coscienza, perché—chi considera la origine loro—tutti sono violenti, da quelli delle republiche nella patria propria in fuora, e non altrove: e da questa regola non eccettuo lo imperadore e manco e preti, la violenza de' quali è doppia, perché ci sforzano con le arme temporale [*sic*] e con le spirituale." [One cannot rule according to conscience, because—if one considers their origin—all states are violent, only excepting the republics of our own land, and I do not except the emperor from this rule, and still less the priests whose violence is twofold, because they constrain us with spiritual as well as temporal arms.] Francesco Guicciardini, *Ricordi,* in *Opere* 108; Guicciardini, *Selected Writings,* ed. Cecil Grayson and trans. Margaret Grayson (New York: Oxford University Press, 1965) 17. I have altered Grayson's translations in almost every case. Although these editions do not deal fully with the philological issues involved in the various redactions of the *Ricordi,* I will use them here because in the text the thematics of dissimulation is not greatly affected by these.

32. Asor Rosa, *"Ricordi"* 2.49.

33. Asor Rosa, *"Ricordi"* 2.48–49.

34. Guicciardini, *Selected Writings* 50; *Ricordi* 138–139: "sempre, quando con altri volete simulare o dissimulare una vostra inclinazione, affaticatevi a

mostrargli, con più potente e efficace ragione che voi potete, che voi avete in animo el contrario: perché quando agli uomini pare che voi conosciate che la ragione voglia così, facilmente si persuadono che le resoluzione [*sic*] vostre siano secondo quello che detta la ragione."

35. Guicciardini, *Selected Writings* 15; *Ricordi* 106: "nega pure sempre quello che tu non vuoi che si sappia, o afferma quello che tu vuoi che si creda."

36. Guicciardini, *Selected Writings* 28; *Ricordi* 118: "è lodato assai negli uomini, e è grato a ognuno, lo essere di natura liberi e reali e, come si dice in Firenze, schietti. È biasimata da altro canto, e è odiosa, la simulazione, ma è molto più utile a se medesimo; e quella realità giova più presto a altri che a sé. Ma perché non si può negare che la no sia bella, io loderei chi ordinariamente avessi el traino suo nel vivere libero e schietto, usando la simulazione solamente in qualche cosa molto importante, le quali accaggiono rare volte. Così acquisteresti nome di essere libero e reale, e ti tireresti drieto quella grazia che ha chi è tenuto di tale natura: e nondimeno, nelle cose che importassino più caveresti utilità dalla simulazione, e tanto maggiore quanto, avendo fama di non essere simulatore, sarebbe più facilmente creduto alle arti tue."

37. Guicciardini, *Selected Writings* 28; *Ricordi* 119: "ancora che uno abbia nome di simulatore o di ingannatore, si vede che pure qualche volta gli inganni suoi trovano fede. Pare strano a dirlo, ma è verissimo."

38. Guicciardini, *Selected Writings* 35; *Ricordi* 124: "è grandissima prudenza e da molti poco osservata, sapere dissimulare le male satisfazione [*sic*] che hai di altri, quando el fare così non sia con tuo danno e infamia; perché accade spesso che in futuro viene occasione di averti a valere di quello, il che difficilmente ti riesce, se lui già sa che tu sia male satisfatto di lui."

39. Guicciardini, *Selected Writings* 46; *Ricordi* 135: "dico bene che è prudenza non parlare se non per necessità delle cose propie [*sic*], e quando se ne parla, non ne dare conto se non quanto è necessario al ragionamento o intento che allora si ha, riservando sempre in se medesimo tutto quello che si può fare sanza dire. Più grato è fare altrimenti, più utile el fare così."

40. Guicciardini, *Selected Writings* 17; *Ricordi* 108: "Non dire a alcuno le cose che tu non vuoi che si sappino, perché sono varie le cose che muovono gli uomini a cicalare . . . e se tu sanza bisogno hai detto uno tuo segreto a un altro, non ti debbi punto maravigliare se colui, a chi importa el sapersi manco che a te, fa el medesimo."

41. Guicciardini, *Selected Writings* 25; *Ricordi* 116: "uno principe o chi è in faccende grande non solo debbe tenere segrete le cose che è bene che non si sappino, ma ancora avezzare sé e i suoi ministri a tacere tutte le cose etiam minime e che pare che non importino, da quelle in fuora che è bene che siano note. Così, non si sapendo da chi ti è intorno né da' sudditi e fatti tuoi, stanno sempre gli uomini sospesi e quasi attoniti, e ogni tuo piccolo moto e passo è osservato."

42. Guicciardini, *Selected Writings* 28; *Ricordi* 118: "fa il tiranno ogni possibile diligenza per scoprire el segreto del cuore tuo, con farti carezze, con ragionare teco lungamente, col farti osservare da altri che per ordine suo si intrinsicano

teco, dalle quali rete [*sic*] tutte è difficile guardarsi: è però se tu vuoi che non ti intenda, pènsavi diligentemente e guardati con somma industria da tutte le cose che ti possono scoprire, usando tanta diligenza a non ti lasciare intendere quanta [*sic*] usa lui a intenderti."

43. Sfez 35–39.

44. Bireley 45. The most well-known French opponent of Machiavelli was Innocent Gentillet, *Discours contre Machiavel* (1576), eds. Antonio D'Andrea and Pamela D. Stewart (Florence: Casalini Libri, 1974). For example, Gentillet remarked (358): "Et d'autant que Machiavel dit que le Prince doit savoir l'art de tromperie, on pourroit icy demander (pour s'en garder) quels sont les preceptes de cest art. A quoy je respon pour Machiavel, qu'on n'en peut pas donner preceptes pratiquables par le menu, pour les appliquer à chascun afaire où peut eschoir tromperie: mais les principes de cest art (que les philosophes appellent en philosophie Axiomes) ce sont ceux-cy, Se parjurer hardiment, Dissimuler finement, Cavaller les esprits, Rompre foy et promesse, et autres semblables." [And inasmuch as Machiavelli says that the prince must know the art of deception, one could ask here (in order to keep oneself from it) what the precepts are of this art. To this I answer for Machiavelli that one cannot provide usable precepts with all particulars, in order to apply them to every affair in which there may fall some fraud. But the principles of this art (which philosophers call "axioms" in philosophy) are the following: freely perjure oneself, skillfully dissimulate, ensnare others' minds, break faith and promises, and others of this sort.]

45. See chap. 1n44, for a brief bibliography of studies of Tacitism. Guicciardini had read and admired Tacitus, whose works had been circulating in Italy since the fourteenth century. For Vico's remark on Tacitus, see the *Autobiografia,* in *Raccolta di opuscoli scientifici e filologici,* ed. Angelo Calogerà and Fortunato Mandelli, 51 vols. (Venice: C. Zane and S. Occhi, 1728–1754), now in *Liber Liber,* ed. Claudio Paganelli, 20 October 1997, http://www.liberliber.it/biblioteca/v/vico/index.htm.

46. Botero, *Della Ragion di Stato* 1 (I.1).

47. Bireley (50) reports that "fifteen Italian editions appeared before 1700, ten before the death of the author in 1617." The Spanish translation alone went through six editions by 1606.

48. Viroli 252. See, above all, Giovanni Botero, *The Reason of State,* trans. P. J. and D. P. Waley, and *The Greatness of Cities,* trans. Robert Peterson (London: Routledge Kegan Paul, 1956). Botero's knowledge of Tacitus may have come from his contacts in Paris, as he himself suggests in *Della Ragion di Stato:* "[hor di quà, hor di là da monti]: Dove, tra l'altre cose da me osservate, mi hà recato somma meraviglia, il sentire tutto il dì mentovare Ragione di Stato, & in cotal materia citare hora Nicolò Machiavelli, hora Cornelio Tacito" (fol. 2r–v). [(While traveling in Italy and beyond the Alps) among the things that I have observed, I have been greatly astonished to find Reason of State a constant subject of discussion and to hear the opinions of Niccolò Machiavelli and Cornelius Tacitus frequently quoted (xiii).] See also Arnaldo Momigliano, "The First

Political Commentary on Tacitus," *Contributo alla storia degli studi classici* (Rome: Edizioni di Storia e Letteratura, 1955) 53–54, and Schellhase 125–126.

49. Birely 238. See also A. Enzo Baldini, ed., *Botero e la 'ragion di stato'* (Florence: Olschki, 1992) and Borelli, *Ragion di stato e leviatano* 63–94.

50. Botero, *The Reason of State* 3; Botero, *Della Ragion di Stato* 1: "Stato è un Dominio ferma sopra popoli; e Ragione di Stato è notitia di mezzi atti a fondare, conservare, e ampliare un dominio così fatto."

51. Sfez 59–60. For a careful deconstruction of Botero's rhetoric, see Victoria Kahn, *Machiavellian Rhetoric: From the Counter-Reformation to Milton* (Princeton: Princeton University Press, 1994) 70–84.

52. Botero, *The Reason of State* 47; *Della Ragion di Stato* 66: "cosi i consegli de' Prencipi, mentre stanno secreti, sono pieni di efficacia, e di agevolezza: ma non si presto vengono à luce, che perdono ogni vigore, e facilità."

53. Botero, *The Reason of State* 48–49; *Della Ragion di Stato* 66–67: "E perche i Consiglieri, e gli Ambasciatori, i Secretarij, le spie sogliono essere ministri ordinarij de' secreti, debbonsi eleggere à cotali officij persone, e per natura, e per industria cupe, e di molta accortezza. Giova assai la dissimulatione, nella quale Lodovico XI Re di Francia collocava gran parte dell'arte del regnare. E Tiberio Cesare non si gloriava di cosa nessuna più che dell'arte del dissimulare, nella quale egli era eccellente: e dissimulatione si chiama un mostrare di non sapere, ò di non curare quel che tu fai, e stimi; come simulatione è un fingere, e fare una cosa per un'altra. E perche non è cosa più contraria alla dissimulatione, che l'impeto dell'ira, conviene che'l Prencipe moderi sopra tutto questa passione in maniera tale, che non prorompa in parole, ò in altri segni d'animo, ò di affetto." I have modified this translation.

54. Jean-Pierre Chrétien-Goni, "*Institutio arcanae:* Théorie de l'institution du secret et fondement de la politique," *Le Pouvoir de la raison d'état*, eds. Christian Lazzeri and Dominique Reynié (Paris: Presses Universitaires de France, 1992) 135–143.

55. See Adriana E. Bakos, "*'Qui nescit dissimulare, nescit regnare':* Louis XI and *Raison d'état* during the Reign of Louis XIII," *Journal of the History of Ideas* 52.3 (1991): 399–416, for a discussion of the origins of this motto.

56. Rodolfo De Mattei, *Il problema della 'ragion di stato' nell'età della Controriforma* (Milan: Ricciardi, 1979) 187–189. Later in the *Ragion di stato* (II.viii), Botero adds: "dissimulazione si chiama un mostrare di non sapere e di non curare quel che tu sai e stimi, come simulazione è un fingere e fare una per un'altra." [Dissimulation means a display of ignorance and nonchalance concerning that which you know and care about, as simulation is feigning and making one thing for another.]

57. Borrelli, *Ragion di stato e leviatano* 78.

58. Elias, *The Civilizing Process* 475–492.

59. Bireley 225–226: "the anti-Machiavellians had great trouble clearly distinguishing lying from dissimulation, and they disagreed about equivocation. Information they realized to be a precious asset in the political struggle, and they judged dissimulation to be necessary for the protection of secrets. In fact, the

basic distinction between dissimulation and lying came out to be between the concealment of information or the preservation of secrets and the active propagation of falsehood."

60. Yves Charles Zarka, "Raison d'État et figure du prince chez Botero," *Raison et déraison d'État: Théoriciens et théories de la raison d'État aux XVIe et XVIIe siècles,* ed. Yves Charles Zarka (Paris: Presses Universitaires de France, 1994) 104–105, points out that Botero never reflects on the juridical status of the state, only on the techniques for the preservation of its dominion.

61. Françoise Charles-Daubert's introduction, in Gabriel Naudé, *Considérations politiques sur les coups d'état* (1639; Hildesheim: Georg Olms Verlag, 1993) xiv–xv; and Cavaillé, *Dis/simulations* 261–265.

62. Jan H. Waszink, "Virtuous Deception: The *Politica* and the Wars in the Low Countries and France, 1559–1589," *Iustus Lipsius Europae lumen et columen,* eds. Gilbert Tournoy, Jeanine de Landtsheer and Jan Papy, Supplementa Humanistica Lovaniensia 15 (Louvain: Louvain University Press, 1999) 248–249.

63. Justus Lipsius, *Politicorum sive civilis doctrinae libri sex* (Leiden: Christophe Plantin, 1589). The first English translation appeared five years later as *Six Bookes of Politickes or Civil Doctrine,* trans. William Jones (London: by Richard Field for William Ponsonby, 1594). I use here Justus Lipsius, *Politica: Six Books of Politics or Political Instruction,* ed. and trans. Jan H. Waszink (Assen: Royal Van Gorcum, 2004). This is a bilingual edition, and page references are given to both of the facing pages.

64. This count includes translations and editions: see Waszink's introduction, in Lipsius, *Politica* 3.165–198.

65. Michel Senellart, "Le Stoicisme dans la constitution de la pensée politique: Les *Politiques* de Juste Lipse (1589)," *Le Stoicisme aux XVIe et XVIIe siècles. Actes du Colloque CERPHI (4–5 juin 1993),* Cahiers de philosophie politique et juridique 25, ed. Jacqueline Lagrée (Caen: Université de Caen, 1994) 118.

66. Lipsius, *Politica* 230/231: "Nisi quod unius tamen Machiavelli ingenium non contemno, acre, subtile, igneum: & qui utinam Principem suum recta duxisset ad templum illud Virtutis & Honoris!" Here I have altered Waszink's translation, incorporating some of Mark Morford's translation of this same passage, in "Tacitean *Prudentia*" 145.

67. The third edition would later be revised and approved for publication by Catholic censors, after Lipsius had been reunited with the Jesuits: see Waszink, ed. Introduction, in Lipsius, *Politica* 120–124. On Naudé, see Lorenzo Bianchi, *Rinascimento e libertinismo: studi su Gabriel Naudé* (Naples: Bibliopolis, 1996) 156–165, and Cavaillé, *Dis/simulations* 242–244.

68. Lipsius, *Politica* 230–232/233: "in quo vere possim dicere, omnia nostra esse, et nihil. Cum enim invento tota & ordo a nobis sint, verba tamen & sententias varie conquisivimus a scriptoribus priscis. idque maxime ab Historicis: hoc est, ut ego censeo, a fonte ipso Prudentiae Civilis." Here again I have incorporated some of Morford 144–45.

69. Morford 141–42. Bireley (78) adds: "the 4th, the most extensive of the six books, included 750 quotations. Of these, not surprisingly, Tacitus was the most

frequently called upon, with 174 citations. The authors summoned forth most frequently after Tacitus were Cicero, 103 times, and Seneca, 92 times."

70. Lipsius, *Politica* 506/507 (IV.13): "Aevum & homines ignorare mihi videntur, & *dicere tanquam in Platonis 'politeia', non tanquam in Romuli faece sententiam* [Cicero, *Ad. Att.* II, Epist. 1]. Inter quos enim vivimus? nempe argutos, malos: & qui *ex fraude, fallaciis, mendaciis, constare toti videntur* [Pro. Ros. Com.]. Ipsi Principes, cum quibus nobis res, plerique in hac classe: & quidquid leonem praeferant, *Astutam vapido servant sub pectore vulpem* [Persius, Sat. V]." Jacqueline Lagrée, *Juste Lipse: la restauration du stoïcisme* (Paris: Vrin, 1994) 92, adds: "on voit s'opérer là, dès le début des *Politiques,* un glissement, non thématisé mais sensible, d'une tonalité machiavélienne qui va se faire jour nettement dans l'analyse de la prudence du Prince." [From the first one can see at work in the *Politica* a slippage (left unthematized but detectable) toward a Machiavellian tonality that comes clearly to light in the analysis of the prince's prudence.]

71. McCrea 16–17; and Gerhard Oestreich, "The Main Political Work of Lipsius," *Neostoicism and the Early Modern State,* eds. Brigitta Oestreich and H. G. Koenigsberger, trans. David McLintock (New York: Cambridge University Press, 1982) 39–56. Pages 48–49 of Oestreich's essay are specifically devoted to *prudentia mixta.*

72. Lipsius, *Politica* 506/507 (IV.13): "*Per fraudem &¨ dolum regna evertuntur,* notat Philosophus [Aristot. V Polit.]: Tu servari per eadem, nefas esse vis? nec posse Principem interdum *cum vulpe iunctum, pariter vulpinarier* [Adag.]? Praesertim si publicus Usus Salusque suadeat: quae semper cum Principis usu ac salute coniuncta?"

73. See Kahn, *Machiavellian Rhetoric* 67–68.

74. Lipsius, *Politica* 512/513: "Illam appello, QUAE HAUT LONGE A VIRTUTE ABIT, MALITIAE RORE LEVITER ASPERSA. in quo genere mihi est Diffidentia, & Dissimulatio."

75. Lipsius's theory was revised in a work spuriously attributed to Walter Raleigh, *The Cabinet-Council: Containing the Cheif [sic] Arts of Empire, and Mysteries of State; Discabineted in Political and Polemical Aphorisms, grounded on Authority and Experience; And illustrated with the choicest Examples and Historical Observations* (London: Tho. Newcomb for Tho. Johnson, 1658). See McCrea, 47, on the authorship of this work. In chap. 20 its author explained that "albeit roundness and plain dealing be most worthy praise, chiefly in private persons; yet because all men in their actions do not so proceed, it behooveth Wise Men and Princes above others at occasions to semble and dissemble; for as in all actions a Prince ought to be slow and advised; so in consent and beleiving [sic], haste and facility is most dangerous; and though credulity be rather an error then [sic] a fault; yet for Princes it is both unfit and perilous. Wherefore it importeth them to be defended with this caution, *Nihil credendo, atque omnia cavendo. Cic.* [Cicero] Notwithstanding he must not shew himself diffident or distrustful utterly; but as I wish he should not over-slightly believe all men, so ought he not for small causes distrust every man. *Multi fallere docuerunt, dum timent falli. Sen.* [Seneca].

"Dissimulation is as it were begotten by diffidence, a quality in Princes of so great necessity as moved the Emperor *Tiberius* to say, *Nescit regnare, qui nescit dissimulare.*

"The necessity of dissimulation is chiefly to be used with strangers and enemies: it also sheweth a certain discretion in Magistrates sometimes to disguise with friends when no offence doth thereof follow. *Doli non sunt doli, nisi astu colas. Plaut.* [Plautus]

"This kind of craft albeit in every mans conceipt not praisable, is nevertheless tolerable, and for Princes and Magistrates (the same being used to good ends) very necessary. But those cunnings which are contrary to vertue, ought not of honest men to be used" (54–55).

76. Lipsius, *Politica* 512, 514/513, 515: "Ut intentus, inquam, suspensusque ambulet, & paene dixerim, *ut nihil nisi quod in oculos incurret manifestumque erit, credat* [Seneca II. *De Ira*]. . . . Reducat ergo se Princeps, & tutum hoc scuto reddat; *Nihil credendo, atque omnia cavendo* [Cic. Orat. Post. redit. in Senat.]. Amici & fidi videntur? circumspice."

77. Lipsius, *Politica* 516/517.

78. Lipsius, *Politica* 516/517: "Reipsa, inquam, paucis: at in specie, omnibus."

79. Lipsius, *Politica* 516/517: "Haec est, quae *frontem aperit, mentem tegit.*" Charron, for instance, would later include this same phrase in his *De la Sagesse* 557 (III.2.7), and it was repeated many times by others.

80. Lipsius, *Politica* 518/519.

81. Lipsius, *Politica* 516/517. Here he cites Tacitus's words: for the complete text of the passage, see chap. 1, p. 15.

82. Lipsius, *Politica* 516/517: "Displicebit hoc ingenuae alicui fronti, et clamabit: *Ex omni vita Simulatio, Dissimulatioque tollenda est* [Cicero, II *De Officiis*]. De privata, fateor: de publica, valde nego. Numquam regent, qui non tegent: *nec aliter possunt ij, quibus commissa est tota respublica.*"

83. Anguissola, in his manuscript entitled "Della dissimulatione" (1612), as cited in Arcari, *La ragion di stato in un manoscritto inedito di Alessandro Anguissola* III, wrote: "et di maggiore esperienza et di maggior lodi degna et più propria del Prencipe è quella sorte di dissimulatione nella quale, mostrando egli intrepidezza et costanza d'animo all'annuncio di qualche avverso colpo di fortuna o d'altra mala novella, non si comuove [*sic*] per non perturbare l'animo de' sudditi et renderli timidi et diffidenti ma anzi mantenerli confirmati nella primiera virtù et speranza." [That sort of dissimulation in which the prince, displaying intrepidity and constancy of mind at the announcement of some adverse blow of fortune or other bad news, remains unmoved in order to keep his subjects from losing heart and becoming timid and diffident, maintaining instead their commitment to their original virtues and hopes, is more proper to him, and worthy of greater use and greater praise.]

84. Tuck 54 and Sfez 46.

85. Lipsius, *Politica* 516/517: "Ut *ad effectum consiliorum suorum veniant, multa simulent oportet inviti, & dissimulent cum dolore* [Cic. Lib. X. Epist. IX]."

86. Sfez 49–50.

87. Cf. Cavaillé, "Guerre civile et paix de l'âme: Juste Lipse, *De constantia in publicis malis*," *Kairos* 6 (1994): 11–40.

88. Tuck 68. Scipione Ammirato, *Discorsi sopra Cornelio Tacito nuovamente posti in luce* [1594], now in *Opere*, vol. 1.

89. Von Stackelberg, *Tacitus in der Romania* 120–128.

90. "Ragion di Stato altro non essere che contravvenzione di legge ordinaria, per rispetto di pubblico beneficio, ovvero per rispetto di maggiore e più universale ragione." See Rodolfo De Mattei, "Scipione Ammirato," *Dizionario biografico degli italiani*, vol. 3 (Rome: Istituto della Enciclopedia italiana, 1961) 1–4; De Mattei, *Il pensiero politico di Scipione Ammirato, con discorsi inediti* (Milan: A. Giuffrè, 1963) 121–151 (the above citation appears on 124); and Bireley 51.

91. Ammirato, *Opere* 1.59: "e perché alcuno non riceva in sé scandalo, che in questo modo si diano insegnamenti del dissimolare, basterà dir loro che di Dio istesso fu scritto che egli dissimola i peccati degli uomini perche si possan pentire."

92. Ammirato, *Opere* 1.59: "vi sono delle dissimulationi milense, per usar questa voce significantissima a questo proposito."

93. See, in another context, Accetto 59:"ed è parte di grand'intelligenza che si dia a veder di non vedere quando più si vede." [It is part of a great intellect to lead others to see that one does not see, when instead one sees the most.]

94. Ammirato, *Opere* 1.59: "per le quali cose che si son dette, può ciascuno vedere quanto destramente convenga camminare in questo fatto della dissimolazione."

95. De Mattei, *Scipione Ammirato* 421, has published the brief manuscript fragment entitled "Con quanto riguardo si debba procedere introno al celare o scuoprire gl'affari e animo suo altrui." In it Ammirato discusses the use of dissimulation in military affairs, noting that "in tanto è vera questa utilità di non scuoprir interamente tutti i tuoi affari, anzi del saperli molte volte accortamente occultare, che gran parte degli ammaestramenti bellici trae origine da questo ampissimo fonte del saper celare i consigli suoi. Quindi vengono i tanti esempi che ci porge Frontino del nascondere i suoi intendimenti, quelli che mette insieme ancor egli, insegnandoci come abbiamo a fare affinchè mostriamo d'abbondar di quelle cose delle quali siamo manchevoli, quelli con li quali ci ammaestra a saper dissimolar le nostre avversità, quando ci insegna a ingannar coloro i quali sono assediati, e altri." [As for the usefulness of not entirely revealing all of your affairs, and, rather, very often knowing how to hide them shrewdly, a large part of military teaching takes its origin from this very ample source, namely knowing how to keep one's counsels hidden. Drawing from this stock, Frontino assembles and offers to us many examples of how to hide one's understanding: these are to teach us what to do in order to show others that we have in abundance those things that we are in fact lacking, to know how to dissimulate any adversity, to deceive those who are under siege, and so on.]

96. Ammirato, *Della segretezza* 3: "coloro, che trattano coi principi, & anche per altro."

97. Ammirato, *Della segretezza* 4: "il tacere, il velare, il ricuoprire, il nascondere, & l'occultare sono voci simili."

98. Ammirato, *Della segretezza* 15: "l'ufficio di prudente huomo è saper dire, e tacere, quel che di dire, & tacer si conviene."

99. Ammirato, *Della segretezza* 29: "il decoro, o convenevolezza del segreto."

100. Ammirato, *Della segretezza* 24: "e io dico. Non si lasci chi che sia uscir di bocca i segreti, che ha udito dal Principe, perche s'armeranno di tanti coltelli, che gli trapasseranno il cuore."

101. Tuck 73–75.

102. Maravall, "La corriente doctrinal del tacitismo" 675: "en Saavedra y en los escritores del Barrocco, la problemática de la razón de Estado se aplica al comportamento individual." [In Saavedra and in Baroque writers the problematic of reason of state is applied to individual behavior.] See also J. A. Fernández-Santamaria, *Reason of State and Statecraft in Spanish Political Thought, 1595–1640* (Lanham, MD: University Press of America, 1983).

103. Diego de Saavedra Fajardo, *Idea de un príncipe político cristiano, representada en cien empresas:* the preface is dated July 10, 1640, and was written in Vienna, but the work soon saw a revised second edition that appeared in Milan in 1643 (bearing the date 1642). All citations here are from Sagrario López Poza's excellent edition of *Empresas políticas:* this is the title traditionally used to refer to Saavedra's work. The first English-language translation was *The Royal Politician, Represented in One Hundred Emblems,* trans. Sir J. A. Astry, 2 vols. (London: M. Gillyflower and L. Meredith, 1700). Given the unreliable nature of this translation, I have preferred to include my own here.

104. Saavedra 525, 528.

105. Saavedra 527–528: "Pero, porque alguna vez conviene cubrir la fuerza con la astucia, y la indignación con la benignidad, disimulando y acomodándose al tiempo y a las personas, se corona en esta Empresa la frente del léon, no con las artes de la raposa, viles y fraudulentas, indignas de la generosidad y corazón magnánimo del príncipe, sino con las sierpes, símbolo del Imperio y de la majestad prudente y vigilante, y jeroglífico en las Sagradas Letras de la prudencia; porque su astucia en defender la cabeza, en cerrar las orejas al encanto y en las demás cosas mira a su defensa propia, no al daño ajeno."

106. Saavedra 529: "Solamente puede ser lícita la disimulación y astucia cuando ni engañan ni dejan manchado el crédito del príncipe. . . . Esto sucede cuando la prudencia, advertida en su conservación, se vale de la astucia para ocultar la cosa según la circunstancias del tiempo, del lugar y de las personas, conservando una consonancia entre el corazón y la lengua, entre el entendimento y las palabras. Aquella disimulación se debe huir que con fines engañosos miente con las cosas mismas; la que mira a que el otro entienda lo que no es, no la que solamente pretende que no entienda lo que es; y así, bien se puede usar de palabras indiferentes y equívocas, y poner una cosa en lugar de otra con diversa significación, no para engañar, sino para cautelarse o prevenir el engaño, o para otros fines lícitos."

107. Saavedra 530: "Estas artes y trazas son muy necesarias cuando se trata con príncipes astutos y fraudulentos. Porque en tales casos, la difidencia y recato, la disimulación en el semblante, la generalidad y equivocación advertida en las palabras para que no dejen empeñado al príncipe ni den lugar a los desinios

o al engaño, usando de semejantes artes no para ofender ni para burlar la fe pública, qué otra cosa es sino doblar la guardas al ánimo?"

108. Saavedra 530: "Siendo el silencio el principal instrumento de reinar"; "mentir no debe un príncipe; pero se le permite callar o celar la verdad"; "sea, pues, el ánimo del príncipe cándido y sencillo, pero advertido en las artes y fraudes ajenas." See also Juan Antonio de Vera y Zuñiga, *El Enbaxador* (Seville: Francisco de Lyra, 1620), Discurso segundo, 86–111; and Pedro Ribadeneira, *Tratado del Príncipe Cristiano,* in *Obras escogidas,* ed. Vicente de la Fuente (Madrid: Ediciones Atlas, 1952) 520–526.

109. Saavedra 530: "es generoso engaño el de la verdad."

110. Saavedra 531: "El saber ser ignorante a su tiempo es la mayor prudencia. Ninguna cosa más conveniente ni más dificultosa que moderar la sabiduría." Among the many works on Tacitism in the *siglo de oro,* see Maravall, "La corriente doctrinal del tacitismo" 645–667.

111. Saavedra 531–532: "Pero es tal la malicia de la política presente, que no solamente penetra estas artes, sino calumnia la más pura sencillez, con grave daño de la verdad y del sosiego público; no habiendo cosa que se interprete derechamente. Y . . . nacen graves errores en los que buscan a las obras y palabras diferentes sentidos de lo que parecen y suenan. Y, encontrados así los juicios y las intenciones, se arman de artes unos contra otros, y viven todos en perpetuas desconfianzas y recelos."

112. Bakos 401.

113. Saavedra 532: "el más ingenioso en las sospechas, es el que más lejos da de la verdad, porque con la agudeza penetra adentro más de lo que ordinariamente se piensa; y creemos por cierto en los otros lo que en nosotros es engaño de la imaginación."

114. Saavedra 532: "las sombras de la razón de estado suelen ser mayores que el cuerpo, y tal vez se deja éste y se abrazan aquéllas."

115. Saavedra 532: "sin la cual, ni habrá amistad, ni parentesco firme, ni contrato seguro, y quedará sin fuerzas el derecho de las gentes, y el mundo en poder del engaño."

116. Saavedra 532: "no siempre se obra con segundas intenciones."

117. The subtext here would most probably seem to be Matthew 10:16 (*estote ergo prudentes sicut serpentes et simplices sicut columbae*), although it is also reminiscent of John 3:8, *spiritus ubi vult spirat: et vocem ejus audis, sed nescis unde veniat, aut quo vadat* [The wind blows wherever it pleases; you hear its sound, but you cannot tell where it comes from, or where it is going]. See John Dowling, *Diego de Saavedra Fajardo* (Boston: Twayne, 1977) 91.

118. Saavedra 534: "con tanto recato deben los príncipes celar sus consejos, que tal vez ni aun sus ministros los penetren."

119. Jürgen Habermas, *The Structural Transformation of the Public Sphere: An Inquiry into a Category of Bourgeois Society,* trans. Thomas Burger and Frederick Lawrence (Cambridge, MA: MIT Press, 1989) 27–56.

120. Saavedra 537–538: "El arte y astucia más conveniente en el príncipe y la disimulación más permitida y necesaria es aquella que de tal suerte sosiega y compone el rostro, las palabras y acciones contra quien disimuladamente trata

de engañalle, que no conozca haber sido entendido; porque se gana tiempo para penetrar mejor y castigar o burlar el engaño, haciendo esta disimulación menos solícito al agresor, el cual, una vez descubierto, entra en temor, y le parece que no puede asegurarse si no es llevando al cabo sus engaños."

121. Saavedra 538: "esta disimulación o fingida simplicidad es muy necesaria en los ministros que asisten a príncipes demasiadamente astutos y doblados, que hacen estudio de que no sean penetradas sus artes."

122. Saavedra 539: "Esta disimulación es más necesaria en los errores y vicios del príncipe, porque aborrece al que es testigo o sabidor dellos."

123. Saavedra 538: "quieren un absoluto imperio sobre los ánimos, no sujeto a la inteligencia ajena."

124. Cf. D'Orléans 49: "mais l'homme [est] un animal secret & cache, & qui comme les huistres se retire chez soy, & n'ouvre que quand il luy plait, & a qui il luy plaist, & de qui les pensees ne peuvent estre transparentes par la lumiere plus vive, & plus ardents rayons du Soleil."

125. Saavedra 541: "astucia y disimulación es en el león el dormir con los ojos abiertos, pero no intención de engañar, sino de disimular la enajenación de sus sentidos."

126. Saavedra 543: "pocos o ninguno le trata verdad, porque al que se teme no se dice. Y así, no debe dormir en confianza de su poder. Deshaga el arte con el arte y la fuerza con la fuerza. El pecho magnánimo prevenga disimulado y cauto, y resista valeroso y fuerte los peligros."

127. Two relevant studies of slightly earlier aspects of this sacrality are Giovanni Ricci, *Il principe e la morte: corpo, cuore, effigie nel Rinascimento* (Bologna: Il Mulino, 1998), and Jean Nagle, *La civilisation du coeur: Histoire du sentiment politique en France, du XIIe au XIXe siècle* (Paris: Fayard, 1998) 75–103. The classic work on this topic remains Ernst H. Kantorowicz, *The King's Two Bodies: A Study in Medieval Theology* (Princeton: Princeton University Press, 1957).

128. Saavedra 543–544: "es ordinariamente la disimulación hija del temor y de la ambición, y ni ésta ni aquél se han de descubrir en el príncipe. Lo que ha de cautelar la disimulación, cautele el silencio recatado y la gravedad advertida."

129. Tuck 94.

130. Information on Machon and the composition of the *Apologie* is taken from Donaldson 186–88.

131. I refer throughout to the 1643 manuscript (BN 19046–7). I have not used the incomplete, and later, manuscript that is also found in the Bibliothèque Nationale de France (fonds Séguier 642).

132. "Mon premier dessein touchant ceste Apologie estoit de mettre le texte de nostre politique d'un costé de ce Livre, et celuy de la bible, des Docteurs de l'Eglise, des Theologiens, des canonistes, des Ecrivains jesuites et autres de ceste approbation, de l'autre coté; et faire voir sans autre raisonnement et sans autre artifice, pas mesme sans aucune liaison, n'y aucune conclusion de ma façon, que ce grand homme n'a rien escript qui ne soit tiré mot pour mot, ou du moins qui ne correspond a tout ce que ces doctes personnages en avoient dit devant luy, ou bien approuvé du depuis" (352). Donaldson (188–189) has described this as "Biblical Machiavellianism," remarking that "the heart of the defense" is

"that Machiavelli's doctrines are consistent with the classical political tradition, with the political writings of the church fathers, and even with the Bible itself," while Machiavelli himself "was a misunderstood Christian moralist, who in his appreciation for the difficult ethical questions of political life 'spoke like a saint.'"

133. Donaldson 221.

134. Machon 634–638 (book 2, maxim 6): "nostre Autheur ne s'est point amusé à faire de longs discours pour justifier ceste maxime, n'y pour monstrer sa necessité en la conseillant; il l'a crüe si importante et si inseparable non pas seulement des affaires d'estat, mais mesmes des privées et des particuliers, qu'il l'a toujours mise en avant comme une regle generale qui ne peut estre contestée, ny condemnée que pour ceux qui ont aussi peu d'intrigues, que de jugement; et aussi peu d'affaires et de commerce parmy les hommes, qu'ils ont peu d'esprit et de raison devans leurs livres, et devans leurs escripts."

135. Machon 661–662: "la nature a fait aussi dedans l'âme un cabinet secret ou les pensées les plus importantes sont cachées et retenües, jusqu'à tant que la prudence trouve a propos de les produire au jour, pour en executer les conseils. . . . La dissimulation luy sert de rideaux, et la prudence de les cacher sont ses plus beaux habits."

136. Machon 639: "celuy qui scait dissimuler et se donner patience, vault mieux et peult beaucoup d'avantage, que celuy qui n'a que la force, et le courage; estant certain que celuy qui est maistre de ses passions, et qui peult les moderer et les tenir en bride, fera plus d'effect, et ses exploits seront plus grands et plus glorieux, que ceux qui pourroient conquerir des Villes par la seule force de leurs armes."

137. Machon 641–642: "veritablement les hommes s'entre-tueroient les uns les autres, ils seroient tous les jours aux prises, il n'y auroit que rage, fureur, vengeance, meurtres et cruautés parmy eux, ils se differoient d'eux mesmes, et par ainsi pour un vice imaginaire et qui n'est point, ils ruineroient tout ce qu'ils ont de vertu, de iustice, de religion, de sacré, et d'adorable."

138. Machon 641: "et que touste ma vie, comme celle des autres hommes, n'est qu'en contraintes, et qu'en ceremonies . . . n'est-ce pas dissimuler, n'est-ce pas practiquer en effet, ce qu'on veult que je condemne de bouche, et en parolles. Que seroit-ce du monde, sans la dissimulation?"

139. Machon 649: "ne fais pas comme celuy qui n'en a tiré autre avantage sinon la consideration du naturel de ce prince, nottant a la marge, prince dissimulé; j'aimerois mieux y notter ainsi, Dissimulation necessaire au prince; a cause que le meme Tacite dit en un autre endroit, que la dissimulation est la derniere chose qui abandonne les princes."

140. Machon 659–660: "Le prince qui ne scait couvrir ses ieux donne de grands avantages a ceux qui veulent entreprendre, non seulement contre luy, mais aussi contre son estat, attendu la liaison estroiste et inseparable qui s'y rencontre."

141. Machon 662: "le bien et le salut de l'Estat est le centre et le but ou tous leurs conseils, et toutes leurs actions doivent tendre, et ou ils ne peuvent souvent arriver qu'en biaisant, et en dissimulant leurs desseins et leurs entreprises."

142. Machon 659: "confessons donc que l'accortise et la dissimulation sont si necessaires, non pas seulement aux princes, et a leurs ministres, mais encore a toutes sortes d'hommes, tant en general qu'en particulier, que sans elle il est du tout impossible de se pouvoir conduire seurement parmy les hommes, et de parer leurs malices." Cf. Charles-Daubert's introduction, in Naudé xv: "pour Naudé, la Monastique et l'Œconomique, art de savoir bien se gouverner soi-même et sa famille, sont les propédeutiques à la politique."

143. Machon 651: "n'y aiant rien de plus certain que la dissimulation est l'appuy des Rois, des Estats, des biens, des familles, et l'assaisonnement de toutes les actions des hommes, et sa practique est si necessaire en toutes choses, que j'ose bien mettre en avant, que pour ne la point oublier dedans mes petites intrigues, et mes interêts particuliers, j'ay fait escrire en tres grosse lettre dessus la tapisserie qui est en la ruelle de mon lict, que; 'La dissimulation est l'appuy des affaires'; affin qu'en me couchant et en me levant ie ne l'oublie point dedans mes entreprises, comme le sel de la prudence, la base de tous nos desseins, et la consolation des choses qu'on ne nous accorde point." See Orest Ranum, "Les refuges de l'intimité," *Histoire de la vie privée, 3: De la Renaissance aux Lumières,* eds. Philippe Ariès and Georges Duby (Paris: Seuil, 1986) 223: "Chez les Français du XVIe et du XVIIe siècles, la ruelle, c'est-à-dire l'espace entre le mur et le lit, était connue pour être particulièrement intime."

144. Machon 642: "Laissons ceste dissimulation civile et morale, pour venir a la politique, et affin que personne ne tienne estrange si je la conseille st si je la soustiens, j'adjoute aux deux passages susdits, celuy-cy de la sapience qui tesmoigne comme Dieu mesme qui est le tout puissant, et qui dans un moment peult ruiner tout le monde, et reduire au neant ceux qui l'offencent, dissimule neanmoins les pechés des hommes pour les porter au repentir et a la penitence."

145. Cavaillé, *Dis/simulations* 331–332, provides a quite different interpretation of this same passage, arguing that Machon, in "cette anecdote plutôt saugrenue," offers the reader "une ostentation maladroite de la dissimulation" while claiming disingenuously to be incapable of mastering it and practicing it.

146. This phrase of Maravall's is cited by Giulia Calvi, ed., in her introduction to *Barocco al femminile* (Bari: Laterza, 1992) xxiii. See also Cavaillé, *Dis/simulations* 328–329, on the "structure anthropologique" of dissimulation in the *Apologie.*

147. Borrelli, *Ragion di stato e leviatano* 142–148, examines the work of the Bolognese ecclesiastic Evangelista Sartonio, who in his *Il Cittadino di Repubblica regolare sotto il titolo di Pensieri politici ovvero avvedimenti civili* (1625) anticipated much of Machon's argument about the universal necessity and efficacy of dissimulation: "il fondamento morale della virtù cristiana viene richiamato, ma immediatamente oltrepassato perché di fatto considerato inefficace nella produzione di disciplina e di obbedienza; pienamente attivo invece è il codice tecnico della dissimulazione: essa penetra, condiziona e strumentalizza i silenzi, le parole, la gestualità, l'educazione dei fanciulli, il governo dei comportamenti propri e degli altri, ed ancora le forme stesse attraverso le quali gli uomini costruiscono l'immagine e le istituzioni del potere" (147). [The moral foundation of Christian virtue is recalled, but immediately left behind because it is in

fact considered ineffective in the production of discipline and obedience. The technical code of dissimulation is instead fully active: it penetrates, conditions and instrumentalizes silences, words, gestures, education of the young, and government of one's own behavior as well as that of others, not to mention the very forms through which men construct the image and the institutions of power.]

148. Gabriele Zinano, in his *Della ragione de gli Stati* (Venice: Guerigli, 1626), as cited in Arcari, *La ragion di stato in un manoscritto inedito di Alessandro Anguissola* 105, remarked that the statesman had to be "un altro Acheloo. Siccome costui, ora in toro, ora in fiume, ora in altra figura si cangia, e sempre in quella che al suo giudizio poteva guadagnare più vantaggio, così l'huomo di stato, nel maneggiare gli affari suoi, sempre rappresenta se stesso con nuova faccia." [(He must be) another Achelous, for he must transform himself at different moments into a bull, into a river and into other figures; he must decide which one would give him more of an advantage. Thus the statesman must, in the management of his affairs, perpetually represent himself with a new face.] Cf. Jon R. Snyder, "Sincerity in Seventeenth-Century Italy," *Rinascimento: rivista dell'Istituto Italiano di studi sul Rinascimento,* 2nd series, 48 (2003): 265–286, on some contemporary Italian paintings of masks.

149. Aricò 566: "la dissimulazione è un procedimento culturale che rappresenta forse l'esperienza più dolorosa della nuova psicologia codificata dall'uomo del Seicento."

150. See, above all, the bibliography provided in Borrelli, *Ragion di stato e leviatano* 282–312. Borrelli's bibliography stops somewhat abruptly in 1651, but political works dealing with dissimulation continued to appear, such as Salvatore Cadana, *Il Principe Avvisato,* vol. 2 (Turin: Gio. Giacomo Rustis, 1653) 17–32, and von Knichen, 506C–509D.

151. *Breviarium politicorum secundum Rubricas Mazarinicas* (Cologne: Giovanni Selliba, 1684) i: "quem ad me Princeps Italus tractatum hunc politicum in lucem edendum miserat." Modern translations of the work include *Bréviaire des politiciens,* trans. François Rosso (Paris: Arléa, 1996), and *Breviario dei politici/Bréviaire des politiciens,* Italian trans. Annapaola Mettel (Locarno: Armando Dadò Editore, 2001).

152. Giovanni Macchia, "Le vie del potere," in *Breviario dei politici,* ed. Giovanni Macchia (Milan: Rizzoli, 2000) vii–viii. This volume contains the text of the 1698 second printing of the original Italian-language edition first published by Giovanni Selliba in Cologne in 1695.

153. For more on Mazarin's life and times, see Geoffrey Treasure, *Mazarin: The Crisis of Absolutism in France* (New York: Routledge, 1995).

154. Macchia, *Breviario dei politici* xiii.

155. "Lo stampatore a chi legge," *Breviario dei politici* i (1698): "e fra le mani i primi Potentati dell'Europa, non che i Titolati lor Soggetti, Principi di minor grado, e gentil'uomini privati, per ciascuno a proporzione valersene al perfetto governo de' suoi sudditi, e sopra tutti del suo proprio individuo." The printer's preface to the 1684 first Latin edition is substantially different.

156. "Lo stampatore a chi legge," *Breviario dei politici* 4 (1698): "con avere anche la mira proporzionata agli uomini di stato, a' quali con disegno particolare s'indrizza questa mia fatica."

157. *Breviarium politicorum* 17: "actiones humanae civiles."

158. *Breviarium politicorum* 1: "duo olim in sincera Philosophia; duo nunc: *sustine* & *abstine,* olim; nunc *simula* & *dissimula.* Sive *nosce te ipsum, nosce alios,* quae (nisi fallor) etiam priora sustenat." The motto "sustine et abstine" is the Latin translation of the words of the Stoic philosopher Epictetus.

159. Cavaillé, *Dis/simulations* 209.

160. *Breviarium politicorum* 2: "an ira metu, temeritate, aut qua passione labores?"

161. *Breviarium politicorum* 4: "nil ostende in vultu praeter humanitatem, aut etiam affectum."

162. *Breviarium politicorum* 71: "vitia aliena aut dissimula, aut excusa, affectus tuos claude, aut contrarios assume."

163. *Breviarium politicorum* 8: "phantastici sunt, qui sunt scrupolosi, tristes, multae orationis, vocales, qui ungues habent nimium breves, qui faciunt mortificationes externas sine internis."

164. *Breviarium politicorum* 4: "constanti incessu modestiam serva, alioquin acribus oculis observa omnia, & prudenti supercilio curiositatem finias. Tales habentur pro prudentibus, astutis, & accuratis."

165. *Breviarium politicorum* 3: "si offenderis ad bilis effusionem, nil dic nec ullo signo prode iram."

166. *Breviarium politicorum* 100: "si laedaris, optimum dissimulare, quia lis litem generat, & pax amittitur."

167. *Breviarium politicorum* 103: "relinque inimico tempus, ut ipse indignitatem facti advertat, non tamen illi proponas, ne quasi ex tua parte occasio irae soleat esse."

168. *Breviarium politicorum* 124: "affectus simulabis, falsi cultus si diutius sint in publico, tandem adversantur; unde praestat abstinere luce, & alios qui vere tales affectus habent, pellicere ad idem. Optimum erit te interea seriis distrahi, ut ipiusmet affectus, quem legere vis, obliviscaris, sic nemo ut cumque te speculetur, iram, & laetitiam ex te colliget."

169. *Breviarium politicorum* 114: "non semper obtegendum, si quid adversi accidat, ne ipsa dissimulatione credatur verius accidisse."

170. *Breviarium politicorum* 73: "valvas fenestrarum ad intra habe, & qua parte fenestras contingunt nigra sunto, ut non dignoscatur clausa fenestra sit nec ne."

171. *Breviarium politicorum* 35–36: "si quid scribas in loco, quem multi adeunt, erige cartam scriptam, veluti eam describeres, haec omnibus pateat, & ea quae vere scribis jaceant, & ita tegantur, ut sola linea, quam descripsisti pateat, & a quovis accedente legi possit. Quae vero scripsisti libro, vel charta alia obtege, aut charta erecta propius mota.

"Si dum legis aliquis accedat, statim plurima folia transpone, ne tua intentio deprehendatur, imo convenit plures libros esse simul compactos, ut unus praealtero inspiciendus objiciatur."

172. *Breviarium politicorum* 37: "scribere secreta manu tua ne graveris; nisi per zifras scribas; idque tales, quae ab omnibus legi, aut intelligi possunt, quales Trithemius in Polygraphia sua dedit, haec enim magis celant, si aliena manu scribantur. Zifrae quae legi non possunt suspicionem excitant, & interceptionem, nisi apte scribas."

173. *Breviarium politicorum* 4: "omnes stude tibi habere perspectos; tua secreta nulli unquam prode: alia expiscare."

174. *Breviarium politicorum* 10: "astuti plerumque sunt, qui habent affectatam lenitarem, in naso monticulum, & ac res oculos."

175. *Breviarium politicorum* 13: "mendaces plerumque natura sunt, qui dum rident habent fossulas in genis."

176. *Breviarium politicorum* 16: "alterius mentem ut agnoscas, suborna alium, cuius amator est, & per eum secretissima rescies."

177. *Breviarium politicorum* 12: "amicum falsum advertes, nunciet illi tertius a te instructus, te ad extrema esse redactum, iura quibus nitebaris falsa esse deprehensa, si velut, non curaret, audierit, nunquam erit amicus."

178. *Breviarium politicorum* 8: "poteris etiam aliquando mediem agere, talia cibo immiscendo, quae illos exhillarent, & reddant loquaces &c."

179. *Breviarium politicorum* 11: "literas subditorum suorum juvabit interdum intercipere, relegere, & ad eas respondere."

180. "Lo stampatore a chi legge," *Breviario dei politici* 4 (1698): "adoperala dunque, non già per l'altrui inganno, ma per prevenire gl'inganni altrui, e valertene, come di antidoto al veleno della frode, che tanto oggi giorno serpeggia."

181. Jonathan I. Israel, *Radical Enlightenment: Philosophy and the Making of Modernity 1650–1750* (New York: Oxford University Press, 2001) 4, defines the "early" phase of the radical enlightenment as beginning around 1650.

182. See, in this regard, the still valuable essay by Oreste Ranum, "Courtesy, Absolutism, and the Rise of the French State, 1630–1660," *The Journal of Modern History* 52 (1980): 426–451.

183. Cavaillé, *Dis/simulations,* detects this same dilemma in the respective works of Naudé (233) and Machon (300–301).

184. For an overview of the rise and fall of reason-of-state theory in Italy, see Gianfranco Borelli, "La Ragion di Stato: teoria e prassi," *Italia 1650,* eds. Giuseppe Galasso and Aurelio Musi (Naples: CUEN, 2002) 121–142.

185. Giovanni Battista Ricciardi, *Chi non sa fingere non sa vivere, ovvero le cautele politiche* (Perugia: per gli eredi di Sebastiano Zecchini, 1672).

186. Although the play does not provide a date for the action, the king in question would seem to be Alfonso II (1448–1495), who ruled only briefly before abdicating the throne to King Charles VIII of France in 1494. The foreign "Re Carlo" who seeks the throne of Naples is mentioned a number of times.

187. Ricciardi 8:

FLOR. Oh se non è per altro, mi par che si vada in maschera di tutti i tempi.

TRES. Non mi pare fuor del Carnevale di veder maschere nessune, e pure non ho gl'occhi sotto le scarpe. . . .

FLOR. Non è, che tu non vegga, ma viene che non ci fai riflessione.

TRES. Eh và sù le forche.

FLOR. Vogliam giocare, che tu poi dici come me? Oh stà a vedere: Dimmi un poco l'andare in maschera non consiste nel cercare di parere quello che uno non è, per non essere conosciuto dalla gente?

188. Ricciardi 25: "Non mostrare alcun segno, leggendo, di turbartene, né.ti cada nell'animo di farmi ritener dalle guardie, che ti circondano, perché quelli che t'insidiano ti sono vicini, e più importa alla tua sicurezza che non sia noto à costoro questo viglietto [*sic*], che il conoscermi."

189. Ricciardi 25–26: "Feci forza a me stesso, e spinsi la simulatione a far argine contro il torrente del sangue, che nella torbida piena degl'affetti tumultuanti rapidamente correva ad inondarmi sul volto. Finsi di leggere ogn'altra cosa, e mascherando la faccia con un riso sardonico, passai a discorsi indifferenti con i Cavalieri più vicini."

190. Ricciardi 27: "È necessario molte volte tollerar quel male, che più s'inasprerebbe con applicarvi violentemente il remedio [*sic*]"; "è necessario salvare le apparenze esterne, acciò la giustizia non sembri tirannide."

191. Ricciardi 28: "Dopo molto pensare esaminando diversamente i partiti, ho deliberato di fingere di haverti dalla mia gratia, e mostrando d'haverne qualche gran causa, la quale tacerò perche non posso per alcun verso scoprirsi esser finta, ti leverò tutti i tuoi beni."

192. In the final act King Alfonso remarks that he and Enrico are now once more "una cosa istessa" (151): they are so intimate as to be one and the same.

193. Ricciardi 155: "et apprendino i Grandi, che nell'incertezze importanti allo stato fingendo si trova il vero."

194. Ricciardi 86: "In somma la fintione è madre del vero, chi non sa fingere non sa regnare."

195. See chap. II n23, for the only other possible reference in print to *Della dissimulazione onesta* that I have been able to locate—Christian Georg Bessel's *Schmiede des politischen Glücks* (The forge of political fortune, 1666). This work was frequently reprinted in the late seventeenth century, as well as translated into Latin; several copies are now in the holdings of the British Library. Not long after Ricciardi's play appeared in Italy, moreover, the first edition of Elizabeth Cary's *The History of the Life, Reign, and Death of Edward II, King of England, and Lord of Ireland* was published (London: Printed by J.C. for Charles Harper, Samuel Crouch and Thomas Fox, 1680). The title page of this edition displays the epigraph "Qui nescit Dissimulare, nequit vivere, perire melius" [whoever does not know how to dissimulate is unable to live, and is better off dead]. Cary's treatise on politics and statecraft offers further evidence (although likely the epigraph was added by the London printer, since Cary herself was long dead by 1680) of the spread of the rule of dissimulation to the sphere of everyday life in the latter part of the seventeenth century.

Chapter 5

Rossi, *Convito* (1639) 181.

1. R. Po-Chia Hsia, *The World of Catholic Renewal, 1540–1770* (New York: Cambridge University Press, 1998) 198–199. See also Cavaillé, *Dis/simulations* 380–381.

2. Lamarche-Vadel 133–134.

3. See Martin, "Inventing Sincerity" 1330–1338.

4. Rossi, *Convito* (1639) 438: "la sincerità e la franchezza è molto rara [*sic*] nell'intentione degli huomini."

5. Rossi, *Convito* (1657) 383: "la sincerità è peregrina, raminga, e bandita dal Mondo."

6. For an extremely valuable overview of ritual and ceremonial in early modern Europe, see Edward Muir, *Ritual in Early Modern Europe,* rev. ed. (New York: Cambridge University Press, 2005).

7. Accetto 53–54.

8. Homer, *The Odyssey,* trans. Robert Fitzgerald (New York: Anchor Books, 1963) 360: "Now all these lies he made appear so truthful / she wept as she sat listening. The skin / of her pale face grew moist the way pure snow / softens and glistens on the mountains, thawed / by Southwind after powdering from the West, / and, as the snow melts, mountain streams run full: / so her white cheeks were wetted by these tears / shed for her lord—and he close by her side. / Imagine how his heart ached for his lady, / his wife in tears; and yet he never blinked; / his eyes might have been made of horn or iron / for all that she could see. He had this trick— / wept, if he willed to, inwardly."

9. Adelin-Charles Fiorato, "Simulation/Dissimulation," *Dictionnaire raisonné de la politesse et du savoir-vivre,* ed. Alain Montandon (Paris: Seuil, 1995) 834–839, traces the development of this discourse in the eighteenth century in France, but has little to say about the *grand siècle* itself.

10. Madeleine de Scudéry, *Les Conversations sur Divers Sujets,* 2nd ed. (Amsterdam: Daniel du Fresne, 1686) 164: "insensiblement à parler de la dissimulation, dont on accuse plus les Gens de la Cour, que le reste du Monde."

11. De Scudéry 164–165: "pouvez-vous loüer une chose directement opposée à la sincerité; qui fait la douceur de la vie des honnestes Gens; & sans laquelle le commerce du monde ne seroit qu'une tromperie continuelle[?]"

12. De Scudéry 167: "la sincerité emporte de necessité avec elle toute la beauté de la vérité, tous les charmes de la franchise, toute la douceur de la confiance. Elle produit, pour l'ordinaire, une certaine ouverture de coeur, qui paroist dans les yeux. . . . Elle est ennemie de tout artifice, de toute dissimulation."

13. Here as elsewhere, I am speaking about the discourse *on* sincerity and the discourse *on* dissimulation; there are of course many examples of seventeenth-century French imaginative fiction that treat these themes, such as Mme de La Fayette's *La Princesse de Clèves* (1678).

14. Oddly enough, her life became the inspiration for one of E. T. A. Hoffmann's novellas, "Mademoiselle de Scudéry: A Tale of the Times of Louis

XIV," *Tales of Hoffmann,* ed. Christopher Lazare (New York: A. A. Wyn, 1946) 37–102.

15. Fiorato (835) notes that Jean-Baptiste de La Salle, in his *Les Règles de la bienséance et de la civilité chrétienne* (1736), argued for a return to a rigorous Augustinianism that would exclude dissimulation: "la bienséance veut qu'un chrétien ne profère aucune parole qui soit contraire à la verité ou à la sincerité." [Propriety requires a Christian to utter no word that would be contrary to the truth or to sincerity.]

16. Lynn Hunt, *The Family Romance of the French Revolution* (Berkeley and Los Angeles: University of California Press, 1992) 96–97, notes of the French Revolution: "dissimulation was consequently an especially important theme. . . . The ability to conceal one's true emotions, to act one way in public and another in private, was repeatedly denounced as the chief characteristic of court life and aristocratic manners in general. These relied above all on appearances, that is, on the disciplined and self-conscious use of the body as a mask. The republicans, consequently, valued transparency—the unmediated expression of the heart—above all other personal qualities. Transparency was the perfect fit between public and private; transparency was a body that told no lies and kept no secrets. It was the definition of virtue, and as such was imagined to be critical to the future of the republic"; as cited in Martin, "Inventing Sincerity" 134n.

17. Adriana Boidi Sassone and Laura Palmucci Quaglino, *Cherasco. Palazzi e committenze tra Corte e provincia* (Turin: Centro Studi Piemontesi, 1994) 36.

18. Giovanni Romano, ed., *Realismo caravaggesco e prodigio barocco: da Molineri a Taricco nella grande provincia* (Savigliano: L'Artistica, 1998) 278–279.

19. The same could be said for Ittig's nearly contemporary 1709 Leipzig dissertation, *De simulatione et dissimulatione.*

20. Maria Gabriella Contratto, *Sebastiano Taricco* (Cuneo: Società Studi Storici Archeologici ed Artistici della Provincia di Cuneo, 1974) 110, cites a manuscript by G. Adriani—now found in the Biblioteca Civica "G. B. Adriani" di Cherasco—noting the position of the "Gabinetto al piano nobile del palazzo Salmatoris, appena salita la scala maggiore."

21. See Contratto (55) on the ruined state of the frescos in the 1970s, and Sassone and Quaglino (41) on the 1983 acquisition of Palazzo Salmatoris by the municipal government in order to restore the structure and its artworks.

22. Contratto (55) argues that "le varie raffigurazioni ricche di simboli e di metafore, e le varie iscrizioni sembrano avvalorare l'ipotesi di una collaborazione di qualche erudito locale." [The various images, rich in symbols and metaphors, and the various epigraphs would seem to support the hypothesis that some learned local collaborated (with the artist).]

Four out of the eight identifiable ancients depicted on the lower walls are mentioned in Celio Calcagnini's *Descriptio silentii* (1544), and many of the themes, figures, and epigrams that appear in the *Saletta del silenzio* are also treated by Pio Rossi in his *Convito,* whose final revised edition dates to 1672–1677.

23. The fourth of the emblems in this group on the ceiling (now lost) represented a silkworm, accompanied by the motto *se non mi celo, i pregi miei non scopro* (if I do not hide myself, I do not reveal my virtues). See C. G. S. Salmatoris Rossillon, *Monumento dedicato alla pace del 1631 nella città di Cherasco* (Turin: Tipografia Chirio e Mina, 1820) 38, and Contratto 112.

24. Both Salmatoris Rossillon (38) and Contratto (112) refer to this bird as a *colomba,* or dove, but this is clearly wrong. An eagle atop a mountain can be seen in the background, just as described in Plutarch. See also Paris Nogari's elegant *Il silenzio* (1582), in the Sala Vecchia degli Svizzeri in the Palazzo Vaticano in Rome, which displays a crane clutching a stone in its beak.

25. *Eximia est* [virtus] *praestare* [silentia] *rebus*: Ovid, *De arte amandi,* 2.603.

26. Rossi, *Convito* (1639) 437.

27. See Saavedra 540n. The motto accompanying Taricco's emblem of the lion is *contego ne detegant.*

28. Xenocrates' epigram is given by Valerius Maximus (7.2, ext.6): *dixisse me aliquando paenituit, tacuisse numquam.* Both Plutarch, *De tuenda sanitate praecepta* 7 (125D), and Stobaeus, *Florilegium* 33.12, attribute a very similar remark to Simonides, explaining that he had never repented of having kept silent but often had repented of having spoken. However, the exact Latin phrase that appears here is instead found in the *Catonis Disticha* (I.xii.2) by Dionysius Cato: *nulli tacuisse nocet, nocet esse locutum.*

29. Seneca, *Epistol.* 105.6: *Minimum cum aliis loqui, plurimum secum;* Epaminondas, *Ex audiendo doctrina ex loquacitate paenitentia* (from *Ita Maxim.,* although there may be other sources).

30. Proverbs 26:28, *lingua fallax non amat veritatem et os lubricum operatur ruinas;* Judith 8:33, *Vos autem nolo ut scrutemini actum meum.* These occur, for instance, in the 1598 edition of the Clementine Vulgate.

31. Isocrates, *Diligentius serva verborum quam pecuniarum deposita;* Pythagoras, *Aut sile aut affer meliora silentio.* I have been unable to identify the source of the former; the Pythagorean dictum was preserved in Stobaeus (3.34.7), although this Latin translation seems to be adapted from the translation by Canterus. See Ernst Leuschner, "The Pythagorean Inscription on Salvator Rosa's London *Self-Portrait,*" *Journal of the Warburg and Courtauld Institutes* 57 (1994): 278–283. This motto appears in a similar form in Calcagnini's *Descriptio silentii* 42–43.

32. Guazzo 1:84: "non meno d'ammirazione porta seco il saper tacere che 'l ben parlare, perché sì come questo scuopre l'eloquenza e la dottrina, così quello dà segno di gravità e prudenza."

33. Calcagnini, *Descriptio silentii,* in Nigro, *Elogio della menzogna* 36.

34. Robbins 128–130.

35. Although Sassone and Quaglino are unsure about the exact date of the work, Giovanni Taricchi, *Delle opere di fresco del pittore Sebastiano Tarico* [*sic*] (Urbino: Tipografia Rocchetti, 1877) 12, states that the room "già prima era stato dipinto dal Tarico" [*sic*], that is, prior to the June 1706 arrival of the Shroud in Cherasco. Bruno Taricco, *Cherasco: Urba Firmissima Pacis* (Cherasco:

Pro Cherasco, 1993) 173, contends instead that the cycle was inspired by the fact that the Shroud had been deposited there, and was therefore painted sometime after June 1706, but I find this unconvincing.

36. Cherasco could boast in 1706 of many fine churches, including, among numerous others, the recently completed Chiesa della Madonna del Popolo (1702), one of whose architects was Sebastiano Taricco.

37. The split pomegranate was used by the Jesuits, for instance, as a hieroglyph for the crown of thorns. Traditionally it served to signify the blood of Christ or Christian charity (open to all people), the unity of the Church or State or academy (many seeds in one perfect fruit), fertility, marriage, and much more. On the Jesuit use of the split pomegranate, see Mario Praz, *Studies in Seventeenth-Century Imagery*, 2nd rev. ed. (Rome: Edizioni di Storia e Letteratura, 1964) 141. For the general symbolism of the pomegranate, see Mirella Levi D'Ancona, *The Garden of the Renaissance: Botanical Symbolism in Italian Painting* (Florence: Olschki, 1977) 312–318.

38. The term is found in C. A. Heumann, *Der Politische Philosophus* (1724): see Geitner 127 *et passim*, where this sort of practical knowledge is also called "Kardiognostik." For more on the symbolism of the pomegranate and its relationship to the representation of sincerity, see Snyder, "Sincerity" 265–286.

39. This was the same year in which the publishing privilege of the *Encyclopédie* was revoked by the French royal authorities, forcing the editors to look elsewhere to continue its publication.

40. Author of numerous works and a critic of Rousseau, Formey served as secretary of the Academy of Sciences in Berlin from 1748 onward.

41. Johann Heinrich Samuel Formey, "La Dissimulation," *Encyclopédie, ou Dictionnaire raisonné des sciences, des arts et des métiers*, eds. Denis Diderot and Jean le Rond d'Alembert, 2nd ed., vol. 4 (Lucca: Vincenzo Giuntini, 1759) 870: "le *dissimulé* veille sur les autres pour ne les pas mettre à portée de le connoître."

42. Formey 4:870, "dans le caractère d'un homme propre à faire le bonheur de la société, le premier trait que l'on exige, est la franchise et la sincerité."

43. Formey 4:870, "ils n'avoient, dit-on, qu'un coeur & qu'une ame, *erat cor unum & anima una.*"

44. Formey 4:870, "On lui préfère un caractère opposé, par rapport à ce qu'on appelle *les grands affaires*, ou *les négociations importantes;* mais tout ce qu'on en peut conclure, c'est que ces occasions particulières ne sont pas ce qui contribue au bonheur de la société en général. Tout négotiation légitime ne devroit rouler que sur un point, qui est de faire voir à celui avec qui on négocie, que nous cherchons à réunir son avantage avec le notre."

45. Formey 4:870: "Il n'est pas douteux que le secret est souvent nécessaire contre la disposition de ceux qui voudroient interrompre nos entreprises légitimes. Mais la nécessité de la précaution deviendroit incomparablement plus rare, si l'on ne formoit d'entreprises que celles qu'on peut avoüer sans être exposé à aucun reproche. La candeur avec laquelle on agiroit alors, mettroit beaucoup de gens dans nos intérêts."

46. Formey 4:870: "Ce qu j'ai voulu dire dans cet article sur le secret de la *dissimulation,* par rapport à la douceur de la société, se réduit donc à trois ou quatre choses. 1°. Ne point estimer le caractère de ceux qui, sans choix & sans distinction, sont réservés & secrets: 2°. ne faire des secrets que sur des choses qui le méritent bien: 3°. avoir une telle conduite, qu'elle n'ait besoin du secret que le moins qu'il soit possible."

47. Gracián, *Art of Worldly Wisdom* 61; *Oráculo manual* 181 (aphorism 110): "máxima es de cuerdos dejar las cosas antes que los dejen."

Bibliography

Works from before 1800

Accetto, Torquato. *Della dissimulazione onesta* (1641). Ed. Salvatore S. Nigro. Turin: Einaudi, 1997.

Ammirato, Scipione. *Della segretezza*. Venice: Filippo Giunti, 1599.

———. *Discorsi sopra Cornelio Tacito nuovamente posti in luce* (1594). *Opere*. Vol. 1. Galatina: Congedo Editore, 2002.

Anguissola, Alessandro. "Della dissimulatione" (1612). MS M.III.6. Biblioteca Nazionale di Torino.

Arcana Aulica: or Walsingham's Manual of Prudential Maxims, for the States-man and the Courtier. London: James Young, 1652.

Aristotle. *The Nicomachean Ethics*. Ed. and trans. Hippocrates G. Apostle. Dordrecht and Boston: D. Reidel, 1975.

Augustine, Saint. *"Confessions" and "Enchiridion."* Trans. and ed. Albert C. Outler. The Library of Christian Classics 7. Philadelphia: The Westminster Press, n.d.

———. *Contra Mendacium*. Trans. Harold B. Jaffee. *Treatises on Various Subjects*. Ed. Roy J. Deferrari. The Fathers of the Church 16. Washington DC: Catholic University of America Press, 1952. 121–179.

———. *De Mendacio*. Trans. M. S. Muldowney. *Treatises on Various Subjects*. Ed. Roy J. Deferrari. The Fathers of the Church 16. Washington DC: Catholic University of America Press, 1952. 51–110.

"Avvertimenti utili per quelli che vogliono entrare in corte." MS 2096, fols. 324–330 and MS 2371, fols. 1–13. Biblioteca Casanatense, Rome.

Bacon, Francis. *The Essayes or Counsels, Civill and Morall*. Ed. Michael Kiernan. The Oxford Francis Bacon 15. Oxford: Clarendon Press, 2000.

Berbeeck, Martin. *Compendium manualis controversiarum huius temporis de fide ac religione*. Luxembourg: Hubert Reulant, 1625.

Bessel, Christian Georg. *Schmiede des politischen Glücks*. Hamburg: Johann Naumann, 1666.

Bonifacio, Giovanni. *L'arte de' cenni*. Vicenza: Francesco Grossi, 1616.

Botero, Giovanni. *Della Ragion di Stato: Libri Dieci, con Tre Libri delle Cause della Grandezza e Magnificenza delle Città*. Rev. ed. Venice: Gioliti, 1598. Anastatic reprint, Bologna: Arnaldo Forni, 1990.

———. *The Reason of State*. Trans. P. J. and D. P. Waley. [and] *The Greatness of Cities*. Trans. Robert Peterson. London: Routledge Kegan Paul, 1956.

Bréviaire des politiciens. Trans. François Rosso. Paris: Arléa, 1996.

Breviario dei politici. Ed. Giovanni Macchia. Reprint of 1698 2nd ed. (trans. Ilario Amante). Milan: Rizzoli, 2000.

Breviario dei politici/Bréviaire des politiciens. Italian trans. Annapaola Mettel. Locarno: Armando Dadò Editore, 2001.

Breviarium politicorum secundum Rubricas Mazarinicas. Cologne: Giovanni Selliba, 1684.

The Cabinet-Council: Containing the Cheif [sic] Arts of Empire, and Mysteries of State; Discabineted in Political and Polemical Aphorisms, grounded on Authority and Experience; And illustrated with the choicest Examples and Historical Observations. London: Tho. Newcomb for Tho. Johnson, 1658.

Cadana, Salvatore. *Il Principe Avvisato*. 2 vols. Turin: Gio. Giacomo Rustis, 1652–1653.

Calcagnini, Celio. *Opera aliquot*. Basel: G. Froben, 1544.

Canonieri, Pietro Andrea. *Il Perfetto Cortegiano et dell'Ufizio del Prencipe verso 'L Cortegiano*. Rome: Zannetti, 1609.

Capaccio, Giulio Cesare. *Il Principe, tratto da gli Emblemi dell'Alciato, con duecento, e più Avvertimenti Politici e Morali*. Venice: Barezzo Barezzi, 1620.

Cardano, Girolamo. *Arcana politica, sive de prudentia civili liber singularis*. Leiden: Elzevir, 1635.

———. *Opera omnia*. 10 vols. Lyon: Huguetan and Ravaud, 1663. Facsimile reprint, Stuttgart-Bad Canstatt: F. Frommann Verlag, 1966.

———. *Il Prosseneta, ovvero della prudenza politica*. Milan: Silvio Berlusconi Editore, 2001.

———. *Proxeneta, seu de humana sapientia liber, recèns in lucem protractus*. Leiden: Elzevir, 1627.

Cary, Elizabeth. *The History of the Life, Reign, and Death of Edward II, King of England, and Lord of Ireland*. London: Printed by J.C. for Charles Harper, Samuel Crouch and Thomas Fox, 1680.

Cartari, Vincenzo. *Le imagini de i dei de gli antichi [sic]*. Eds. Ginetta Auzzas, Federica Martignago, Manlio Pastore Stocchi, and Paola Rigo. Vicenza: Neri Pozza Editore, 1996.

Casoni, Guido. *Emblemi politici*. Venice: Paolo Baglioni, 1632.

Castiglione, Baldassar. *Il Libro del Cortegiano* (1528). Milan: Garzanti, 1981.

———. *The Book of the Courtier*. Trans. Charles S. Singleton. New York: Anchor Books, 1959.

Charron, Pierre. *De la Sagesse*. Bordeaux: Simon Millanges, 1601.

———. *De la Sagesse*. Ed. Barbara de Negroni. Paris: Librairie Arthème Fayard, 1986.

Chokier, Jean de. *Thesaurus Politicorum Aphorismorum*. Rome: Bartolomeo Zanetti, 1611.

Coignet, Mathieu. *Instruction aux princes pour garder la foy promise, contenant un sommaire de la philosophie Chretienne et morale, & devoir d'un homme de bien. En plusieurs discours politiques sur la vérité et le mensonge*. Paris: Jacques de Puys, 1584.

———. *Politique discourses upon trueth and lying. An instruction to princes to keepe their faith and promise*. Trans. Edward Hoby. London: Ralfe Newberie, 1586.

Collodio, Andrea. *Disputatio Politica Ad C. Corn. Taciti Annal. lib. I. De Tiberii Dissimulatione ad per illustrem ac nobilissimum D. D. Romanum Garzonium. Patronum Optimum*. Lucca: Ottaviano Guidoboni, 1616.

Cureau de la Chambre, Marin. *L'Art de connoistre les hommes*. 2nd rev. ed. Paris: Jacques d'Allin, 1663.

———. *The Art How to Know Men*. Trans. John Davies. London: Thomas Dring, 1665.

Della Casa, Giovanni. *Galateo ovvero de' costumi* (1558). Ed. Carlo Cordié. Milan: Mondadori, 1993.

———. *The Refin'd Courtier, or a Correction of Several Indecencies Crept into Civil Conversation*. Trans. Nathaniel Walker. London: R. Royston, 1663.

Della Porta, Giambattista. *Della fisonomia dell'uomo* (1586; 1610). Ed. Mario Cicognani. Parma: Ugo Guanda, 1988.

Descartes, René. *Oeuvres de Descartes*. Eds. Charles Adam and Paul Tannery. 11 vols. Paris: J. Vrin, 1996.

Diderot, Denis and Jean le Rond d'Alembert, eds. *Encyclopédie, ou Dictionnaire raisonné des sciences, des arts et des métiers*. 2nd ed. Vol. 4. Lucca: Vincenzo Giuntini, 1759.

Ducci, Lorenzo. *Arte aulica, nella quale s'insegna il modo, che deve tenere il Cortigiano per divenire possessore della gratia del suo Principe*. Ferrara: Vittorio Baldini, 1601.

———. *Ars aulica, or the Courtier's Arte*. Trans. Edward Blount. London: Printed by Melch. Bradwood for Edward Blount, 1607.

Erasmus, Desiderius. *Collected Works: Adages II.vii.1 to III.iii.100*. Trans. R. A. B. Mynors. Toronto: University of Toronto Press, 1992.

Faret, Nicolas. *L'Honneste-Homme ou, L'Art de Plaire à la Court.[sic]* Paris: Toussaincts du Bray, 1630.

———. *L'Honnête Homme ou L'Art de Plaire à la Cour*. Ed. Maurice Magendie. Geneva: Slatkine Reprints, 1970.

Formey, Johann Heinrich Samuel. "La Dissimulation." *Encyclopédie, ou Dictionnaire raisonné des sciences, des arts et des métiers*. Eds. Denis Diderot and Jean le Rond d'Alembert. 2nd ed. Vol. 4. Lucca: Vincenzo Giuntini, 1759. 870.

Gentillet, Innocent. *Discours contre Machiavel* (1576). Eds. Antonio D'Andrea and Pamela D. Stewart. Florence: Casalini Libri, 1974.

Gracián, Baltasar. *The Art of Worldly Wisdom: A Pocket Oracle*. Trans. Christopher Maurer. New York: Doubleday, 1992.

———. *El Héroe* (1637). *Obras Completas.* Ed. Arturo del Hoyo. Madrid: Aguilar, 1960.

———. *Obras Completas.* Ed. Arturo del Hoyo. Madrid: Aguilar, 1960.

———. *Oráculo manual y arte de prudencia* (1647). *Obras Completas.* Ed. Arturo del Hoyo. Madrid: Aguilar, 1960.

———. *Oráculo manual y arte de prudencia.* Ed. Benito Pelegrín. Zaragoza: Guara Editorial, 1983.

Guazzo, Stefano. *La civil conversazione* (1574). Ed. Amedeo Quondam. 2 vols. Modena: Franco Cosimo Panini, 1993.

Guicciardini, Francesco. *Ricordi. Opere.* Ed. Vittorio De Caprariis. Milan: Riccardo Ricciardi Editore, 1953.

———. *Selected Writings.* Ed. Cecil Grayson and trans. Margaret Grayson. New York: Oxford University Press, 1965.

Homer. *The Odyssey.* Trans. Robert Fitzgerald. New York: Anchor Books, 1963.

Ittig, Carl. *De simulatione et dissimulatione.* Leipzig: Literis Immanuelis Titii, 1709.

Jonson, Ben. *Timber: or, Discoveries; Made Upon Men and Matter...* (1640). Ed. G. B. Harrison. London: Bodley Head; New York: E. P. Dutton, 1923.

Knichen, Rudolf Gottfried von. *Opus Politicum.* Frankfurt am Main: Johann David Zunner, 1682.

Kuiper, Gijsbert, and Stéphane Le Moine. *Harpocrates, sive explicatio imagunculae argenteae perantiquae.* Utrecht: Franciscus Halma, 1687.

La Bruyère, Jean de. *Les Caractères* (1688). Ed. Robert Garapon. Paris: Garnier, 1962.

La Rochefoucauld, François de. *Maximes et reflexions diverses* (1665). Ed. Henry A. Grubbs, Jr. Princeton: Princeton University Press, 1929.

Lemprière, John. *Lemprière's Classical Dictionary* (1792). London: Bracken Books, 1984.

Lipsius, Justus. *Epistola de fructu peregrinandi et praesertim in Italia* (1578), first printed in *Epistolarum selectarum: centuria prima.* Leiden: Christophe Plantin; London: George Bishop, 1586. 30–36.

———. *Politica: Six Books of Politics or Political Instruction.* Ed. and trans. Jan H. Waszink. Assen: Royal Van Gorcum, 2004.

———. *Politicorum sive civilis doctrinae libri sex.* Leiden: Christophe Plantin, 1589.

———. *Six Bookes of Politickes or Civil Doctrine.* Trans. William Jones. London: by Richard Field for William Ponsonby, 1594.

Lottini, Giovanfrancesco. *Avvedimenti civili.* Florence: Bartolomeo Sermartelli, 1574.

Machiavelli, Niccolò. *Il Principe* (1532). *Le grandi opere politiche.* Eds. Gian Mario Anselmi and Carlo Varotti. Vol. 1. Turin: Bollati Boringhieri, 1992.

Machon, Louis. *Apologie pour Machiavel en faveur des Princes et des Ministres d'Estat.* Paris 1643. MS 19046–7. Bibliothèque Nationale de Paris.

Malvezzi, Virgilio. *Il Tarquinio superbo* (1634). *Opere historiche e politiche.* Geneva: Pietro Chouët, 1656.

Miscellanea di storia italiana edita per cura della Regia Deputazione di storia patria. Series 1. Vol. 1. Turin: Stamperia Reale, 1862.

Montaigne, Michel de. *Les Essais* (1580). Ed. Pierre Villey. 3rd rev. ed. 3 vols. Paris: Presses Universitaires de France, 1999.

——. *The Complete Works: Essays, Travel Journal, Letters.* Trans. Donald M. Frame. New York: Knopf, 2003.

Naudé, Gabriel. *Considérations politiques sur les coups d'état* (1639). Hildesheim: Georg Olms Verlag, 1993.

Orléans, Louis de. *Le Banquet et après dinée du Conte d'Arete, où il se traicte de la dissimulation du Roy de Navarre, & des moeurs de ses partisans.* Paris: Guillaume Bichon, 1594.

Pasquale, Carlo. *C. C. Taciti ab excessu divi Augusti Annalum libri quatuor priores, et in hoc observationes.* Paris: Robert Colombel, 1581.

——. *Gnomae, seu, axiomata politica: et Taciti Annalibus excerpta,* in *C. Cornelii Taciti et C. Velleii Paterculi scripta quae exstant.* Paris: Pierre Chevalier, 1608.

Philibert de Vienne. *Le Philosophe de Court* (1547). Ed. Pauline M. Smith. Geneva: Librairie Droz, 1990.

Pino da Cagli, Bernardino. *Del Galant'huomo overo Dell'Huomo Prudente, et Discreto.* Venice: Sessa, 1604.

Plato. *Collected Dialogues.* Eds. Edith Hamilton and Huntington Cairns. Bollingen Series 71. Princeton: Princeton University Press, 1961.

Plutarch. *Moralia.* Trans. W. C. Hembold. Cambridge, MA: Harvard University Press, 1939.

Pontano, Giovanni. *De Prudentia.* Naples: Sigismondo Mayr, 1505.

——. *Opera omnia soluta oratione composita.* Venice: Aldus Manutius, 1518–19.

Puttenham, George. *The Arte of English Poesie* (1589). *English Renaissance Literary Criticism.* Ed. Brian Vickers. New York: Oxford University Press, 2003.

Refuge, Eustache de. *Traicté de la Cour.* Paris, 1616.

——. *Traicté de la Cour, ou Instructions des courtisans.* 3rd rev. ed. Paris: Abraham Saugrain, 1619.

——. *A Treatise of the Court, or Instructions for Courtiers. Digested into Two Books.* Trans. John Reynolds. London: Aug. Matthewes for William Lee, 1622.

Ribadeneira, Pedro. *Tratado del Principe Cristiano* (1595). *Obras escogidas.* Ed. Vicente de la Fuente. Madrid: Ediciones Atlas, 1952.

Ricciardi, Giovanni Battista. *Chi non sa fingere non sa vivere, ovvero le cautele politiche.* Perugia: per gli eredi di Sebastiano Zecchini, 1672.

Rosa, Salvator. *Il teatro della politica. Sentenziosi afforismi [sic] della prudenza.* Ed. Giorgio Baroni. Scelta di curiosità letterarie inedite o rare dal secolo XIII al XIX, Dispensa 281. Bologna: Commissione per i testi di lingua, 1991.

Rosello, Lucio Paolo. *Due dialoghi.* Venice: Comin da Trino, 1549.

Rossi, Pio. *Il convito morale per gli etici, economici e politici.* Venice: Guerigli, 1639.

——. *Il convito morale per gli etici, economici e politici.* Venice: Guerigli, 1657.

Saavedra Fajardo, Diego de. *Empresas políticas* (1640). Ed. Sagrario López Poza. Madrid: Ediciónes Cátedra, 1999.

——. *The Royal Politician, Represented in One Hundred Emblems.* Trans. Sir J. A. Astry. 2 vols. London: M. Gillyflower and L. Meredith, 1700.

Sarpi, Paolo. *Lettere ai Gallicani.* Ed. Boris Ulianich. Wiesbaden: F. Steiner, 1961.

Scudéry, Madeleine de. *Les Conversations sur Divers Sujets.* 2nd ed. Amsterdam: Daniel du Fresne, 1686.

Senault, François. *De l'Usage des passions.* Rouen: Par la Société, 1656.

Seneca, Lucius Annaeus. *Dialoghi morali.* Ed. Carlo Carena and trans. Gavino Manca. Turin: Einaudi, 1995.

Shakespeare, William. *The Norton Shakespeare.* Eds. Stephen Greenblatt, Walter Cohen, Jean E. Howard, and Katharine Eisaman Maus. 2nd ed. New York: W. W. Norton, 2008.

Siena, Sisto da. *Bibliotheca Sancta.* Venice: Johann Gryphius, 1566.

Stradling, John. *A Direction for Travailers.* London: R. Bourne for Cutbert Burbie, 1592.

Tacitus, Publius Cornelius. *The Histories.* Trans. Clifford H. Moore. [and] *The Annals.* Trans. John Jackson. Cambridge, MA: Harvard University Press, 1937.

Tasso, Torquato. *Tasso's Dialogues: A Selection with "The Discourse on the Art of the Dialogue."* Trans. Carnes Lord and Dain A. Trafton. Berkeley and Los Angeles: University of California Press, 1982.

Tertullian. *Disciplinary, Moral and Ascetical Works.* Trans. Rudolph Arbesmann, Emily J. Daly, and Edward A. Quain. The Fathers of the Church 40. New York: The Fathers of the Church, Inc., 1959.

Vannozzi, Bonifacio. *Della Supellettile degli Avvertimenti Politici, Morali, et Christiani.* 3 vols. Bologna: Eredi di Giovanni Rossi, 1609–1613.

Ventura, Comin. *La Prima Parte del Thesoro Politico.* Milan: Girolamo Bordone, 1600.

———. *La Seconda Parte del Thesoro Politico.* Milan: Girolamo Bordone and Pietromartire Locarni, 1601.

Vera y Zuñiga, Juan Antonio de. *El Enbaxador.* Seville: Francisco de Lyra, 1620.

Vico, Giambattista. *Autobiografia. Raccolta di opuscoli scientifici e filologici.* Eds. Angelo Calogerà and Fortunato Mandelli, 51 vols. Venice: C. Zane and S. Occhi, 1728–1754. Now in *Liber Liber.* Ed. Claudio Paganelli. 20 October 1997. http://www.liberliber.it/biblioteca/v/vico/index.htm.

Works from after 1800

Arcari, Paolo Maria. *La ragion di stato in un manoscritto inedito di Alessandro Anguissola.* 2nd ed. Rome: Nuove Grafiche, 1939.

Archer, John Michael. *Sovereignty and Intelligence: Spying and Court Culture in the English Renaissance.* Stanford: Stanford University Press, 1993.

Arditi, Jorge. *A Genealogy of Manners: Transformations of Social Relations in France and England from the Fourteenth to the Eighteenth Century.* Chicago: University of Chicago Press, 1998.

Aricò, Denise. "Anatomie della 'dissimulazione' barocca (in margine all'*Elogio della dissimulazione* di Rosario Villari)." *Intersezioni* 8.3 (1988): 565–566.

Bacchelli, Franco. "Science, Cosmology, and Religion in Ferrara, 1520–1550." *Dosso's Fate: Painting and Court Culture in Renaissance Italy.* Eds. Luisa

Ciammitti, Steven F. Ostrow and Salvatore Settis. Trans. Jon R. Snyder. Issues and Debates 5. Los Angeles: The Getty Research Institute for the History of Art and the Humanities, 1998. 333–354.

Bakos, Adriana E. "*'Qui nescit dissimulare, nescit regnare'*: Louis XI and *Raison d'état* during the Reign of Louis XIII." *Journal of the History of Ideas* 52.3 (1991): 399–416.

Baldini, A. Enzo, ed. *Botero e la 'ragion di stato.'* Florence: Olschki, 1992.

Balsamo, Jean. "Les Origines parisiennes du *Tesoro politico* (1589)." *Bibliothèque d'Humanisme et Renaissance* 57.1 (1995): 7–23.

Barberis, Walter. Introduction. *Il Libro del Cortegiano*. By Baldassar Castiglione. Turin: Einaudi, 1998. vii–lxvi.

Battista, Anna Maria. *Politica e morale nella Francia dell'età moderna*. Ed. Anna Maria Lazzarino Del Grosso. Genoa: NAME, 1998.

Belligni, Eleonora. *Lo scacco della prudenza: Precettistica politica ed esperienza storica in Virgilio Malvezzi*. Florence: Olschki, 1999.

Berger, Harry Jr. *The Absence of Grace: Sprezzatura and Suspicion in Two Renaissance Courtesy Books*. Stanford: Stanford University Press, 2000.

Biagioli, Mario. "Etiquette, Interdependence, and Sociability in Seventeenth-Century Science." *Critical Inquiry* 22 (1996): 193–238.

Bianchi, Lorenzo. "Elementi stoici nel pensiero di Gabriel Naudé." *Individualismo, assolutismo, democrazia*. Eds. Vittorio Dini and Domenico Taranto. Naples: Edizioni Scientifiche Italiane, 1992. 27–51.

——. *Rinascimento e libertinismo: studi su Gabriel Naudé*. Naples: Bibliopolis, 1996.

——. "Tra Rinascimento e Barocco. Forza e dissimulazione nelle *Considérations politiques* di Gabriel Naudé." *Studi filosofici* 21 (1998): 129–151.

Bigalli, Davide, ed. *Ragione e 'civiltas.' Figure del vivere associato nella cultura del Cinquecento europeo*. Filosofia e scienza nel Cinquecento e nel Seicento, Serie 1, Studi 28. Milan: FrancoAngeli, 1986.

Biondi, Albano. "Il *Convito* di Don Pio Rossi: società chiusa e corte ambigua." *La corte e il 'Cortegiano': 2 — un modello europeo*. Ed. Adriano Prosperi. Rome: Bulzoni, 1980. 93–112.

——. "La giustificazione della simulazione nel Cinquecento." *Eresia e Riforma nell'Italia del Cinquecento*. Miscellanea 1. DeKalb: Northern Illinois University Press, 1974. 7–68.

Biow, Douglas. "From Machiavelli to Torquato Accetto: The Secretarial Art of Dissimulation." *Educare il corpo, educare la parola nella trattatistica del Rinascimento*. Eds. Giorgio Patrizi and Amedeo Quondam. Biblioteca del Cinquecento 80. Rome: Bulzoni Editore, 1998. 219–238.

Birely, Robert. *The Counter-Reformation Prince: Anti-Machiavellianism or Catholic Statecraft in Early Modern Europe*. Chapel Hill: University of North Carolina Press, 1990.

Bisello, Linda. *Sotto il 'manto' del silenzio: storia e forme del tacere (secoli XVI–XVII)*. Florence: Olschki, 2003.

Bodei, Remo. *La geometria delle passioni. Paura, speranza, felicità: filosofia e uso politico*. Rev. ed. Milan: Feltrinelli, 1992.

Boidi Sassone, Adriana, and Laura Palmucci Quaglino. *Cherasco. Palazzi e committenze tra Corte e provincia*. Turin: Centro Studi Piemontesi, 1994.

Bok, Sissela. *Secrets: On the Ethics of Concealment and Revelation*. New York: Pantheon Books, 1982.

Bolzoni, Lina. *La stanza della memoria: modelli letterari e iconografici nell'età della stampa*. Turin: Einaudi, 1995.

Borrelli, Gianfranco. "Bibliografia saggistica sulla letteratura della 'Ragion di Stato.'" *Archivio della Ragion di Stato* 1 (1993): 15–92.

———. *Ragion di stato e leviatano: conservazione e scambio alle origini della modernità politica*. Bologna: Il Mulino, 1993.

———. "La Ragion di Stato: teoria e prassi." *Italia 1650*. Eds. Giuseppe Galasso and Aurelio Musi. Naples: CUEN, 2002. 121–142.

———. "Tecniche di simulazione e conservazione politica in Gerolamo Cardano e Alberico Gentili." *Annali dell'Istituto storico italo-germanico in Trento* 12 (1986): 87–145.

Bryson, Anna. *From Courtesy to Civility: Changing Codes of Conduct in Early Modern England*. Oxford: Clarendon Press, 1998.

Buck, August. "Die Kunst der Verstellung im Zeitalter des Barocks." *Studien zu Humanismus und Renaissance: Gesammelte Aufsätze aus den Jahren 1981–1990*. Eds. Bodo Guthmüller, Karl Kohut, and Oskar Roth. Wolfenbütteler Abhandlungen zur Renaissanceforschung 11. Wiesbaden: Otto Harrassowitz, 1991. 486–509.

Burke, Peter. *The Art of Conversation*. Ithaca, NY: Cornell University Press, 1993.

———. *The Fortunes of the "Courtier": The European Reception of Castiglione's "Cortegiano."* The Penn State Series in the History of the Book. University Park: Penn State University Press, 1995.

Bury, Emmanuel. *Littérature et politesse: L'invention de l'honnête homme (1580–1750)*. Paris: Presses Universitaires de France, 1996.

Calvi, Giulia, ed. Introduction. *Barocco al femminile*. Bari: Laterza, 1992. i–xxvii.

Cantarino, Elena, and Emilio Blanco, eds. *Diccionario de conceptos de Baltasar Gracián*. Madrid: Ediciones Cátedra, 2005.

Cavaillé, Jean-Pierre. "De la construction des apparences au culte de la transparence. Simulation et dissimulation entre le XVIe et le XVIIIe siècle." *Littératures Classiques* 34 (1998): 73–102.

———. "De la dissimulation honnête." *Sigila* 8 (2001): 65–80.

———. *Dis/simulations. Jules-César Vanini, François La Mothe Le Vayer, Gabriel Naudé, Louis Machon et Torquato Accetto: Religion, morale et politique au XVIIe siècle*. Paris: Honoré Champion, 2002.

———. "Guerre civile et paix de l'âme: Juste Lipse, *De constantia in publicis malis*." *Kairos* 6 (1994): 11–40.

———. "Histoires d'équivoques." *Cahiers du Centre de Recherches Historiques* 33 (2004): 155–173.

———. "Louis Machon (1603–après 1672). Autopsie d'une non-publication." *Groupe de recherches interdisciplinaires sur l'histoire du littéraire: de la publication entre Renaissance et Lumières*. Eds. Christian Jouhaud and Alain Viala. Paris: Fayard, 2002. 93–109, 318–321.

———. "Ruser sans mentir: de la casuistique aux sciences sociales. Le recours à l'équivocité entre efficacité pragmatique et souci éthique." *Les raisons de la ruse: une perspective anthropologique et psychanalytique.* Eds. Serge Latouche, Pierre-Joseph Laurent, Olivier Servais, and Michael Singleton. Paris: Éditions La Découverte/M.A.U.S.S., 2004. 93–116.

———. "Simulatio/dissimulatio: notes sur feinte et occultation, XVIe–XVIIIe siècle." *Il vocabolario della République des lettres. Terminologia filosofica e storia della filosofia: problemi di metodo.* Ed. Marta Fattori. Lessico intellettuale europeo 70. Florence: Olschki, 1997. 115–131.

———. "Théorie et pratique de la dissimulation dans le *Spaccio della bestia trionfante.*" *Mondes, formes et société selon Giordano Bruno.* Eds. Tristan Dagron and Hélène Védrine. Paris: Vrin, 2003. 47–63.

Cavaillé, Jean-Pierre, ed. *Bibliographie: "Mensonge, tromperie, simulation et dissimulation."* Les dossiers du GRIHL [Groupe de Recherches Interdisciplinaires sur l'Histoire du Littéraire]. 21 January 2008. http://dossiersgrihl.revues.org/document2103.html.

Cavallo, JoAnn. "Joking Matters: Politics and Dissimulation in Castiglione's *Book of the Courtier.*" *Renaissance Quarterly* 53.2 (2000): 402–424.

Chastel, André. "Signum harpocraticum." *Studi in onore di Guilio Carlo Argan.* Eds. Silvana Macchioni and Bianca Tavassi La Greca. Vol. 1. Rome: Multigrafica Editrice, 1984. 147–156.

Chrétien-Goni, Jean-Pierre. "*Institutio arcanae:* Théorie de l'institution du secret et fondement de la politique." *Le Pouvoir de la raison d'état.* Eds. Christian Lazzeri and Dominique Reynié. Paris: Presses Universitaires de France, 1992. 135–143.

Clark, Stuart. *Vanities of the Eye: Vision in Early Modern European Culture.* New York: Oxford University Press, 2007.

Cochrane, Eric. *Florence in the Forgotten Centuries 1527–1800.* Chicago: University of Chicago Press, 1973.

Contratto, Maria Gabriella. *Sebastiano Taricco.* Cuneo: Società Studi Storici Archeologici ed Artistici della Provincia di Cuneo, 1974.

Corbin, Alain, Jean-Jacques Courtine, and Georges Vigarello, eds. Preface. *Histoire du corps, 1: De la Renaissance aux Lumières.* Paris: Éditions du Seuil, 2005.

Costo, Tomaso, and Michele Benvenga. *Il segretario di lettere.* Ed. Salvatore S. Nigro. Palermo: Sellerio, 1991.

Courcelles, Dominique de, ed. *D'un principe philosophique à un genre littéraire: les 'secrets.'* Paris: Honoré Champion, 2005.

Courtine, Jean-Jacques and Claudine Haroche. *Histoire du visage: exprimer et taire ses émotions, XVIe–début XIXe siècle.* Paris: Rivages, 1988.

D'Angelo, Paolo and Stefano Velotti. *Il 'non so che': storia di un'idea estetica.* Palermo: Aesthetica Edizioni, 1997.

Dandelet, Thomas J., and John A. Marino, eds. Introduction. *Spain in Italy: Politics, Society and Religion, 1500–1700.* Leiden: Brill, 2007. 1–18.

Delft, Louis Van. "De la dissimulation." *La sincerité: l'insolence du coeur.* Eds. Christine Baron and Catherine Doroszczuk. Paris: Éditions Autrement, 1995. 73–85.

———. *Le moraliste classique*. Geneva: Droz, 1982.

———. "La notion de 'dissimulation honnête' dans la culture classique." *Prémices et floraison de l'Âge classique: mélanges en l'honneur de Jean Jehasse*. Ed. Bernard Yon. Saint-Étienne: Publications de l'Université de Saint-Étienne, 1995. 253–267.

De Mattei, Rodolfo. *Il pensiero politico di Scipione Ammirato, con discorsi inediti*. Milan: A. Giuffrè, 1963.

———. *Dal premachiavellismo all'antimachiavellismo*. Florence: Sansoni, 1969.

———. *Il problema della 'ragion di stato' nell'età della Controriforma*. Milan: Riccardo Ricciardi Editore, 1979.

———. "Scipione Ammirato." *Dizionario biografico degli italiani*. Vol. 3. Rome: Istituto della Enciclopedia italiana, 1961. 1–4.

Dewald, Jonathan. *The European Nobility, 1400–1800*. New York: Cambridge University Press, 1996.

Dini, Vittorio. *Il governo della prudenza: virtù dei privati e disciplina dei custodi*. Milan: FrancoAngeli, 2000.

Dini, Vittorio, and Giampiero Stabile. *Saggezza e prudenza: studi per la ricostruzione di un'antropologia in prima età moderna*. Naples: Liguori, 1983.

Donaldson, Peter S. *Machiavelli and Mystery of State*. New York: Cambridge University Press, 1988.

Dooley, Brendan, ed. and trans. *Italy in the Baroque: Selected Readings*. New York: Garland Publishing, 1995.

Dowling, John. *Diego de Saavedra Fajardo*. Boston: Twayne, 1977.

Duindam, Jeroen. *Myths of Power: Norbert Elias and the Early Modern European Court*. Trans. Lorri S. Granger and Gerard T. Moran. Amsterdam: Amsterdam University Press, 1994.

Dunning, Eric and Stephen Mennell, eds. *Norbert Elias*. 4 vols. Thousand Oaks, CA: SAGE Publications, 2003.

Dzelzainis, Martin. "Bacon's 'Of Simulation and Dissimulation.'" *A Companion to English Renaissance Literature and Culture*. Ed. Michael Hattaway. Oxford and Malden, MA: Blackwell, 2003. 233–240.

Egido, Aurora. *Las caras de la prudencia y Baltasar Gracián*. Madrid: Editorial Castalia, 2000.

Egido, Aurora, and María del Carmen Marín Pina, eds. *Baltasar Gracián: Estado de la cuestión y nuevas perspectivas*. Zaragoza: Institución "Fernando el Católico," 2001.

Egido, Aurora et al., eds. *Baltasar Gracián IV Centenario (1601–2001)*. Zaragoza: Instituto de Estudios Altoaragoneses, 2003.

Elias, Norbert. *The Civilizing Process*. Trans. Edmund Jephcott. Oxford: Blackwell, 1994 (rev. ed. 2000).

———. *The Court Society*. Trans. Edmund Jephcott. Oxford: Blackwell, 1983. Reissued in *The Collected Works of Norbert Elias*. Ed. Stephen Mennell. Vol. 2. Dublin: University College Dublin Press, 2006.

Esposito, Roberto. *Ordine e conflitto. Machiavelli e la letteratura politica del Rinascimento italiano*. Naples: Liguori, 1984.

Euringer, Martin. *Zuschauer des Welttheaters: Lebensrolle, Theatermetapher und gelingendes Selbst in der Frühen Neuzeit*. Darmstadt: Wissenschaftliche Buchgesellschaft, 2000.

Fantoni, Marcello. *La corte del granduca: forma e simboli del potere mediceo fra Cinque e Seicento*. Biblioteca del Cinquecento 62. Rome: Bulzoni, 1994.

Fernández-Santamaria, J. A. *Reason of State and Statecraft in Spanish Political Thought, 1595–1640*. Lanham, MD: University Press of America, 1983.

Fintoni, Monica. "Teorie della dissimulazione tra XVI° e XVII° secolo." Diss. Università degli Studi di Trieste, 1996.

Fiorato, Adelin-Charles. "Simulation/Dissimulation." *Dictionnaire raisonné de la politesse et du savoir-vivre*. Ed. Alain Montandon. Paris: Seuil, 1995. 801–846.

Foà, Simona. "Lorenzo Ducci." *Dizionario biografico degli italiani*. Vol. 4. Rome: Istituto della Enciclopedia Italiana, 1992. 740–741.

Fontana, Alessandro, and Jean-Louis Fournel. "Piazza, Corte, Salotto, Caffè." *Letteratura italiana*. Ed. Alberto Asor Rosa. Vol. 5. Turin: Einaudi, 1986. 635–686.

Foucault, Michel. *Discipline and Punish: The Birth of the Prison*. Trans. Alan Sheridan. New York: Vintage Books, 1979.

———. *Fearless Speech*. Ed. Joseph Pearson. Los Angeles: Semiotext(e), 2001.

Fournel, Jean-Louis. "Place et Palais." *50 Rue de Varennes* 1 (1985): 37–50.

Fumaroli, Marc. *Le genre des genres littéraires français: la conversation*. Oxford: Clarendon Press, 1992.

Fumerton, Patricia. *Cultural Aesthetics: Renaissance Literature and the Practice of Social Ornament*. Chicago: University of Chicago Press, 1991.

Garver, Eugene. *Machiavelli and the History of Prudence*. Madison: University of Wisconsin Press, 1987.

Geitner, Ursula. *Die Sprache der Verstellung: Studien zum rhetorischen und anthropologischen Wissen im 17. und 18. Jahrhundert*. Tübingen: Max Niemeyer Verlag, 1992.

Ginzburg, Carlo. *Il Nicodemismo. Simulazione e dissimulazione nell'Europa del '500*. Turin: Einaudi, 1970.

Goffman, Erving. *The Presentation of the Self in Everyday Life*. Garden City, NY: Doubleday, 1959.

Goldsmith, Elizabeth C. *Exclusive Conversations: The Art of Interaction in Seventeenth-Century France*. Philadelphia: University of Pennsylvania Press, 1988.

Gouverneur, Sophie. *Prudence et subversion libertines: la critique de la raison d'État chez François de la Mothe le Vayer, Gabriel Naudé et Samuel Sorbière*. Paris: Honoré Champion, 2005.

Grafton, Anthony. *Cardano's Cosmos: The Worlds and Works of a Renaissance Astrologer*. Cambridge, MA: Harvard University Press, 1999.

Greenblatt, Stephen. "Invisible Bullets: Renaissance Authority and Its Subversion." *Shakespearean Negotiations: The Circulation of Social Energy in Renaissance England*. Berkeley and Los Angeles: University of California Press, 1988. 21–65.

———. *Renaissance Self-Fashioning: From More to Shakespeare*. Chicago: University of Chicago Press, 2005.

Gregori, Carlo. "L'elogio del silenzio e la simulazione come modelli di comportamento in Gerolamo Cardano." *Sapere e/è potere: discipline, dispute e professioni nell'università medievale e moderna—il caso bolognese a confronto. Vol.3: dalle discipline ai ruoli sociali. Atti del 4° convegno, Bologna 13–15 aprile 1989.* Ed. Angela De Benedictis. Bologna: Comune di Bologna/Istituto per la Storia di Bologna, 1990. 73–84.

Groebner, Valentin. *Who Are You? Identification, Deception and Surveillance in Early Modern Europe.* Trans. Mark Kyburz and John Peck. New York: Zone Books, 2007.

Guidi, José. "Les Différentes rédactions du *Livre du Courtisan.*" *De la Politesse à la politique: Recherches sur les langages du 'Livre du Courtisan'.* Eds. Paolo Grossi and Juan Carlos D'Amico. Caen: Presses Universitaires de Caen, 2001. 19–30.

Habermas, Jürgen. *The Structural Transformation of the Public Sphere: An Inquiry into a Category of Bourgeois Society.* Trans. Thomas Burger and Frederick Lawrence. Cambridge, MA: MIT Press, 1989.

Hallyn, Fernand. *Descartes: dissimulation et ironie.* Geneva: Droz, 2006.

Hinz, Manfred. "Il cortigiano e il tacitismo." *Traités de savoir-vivre en Italie. I trattati del saper vivere in Italia.* Ed. Alain Montandon. Clermont-Ferrand: Association des Publications de la Faculté des Lettres et Sciences Humaines de Clermont-Ferrand, 1993. 191–198.

———. *Die menschlichen und die göttlichen Mittel: Sieben Kommentare zu Baltasar Gracián.* Bonn: Romanistischer Verlag, 2002.

———. *Rhetorische Strategien des Hofmannes: Studien zu den italienischen Hofmannstraktaten des 16. und 17. Jahrhunderts.* Stuttgart: J. B. Metzler, 1992.

Hoffmann, E. T. A.. "Mademoiselle de Scudéry: A Tale of the Times of Louis XIV." *Tales of Hoffmann.* Ed. Christopher Lazare. New York: A. A. Wyn, 1946. 37–102.

Horodowich, Elizabeth A. *Language and Statecraft in Early Modern Venice.* New York: Cambridge University Press, 2008.

Houdt, Toon van, Jan L. DeJong, Zoran Kwak, Marijke Spies, and Marc van Vaeck, eds. *On the Edge of Truth and Honesty: Principles and Strategies of Fraud and Deceit in the Early Modern Period.* Leiden: Brill, 2002.

Hsia, R. Po-Chia. *The World of Catholic Renewal, 1540–1770.* New York: Cambridge University Press, 1998.

Hunt, Lynn. *The Family Romance of the French Revolution.* Berkeley and Los Angeles: University of California Press, 1992.

Israel, Jonathan I. *Radical Enlightenment: Philosophy and the Making of Modernity 1650–1750.* New York: Oxford University Press, 2001.

Jardine, Lisa, and Alan Stewart. *Hostage to Fortune: The Troubled Life of Francis Bacon.* New York: Hill and Wang, 1999.

Javitch, Daniel. "*Il Cortegiano* and the Constraints of Despotism." *Castiglione: The Real and the Ideal in Renaissance Culture.* Eds. Robert W. Hanning and David Rosand. New Haven: Yale University Press, 1983. 17–28. Reprinted in *The Book of the Courtier: The Singleton Translation.* Ed. Daniel Javitch. New York: W. W. Norton, 2002. 319–328.

Kahn, Victoria. *Machiavellian Rhetoric: From the Counter-Reformation to Milton.* Princeton: Princeton University Press, 1994.

———. *Rhetoric, Prudence and Skepticism in the Renaissance.* Ithaca: Cornell University Press, 1985.

Kaiser, Wolfgang, ed. *Pratiques du secret XVe–XVIIe siècles.* Special issue of *Rives nord-méditerranéennes* 17 (2004): 1–149.

Kantorowicz, Ernst H. *The King's Two Bodies: A Study in Medieval Theology.* Princeton: Princeton University Press, 1957.

Knox, Dilwyn. *Ironia: Medieval and Renaissance Ideas on Irony.* Leiden: E. J. Brill, 1989.

Kruse, Margot. "Justification et critique du concept de la dissimulation dans l'oeuvre des moralistes du XVIIe siècle." *La Pensée religieuse dans la littérature et la civilisation du XVIIe siècle en France.* Eds. Manfred Tietz and Volker Kapp. Tübingen: Papers on French Seventeenth-Century Literature, 1984. 147–170.

Lagrée, Jacqueline. *Juste Lipse: la restauration du stoïcisme.* Paris: Vrin, 1994.

———. ed. *Le Stoïcisme aux XVIe et XVIIe siècles. Actes du Colloque CERPHI (4–5 juin 1993).* Cahiers de philosophie politique et juridique 25. Caen: Université de Caen, 1994.

Lamarche-Vadel, Gaëtane. *De la duplicité: les figures du secret au XVIIe siècle.* Paris: La Différence, 1994.

Landolfi, Mario. "La dissimulazione: ovvero il trionfo della prudenza nell'opera di Torquato Accetto." *Riscontri* 4 (2002): 9–19.

Laspalas Pérez, Javier. "Cortesía y sociedad: las 'Artes de vivir' de Gerolamo Cardano y Eustache de Refuge." *Cuadernos de Historia Moderna. Anejos* 3 (2004): 39–57.

———. "El problema de la insinceridad en cuatro tratados de cortesía del Renacimiento." *Aportaciónes a la historia social del lenguaje: España siglos XIV–XVIII.* Eds. Rocío García Bourrellier and Jésus M. Usunáriz. Madrid: Iboamericana; Frankfurt: Vervuert, 2005. 27–55.

Lausberg, Heinrich. *Elemente der Literarische Rhetorik.* 2nd ed. Munich: Max Hüber Verlag, 1971.

Lazzeri, Christian, and Dominique Reynié, eds. *Le pouvoir de la raison d'État.* Paris: Presses Universitaires de France, 1992.

Lefebvre, Charles. "Dissimulation." *Dictionnaire de droit canonique.* Ed. R. Naz. Paris: Librairie Letouzey et Ané, 1949.

Leuschner, Ernst. "The Pythagorean Inscription on Salvator Rosa's London Self-Portrait." *Journal of the Warburg and Courtauld Institutes* 57 (1994): 278–283.

Levi D'Ancona, Mirella. *The Garden of the Renaissance: Botanical Symbolism in Italian Painting.* Florence: Olschki, 1977.

Macchia, Giovanni. Introduction. *I moralisti classici da Machiavelli a La Bruyère.* Milan: Adelphi, 1988.

———. *Le Théâtre de la dissimulation.* Trans. Paul Bédarida. Paris: Gallimard, 1993.

———. *Tra Don Giovanni e Don Rodrigo: scenari secenteschi.* Milan: Adelphi, 1989.

Maravall, José Antonio. "La corriente doctrinal del tacitismo político en España." *Cuadernos Hispanoamericanos* 238–240 (1969): 645–667.

————. *The Culture of the Baroque.* Trans. Terry Cochran. Theory and History of Literature 25. Minneapolis: University of Minnesota Press, 1986.

Marquer, Éric. "Vers une moralisation du secret aux XVIe et XVIIe siècle." *D'un principe philosophique à un genre littéraire: les 'secrets.'* Ed. Dominique de Courcelles. Paris: Honoré Champion, 2005. 473–483.

Martin, John J. "Inventing Sincerity, Refashioning Prudence: The Discovery of the Individual in Renaissance Europe." *The American Historical Review* 102.5 (1997): 1309–1342.

————. *Myths of Renaissance Individualism.* New York: Palgrave Macmillan, 2004.

Martin, Raymond, and John Barresi. *The Rise and Fall of Soul and Self: An Intellectual History of Personal Identity.* New York: Columbia University Press, 2006.

Mazzacurati, Giancarlo. *Il Rinascimento dei moderni. La crisi culturale del XVIo secolo e la negazione delle origini.* Bologna: Il Mulino, 1985.

McCrea, Adriana. *Constant Minds: Political Virtue and the Lipsian Paradigm in England, 1584–1650.* Toronto: University of Toronto Press, 1997.

Mellor, Ronald. *Tacitus.* New York: Routledge, 1993.

Mennell, Stephen, ed. *The Collected Works of Norbert Elias.* Vol. 2. Dublin: University College Dublin Press, 2006.

Momigliano, Arnaldo. *Contributo alla storia degli studi classici.* Rome: Edizioni di Storia e Letteratura, 1955.

Montandon, Alain, ed. *Étiquette et politesse.* Clermont-Ferrand: Association des Publications de la Faculté des Lettres et Sciences Humaines de Clermont-Ferrand, 1992.

————. "Pour une histoire des traités de savoir-vivre italiens: esquisse bibliographique." *Traités de savoir-vivre en Italie. I trattati del saper vivere in Italia.* Clermont-Ferrand: Association des Publications de la Faculté des Lettres et Sciences Humaines de Clermont-Ferrand, 1993. 309–334.

Moos, Peter von. "*Occulta cordis:* contrôle de soi et confession au Moyen Âge." *Médiévales* 29 (1995): 131–140; 30 (1996): 117–137.

Morford, Mark. "Tacitean *Prudentia* and the Doctrines of Justus Lipsius." *Tacitus and the Tacitean Tradition.* Eds. T. J. Luce and A. J. Woodman. Princeton: Princeton University Press, 1993. 129–151.

Mozzarelli, Cesare. "Aristocrazia e borghesia nell'Europa moderna." *Storia d'Europa. Vol. 4: L'età moderna.* Eds. Maurice Aymard and Perry Anderson. Turin: Einaudi, 1995. 327–362.

Muir, Edward. *Ritual in Early Modern Europe.* Rev. ed. New York: Cambridge University Press, 2005.

Müller, Wolfgang G. "Dissimulation as a Theme and Rhetorical Device in Kyd's *Spanish Tragedy.*" *Arbeiten aus Anglistik und Amerikanistik* 10.1–2 (1985): 21–41.

————. "Ironie, Lüge, Simulation, Dissimulation und verwandte rhetorische Termini." *Zur Terminologie der Literaturwissenschaft.* Ed. Christian Wagenknecht. Stuttgart: Metzler, 1989. 189–208.

Nagle, Jean. *La civilisation du coeur: Histoire du sentiment politique en France, du XIIe au XIXe siècle.* Paris: Fayard, 1998.

Nigro, Salvatore S. "*Della dissimulazione onesta* di Torquato Accetto." *Letteratura italiana*. Ed. Alberto Asor Rosa. Vol. 2. Turin: Einaudi, 1993. 973–990.

Nigro, Salvatore S., ed. "*Scriptor necans.*" *Della dissimulazione onesta*. By Torquato Accetto. Genoa: Costa & Nolan, 1983. 19–26.

———. "Usi della pazienza." *Della dissimulazione onesta*. By Torquato Accetto. Turin: Einaudi, 1997. xi–xxx.

Nigro, Salvatore S., ed. and trans. *Elogio della menzogna*. Palermo: Sellerio, 1990.

Oestreich, Gerhard. "The Main Political Work of Lipsius." *Neostoicism and the Early Modern State*. Eds. Brigitta Oestreich and H. G. Koenigsberger. Trans. David McLintock. New York: Cambridge University Press, 1982. 39–56.

Olivero, Giuseppe. *Dissimulatio e tolerantia nell'ordinamento canonico*. Università di Catania: Pubblicazioni della Facoltà di Giurisprudenza 18. Milan: A. Giuffré, 1953.

Ornaghi, Lorenzo. "La 'bottega di maschere' e le origini della politica moderna." *Famiglia del Principe e famiglia aristocratica*. Ed. Cesare Mozzarelli. Rome: Bulzoni, 1988. 9–23.

Ossola, Carlo, ed. *La corte e il 'Cortegiano.' 1—la scena del testo*. Rome: Bulzoni, 1980.

———. *Dal 'cortegiano' all' 'uomo di mondo': storia di un libro e di un modello sociale*. Turin: Einaudi, 1987.

Pagden, Anthony. *Spanish Imperialism and the Political Imagination: Studies in European and Spanish-American Social and Political Theory 1513–1830*. New Haven: Yale University Press, 1990.

Paternoster, Annick. "Il teatro della retorica non-apparente. La struttura del dialogo nel *Cortegiano*." *Lingua e stile* 26.1 (1991): 35–55.

Patrizi, Giorgio, and Amedeo Quondam, eds. *Educare il corpo, educare la parola nella trattatistica del Rinascimento*. Rome: Bulzoni Editore, 1998.

Patrizi, Giorgio. "*Galateo* di Giovanni della Casa." *Letteratura italiana. Le opere*. Ed. Alberto Asor Rosa. Vol. 2. Turin: Einaudi, 1993. 453–477.

———. "*Il Libro del Cortegiano* e la trattatistica sul comportamento." *Letteratura italiana*. Ed. Alberto Asor Rosa. Turin: Einaudi, 1984. 3.2: 855–890.

———. "Il valore della norma: etichetta come comunicazione e rappresentazione tra *Cortegiano* e *Galateo*." *Étiquette et politesse*. Ed. Alain Montandon. Clermont-Ferrand: Association des Publications de la Faculté des Lettres et Sciences Humaines de Clermont-Ferrand, 1992. 33–42.

Pavel, Thomas. *L'Art de l'éloignement. Essai sur l'imagination classique*. Paris: Gallimard, 1996.

Pons, Alain. "Le Thème de la communication dans le *Galatée* de Giovanni della Casa." *Savoir Vivre I*. Ed. Alain Montandon. Meyzieu: Césura Lyon Édition, 1990. 11–23.

Porter, Martin. *Windows of the Soul: Physiognomy in European Culture 1470–1780*. Oxford: Clarendon Press, 2005.

Praz, Mario. *The Flaming Heart*. New York: W. W. Norton, 1973.

———. *Studies in Seventeenth-Century Imagery*. 2nd rev. ed. Rome: Edizioni di storia e letteratura, 1964.

Prieto, Paolo. *I servizi segreti di Venezia. Spionaggio e controspionaggio: cifrari, intercettazioni, delazioni, tra mito e realtà*. Milan: Il Saggiatore, 1994.

Procacci, Giuliano. *Machiavelli nella cultura europea dell'età moderna*. Bari: Laterza, 1995.

Prosperi, Adriano, ed. *La corte e il 'Cortegiano.' 2—un modello europeo*. Rome: Bulzoni, 1980.

Quondam, Amedeo. *La conversazione: un modello italiano*. Rome: Donzelli, 2007.

Raab, Felix. *The English Face of Machiavelli: A Changing Interpretation, 1500–1700*. London: Routledge Kegan Paul; Toronto: University of Toronto Press, 1964.

Ranum, Orest. "Courtesy, Absolutism, and the Rise of the French State, 1630–1660." *The Journal of Modern History* 52 (1980): 426–451.

———. "Les refuges de l'intimité." *Histoire de la vie privée, 3. De la Renaissance aux Lumières*. Eds. Philippe Ariès and Georges Duby. Paris: Seuil, 1986. 211–265.

Raponi, Nicola. "Alessandro Anguissola." *Dizionario biografico degli italiani*. Vol. 3. Rome: Istituto della Enciclopedia Italiana, 1961. 315–316.

Reiss, Timothy J. *Mirages of the Selfe: Patterns of Personhood in Ancient and Early Modern Europe*. Stanford: Stanford University Press, 2003.

Revel, Jacques. "Les usages de la civilité." *Histoire de la vie privée, 3. De la Renaissance aux Lumières*. Eds. Philippe Ariès and Georges Duby. Paris: Seuil, 1986. 169–209.

Ricci, Giovanni. *Il principe e la morte: corpo, cuore, effigie nel Rinascimento*. Bologna: Il Mulino, 1998.

Richards, Jennifer. *Rhetoric and Courtliness in Early Modern Literature*. New York: Cambridge University Press, 2003.

Rigoni, Mario Andrea. "Una finestra aperta sul cuore." *Lettere italiane* 26.4 (1974): 434–458.

Rinaldi, Rinaldo. "Scrivere contro: Machiavelli in Castiglione." *De la Politesse à la politique: Recherches sur les langages du 'Livre du Courtisan'*. Eds. Paolo Grossi and Juan Carlos D'Amico. Caen: Presses Universitaires de Caen, 2001. 31–49.

Robbins, Jeremy. *Arts of Perception: The Epistemological Mentality of the Spanish Baroque, 1580–1720*. New York: Routledge, 2007.

Romano, Giovanni, ed. *Realismo caravaggesco e prodigio barocco: da Molineri a Taricco nella grande provincia*. Savigliano: L'Artistica, 1998.

Rosa, Mario. "Chiesa e stati regionali nell'età dell'assolutismo." *Letteratura italiana*. Ed. Alberto Asor Rosa. Vol. 1. Turin: Einaudi, 1982. 257–389.

Rudich, Vasily. *Dissidence and Literature under Nero: The Price of Rhetoricization*. New York: Routledge, 1997.

———. *Political Dissidence under Nero: The Price of Dissimulation*. New York: Routledge, 1993.

Saccone, Eduardo. *Le buone e le cattive maniere: letteratura e galateo nel Cinquecento*. Bologna: Il Mulino, 1992.

Salmatoris Rossillon, C. G. S. *Monumento dedicato alla pace del 1631 nella città di Cherasco*. Turin: Tipografia Chirio e Mina, 1820.

Santoro, Mario. *Fortuna, ragione e prudenza nella civiltà letteraria del Cinquecento.* Naples: Liguori, 1967.

Schellhase, Kenneth C. *Tacitus in Renaissance Political Thought.* Chicago: University of Chicago Press, 1976.

Scholar, Richard. *The "Je-Ne-Sais-Quoi" in Early Modern Europe: Encounters with a Certain Something.* New York: Oxford University Press, 2005.

Schulte, Hansgerd. *El Desengaño: Wort und Thema in der Spanischen Literatur des Goldenen Zeitalters.* Freiburger Schriften zur Romanischen Philologie 17. Munich: Wilhelm Fink Verlag, 1969.

Schulz-Buschhaus, Ulrich. "Über die Verstellung und die ersten 'Primores' des *Héroe* von Gracián." *Romanische Forschungen* 91.4 (1979): 411–430.

Scragg, Leah. "Edward Blount and the History of Lylian Criticism." *Review of English Studies* 46.181 (1995): 1–10.

Senellart, Michel. "Noble mensonge et prudence politique." *La sincerité: l'insolence du coeur.* Eds. Christine Baron and Catherine Doroszczuk. Paris: Éditions Autrement, 1995. 54–72.

———. "Simuler et dissimuler: l'art machiavélien d'être secret à la Renaissance." *Histoire et secret à la Renaissance: Études sur la représentation de la vie publique, la mémoire et l'intimité dans l'Angleterre et l'Europe des XVIe et XVIIe siècles.* Ed. François Laroque. Paris: Presses de la Sorbonne Nouvelle, 1997. 99–106.

———. "Le Stoicisme dans la constitution de la pensée politique: Les *Politiques* de Juste Lipse (1589)." *Le Stoicisme aux XVIe et XVIIe siècles. Actes du Colloque CERPHI (4–5 juin 1993).* Cahiers de philosophie politique et juridique 25. Ed. Jacqueline Lagrée. Caen: Université de Caen, 1994. 109–130.

Serés, Guillermo, ed. *"Levante sus primores la agudeza": Baltasar Gracián (1601–2001).* Special issue of *Ínsula* 655–656 (July–August 2001).

Sfez, Gérald. *Les Doctrines de la raison d'État.* Paris: Armand Colin, 2000.

Shuger, Debora. *Censorship and Cultural Sensibility: The Regulation of Language in Tudor-Stuart England.* Philadelphia: University of Pennsylvania Press, 2006.

Simoncelli, Paolo. *Evangelismo italiano del Cinquecento: questione religiosa e nicodemismo politico.* Rome: Istituto Storico Italiano per l'età moderna e contemporanea, 1979.

Simonetta, Marcello. *Rinascimento segreto: il mondo del segretario da Petrarca a Machiavelli.* Milan: FrancoAngeli, 2004.

Smith, Pauline M. *The Anti-Courtier Trend in Sixteenth Century French Literature.* Travaux d'Humanisme et Renaissance 84. Geneva: Droz, 1966.

Snyder, Jon R. "Appunti sulla politica e l'estetica della dissimulazione tra Cinque e Seicento." *Cheiron* 11.22 (1994): 23–43.

———. "Il disincanto del corpo: simulazione e dissimulazione nella *Civil conversazione* di Stefano Guazzo." *Stefano Guazzo e Casale tra Cinque e Seicento.* Ed. Daniela Ferrari. Rome: Bulzoni, 1997. 309–321.

———. "Norbert Elias's *The Civilizing Process* and the Critique of Conduct." *Educare il corpo, educare la parola nella trattatistica del Rinascimento.* Eds. Giorgio Patrizi and Amedeo Quondam. Biblioteca del Cinquecento 80. Rome: Bulzoni, 1998. 289–307.

————. "Sincerity in Seventeenth-Century Italy." *Rinascimento: rivista dell'Istituto Italiano di studi sul Rinascimento*. 2nd series, 48 (2003): 265–286.

————. "Truth and Wonder in Naples circa 1640." *Culture and Authority in the Baroque*. Eds. Massimo Ciavolella and Patrick Coleman. Toronto: Toronto University Press, 2005. 85–105.

Sommerville, Johann P. "The 'New Art of Lying': Equivocation, Mental Reservation and Casuistry." *Conscience and Casuistry in Early Modern Europe*. Ed. Edmund Leites. New York: Cambridge University Press; Paris: Editions de la Maison des Sciences de l'Homme, 1988. 159–184.

Sozzi, Lionello. "La Polémique anti-italienne en France au XVIe siècle." *Atti dell'Accademia delle Scienze di Torino* 106 (1972): 99–190.

Stackelberg, Jürgen von. *Französische Moralistik im europäischen Kontext*. Darmstadt: Wissenschaftliche Buchgesellschaft, 1982.

————. *Tacitus in der Romania*. Tübingen: Max Niemeyer Verlag, 1960.

Stegmann, André. "Le Tacitisme: programme pour un nouvel essai de définition." *Machiavellismo e antimachiavellismo nel Cinquecento. Atti del convegno di Perugia, 30.9–1.10.69*. Special issue of *Il pensiero politico* 2.3 (1969): 117–130.

Summers, David. *The Judgment of Sense: Renaissance Naturalism and the Rise of Aesthetics*. New York: Cambridge University Press, 1987.

Taricchi, Giovanni. *Delle opere di fresco del pittore Sebastiano Tarico [sic]*. Urbino: Tipografia Rocchetti, 1877.

Taricco, Bruno. *Cherasco: Urba Firmissima Pacis*. Cherasco: Pro Cherasco, 1993.

Taylor, Charles. "The Person." *The Category of the Person: Anthropology, Philosophy, History*. Eds. Michael Carrithers, Steven Collins, and Steven Lukes. New York: Cambridge University Press, 1985. 257–281.

————. *Sources of the Self: The Making of the Modern Identity*. Cambridge, MA: Harvard University Press, 1989.

Treasure, Geoffrey. *Mazarin: The Crisis of Absolutism in France*. New York: Routledge, 1995.

Tuck, Richard. *Philosophy and Government 1572–1651*. New York: Cambridge University Press, 1993.

Uhlig, Claus. "Moral und Politik in der europäischen Hoferziehung." *Literatur als Kritik des Lebens*. Eds. Rudolf Haas, H.-J. Müllenbrock, and Claus Uhlig. Heidelberg: Quelle und Meyer, 1975. 27–51.

Vagnoni, Debora. "Immagini neoplatoniche e teologia negativa nella dissimulazione di Torquato Accetto." *Linguistica e letteratura* 1–2 (2004): 89–118.

————. "Il plagio del *De patientia* di Celio Calcagnini nel secondo dei *Due dialoghi* di Lucio Paolo Rossello." *Furto e plagio nella letteratura del classicismo*. Ed. Roberto Gigliucci. Rome: Bulzoni, 1998. 347–355.

Vedova, Giuseppe. *Biografia degli scrittori padovani*. 2 vols. Padua: Minerva, 1832–1836.

Velotti, Stefano. *Sapienti e bestioni : saggio sull'ignoranza, il sapere e la poesia in Giambattista Vico*. Parma: Pratiche, 1995.

Vickers, Brian, ed. *English Renaissance Literary Criticism*. New York: Oxford University Press, 2003.

Vígh, Éva. *Barocco etico-retorico nella letteratura italiana.* Szeged: JATE Press, 2001.

Villari, Rosario. *L'elogio della dissimulazione: la lotta politica nel Seicento.* Bari: Laterza, 1987.

Viroli, Maurizio. *From Politics to Reason of State. The Acquisition and Transformation of the Language of Politics, 1250–1600.* New York: Cambridge University Press, 1992.

Waszink, Jan H. "Virtuous Deception: The *Politica* and the Wars in the Low Countries and France, 1559–1589." *Iustus Lipsius Europae lumen et columen.* Eds. Gilbert Tournoy, Jeanine de Landtsheer, and Jan Papy. Supplementa Humanistica Lovaniensia 15. Louvain: Louvain University Press, 1999. 248–267.

Whigham, Frank. "Interpretation at Court: Courtesy and the Performer-Audience Dialectic." *New Literary History* 14.3 (1983): 623–639. Republished in revised form in his *Ambition and Privilege: The Social Tropes of Elizabethan Courtesy Theory.* Berkeley and Los Angeles: University of California Press, 1984.

Zagorin, Perez. *Francis Bacon.* Princeton: Princeton University Press, 1998.

———. "The Historical Significance of Lying and Dissimulation." *Social Research* 63.3 (1996): 863–912.

———. *Ways of Lying: Dissimulation, Persecution, and Conformity in Early Modern Europe.* Cambridge, MA: Harvard University Press, 1990.

Zarka, Yves Charles. "Raison d'État et figure du prince chez Botero." *Raison et déraison d'État: Théoriciens et théories de la raison d'État aux XVIe et XVIIe siècles.* Ed. Yves Charles Zarka. Paris: Presses Universitaires de France, 1994. 101–120.

Index

Italicized page numbers refer to illustrations.

Text: 10/13 Galliard
Display: Galliard
Compositor: Binghamton Valley Composition, LLC